ENCOUNTER

GRIN AND BEAR IT   BY LICHTY

"Like man, let's dig this basic English course! . . . Might be
groovy knowing another language besides our own!"

ENCOUNTER

Readings for
Thinking/Talking/Writing

Joan G. Roloff

Director of Developmental Education
William Rainey Harper College
Palatine, Illinois

Unit Illustrations by
Kay S. Kutch
Student, William Rainey Harper College

Glencoe Press
A Division of The Macmillan Company
Beverly Hills, California

To my husband:

Whose patience and sense of humor in the midst of chaos, and whose loving encouragement of my commitment to my work have made this book possible.

Glencoe Press
A Division of The Macmillan Company
8701 Wilshire Boulevard
Beverly Hills, California   90211
Collier-Macmillan Canada, Ltd., Toronto, Canada

Library of Congress catalog card number: 78-101718

First printing, 1970

CONTENTS

PREFACE

Caught up in the complexities of today's world, every college student must inevitably make a multitude of decisions about his own life and his relationship to the society of which he is a part. These decisions are far more complicated, far more difficult to make than they were even a few years ago; and the consequences of each student's individual decisions, multiplied by thousands or millions, have ramifications which, inevitably, will strongly influence the future direction of our country and our world.

In our new "global village," effective communication is essential in working toward solutions of the complex problems in which we are involved. Thus the college English class is in an important and vulnerable position: important, because the skills of reading, thinking, discussing and writing are now the *essential tools* for coping with the contemporary world; and vulnerable, because the failure of the class to help the student to read, to think, to talk, and to write with greater discrimination and skill means the failure to help young men and women develop into functioning citizens in the problem-torn society they must face.

Encounter is designed with three premises in mind. First, the student must have something interesting and relevant to think, talk, and write *about* before he can or will wish to do so effectively. Second, there *are* subjects which offer an imperative challenge to involvement for students: subjects which almost demand their attention, their thought, their response, because of their immediate importance to the student personally and to his world. Third, the *content* of communication must be primary; the problems of correct form should be dealt with as they relate to the effectiveness of the content.

Because many students enter college with inadequately developed communication skills, particularly in the areas of reading and writing, the selections in this text have been chosen not only for their interest and relevance to the student, but also on the basis of their accessibility, in terms of vocabulary level and structure. At the end of each selection, there are questions "For Thinking, Talking, Writing." In order to allow for the greatest possible flexibility within the classroom, these questions are designed to be equally as useful for either discussion or writing. They deal only with content; matters of form and structure are dealt with in detail in the Instructor's Manual, to provide for a variety of emphasis according to the situation in the particular classroom.

In addition, the sections may be dealt with in any order the instructor considers appropriate, since each is largely self-contained; and there is a sufficient number of selections within each section to allow for considerable choice, if time or inclination prevents use of all of the material.

Abraham Maslow once said that the purpose of education is the development of full humanness. It is hoped that this text will provide a basis for that kind of educational experience, so that students will emerge from their encounter with *Encounter* more aware of self, more aware of others, more fully human — and better able to communicate that humanness.

JOAN G. ROLOFF

ENCOUNTER

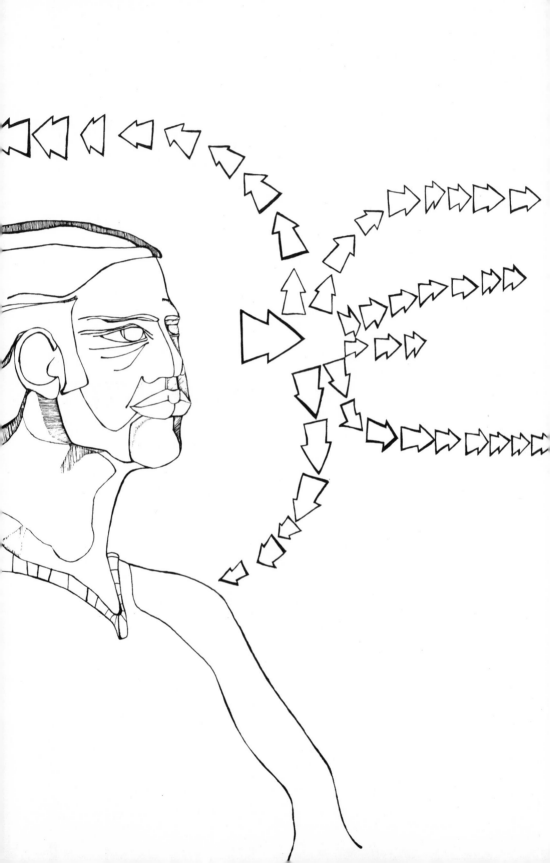

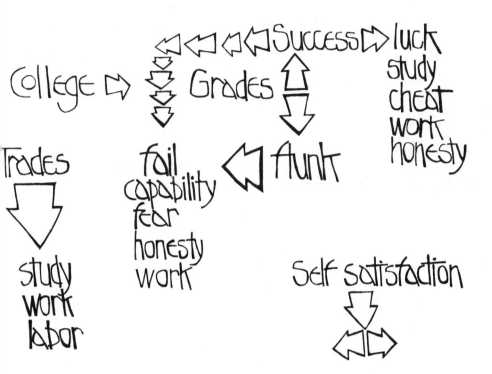

COLLEGE:

what's it all about, anyway?

Introduction

Here you are in college. Perhaps it's your first semester, or perhaps you've been in college before. In either case, you find yourself in classes, probably at desks or tables, with instructors, classmates, books, and assignments.

But — what's it all about, anyway? Of course a college education cannot be the answer to everything. We all, from time to time, might want to echo a statement by A. E. Newton:

> I wish that someone would give a course in how to live. It can't be taught in the colleges: that's perfectly obvious, for college professors don't know any better than the rest of us.
>
> —*The Book-Collecting Game,* 1928

This first section of your text attempts to help you explore the question, "What's it all about, anyway?" As you read the articles in this section, you will deal with some questions you may never have thought about, and some to which you may have given a great deal of thought. Is the present "system" of college a good one, or does it need a lot of changes? How do I feel about all the rebellion on college campuses? What happens when the college I want to attend turns me down? Why am I getting such lousy grades? What are some techniques for getting good grades on final exams? Why should we have grades at all — should the grading system be abolished? Should I really be going to college?

The important thing to keep in mind as you explore each of these questions through the following articles is how they relate to *you. You* are the one attending college; *you* are the one who should be making decisions about your education. Read — think — talk — write. Maybe when you've been through this section, you'll be a lot clearer on "What's it all about, anyway?"

"Let's toss!...Heads we set fire to the administration building, tails we work on our exams and send our laundry home!"

GRIN & BEAR IT courtesy of George Lichty and Publishers–Hall Syndicate.

For Thinking, Talking, Writing

This cartoon illustrates the confusion that many students are now feeling about the college "system" and how they should respond to it. The next three articles discuss some of the problems of higher education in the United States today and make some suggestions for coping with the problems and improving the system. As you read these articles and think through the questions, try to relate your *own* experiences, your *own* problems concerning school, to each of the topics discussed.

The System Really Isn't Working

Judson Jerome

Most of us recognize that we might have been better educated; but do we recognize that we might have improved our education not by pursuing more of the same but by going about learning in completely different ways? For example, why have we not resented—and changed—education conducted almost without reference to politics, religion, sex, personal ethics, family relationships—without reference, in short, to the areas of experience which matter as one prepares for citizenship, parenthood, or any other role outside the school? How many of us truly feel that our college education was relevant to real human concerns?...

I hear students telling me what I never had the guts or imagination to say, though I recognize its truth: the system isn't working. The whole network of departments, field, areas, credits, requirements, courses, grades, which we have accepted as educational design, does not relate coherently to human learning....

Yet never have conditions been so propitious for revaluations.... Take the classroom. We are accustomed to think of it as the focus of education, but to what extent are we victims of our inherited architecture? What compulsion is there to populate those cubicles containing rows of chairs, blackboards and a desk or lectern up front every MWF 9-10? Why, indeed, meet in groups of 15 to 40, with some faculty member making assignments, giving nonlectures, and conducting nondiscussions?...

Why think of education in terms of courses?...

In the next few years we will probably see more and more classrooms — throughout our colleges — emptied of their present function. Even if students were to accept course structures as they now exist, they are becoming too numerous to be accommodated — and more efficient ways are being found of feeding the passive ones. More important, new definitions of education are being forced upon us which bypass much of the sort of activity associated with classrooms. "Field Study Centers" or "beachheads" are springing up in ghettos and rural pockets of poverty; groups of students and faculty move in to combine service with learning in such ways that the acquisition of knowledge is inseparable from its active use, and units such as courses are patently inconceivable. More and more information is being programmed for independent study, free-

Reprinted by permission of the author and Ann Elmo Agency.

ing faculty time — at least in theory — for informal interaction with students in a variety of settings, none of which is likely to be the classroom. Educational games, in which individual and group responses to tactical questions are tested against a computer's store of probable consequences, demand new equipment, new furnishings and kinds of rooms. Imagine classroom buildings being broken up into living units, lounges, reading rooms, blocks of carrels. We have much to learn about the ways people can relate to one another and learn effectively.

Relevance, as our students have taught us, is the key word.... They will not accept the compulsion they once accepted. As adults we have passed a threshold of dignity: there is some guff we will not swallow. That threshold seems to be passed now at younger and younger ages. It never occurred to me or to my generation to question the authority of teachers, parents, the draft, the police — but today 14-year-old people (I hesitate to call them kids; one lives in my home) raise valid questions about such authority and insist on their right to answers. If it weren't for the draft and disdain for the choices available in the job market, the exodus from conventional settings of higher education would be rapid. Perhaps we should ponder why college students have ever tolerated their second-class citizenship. College education is adult education. Few people who consider themselves adults would put up with the rules and regulations, the attendance requirements, dress standards, dormitory hours, the made-work, the time-serving, the arbitrary and unilateral "assignments," the nit-picking formats of term papers and registration forms, the host of practices which might have some dubious utility in grammar school but which are ludicrous when mindlessly extended to men and women of 18 years and more of age.

There is a basic lesson we can draw from the many instances when college students have been treated like adults and have used their responsibility well. Antioch's work-study program sends every student, even freshmen, off to strange cities and new jobs every other quarter — a plan that has worked for nearly 50 years because college students on their own prove themselves to be adults. The free colleges and universities, in spite of some of their rebellious excesses, have generally succeeded in providing substantial education of high quality, largely under student control. Harris Wofford, in designing a new college which opened this year at Old Westbury, Long Island, has involved student advisers in every stage of the planning — and is grateful for their insight and their help. Inner colleges such as the one at Antioch and Bensalem, at Fordham, use the dormitory as a learning center and, with a free approach to what should be studied and how, have shown the possibilities of real partnerships between students, faculty and administrators. In these developments we can see that the generation gap is miraculously healed as soon as one disregards it. . . .

Some of us over 30 would like to become trustworthy again — and to exercise influence, if authority is denied us, with a generation in some danger of running amuck, cut off from any counsel except its own. If we feel strongly enough to give this concern radical effort — exercising a kind of Faculty Power — we can set out to learn the new skills and to create the new patterns of satisfaction and professional reward, the new ways of looking at our own fields. We will have to leap into the discussion as our culture struggles to redefine itself.

For Thinking, Talking, Writing

1. Have you ever given any *real* thought to what your education is all about — or have you always just accepted passively the fact that school is "there" and that you "go to school"? After reading this article, can you state ways in which you feel your education so far has *not* been really relevant, really appropriate, to your own life? Can you state ways in which it *has* been relevant to you, helpful to your life?

2. Think about the situations in your life in which you have really learned a *lot* about something important to you. Were these situations usually in school? Probably not. Describe what these situations were like — try to figure out *why* you learned so much. Relate what you come up with to what might be done *in* school; can you find any new ideas for making school more interesting, more effective, more of a real education for *you*?

3. State your own feelings and opinions about the situations described in the following statements from the article:

   (a) "If it weren't for the draft and disdain for the choices available in the job market, the exodus from conventional settings of higher education would be rapid." [In other words, if you didn't have to go to college either to stay out of the draft or to try to get a better job, would you go at all? Why or why not?]

   (b) "College education is adult education. Few people who consider themselves adults would put up with . . . the host of practices which might have some dubious utility in grammar school but which are ludicrous when mindlessly extended to men and women of 18 years and more of age."

   (c) "We can see that the generation gap is miraculously healed as soon as one disregards it."

Professional Troublemakers on Campus

Ann Landers

DEAR ANN LANDERS: I'm a middle-aged square who would like your opinion on the current campus upheavals. What's behind this so-called alienation of youth? Have we botched things so badly that everything ought to be junked—including our university system?

I'm horrified by what I read in the newspapers and see on TV. Is there any justification for these campus revolutions? Do college students have the right to virtually close down our institutions of higher learning?

I've always been a champion of youth, but my faith has been shaken. Please, Ann Landers, express yourself. You've been noticeably silent on a subject of enormous social significance.   BEWILDERED

DEAR BEWILDERED: Welcome to the club. I, too, have always had great faith in our youth. And I still have. They are brighter than we were, more assertive, more articulate, and they possess a far deeper commitment to social justice.

The vast majority of campus kids are decent, law-abiding citizens who want an education. And this is what makes the campus rioting reprehen-

sible. The hell-raisers—those who have been destroying property and obstructing justice — are clearly in the minority on every campus where there has been trouble.

In a free society, citizens have the right to dissent, to express opposition to practices which they consider unjust. But wanton destruction of property, rifling of files, threatening college presidents and faculty members is not valid protest. It is lawlessness and must not be tolerated.

I believe students who break the law should be treated as lawbreakers. There must be no shilly-shallying, no dilly-dallying, no amnesty granted. When we bow to the demands of the nihilists and reward criminal tactics, we encourage others to follow their lead. When we knuckle under to rioters who spit in the face of authority we are being unfair to students who want to learn, to taxpayers and alumni who support these schools, and to the embattled faculty members and administrators who wind up at the mercy of roughnecks.

Reprinted courtesy of Ann Landers, Publishers–Hall Syndicate, and the *Chicago Sun-Times.*

Unless we take a firm stand against these anarchists, many of whom are not even students but professional troublemakers, we will see an end to the university and the birth of fascism.

For Thinking, Talking, Writing

1. On the basis of the article you have just read, "The System Really Isn't Working," and your other background knowledge, take a stand for or against Miss Landers' point of view about the way student riots should be handled.
2. React to the following statements from the article:
   (a) "[Today's youth] are brighter than we were, more assertive, more articulate, and they possess a far deeper commitment to social justice."
   (b) "In a free society, citizens have the right to dissent, to express opposition to practices which they consider unjust. But wanton destruction of property...is not valid protest. It is lawlessness and and must not be tolerated."
   (c) "When we knuckle under to rioters who spit in the face of authority we are being unfair to students who want to learn...."

How Should a University Administrator Respond to Radical Activism Among Students?

Robert M. Hutchins

Everything that is wrong with the American university has been wrong with it for at least fifty years. The difference is that until recently almost nobody cared. The university was a peripheral institution. Neither government nor industry was interested in it. The students could afford to waste their time and, in any event, seemed satisfied with bright college years.

Though voices were raised complaining about the futility of the curriculum, the mediocrity of teaching, the triviality of research, the evils of specialization, the egocentricity of departments, the backwardness of faculties, the forwardness of trustees, and the tyranny of presidents, nothing happened. The university entered the postwar period with all its accumulated sins upon its head.

It was, at that date, simply a place where people assembled to put in time. Theirs not to reason why. If you had asked anybody connected with the institution what it was for, he would have replied that it was for the purpose of qualifying people for various jobs; but he would seldom have claimed that there was more than a nominal connection between the subjects studied and the requirements of the jobs....

At the end of the Second World War, the university moved from the periphery to the center. The university would unlock all the secrets of nature and train all the people needed to turn discoveries into weapons and money. It would lead the way to national power and prosperity and would see to it that we got there before the Russians. From a hotbed of radicalism the university became overnight the central factory of the knowledge industry, which was to be the foundation of our future. At the same time, the educational system, with the university at the top, became the national screening device through which individuals were to be put in the proper productive relationship to the national program of power and prosperity.

The Center Magazine, a publication of the Center for the Study of Democratic Institutions, 1969.

A ramshackle building on the outskirts of town may pass without remark. If you suddenly announce that it is the national Capitol, people are likely to find fault with it. There will be still more objection if you insist that everybody who wants to amount to anything should spend at least four years in it. Things get worse if the purpose of these proclamations is not shared by the best and brightest of those who are expected to respond to them.

The world has moved too fast for the university. The leaders of the younger generation see that the problem is not to get wealth and power; of these the United States seems to have plenty already. The problem is justice, or what to do with wealth and power. An institution that evidently has little interest in this question cannot command the allegiance of the young. Particularly is this the case when all the defects and shortcomings of the prewar university remain.

The only kind of institution that can command the allegiance of the young is one that can convince them that it is seriously trying to become a center of independent thought and criticism. By definition, the curriculum and organization of such an institution cannot be simply a compromise among forces at work in the community. Students should participate in discussions of the constitution and course of study. If they make irrational demands, they should be rejected like the irrational demands of politicians and industrialists.

Attempts to disrupt the institutions are not likely to be made if the students believe that the university is bent on becoming a center of independent thought and criticism. If such attempts are made, they will not receive widespread or durable support.

If in spite of the best efforts of all concerned, or all but a few, the university is disrupted, the police should on no account be called in. They cannot be trusted, and an invitation to them to enter in the name of "law and order" is evidence that the university has given up trying to become a center of independent thought and criticism, for such a center can live only by discussion. The Reagan-Hayakawa syndrome produces a university that is worse than none at all.

If, therefore, a university is victimized by a group who insist on irrational demands or who simply want to disrupt the institution, the thing to do is to close the place down and call for a constitutional convention. In state colleges and universities the convention should consist of politicians, regents or trustees, administrators, professors, junior members of the faculty, and students.

This is what higher education in America needs, serious discussion about what it is for and how to organize to achieve its objectives.

Such discussion has never taken place. No college or university could emerge unchanged from the kind of scrutiny and debate a constitutional convention would require.

Ancient sins of omission and commission might be absolved at last. Modern crimes against humanity might be corrected. The university, instead of reflecting misguided purposes and abandoned ideals, might fashion the mind of the new age.

For Thinking, Talking, Writing

1. Discuss *your* feelings and beliefs about Dr. Hutchins' statement that "The leaders of the younger generation see that the problem is not to get wealth and power...the problem is justice, or what to do with wealth and power."
2. Do you believe, as Dr. Hutchins does, that college should be "a center of independent thought and criticism"? What other important purposes does a college serve?
3. Do you agree with Dr. Hutchins that the police should never be called in during university disruptions? Why or why not? What do you think of his proposal that in case of serious disruption, a college should simply be closed down and a constitutional convention called?
4. Engage in what Dr. Hutchins calls serious discussion about what higher education in the United States is *for* and how to organize it to achieve its objectives.

On Being Unchosen by
the College of One's Choice

Joan Didion

"Dear Joan," the letter begins, although the writer did not know me at all. The letter is dated April 25, 1952, and for a long time now it has been in a drawer in my mother's house, the kind of back-bedroom drawer given over to class prophecies and dried butterfly orchids and newspaper photographs that show eight bridesmaids and two flower girls inspecting a sixpence in a bride's shoe. What slight emotional investment I ever had in dried butterfly orchids and pictures of myself as a bridesmaid has proved evanescent, but I still have an investment in the letter, which, except for the "Dear Joan," is mimeographed. I got the letter out as an object lesson for a 17-year-old cousin who is unable to eat or sleep as she waits to hear from what she keeps calling the colleges of her choice. Here is what the letter says: "The Committee on Admissions asks me to inform you that it is unable to take favorable action upon your application for admission to Stanford University. While you have met the minimum requirements, we regret that because of the severity of the competition, the Committee cannot include you in the group to be admitted. The Committee joins me in extending you every good wish for the successful continuation of your education. Sincerely yours, Rixford K. Snyder, Director of Admissions."

I remember quite clearly the afternoon I opened that letter. I stood reading and re-reading it, my sweater and my books fallen on the hall floor, trying to interpret the words in some less final way, the phrases "unable to take" and "favorable action" fading in and out of focus until the sentence made no sense at all. We lived then in a big dark Victorian house, and I had a sharp and dolorous image of myself growing old in it, never going to school anywhere, the spinster in *Washington Square*. I went upstairs to my room and locked the door and for a couple of hours I cried. For a while I sat on the floor of my closet and buried my face in an old quilted robe and later, after the situation's real humiliations (all my friends who applied to Stanford had been admitted) had faded into safe theatrics, I sat on the edge of the bathtub and thought about swallowing the contents of an old bottle of codeine-and-Empirin. I saw myself in an oxygen tent, with Rixford K. Snyder hovering outside, although how the news was to reach Rixford K. Snyder was a plot point that troubled me even as I counted out the tablets.

Of course I did not take the tablets. I spent the rest of the spring in sullen but mild rebellion, sitting around drive-ins, listening to Tulsa evangelists on the car radio, and in the summer I fell in love with someone who wanted to be a golf pro, and I spent a lot of time watching him practice putting, and in the fall I went to a junior college a couple of hours a day and made up the credits I needed to go to the University of California at Berkeley. The next year a friend at Stanford asked me to write him a paper on Conrad's *Nostromo*, and I did, and he got an A on it. I got a B— on the same paper at Berkeley, and the specter of Rixford K. Snyder was exorcised.

So it worked out all right, my single experience in that most conventional middle-class confrontation, the child vs. the Admissions Committee. But that was in the benign world of country California in 1952, and I think it must be more difficult for children I know now, children whose lives from the age of two or three are a series of perilously programmed steps, each of which must be successfully negotiated in order to avoid just such a letter as mine from one or another of the Rixford K. Snyders of the world. An acquaintance told me recently that there were ninety applicants for the seven openings in the kindergarten of an expensive school in which she hoped to enroll her four-year-old, and that she was frantic because none of the four-year-old's letters of recommendation had mentioned the child's "interest in art." Had I been raised under that pressure, I suspect I would have taken the codeine-and-Empirin on that April afternoon in 1952. My rejection was different, my humiliation private: No parental hopes rode on whether I was admitted to Stanford, or anywhere. Of course my mother and father wanted me to be happy, and of course they expected that happiness would necessarily entail accomplishment, but the terms of that accomplishment were my affair. Their idea of their own and of my worth remained independent of where, or even if, I went to college. Our social situation was static, and the question of "right" schools, so traditionally urgent to the upwardly mobile, did not arise. When my father was told that I had been rejected by Stanford, he shrugged and offered me a drink.

I think about that shrug with a great deal of appreciation whenever I hear parents talking about their children's "chances." What makes me uneasy is the sense that they are merging their children's chances with their own, demanding of a child that he make good not only for himself but for the greater glory of his father and mother. Of course it is harder to get into college now than it once was. Of course there are more children than "desirable" openings. But we are deluding ourselves if we pretend that desirable schools benefit the child alone. ("I wouldn't care at all about his getting into Yale if it weren't for Vietnam," a father told me not long ago, quite unconscious of his own speciousness; it would have been malicious of me to suggest that one could also get a deferment at Long Beach State.) Getting into college has become an ugly business, malignant in its consumption and diversion of time and energy and true interests, and not its least deleterious aspect is how the children themselves accept it. They talk casually and unattractively of the "first, second and third choices," of how their "first-choice" application (to Stephens, say) does not actually reflect their first choice (their first choice was Smith, but their adviser said their chances were low, so why "waste" the application?); they are calculating about the expectation of rejections, about their "backup" possibilities, about getting the right sport and the right extracurricular activities to "balance" the application, about juggling confirmations when their third choice accepts before their first choice answers. They are wise in the white lie here, the small self-aggrandizement there, in the importance of letters from "names" their parents scarcely know. I have heard conversations among 16-year-olds who were exceeded in their skill and manipulative self-promotion only by applicants for large literary grants.

And of course none of it matters very much at all, none of these early successes, early failures. I wonder if we had better not find some way to let our children know this, some way to let them work through their own rejections and sullen rebellions and interludes with golf pros, unassisted by anxious promptings from the wings. Finding one's role at 17 is problem enough, without being handed somebody else's script.

For Thinking, Talking, Writing

1. Have you at some time had an experience similar to the author's — either not being accepted by a college or perhaps flunking out of one? If you have, describe your feelings about the situation, and the steps you took to get over your humiliation, or hurt, or anger.
2. Do you agree or disagree with the author's statement that "... of course none of it matters very much at all, none of these early successes, early failures"? Explain your opinion about this.
3. What is the important point in this article *beyond* the matter of being accepted or rejected by a college? What is the author attempting to say about our behavior in the face of failure in all kinds of human situations?

If I'm So Smart, How Come I Flunk All the Time?

Charles W. Slack

Mission Impossible: Can twenty flunking students of varying intelligence raise their math and English a full year's level in only thirty working days?

Dr. Lloyd Homme, chief of a special educational "fix-it" laboratory in Albuquerque, New Mexico, said Yes and put teams of behavioral scientists together with the flunking students to work on the problem. Any available technology could be used—teaching machines, programmed instruction, computer-assisted methods—to cram a year's knowledge into the boys.

After technology was applied, were the experiments a success? The scientists said Yes but the students said No. When grades were measured using standardized tests under strict laboratory conditions, marks went up more than one year on the average. Meanwhile, back at school, the students were still barely passing, at best.

"The experiment was fine for the scientists. They proved their theory on paper and made a name for themselves, but most of us were still flunking in class," remarked one seventeen-year-old.

The only clue to the mystery was this common remark: "The teachers ignore us—they've got it in for us."

At first the scientists on the team thought the complaint was just sour grapes and told the boys to work harder. When grades still failed to rise, the scientists felt there might be some truth in what the young team members were saying. Not that teachers were to blame, necessarily, but there still might be some negative bias. "You should see what goes on in class!" said the boys.

"The only thing to do was to take them up on it, go into the classroom with them and see what was holding back their grades," said Dr. Homme.

Hence, bearded behavioral scientists with Master's degrees and Ph.D.'s ended up in the back row of math and English classes. Their notes, however, did not pertain to algebra and Shakespeare. Instead, they made observations about the behavior of students and teachers.

When all results were in and tabulated, Homme was surprised to discover that two simple actions made the difference.

"With few exceptions, our students acted like dummies," said Dr. Homme, "even though we knew they were ahead of the rest in knowledge. They were so used to playing the class idiot that they didn't know how to display their new-found gains. Their eyes wandered, they appeared distracted or even belligerent. One or two read magazines hidden under their desks, justifying their surreptitious behavior, most likely, on the basis they already knew the classwork. They rarely volunteered and often had to have questions repeated because they weren't listening. Teachers, on the other hand, did not trust our laboratory results. Nobody was going to tell them that 'miracles' could work on Sammy and Jose."

In the eyes of teachers, students seemed to fall into three groups. We'll call them: *bright-eyes, scaredy-cats* and *dummies.*

BRIGHT-EYES had perfected the trick of:

1. "eyeballing" the instructor at all times, even from the minute he entered the room.
2. never ducking their eyes away when the instructor glanced at *them.*
3. getting the instructor to call on them when they wanted, *without* raising their hands.
4. even making the instructor go out of his way to call on someone else to "give others a chance" (especially useful when bright-eyes themselves are uncertain of the answer).
5. readily admitting ignorance so as not to bluff — but in such a way that it sounds as though ignorance is rare.
6. asking many questions.

   SCAREDY-CATS (*the middle group*)

1. looked toward the instructor but were afraid to let him "catch their eyes."
2. asked few questions and gave the impression of being "under achievers."
3. appeared uninvolved and had to be "drawn out," hence were likely to be criticized for "inadequate participation."

   DUMMIES (*no matter how much they really knew*)

1. never looked at the instructor.
2. never asked questions.
3. were intransigent about volunteering information in class of any kind.

To make matters worse, the tests in school were *not* standardized and not given nearly as frequently as those given in the laboratory. School test-scores were open to teacher bias. Classroom behavior of students counted a lot toward their class grades. There was no doubt that teachers were biased against the dummies. The scientists concluded that no matter how much knowledge a dummy gained on his own, his grades in school were unlikely to improve unless he could somehow change his image into a bright-eyes. This would mean...

1. Look the teacher in the eye.
2. Ask questions and volunteer answers (even if uncertain).

"Teachers get teacher-training in how to play their roles. Why shouldn't students get student-training in how to play bright-eyes?" asked Homme.

Special training sessions were held at the laboratory. Dummies were drilled in eyeballing and hand-raising, which, simple as they sound, weren't easy to do. "I felt so square I could hardly stand it," complained one of the dummies. "That was at first. Later, when I saw others eyeballing and hand-raising and really learning more, I even moved my seat to the front. It flipped the teacher out of her skull. She couldn't get over it."

Those who found eyeballing especially difficult were taught to look at the instructor's mouth or the bridge of his nose. "Less threatening to the student," explained Homme. "It seems less aggressive to them."

Unfortunately, not all of the dummies were able to pick up new habits during the limited training period. Some learned in the laboratory but were unable to use the technique in the classroom. These became scaredy-cats — at least a step up. But for the majority, grades improved steadily once they got the hang of their new techniques. The students encouraged and helped each other to hand-raise and eyeball.

Teachers' comments reflected the improvement. "There is no doubt that student involvement was increased by the program and as a result grades went up."

By way of advice to others wishing to improve their own eyeballing and hand-raising to get better marks, student Jose Martinez suggests: "Don't try to do it all at once. You'll shock the teacher and make it tough for yourself. Begin slowly. Work with a friend and help each other. Do it like a game. Like exercising with weights — it takes practice but it's worth it."

Homme agrees. "In fact, results are guaranteed for life," he says.

For Thinking, Talking, Writing

1. Have you ever thought about the fact that getting good grades in school involves more than just knowing the material — that it's also a matter of learning *techniques* to let the instructor know that you know something about the subject? Think about college in this way for a few moments — as a "game" to be learned as well as a place where you pursue your education. If you think of it in this way, can you think of other techniques besides the ones the author mentions which might be useful in playing this "game"?

2. How might the techniques that help you do well in school apply equally well to other situations, such as jobs, dates, and so on? Explore this question; what does it have to do with general techniques of effective communication?

3. How would you categorize yourself: as a "bright-eyes," a "scaredy-cat," or a "dummy"? Why? What might you do, specifically, to move yourself up, if necessary?

How to Cram:
Five Neverfail Methods

Craig Karpel

Never again the agonizing, down-to-the-wire, up-tight grind. Thousands hissed this pronouncement through gritted teeth and blue lips last semester, the semester before and the one previous to that. But here it is a week before exams and it's pouring blue books and ignorance once again.

Willis saw one chance for salvation — or at least postponement.

So he slapped BandAids on his wrists and made it over to the school psychiatrist, who prescribed plenty of liquids, draft-free surroundings, and several books on How to Study. While Willis rummages through his medicine cabinet in search of a single-edged razor blade, we skim the books for the good parts.

"And while we're on the subject of what not to do," say Abraham Lass and Eugene Wilson in *The College Student's Handbook*, "let us strongly urge you to... avoid last-minute cramming." In *How to Study in College*, Walter Pauk, director of the Reading-Study Center at Cornell University, tells us that "if your goal in college is to gain knowledge — as it should be — cramming will not help you."

All things in moderation. Early to bed, early to rise. A penny saved is a penny earned. Waste not, want not. Plan for a rainy day.

Books on How to Study are like books on Where You Came From — if you don't already know, chances are it's too late by the time you get to the book.

But perhaps you do know, and are, right at this minute, nestling snugly amid the cramming paraphernalia. Because for you, as for others who concentrate best "under pressure," cramming has proven to be the most effective, indeed the *only* method of study. And though the practice has been devalued, defamed and discounted as ineffectual and unreliable, there is something to be said, psychologically *and* physiologically, for the tension that spurs you to action.

Studies in retention have indicated that (*a*) you remember more if you study just before the exam, retain less after a time-lapse, and (*b*) you learn and retain any part of the full body of material better if you study all the material at once than if you study each part at different intervals.

Therefore, experiments confirm the benefits of cramming for a *particular exam*, since you are not confused by material from another course, since it is fresh in your mind, having just studied it the night before, and since you've learned the full term's work at one sitting.

So we come to the first sitting. You have one week to learn a term's work. Considering your alternative may be Daddy's business if you flunk, you'd better make good use of this time.

The first step is to find out where you're at — how much you know, don't know, aren't sure about. You might check on your knowledge against your instructors' course outlines or your own notes. Then decide how much attention each course merits — a great deal for high-credit, required and major courses; much less for low-credit, elective and minor courses. Draw up a schedule that takes both factors into account. If your grade in a course is very important, you might devote a lot of time to it even though you're already rather well prepared. Or you might hardly bother with a subject about which you are almost totally ignorant because how well you do in it isn't terribly important. There are even times when you may ignore a course entirely in order to salvage four others. Make up a day-to-day, hour-by-hour schedule of how you're going to spend your cramming time, right up to the hour of your last exam. Schedule study in courses which bore you in the morning. It's almost impossible to study late at night for a course that puts you to sleep on the best of days. The same principle applies to difficult subjects, which should be attended to when you're wide awake and receptive. At the end of the day, you can reward yourself for all you've done to get there by concentrating on the easier, more pleasant material.

At this point, you must decide *how* to cram. Following is a starter set of five crams — combine elements of each to come up with the right combination for specific courses.

The Know-It-All Cram

You've been to all the lectures, done all the readings. You've accumulated copious and painstakingly outlined notes — other people come to *you* to borrow them. Every time you open a book to review you get a feeling of *déja vú*. Rolf Fuessler, twenty-one, senior at the State University of New York at Stony Brook and editor-in-chief of the campus newspaper, says that when this happens, he just looks at his notes and underlinings the night before the exam, then goes to the movies. This strategy may serve you well if you're rather casual about grades. But if you're struggling for every point, take advantage of a principle educational psychologists call "overlearning." Past the point where you've succeeded at committing a body of material to memory, the more times you go over it, the longer and greater your retention will be. Eugene H. Ehrlich, who's in charge of the Reading and Study Habits Improvement program at Columbia University, suggests you do this by spending your time trying to psych out the exam — figuring out what questions will be asked and outlining answers for them. If you're preparing for an essay test, Ehrlich says, spend your time outlining essays you have to be prepared to write. If your exam will consist of brief essays, try identifying all possible subjects and making notes on the paragraphs you will write. If you're going to have a quick-scoring test with multiple-choice and one-word answers, go over the material you could be quizzed on, looking for possible questions. Fuessler goes to *Bartlett's Quotations* to find lines he may be quizzed on in a Shakespeare exam. If you're up for an oral test, think through all the topics you're held accountable for and what you might want to say about them. Then compare your answers with your notes, text and readings. Jot down points you may have missed or mistakes you may have made. Any question you find difficulty answering will provide a point of departure for some selective, intensive reviewing. In every instance, the introduction of a provocative, related book would be not only helpful but a lot more interesting. Your frame of reference is widened, you have studied the material from a different angle and you can arrive at *original* ideas. All of which makes the difference between intake and digestion (add Food for Thought to that list of slogans), memorizing and thinking, between being tired and drained and being tired and knowledgeable.

The My-Mind-Is-a-Total-Blank Cram

You've been going to the lectures and keeping up with assignments, but the material is foreign; you're certain a mistake has been made — you never read this. A good technique for improving retention is *immediate recall* — checking your memory on a topic immediately after you've studied the material.

A skeleton outline of the term's work on one piece of paper indicates weak areas and triggers responses to key words, phrases. Start by separating the course into its major sections. Read your notes on a section a few times until you feel you've fully committed them to memory. Now, without looking at your original notes, write out a summarizing outline. When you've followed this procedure for each section, divide your summary in half. Go over each half successively until it's set in your head. Then lay it aside and make an even more concise outline. When you've crammed this last summary firmly into your (we hope) receptive skull, construct a one-page outline that will key your memory for the entire course. Now take this one-page skeleton and *use it to reconstruct* the material of the entire course. When you've finished, you should have something like a facsimile of your original notes. If you've forgotten anything important, insert a brief reference to it in your final key. During the exam, you should be able to reconstruct the entire course from memory if necessary.

The Let-Me-Borrow-Your-Notes Cram

Your attendance has been spotty, your note-taking haphazard, and only a few books on the reading list are crossed off. The first step is to get a good set of notes from someone whose accuracy and grasp of the subject you trust. If the other person needs the notes to study with, so much the better. But steer clear of the copying machine and copy them out yourself; as you do you'll find yourself beginning to assimilate them. Then go the skeleton-key route as if the notes were your own. Second step: Fill in the holes in your readings. You won't have time to read the entire list, so start by establishing some priorities. Which are the most important books on the list? Which books, chapters of books, were given the most attention in class? Out of ten books, you might end up reading two, reading two or three significant chapters in three, skimming through three, and skimming a few chapters in two. When you're pressed for time, don't read a secondary source if the primary source is easier and shorter. Plato's *Republic* goes down easier than most books on Greek philosophy.

"Review notes" can also be helpful. Jules Dienstag, Columbia, '68, is secretary of the school's august Academic Affairs Committee. He is grade-conscious, as premeds perforce must be, and has never rated less than a B — in any course. "I'll take a 'trot' (student slang for review notes)," Dienstag says, "and fill in the outline from memory with anything that is in the lectures or readings but isn't there." When you come to a topic in the trot outline which you can't flesh out adequately, go back to class notes or the readings and refresh your memory.

The Oh-Well-Maybe-I-Can-Get-a-D Cram

You've ignored the course entirely. Your instructor couldn't spot you as a member of the class in a lineup. Your notebook is full of doodles. You've just borrowed a copy of the reading list. You hadn't realized so many books could be written on one subject, let alone be *assigned*. You'll be satisfied just to squeak through. Best bet is to start borrowing a copy of the most discoursive set of notes you can find — they'll make you feel more confident than an outline. Read the notes until you think you know them, then put them aside and practice outlining them from memory until you can do it without a slip. Find someone trustworthy to tell you the relative importance of the books on the reading list — you may be running scared for nothing. There may only be a few you'll actually be tested on, perhaps none at all. "I had a biology instructor who assigned a really murderous reading list — you could have spent the entire semester just reading those books," one former colleague told me. "So one day I went to him and said, 'You can't really expect us to *read* all that, can you?'

" 'No!' he laughed. 'Of course I can't. I just want you to go through some of the books as background material. The only thing I'm going to hold you responsible for is the lectures.' "

You'll get your priorities straight, then go through the list as in the Let-Me-Borrow-Your-Notes Cram. Only you may read only one book through, read a few chapters in four or five, skim two or three books, and skim a few chapters in a book or two.

If you have quite a few books to cover and not enough guidance about what is important, use indexes. Look up the topic or person you're supposed to be studying and read only the pertinent pages. If you have only a vague idea what the course is about, the index will be helpful — just look for the items that have the most page numbers after them and read those. Students have passed courses on little more than a few stray facts gleaned from index-hunting.

Another possible ploy before resigning yourself to academic probation is to borrow other classmates' term papers, hoping they'll help answer questions on the exam. You're not plagiarizing by paraphrasing a few of Alice's ideas any more than Alice was in paraphrasing a few of Freud's (although a direct line to Freud would be more reliable).

The Gang-Cram

Regardless of how well prepared you are, communal study can be very productive. Groups of under five people seem to work best. First thing is to meet and assign a section of the course to each person. A few days later, each gang-crammer distributes to the others a complete outline of the material he covered, then goes over the outline point by point with the group. At the next gang-cram, a day or two later, each person comes prepared with questions he thinks may appear on the test, and the group plots out answers together. You'll find that working with friends will put a great deal of pressure on you to perform. You're more likely to prepare a good outline if you know that four other people are depending on you. Working in a group will aid your memory, too. Did you ever forget what was said at a bull session that took place at midnight by 9 A.M. the next morning? Fatigue is less a problem when you're gang-cramming — the contact with other people in the same boat keeps you alert. And you're more likely to fall asleep testing yourself on French vocabulary than when being tested by a friend.

Sleep is the curse of the cramming class. How-to-Study book authors can't seem to get together on what to do about it. Says Colin E. Woodley in *How to Study and Prepare for Exams:* "When your study table calls for a type of study requiring a high degree of concentration (such as memorizing), and you dutifully sit down at your desk, even though you are extremely tired, there is only one thing to do — go to bed." Not so, says Mr. Pauk. "One word of warning: Too many students rationalize that it is better to give in to the urge to sleep and that when they wake up they will be refreshed. Few students report this happy result. Rather, they awake to a formidable pile of work undone. It is far better to combat the desire to sleep, get the work done, and then go to bed at the usual time."

Neither of these gentlemen gets at the root of the matter. The main problem is how to avoid the urge to sleep in the first place. There are two ways to combat fatigue besides sleep — food and exercise. First, don't neglect your three squares. On the contrary — make it four, and bring your books to the table. Second, lay in a supply of energy food and munch it constantly while you lucubrate — you later work off any weight you've gained jumping for joy over your grades. Third, exercise while you study. This may mean taking a break for a few minutes every hour and walking, or even doing calisthenics. Keep the windows open; plenty of air and low temperatures will help keep your head clear.

What about stimulants? Dienstag doesn't believe in any ("I don't even take coffee") while Fuessler takes black coffee by the pot. Coffee won't harm you, but if you find too much of it puts your nerves on edge or reduces your ability to concentrate, reduce your intake or lay off entirely. Caffeine pills are less desirable — they're more concentrated and leave out the sugar. You'll have to make your own decision about whether to use amphetamines. Dienstag and Fuessler have managed to study long and hard without once popping a Dex. Dr. Anthony Philip, Director of Columbia's Counseling Services, is also down on speed.

"I have no doubt," he says, "that the use of amphetamines is widespread around exam time. And I have no doubt they keep you awake. The question is, do they help you learn? There are experiments in which it has been shown that when subjects are asked to solve mathematical problems under the influence of these drugs, they get the impression they're doing exceptionally well, while in fact they're doing quite poorly. But there are experiments whose conclusions are just the opposite — that the amphetamines enhance learning capacity. The evidence is contradictory."

Regardless of how you stay awake while you cram, nights before exams are times for sleep. If you can possibly manage to, knock off about 1 A.M. the night before.

And dream: *You have taken your seat in the fetid gym and amid the rustling papers you put a nickel in your head, pull the handle. Your eyes come up lemons and you cup your hands just as a cascade of facts gush out, overflow onto your blue book and array themselves in brilliant prose.*

You're brilliant; you've made Dean's List. Go to sleep. You have to register tomorrow.

For Thinking, Talking, Writing

1. How do *you* study best — gradually, during the semester, or "under pressure," cramming? If all the "How to Study" books claim that cramming is the *poorest* way to study, why do you suppose that so many students continue to use this method?

2. Mr. Karpel points out that although you remember more if you study just before the exam, you retain less of the material studied that way after a time-lapse. Thus part of learning good study techniques involves making judgments: is the material you are studying in any particular course something you want to be sure you know later, or is it something you're only trying to "get through" for now? Evaluate each of the courses you are now taking in these terms: "remember later" or "get through now." This should help you plan your study time during the semester — gradual and careful study in the courses in which you really need to learn the material permanently; casual study and perhaps last-minute cramming for those courses which are not important to your future.

3. Have you learned any new study techniques through reading this material — techniques which perhaps you've never thought of before? If so, list them and explain why you think they might be useful to *you* in your college career.

Why Grades
Should Be Abolished

Sydney J. Harris

A teacher I know has sent me a recent book called *Making the Grade*, which is a nice pun in itself — for young people today can't make the grade unless they make the grade. And the grade has become more important than anything else in the educational process.

For many long and wearisome years, I have chanted the refrain that grades should be abandoned in the school system. Everything they accomplish is negative, and they have absolutely no meaning outside the narrow framework of the course or the school.

In *Making the Grade*, the three authors — all educators, by the way — after examining possible alternatives and compromises, finally recommend the complete abolition of the grading system. Their main charges against it are five in number:

1. It "institutionalizes" the students and moves them through the college anonymously, like beef stamped on the butt and processed in a meat-packing plant.

2. It focuses course work around the goal of "earning a grade" rather than learning the subject. The grade, which is just a symbol, becomes an object in itself, and distorts the learning process.

3. The relationship with the faculty is determined by the struggle for a "good grade"; there is little dialogue and less searching for wisdom, but merely memorization and playing back to the teacher his own set of values, preconceptions and criteria — which may differ vastly from teacher to teacher in the same general subject.

4. Study habits vary, depending upon how much the student wants to get a "good grade" or how much of a "snap course" a certain subject is; it may be easier to get an "A" without working in one course than to get a "C" when working hard in another. This bears no relation to the intrinsic merit of the subject.

5. Student morale is depressed by a growing awareness, throughout college, of the whimsical and arbitrary ways in which grades are awarded by different teachers and different departments. For this reason, scholarship is replaced by

SYDNEY J. HARRIS courtesy of *Chicago Daily News* and Publishers–Hall Syndicate.

gamesmanship, and even the awarding of the ultimate degree becomes cheapened and trivialized in the eyes of most students.

Of course, the trouble begins in the early school years, when young pupils are invited to compete with one another for gold stars and high grades, instead of cooperating with one another and with each teacher to bring out the optimum resources of each pupil. As long as schooling is considered a "contest," genuine education must suffer.

For Thinking, Talking, Writing

1. You are in a particularly good position to speak on the subject of whether or not grades should be abolished, because you have been struggling with the "grade problem" for years. State your own opinion on each of the five reasons Mr. Harris gives for abolishing grades. Are these reasons valid? Why or why not?
2. In this article, Mr. Harris does not discuss any alternative method of evaluation, if grades were abolished. What would you suggest as an alternative? Or does a student's work in school need to be evaluated at all? Why or why not?
3. Do you agree with Mr. Harris that "As long as schooling is considered a 'contest,' genuine education must suffer"? Or is the spirit of competition necessary as a motivation for learning? Defend your answer.

Calculated Risk

Fredelle Maynard

The other day I saw a huge billboard — just the photograph of a baby's feet and the legend, "$18,000 for college. Will you have it when he needs it?" I suppose the parents of very young children, seeing that sign, don't worry too much. After all, they've got years and years to save up. But for the parents of teenagers, the thought of having to spend that much money in a few years is staggering.

Nonetheless, I doubt whether many people stop to ask themselves, as my husband, Hal, and I did last spring, "Do we *have* to spend it? Have we got that kind of money?" And most of all, "Does our son *need* to go to college?"

It's easy, these days, to assume that every secondary-school graduate must continue his education — that college is an inalienable right, like life, liberty and the pursuit of happiness. Hal and I have always acted on that assumption; we started our marriage determined to give our children all the things we never had, including a college education. We both grew up during the hungry thirties, and we know a lot about the struggle to earn a living. Hal went to work straight out of high school and came up the hard way from stock boy to assistant manager in a large department store. But without a college degree, the upper level jobs will always be closed to him. Naturally, then, we'd planned that of our three children, Larry at least — the eldest and the only boy — would get a better start.

"It doesn't matter so much for the girls," Hal would say as we put aside ten or fifteen dollars every month for the education fund. "I'd like them to go to college, but after all, they'll get married. It's Larry I'm concerned about. I don't want him to be boxed in the way I am. If you want to move ahead you've got to have the right credentials."

Not that we had unrealistic ambitions for our son. He wasn't much of a student, even in grade school. We didn't think in terms of the professions, like medicine or law. But there seemed no reason why an averagely bright kid couldn't make it through a business-school curriculm, or maybe liberal arts. Purely as an investment, college seemed the logical goal. We knew that a college graduate can be expected to earn, over a lifetime, $100,000 more than a high school graduate. And we figured — this was when Larry was still reading Dick and Jane — that $8,000 would see him through.

Of course we couldn't have anticipated that college costs would rise so rapidly, or that our own income simply wouldn't keep pace with the demands of a growing family. Every time we managed to save a little extra, along came an emergency that swallowed up the surplus: in eighth grade, Larry hurt himself playing football — which left him with a bad knee and cost us a fortune in medical bills, and Moira's teeth needed straightening. By the time Larry entered high school, our education fund stood at just over $2,000, a long way from the goal. Still, we didn't worry too much. Tuition at our state university is a lot lower than at private colleges. Larry could work summers and earn something toward his expenses. Anyway, weren't there all kinds of grants and loans available?

Our first disappointment had to do with those summer earnings. Larry is not a fireball. He's the kind of boy who is perfectly willing to work if only somebody else will take care of the tiresome preliminaries — like finding a job. In his sophomore year, for instance, we started talking summer work in March, but Larry's response was always a casual, "It's too early. No one's hiring yet for July."

By June, when he went job-hunting in earnest, the hiring was all over. He spent that summer sleeping till noon and hanging around a local garage.

The next year we urged him to apply for post office work, which paid over two dollars an hour. Larry sent away for the application, even boned up on the practice tests — and then forgot to take the civil-service exam on the required date. That meant two months of lawn mowing and odd jobs. He cleared just $217 for the summer.

"Don't worry, Mom," he said. "There's a chance of a good job at the Triple W ski lodge over Christmas vacation."

Suddenly, though, it was his senior year. Hal and I looked at our bankbook and began to worry in earnest. Maybe Larry should take on some kind of after-school work? But his grades were shaky, and finally we both agreed that what we couldn't afford, this last crucial year, was for the boy to be distracted and maybe not accepted by a college. "I think," Hal said, "we'd better go see the school guidance counselor, look into scholarship and loan possibilities."

Our appointment with Mr. Bates, the guidance counselor, was not cheering. Yes, there were college scholarships available for youngsters from low- and middle-income families, but they were based on merit as well as need. Larry, with his low-C average, couldn't possibly qualify.

"In fact," Mr. Bates said, frowning at the folder of grades in front of him, "I honestly doubt if your son will make the state university. Marks...class standing...college-board scores...the picture's not too bright. I'd advise Larry to make three or four other applications, to colleges with less rigorous entrance standards. As for the loans — yes, you could apply for a low interest loan, guaranteed by the state or Federal government. But the maximum there is a thousand dollars a year."

Larry wrote away to the colleges his counselor suggested, and we made another grim discovery. Even *applications* cost money. Every time Larry filled out an application form, we had to write another check for ten or fifteen dollars — nonrefundable. Two of the colleges insisted on interviews, involving longish trips we hadn't budgeted for. As the magic date of notification approached, Hal said bleakly, "I begin to see what the next four years will be like. Larry hasn't started and we've spent a couple of hundred dollars already."

There was worse to come. On April 15, Larry received formal notices from the schools he'd applied to. The state university and two others sent a flat No. One college put him on its waiting list. The fifth accepted him — on condition he take a remedial English course before the fall term began.

After the first shock of the rejections wore off, Larry recovered his spirits. "This'll be really great. I mean, most of the guys go to State. I sort of like the idea of going farther away, getting to see a different part of the country."

Hal was scratching figures on a note pad. "You know, son," he said, "this changes the picture. There's that summer school business, for instance...."

Larry shrugged. "Gee, Dad, that's no big deal. Sure, I'd rather not hack away at English for eight weeks — but it's worth it."

"That's not what I meant," Hal went on. "It's a matter of money. This means you can't take on a summer job. In fact, instead of earning four or five hundred toward tuition, you're going to *spend* that much extra at summer school. And you'll have higher expenses next year. Tuition alone is a thousand dollars more than at State, and there's transportation to figure. It all adds up."

The night Hal and I sat down together for what a politician might call an agonizing reappraisal. Hal's annual income, before taxes, was $9,350. College for Larry — including books, clothes, transportation and so on — could run $4,000 a year or more. A student loan would cover a quarter of that. We could manage, from savings, another thousand a year — provided we had no unexpected crises. Where would the rest come from?

"As I see it," Hal said at last, "there are just three alternatives. We can borrow — possibly remortgage the house. I can take on another job nights or weekends. Or you can go back to work."

I spoke without a moment's thought — instinctively saying something we'd never even considered. "There's a fourth alternative. Larry doesn't have to go to college."

"You mean, not this year?"

"I don't know what I mean. Maybe just not go, period."

Hal put down his pencil. "But we've always assumed...."

Suddenly I felt on firm ground. "Of course we have. So has Larry. But the simple fact of the matter is, it doesn't make sense. Not now, anyway. If Larry goes to college, the rest of us have to make big sacrifices. You certainly can't moonlight; you work hard enough as is. If I take a job, the household suffers and so do the girls. Faith and Moira still like to find mother in the kitchen when they come home from school. And in a few more years, they'll be graduating. Faith talks nursing school. Moira's such a good student she should have a chance at college."

"Do you mean Larry should give up the whole idea?"

"Not necessarily," I said. "Maybe he could work and plan to go to college once he's saved enough money. Besides, working just might give him a clearer idea of *why* he wants to go in the first place. Now, it's just a matter of 'Everybody else is going. Why shouldn't I?' "

It's funny how, once we'd made the decision, it seemed so obviously right. Larry took it hard at first, until we explained that we weren't punishing him for not getting better grades or not earning more money. In fact, like most teenagers, he'd had no idea of what the family finances were like. When we showed him our budget figures, he seemed grateful for being treated like a responsible adult.

For just seven months now, Larry's been working at a local tool-and-die plant. Even in that time, we've seen him do more growing up than in two years of meandering through high school. Now there seems to be direction in his thinking.

"My job isn't hard," he said the other day. "It's just so *boring*. I'd sure hate to spend the rest of my life on nuts and bolts." Then, after a minute: "I've been thinking about taking a university extension course next year. That way I can get that remedial English out of the way, and be all set for college in case I ever...."

It's still too early to know whether Larry will indeed continue his education. Maybe he'll decide college isn't important enough to justify a considerable sacrifice of time and money. But if he wants to go badly enough, he'll make the sacrifice (with whatever help we can give him). And in that case, chances are he'll take the studying seriously. He won't be just a passenger enjoying a free ride, but the captain of the ship— choosing his own port and heading straight for it.

For Thinking, Talking, Writing

This article poses a basic question you may not really have thought about: whether or not college is the right road for *you*. Many students, like Larry, just *assume* they will go to college, whether they like school and are good at it or not, either because their parents assume they will go or because pressures from society indoctrinate us with the idea that college is the "thing to do." Analyze your own beliefs and attitudes about college by expressing *your* point of view on the following questions:

1. Should "everybody" (meaning every high school graduate) go to college if he or she can? Why or why not?
2. Is a college education more important for men than for women? Why or why not?
3. Forgetting about the problems of the draft for a moment, what are the real *reasons,* as you see them, for going to college? What is *your* particular reason?
4. Can you think of good reasons for *not* going to college? Can you suggest sensible alternatives—other choices besides college—that will lead to a worthwhile, rewarding life?
5. Do you agree that postponing college for a while—working or putting in service time instead—can be valuable to the process of growing up and knowing what you *want* from college?
6. If you had been Larry's parents, would you have made the choice they did? If not, what would *you* have done?

THE GENERATION

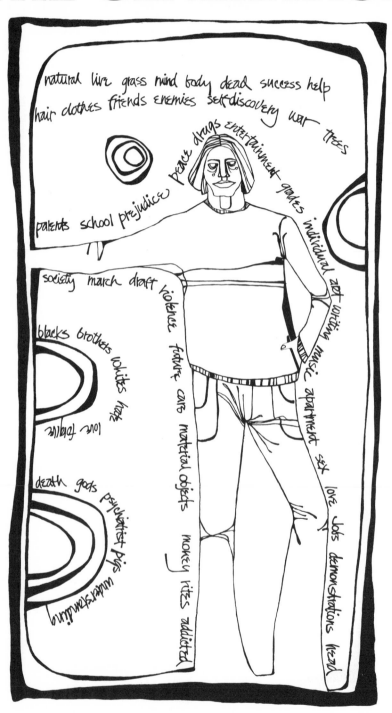

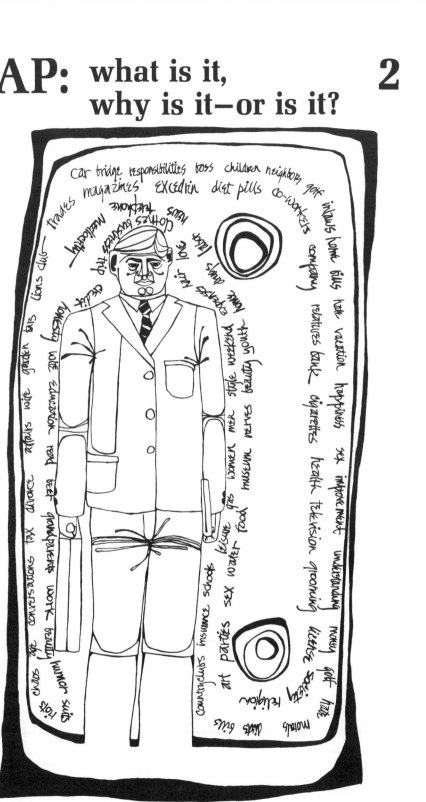

Introduction

Years ago George Bernard Shaw said, "If parents would only realize how they bore their children." Yet the interesting thing about the generation gap is the question, does it really exist? Or, perhaps more to the point, does it exist to any greater extent today than it did in the past? Even in Biblical days, young people were referred to as "A stubborn and rebellious generation" (Psalms, 78:8); and the quotations that introduce this section indicate that we have always been concerned with the gap between older and younger people.

Still, many people feel that the generation gap is worse now than it has ever been before. If it is, perhaps the reason is the tremendous explosion of knowledge during the twentieth century, an explosion which has made life for young people nowadays so *very* different from life as it was when their parents were young.

Comments by teen-agers give a bit of insight into how some members of the younger generation feel about the generation gap:

> "A lot of parents are using sociological terms, like 'the generation gap' as an excuse for their inadequacies. We're not *that* far away from our parents, if they would take the time to see why we are what we are," says Pam Roberts, of Findlay, Ohio.

> And Elaine Malm, from Allentown, Pennsylvania, states, "Too many teens are so anti-Establishment that they can't take any advice from adults. Sure, we have to find our own morals, but in the process do we have to cut out all communication with adults?"*

In this section you will explore the generation gap as it has been written about recently. As you do, keep in mind these questions: *Is* there really a generation gap, or are the differences in opinion between the generations due to something other than a difference in age? Is the younger generation really any wiser now than the older generation thought they were when they were young? Since the "generation gap" is causing so many hostilities between people, what can be done to reduce or eliminate it, so that people can work more closely together to correct some of the problems of our society?

Read—think—talk—write. Can *you* solve the "generation gap"—at least for yourself?

*Reprinted with permission from *McCall's*. Copyright © 1968 by McCall Publishing Company.

Now, About That Gap

Compiled by Ruth Block

"What is more enchanting than the voices of young people when you can't hear what they say!"
—Logan Pearsall Smith.

"Youth loves honor and victory more than money. It really cares next to nothing about money, for it has not yet learned what the lack of it means."
—Aristotle.

"The use of a university is to make young gentlemen as unlike their fathers as possible."
—Woodrow Wilson.

"When I was a boy of fourteen my father was so ignorant I could hardly stand to have the old man around. But when I got to be twenty-one, I was astonished at how much the old man had learned in seven years."
—Mark Twain.

"Youth is wholly experimental."
—Robert Louis Stevenson.

"I remember my youth and the feeling that will never come back any more—the feeling that I could last forever, outlast the sea, the earth, and all men."
—Joseph Conrad.

"Come on now all you young men, all over the world. . . . Twenty to twenty-five! These are the years! Don't be content with things as they are. 'The earth is yours and the fulness thereof.' Enter upon your inheritance, accept your responsibilities. Raise the glorious flags again, advance them upon the new enemies, who constantly gather upon the front of the human army, and have only to be assaulted to be overthrown. . . . You will make all kinds of mistakes; but as long as you are generous and true, and also fierce, you cannot hurt the world or even seriously distress her. She was made to be wooed and won by youth. She has lived and thrived only by repeated subjugations."
                              —Winston Churchill.

"Everybody's youth is a dream, a form of chemical madness."
                    —F. Scott Fitzgerald.

"All the young are in the same position as the Negro. The discrepancy between the riches of the TV feast and the poverty of the school experience is creating great ferment, friction and psychic violence."
                    —Marshall McLuhan.

"When one is twenty, ideas of the outside world and the effect one can have on it take precedence over everything else."
                    —Stendhal.

"Almost everything that is great has been done by youth."
                    —Benjamin Disraeli.

"The black melancholy of young men has many apparent causes, but the many are really one: that the young men wish and will more than they can do."
—*Carl Van Doren.*

"The young leading the young, is like the blind leading the blind; they will both fall into the ditch."
—*Lord Chesterfield.*

"These students, ill at ease in their factory-like universities and lost in the midst of the lonely crowd, could be compared to the workers in the first factories at the start of the 19th century. The workers destroyed the machines; [the students] symbolically break their working tools and the instrument of their servitude, the tables and the chairs."
—*Raymond Aron (May, 1968).*

"Everyone believes in his own youth that the world began to exist only with his own coming, and that in reality everything exists on his account."
—*Goethe.*

"Youth thinks intelligence a good substitute for experience, and his elders think experience a substitute for intelligence."
—*Lyman Bryson.*

For Thinking, Talking, Writing

What is *your* reaction to what each of these well-known men says about young people?

Generation Gap?
Ask Any Grandparent

Erma Bombeck

We hear a lot of static about the generation gap between parents and their children.

Can you imagine what it's like between grandparent and grandchild? One grandmother in Jackson, Mich., implored me to "write something about us. My grandchildren think I fought off the dinosaurs!"

The only solace I can give you is that age is a relative thing. When I was 9, I asked my grandmother if she had ever visited the Garden of Eden.

I envisioned her at birth: a small baby with long gray hair secured in a bun, an apron and sturdy black-tie shoes. She had bypassed childhood and started her first year of life over a washboard and a hot kitchen stove. I calculated her to be about 100 years old. (She was 40.)

When I was 18, I promoted her from Bibical times to the birth of America, pleading always for stories of her capture by Indian tribes and how it really was at Little Big Horn.

I used to feel sorry for Grandma. She was so serious and moralistic, she had skirted love and sex for mundane things like making soap and barrel staves. As for Grandma's five children, I rationalized she had conceived them without sin.

When I was 22, a curious thing happened. I had a child. It took about 20 years off Grandma's life. It put her somewhere between the Boston Tea Party and Appomattox.

We actually began to have some dialog. I discovered she had once danced, had spit curls, kissed a boy, gone to school, been on a honeymoon, gained weight during pregnancy and giggled in church. She began to take on human qualities! Within 10 years, she was almost my contemporary.

The trouble with youth (today's and yesterday's) is that they are so self-centered they equate everything with themselves.

They cannot imagine growing up without brush rollers, transplants, television, pizzas, drive-ins or credit cards. What a drag. No Buckleys, no astronauts, no miniskirts, no Peanuts, no dissent.

Reprinted with permission from Newsday, Inc.

They don't know it, but the "now" generation is not so far away from the "has been" group.

For every John Glenn and Frank Borman, there was an Orville and Wilbur Wright, for every Dr. Christiaan Barnard, there was a Dr. Louis Pasteur, for every Betty Friedan a Carrie Nation, for every Vietnam a San Juan Hill, for every Steve McQueen a Charles Bickford.

If anyone is keeping score, today's old people (can't stand calling them Senior Citizens) are leading the pack. They're moving in the most devastating transition of all times and holding their own.

The other day my 10-year-old asked his grandmother if he could borrow her flag with 13 stars to take to school with him. He's just about on schedule. Two years ago he wanted to know if granddad was a Viking or did he go to college.

For Thinking, Talking, Writing

1. Did you feel that grandparents were this "old" while you were growing up? Mrs. Bombeck says that after she was grown, her grandmother seemed younger; have you had that experience yet?
2. How many of the "older" famous people that Mrs. Bombeck mentions can you identify?
   (a) Orville and Wilbur Wright
   (b) Dr. Louis Pasteur
   (c) Carrie Nation
   (d) Charles Bickford
3. Although Mrs. Bombeck intends this primarily as a humorous article, she says some important things about feelings between generations. What are they?

The Lighter Side of the Generation Gap

Writer and Artist: David Berg

For Thinking, Talking, Writing

1. "The Lighter Side of the Generation Gap" originally appeared in MAD magazine. How do you usually define "mad"? What is the dictionary definition? By what definition are these selections "mad"?

2. In these selections which side of the generation gap seems more "right" to you? What are the "gaps" in attempting to reconcile "right" and "wrong"?

3. How would you define "hippie"? How does the treatment of the hippies in these selections agree or disagree with your beliefs about them? In these selections, how is a "hippie" defined? (Your definition should be the result of a *careful* reading of the pictures.)

I Don't Trust
Anyone Under 30

Cecelia Holland

Militant, committed, articulate and radical, the generation under 30 claims to be the hope of the world. Our parents believe it. They contrast the purity of our motives and the energy of our commitments with their own corrupted morality and corroded traditions and decide that everything we say *must* be right. "Don't let the kids down," says an advertisement for Gene McCarthy. Not since the Children's Crusade in the early 13th century has an older generation entrusted so much of its salvation to the young. Not since the Renaissance have we wielded so much influence over our elders. (Did Cesare Borgia trust anybody over 30?)

Much of the work in the civil-rights crusade is done by people under 30 years of age. Almost all the protesters of the Vietnam war (and the great majority of those fighting in it) are under 30. There are very few hippies over 30, and the hippie movement stands out as the single most visible protest against the syndrome commonly called the American Way of Life. My generation is the most idealistic, the most dynamic and the most liberal in history; just ask us, we'll tell you. We're strong on freedom and long on love, and there are enough of us around to change the very definitions of the words to make these statements fact.

Are we strong on freedom? It would be hard to find a young person outside the South who isn't all for the Negro revolution. The freedom to protest the Vietnam war—to protest anything (except the protesters)—is as hallowed as the bones of a saint. Yet to hold a conservative viewpoint, however honestly, can only be a sign of cowardice. Anybody over 30 will ask first what your opinion is on the war. Anybody under 30 will automatically assume you're against it; if you aren't, you're a heretic.

Freedom and free speech should mean that anyone can hold any opinion he wants on the Negro or the war in Vietnam, as long as he doesn't try to enforce his views on anybody else. But our generation's conception of freedom goes more like this: "Do your own thing and all will be well, as long as your own thing is certified pure by the rest of us."

But what if your own thing doesn't happen to conform to that of the world, the militant students, the nonstudents or any other faction?

REPRINTED WITH PERMISSION OF THE SATURDAY EVENING POST 1968 Curtis Publishing Company.

There are, after all, people in this world who manage to live entirely within the existing social structure, and who do so by choice. There are people who find it possible to go through life neither rebelling nor conforming. Are they all hypocrites? To the under-30 group, nonalignment is as abhorrent as slavish devotion to the *status quo*.

Let's face it, my generation is *not* strong on freedom. Basically, we simply want to do what we like, without being bothered by anything silly like antique conventions and laws. But why the devil can't we just say so and let it go at that? Why do we dress our preferences in the vestments of a quasi-religion?

Part of the reason, I suspect, is that we're still bound by at least one antique convention: doing things for the right reasons, the socially acceptable motives. We have a party line, certain things and opinions that must be professed under certain conditions. Deviation labels one unfit. Anybody who's ever ventured into the wilderness of conversation with more than one hip or militant student or political fanatic or fellow-traveler knows that there is a striking similarity, not only in the lines of argument taken on almost all subjects but in the words and slogans used, not only within each faction but across partisan lines. Doctrine has hardened into dogma. (I am a fellow-traveler with the "straights," which means that sometimes I'm self-consciously hip; and making the transition from one vernacular to the other is difficult enough to suggest that the differences are not merely linguistic. Hip-think doesn't require logic or clarity, which makes it easier, of course, to sound profound.)

The drug issue is a good example of our dogmatism. If you don't smoke or pop pills, you're narrow-minded, tradition-bound and a chicken. Your reasons for denying the Nirvana of drugs make no difference. There are people for whom "grass," "acid," "speed" and their relatives hold no interest, just as there are people who dislike roast beef. Usually they manage to commune with the infinite quite well without an interpreter. Yet these people are as square to the drug-user as the housewife who won't wear short skirts because the neighbors might talk.

What does love mean to the Love Generation? It can mean purging oneself of hatred and prejudice and welcoming everyone else as a brother, and it can mean preaching the gospel while pushing Methedrine. It can mean the L.A. Diggers, a group of well-off, sympathetic people who give runaway kids a place to stop and catch their breath, and it can mean the "rank sweat of an enseamed bed." There's something of calf-love in all of our uses of the word, and something else that's just a little weird: The widely published off-campus living arrangements of college students like Barnard's Linda Leclair is another indication, with *Playboy* magazine and Ingmar Bergman, that sex is rapidly becoming a spectator sport. Why is it we can't love without announcing it to the world in infinite detail?

Love, as the song-makers know, is a private thing, and those who proclaim it in public tend to slip a little in the practice. Whatever the Columbia students were thinking about when they threw rocks, mailboxes and desks at the cops during their recent fit of self-expression, it wasn't love. If it was, it lost a lot in the translation.

Actually, when you cut out the preaching and look at the action, we're all sharpshooters—in the old sense—and our major target is that famous bogeyman, the world we never made. We think our parents made it—the hypocrisy, the prejudice, the materialism, the hatred, the uncertainty—and we know we have the answers for improving it. It takes the wisdom that comes with some age to realize that if the solution looks simple you probably don't understand the problem. And it takes the kind of minds we haven't got to realize that what you say means less than what you do.

The hip world isn't the whole of our generation, but it's a good microcosm. Its values and flaws characterize us all. The hippie drops out of society. But luckily for him, society sticks around, because the hippie is a parasite. The straight world supports him. Without this country's prosperity, there could be no hippies. They'd have nobody to bum from, nobody to give them easy jobs to tide them over the winter. There would be no leisure time in which to practice being hip, and no straight public to be titillated and fleeced. The hip world is neither self-supporting nor self-perpetuating, and it's hypocritical to claim that it is.

This kind of hypocrisy creeps into almost all our debunking of the Bad World. The institutions that create the atmosphere conducive to protest are inextricably bound up with the institutions we protest against. If it weren't for the Establishment, what would we fight against? And if we couldn't fight, who knows but—horrors—we might become Establishment ourselves? History is full of rebellious crusades that demolished the *status quo* and wound up becoming the *status quo* themselves.

To protect ourselves, we try to cover the deck with protests—prove our unimpeachable nobility by knocking everything in sight as ignoble. How well do we listen to what we say?

Materialism in this country has taken the odd turn of becoming a form of idealism: things put aside for tomorrow. Our parents live for tomorrow, in a thingy kind of way. They dream of the bright world ahead, a utopia which we find rather pathetic because we quit believing in utopias a long time ago. We live for today. We grab what we can get, now. Tomorrow never comes anyway. And when it does, it's just like today. Actually we aren't even particularly cynical about it, just sad.

The deadly corollary to this kind of thinking is that what you have to work for isn't worth having. (A woman's magazine recently declared that the emphasis is on "roles, not goals," a decent square translation of "do your own thing.") We think knowledge that must be learned isn't valuable; only intuitive, revealed knowledge is worth while. The college "grind" is a pitiable figure. It's so much easier to fake your way through. College isn't a place where you learn; it's an object to be revolutionized. You don't find knowledge, it comes to you, complete with bright colors and dogs barking flowers.

If we work, we do just enough to survive. A job exists to keep one fed—we accept employment as a token reason for accepting a living. We're a generation of grasshoppers.

We love Marshall McLuhan because he makes it impossible, and therefore unnecessary, to think logically. Our passion for J. R. R. Tolkien is, I think, due not to the clear-cut moral position he espouses but to the blatantly mythological character of his books; they aren't about the real world, which makes them safe to handle. ("We can dig the morality, but we don't have to do anything about it, because we aren't mythological people," says my sister, who is 17.) The fads borrowed from Oriental and Indian cultures are deliberate archaisms. We long for the safe, still, dead worlds in which all values are only reflections of eternity. We don't like change, and we doubt we can cope with it, so we pretend it doesn't exist. Reality has become elusive, painful, a blind god that isn't dead but probably isn't human either, so we prefer ambiguity.

If we're grasshoppers, what about the ants? "Of course they're straight—they're parents." Nobody over 30 can possibly have access to the Truth. Actually, we don't dislike our parents so much as we resent them—their money-fever, their ability to muddle (and meddle in) almost everything and, above all, their timidity. J. Alfred Prufrocks, the batch of them. It's the lack of authority they display that revolts us, and their readiness to be fooled. If our parents were a bolder, tougher generation, we would be a meeker, sweeter pack of grasshoppers.

The harshness of our indictment of our parents stems from our essential innocence, and our innocence stems from ignorance. We're the best-educated generation around, judging by the number of years we spend in schools, but we really don't know much. Colleges insist on graduating students who can't write an intelligible English sentence, who don't speak three words of a foreign language, who have read neither Marx nor Keynes nor Freud nor Joyce, and who never will. It isn't necessarily the colleges' fault: The books and the professors are there, but we've lost the ability to take advantage of them. Nevertheless, we feel ourselves entitled to hold an opinion on everything, whether we know anything about it or not. And we've discovered that the less we know about something, the easier it is to hold a strong opinion about it.

The Berkeley sit-in in defense of free speech was followed by the protest against the presence of a Navy recruiting booth on campus; many of the same students (and non-students) took part in both. Isn't this in some small, tinny way inconsistent? This may be an unfair parallel, but this kind of behavior reminds me of the U.S.S.R., where Benjamin Spock is considered a hero because he defies the United States Government; and where Soviet writers who publish anything in opposition to the Party are tried and punished as traitors.

Heaven preserve us from our own children.

For Thinking, Talking, Writing

This article was written by a 24-year-old woman who is already a successful author. Thus she is not only a member of the "under-30" generation, she is also successful within the social structure as it now exists. In a way, then, she speaks from *both* sides of the fence.
1. Discuss the following statements from Miss Holland's article:
   (a) "... If the solution looks simple you probably don't understand the problem."
   (b) "... What you say means less than what you do."
   (c) "... The less ... [you] know about something, the easier it is to hold a strong opinion about it."
2. Do you agree with Miss Holland that the values and flaws of the hip world characterize the whole younger generation? Analyze your own friends and classmates—do they seem to you to be intolerant of the freedom of others to hold opinions different from their own, hypocritical about society, unwilling to work for anything, unwilling to try to think logically, withdrawers from reality, prejudiced against people over 30, and intellectually ignorant?
3. In order to understand some of Miss Holland's points, it is necessary that you know her *allusions* (the items she refers to that she expects the reader already to know something about). If you don't recognize the following people and things, look them up; then relate each of these allusions to the point she is making:
   (a) The Children's Crusade in the 13th century
   (b) Cesare Borgia
   (c) Nirvana
   (d) Ingmar Bergman
   (e) Marshall McLuhan
   (f) J. R. R. Tolkien
   (g) J. Alfred Prufrock
   (h) Karl Marx
   (i) John Maynard Keynes
   (j) Sigmund Freud
   (k) James Joyce
   (l) Benjamin Spock

Who Actually Creates Gaps?

Mike Royko

A student berated me recently for the failure of my generation to stamp out war, poverty, injustice and prejudice.

He said we were do-nothings when we were his age. And because of us, his generation now had so much evil-curing to do.

I couldn't think of any excuses, so I just mumbled that I'd been busy and couldn't get around to everything.

But the truth is, I had never given any thought to being part of a particular generation, so I couldn't say much about its accomplishments.

That's a mistake. We must speak up for our generations. With all the generation gaps that exist, we need clearly defined generations to fit around them.

So from now on, I'm going to be ready to defend my generation.

Unfortunately, I'm not sure what to say about it. There aren't many generations that were less exciting. I'm not even sure of its name.

It's the group that was born just before and after the Depression began. People who are part of it are now saying: "Forty? The prime of life."

If any generation had an inferiority complex, mine did.

For one thing, it was really small. Today's young generation is enormous because everybody wanted babies after World War II, and just about everybody had them.

Half the kids born in my generation were "accidents." That's a hearty welcome for you.

A Depression childhood left its mark. Maybe we were too young to have to scratch for a living, but everyone we knew did.

That's why we have different economic attitudes than the young generation.

They spend money foolishly and they enjoy doing it.

We spend money foolishly, too, and we enjoy doing it. But then our stomachs hurt.

Then came the war, and everybody had a brother, uncle or father in it. But as adolescents, we did nothing but collect old fat, old papers, old tires, and give dirty looks to neighborhood 4-Fs.

A few years later, our war came along. And those of us who took part were pioneers. It was the first time we took half a loaf.

Reprinted with permission from the *Chicago Daily News*.

But were we viewed as victims or martyrs? No. We were hailed as losers. Coming back from Korea, and expecting people to be interested, was about like coming back from a Wisconsin vacation with color slides.

Many members of my generation are still haunted by the question of why they did not rebel against their dirty little war, why they didn't march in the streets, burn draft cards, and all that. It was just as bad a war, and the women were ugly.

The question doesn't haunt me. I know why we didn't.

By then, the country was firmly in the hands of those who scraped through a depression and won a popular war.

Actually, they are still running things. But our young protesters are their children and they have become tolerant and understanding.

My generation wasn't their children. We were their young brothers, maybe, or their nephews.

I think they would have punched us in the mouth.

Besides, we were outnumbered. We were always outnumbered. Even in politics.

Today's young generation has had several political leaders they could follow, beginning with John F. Kennedy, and followed by his brother, and Senators McCarthy, Muskie, and McGovern.

We, too, had a forward-thinking, exciting, charismatic political figure. The trouble was, Adlai Stevenson kept losing.

Today's generation has even had its political villain in President Johnson. It could stand in Grant Park and chant an obscenity: "(beep-beep) LBJ," and feel good about it.

We had only Ike, and it was inconceivable that anyone could chant "(beep-beep)" at Ike. We would have chewed on soap.

And so we slid comfortably into something resembling maturity, without doing a thing. At least, that is what the young student radical told me.

But you have to wonder where some of today's righteous movements would be without a few members of my generation—such as Martin Luther King, Robert F. Kennedy, Malcolm X, Lenny Bruce, all heroes of today's generation.

In fact, it makes you wonder exactly who is creating the gaps.

For Thinking, Talking, Writing

Mr. Royko points out that some of today's most-loved heroes are "over 30." Does this fact say anything about the generation gap? Is a generation gap more likely to be related to point of view than it is to actual age? Explain your "yes" or "no" answer.

"She Was Never Bad But Once"

Ridgely Hunt

A mongoloid is a person born with a severe mental deficiency and with the physical characteristics of slanting eyes, a broad, short skull, and broad hands with short fingers. Mongoloids are usually happy children, but they do not usually live a normal life span.

W. Ely Lewis still lives on Water Street in Hart, Mich., in the same house where his daughter died 10 years ago. It's a quiet street, shaded by elms on one side and by maples on the other, with a pair of rusty, disused railroad tracks running right down the middle. One block to the south it deteriorates into a dirt road, but up where Lewis lives the neighborhood is well preserved, permeated on a warm spring morning by children's voices and the occasional wham of a screen door.

"I used to have the nicest garden in town," says Lewis. "I used to love to spade. I've got a dandy shovel, and I could spade backwards or forwards, either way, and I could spade all day long up to three or four years ago, and I just enjoyed it." But old age has shortened his breath and weakened his legs. Just to walk downtown and back exhausts him. He uses a hearing aid when he can find it, but cataracts are occluding his vision, and for some reason which the doctors down in Muskegon have not made clear to him, they cannot operate. His stomach muscles remain hard as a rock, however, and he likes to invite a visitor to punch him in the belly. He lives alone, cooking a piece of ham steak for his lunch [baked, never fried] and banging out letters on his typewriter at the dining room table. His mind remains as sharp as it ever was, though increasingly he dwells in the past, which is where most of his life now lies. He has lost his cousin, his sister, his wife, and his only child. "But," he adds resolutely, "you can't expect to have all those people when you get as old as I am." He is 86. And in a sense, the death of his daughter contained an element of mercy. Her name was Geraldine Mary, and Lewis now thinks she was a mongoloid, though he says, "I never knew she was that kind—never realized it until after she died."

Geraldine was born in 1922 in the house next door to the one where Lewis now lives. He was 40 years old then and his wife was 38, an age at which the odds of giving birth to a mongoloid child begin to rise dangerously. "The doctor that officiated was one of our very best friends, and it just broke his heart when he realized right away the condition that she was in because he knew how much we'd planned on having a child.

"When she was 3 months old, we took her to Grand Rapids to what we thought was the best baby specialist in the state, and he spent two hours on her and called in another doctor, and he hated to tell us that she'd never walk or talk or hold up her head, and to go home and wean her at once. (I knew here it was for my wife's sake because she had coughed nearly all the time she'd been carrying this baby—had an awful cough. It probably was tuberculosis coming on, but she didn't get that fixed up till later.) But they didn't know Mrs. Lewis' disposition when they told her that, and she said, 'If it makes any difference to *her*, why I'll keep right on,' and she nursed her. She went from an ordinary 115 pounds to 99 pounds after Geraldine was born.

"Most of our friends and relatives said: 'Put her in a home. It's too much of a job for you.' But we knew that if we put her in a home, she'd just shrivel up and wouldn't have been happy. We wouldn't have been either. Yes, I've got letters from some of our closest relatives and best friends, and they said we were trying to do too much for our own benefit. They were sincere in it. I can see their point of view, but they hadn't been through the mill like we had."

Going through the mill with Geraldine had its hardships, but mostly Lewis remembers it with pleasure and pride. He remembers especially a night of triumph and vindication when next he saw the baby expert from Grand Rapids.

"When Geraldine was about 8 years old, this doctor came to Hart to give a lecture in the church, and I asked him to come down and see that child that would 'never walk or talk or hold up her head.' And he came down here and sat down in a chair, and I got Geraldine up and told her that Doctor Gordon had come from Grand Rapids to see her. She acknowledged the introduction and said, 'I'm glad, Doctor, you're here, and it's nice for you to come see me clear from Grand Rapids.' Then he looked her over, and he could hardly believe she was in such shape. Of course, her hands were all crippled up, and her feet were small, but her head wasn't very much ill-shaped.

"He asked her a few questions, and then I began to show her off. I said, 'She can tell all the townships in the county. She can name all the states in the Union without a mistake, and she can spell most of the names of the states.' And after he'd been here half an hour or so, I said to Geraldine—we had a piano then—'Would you like to play a piece on the piano for the doctor?' And she says, 'Yes, doctor, what do you want me to play? "Silent Night"? I think I can do that the best.' She couldn't reach an octave, mind you, but she could make a piano sing.

"And then I had her spell quite a number of the states like Massachusetts and California. She could spell them. Then I asked her how much two times two was, and she said, 'I don't know, Daddy.'

" 'What's two *plus* two?'

" 'I don't know. Don't *ask* me those questions in arithmetic. You know I can't get that.'

"She couldn't ever write. She couldn't read. The three R's—reading, 'riting, and 'rithmetic," Lewis muses with a sad chuckle.

"Then I asked him, did he make a mistake about that child? He said, 'No.'

" 'Why,' I said, 'don't you remember what you told us?'

" 'Just as though it was yesterday.'

" 'Well,' I said, 'she can do quite a few things.'

" 'Yes,' he said, 'but I didn't know she was going to have the care of 1 in 100,000.' "

Lewis has spent most of his life holding public office of one sort or another: village clerk in Pentwater, recorder of deeds for Oceana county, postmaster of Hart. He ran for public office 34 times, never lost a primary, and lost only three elections. Even those three defeats came not at the hands of the Democrats but of the Pentwater Progressives, who hit a winning streak in 1912. But all his victories dwindle in the glow of that triumphal night when Geraldine displayed her accomplishments for the specialist from Grand Rapids. " 'I didn't know she was going to have the care of 1 in 100,000.' That's just the words he said."

Lewis sees nothing extraordinary in the care they gave their daughter. "It was easy. She had a regular photographic mind about those things," he says. "I spent a lot of time, and so did my wife, and we took a lot of patience. If she asked any questions, we answered them—took the time to."

They tried to put her in school, but despite special tutoring, she couldn't keep step with her classmates. "Now one of the teachers that taught her," Lewis recalls, "she said, 'The part that Geraldine knows, I never taught a smarter child.' She says, 'She's got the keenest mind I ever knew.' " But the three R's exceeded her grasp; her abilities focused on such subjects as history and geography, which she could memorize as Lewis recited them for her. She also knew the make and model of just about every automobile in Hart. Lewis taught her that, too.

The piano she learned by watching her cousin Muriel Martin, who came to live with the Lewises and was reared by them. "Boy, we were lucky to get Muriel to stay with us," Lewis says fervently. "She was just two years older than Geraldine was. They just came together — never a bit of jealousy. She's all I've got left now." Muriel married a man named Burton L. Henry, raised four handsome, strapping sons, and now lives over in Shelby. After her piano lessons, Lewis remembers, Muriel would "come home and practice on her lesson. Geraldine would sit down with her to her left, listen two or three times, and she'd sit down and play it as good as Muriel did."

But despite her accomplishments, Geraldine required constant care in virtually every aspect of her existence. She could wash a dish but couldn't dry it, eat a meal but couldn't cook it, brighten a house but couldn't clean it. In early childhood she walked alone to school and rode a tricycle around the neighborhood, but after an operation to repair a faulty kneecap, Lewis says, "she lost her nerve and she wouldn't walk alone. She'd walk with my hand, but to her dying day, she wouldn't take a step alone. When my wife was in the hospital with tuberculosis for 10 months, I tried every day — I had to stay home and take care of her then — every day I tried to get her to walk two or three steps. No, she wouldn't do it." To move around the house she pushed her rocking chair ahead of her. Lewis still has the very chair in his parlor in the house on Water Street. "She'd take that chair and get around the house just like nothing. Telephone ring, and she'd just take that chair over to it almost as fast as you can walk."

Geraldine didn't allow her disabilities to depress her. "Just once, she said, 'Mother'— I think she was about 12 years old — she said, 'Why can't I do things and go places like the other kids?' It kind of stumped Mrs. Lewis. She tried to explain to her what a nice time she had and how many friends she had and so forth, and Geraldine never mentioned it afterward. She didn't feel any inferiority complex at all."

Even so, she preferred the company of older people. "She had several different girls at different times," Lewis says, "who were very nice to her and loved to come on the porch here and sit and visit with her, and she was a good visitor. She was able to hold her own in conversation with anybody." But her best friends were three elderly ladies, and only these three would Geraldine invite to her birthday parties. Most of her love she reserved for her parents.

"Oh, she was the most affectionate kid you ever saw. And she thought she had the nicest daddy and the nicest mother and all that, and she would tell us about it. And she wouldn't stand for any of her friends being abused, mentally or any other way. She thought I was picking on her mother once when we were fooling her a little bit, and holy Judas if she didn't wade into me and hit me just as hard as she could! 'You can't hurt my mother, Dad!' "

But that was an uncharacteristic outburst for Geraldine. "She was so good," Lewis says. "She never was bad but once, and we never could understand what was wrong with her. We never found out. She wouldn't tell us. Something went wrong." To this day the incident stands out in his mind as one of the landmarks in his journey with his daughter.

"She never was bad but that one time when she went to the dining table and took the doily off and threw it on the floor. Mrs. Lewis just picked it up and said, 'Geraldine, you mustn't do that.' And she did it 8 or 10 times, and toward the last Mrs. Lewis got a big newspaper and rolled it up hard and slapped her on the hands. She did it three or four more times, and then she began to realize that that wasn't getting anywhere, and then I began to shame her, and in a little while she says, 'Daddy, I'm sorry.'

" 'Well,' I said, 'now won't you tell us what's wrong?'

" 'No.'

" 'Well, what makes you act so bad?'

" 'I won't tell.'

"And she never would. We never found out what was wrong with that girl that time. Just couldn't figure it out. That was the only time she was ever real naughty."

Not that Geraldine was servile. "She had a mind of her own," says her father, "but still she was good. Now I took her to the beach and took her into the cold water, and she didn't like it, and she wouldn't go in. And I'd get her on my shoulders to try to get her to go out there, and she'd take me right by the hair, and she said, 'Daddy, I'll pull your hair out if you don't go back.' Maybe that's what became of it."

She preferred the pleasures of the land, especially swings. "She loved to swing," says Lewis. "I had five swings around this house so she could swing. I think that was a mistake because the swing out back was about 20 feet high, and she would kick against the ground with that one foot, and that was the crookedest foot all the time. She always did that. I'm sorry now. But it might not have made any difference.

"There was a swing over in John Gurney Park that was 60 feet high. The fellow built it said it was the highest swing in Michigan, and I used to take her and Muriel over there, and boy, how Geraldine did love to swing in that!"

And so Geraldine and her parents lived out the years in the house on Water Street, each one satisfied with life as it came. No matter what happened to them, Mrs. Lewis would say: "Well, it will come out all right. It always *has*, hasn't it?" And it always did.

Only one shadow troubled them: the question of who would care for Geraldine when they were gone. They didn't like to think of her being put in a home. "Muriel would have taken her," Lewis says, "but it would have made a difference in her family — to bring four boys up there with a girl that had to be waited on." As it turned out, they needn't have worried. Geraldine died before either of her parents at the age of 36.

"One thing to be satisfied about or be happy about, though of course it's pretty tough," says Lewis, "is that she went at just the right time. We were both here."

Lewis doesn't know what killed her. "I don't think it was her heart. I think it was down in her stomach. Her stomach swelled up, and I think it was probably a tumor or something of that kind. She complained for about a week that there was something wrong with her stomach. 'Will you rub it for me, Daddy?'

"She wasn't in pain. She was sitting on a chair right at the head of the bed. I was talking to her, and I just saw her die. Inside of five minutes from the time she was talking, she was dead. And I laid her on the bed, and some black stuff came out of her mouth. Something must have broken inside."

Something broke inside Lewis that night too, and it never was the same again.

For Thinking, Talking, Writing

1. This article tells the story of a family that never experienced a generation gap. What special circumstances helped the members of this family remain so close to each other?
2. What did the doctor mean when he said, "I didn't know she was going to have the care of 1 in 100,000"? The article gives some clues about the emotional care Geraldine had from her parents, as well as the physical care she needed. Which was more important, do you think?
3. If the strong sense of loving and caring and giving which was present in the Lewis family is also present in a family with normal children, do you think this helps eliminate the "generation gap" problem? Why or why not?

"WHAT DO THEY KNOW ABOUT WHAT COUNTS? THEY'RE ESTABLISHMENT."

the small society   by Brickman

For Thinking, Talking, Writing

1. Mr. Mauldin's cartoon suggests, in a way, that the generation gap is inevitable. After the reading, thinking, talking, and writing you have done in this section, do you think this is necessarily so? If so, why? If not, how do you think it can be avoided?
2. What aspect of Mr. Mauldin's cartoon is highly improbable?
3. Two different kinds of generation gaps are suggested by Mr. Mauldin's cartoon and by Mr. Brickman's "the small society." Which kind is the more realistic one? Which is the more emotional one? Which is the more artificial one?

3

SOCIETY:
where do I fit in?

Introduction

Once it was easy to explain the society we lived in: there were clearly defined goals, clearly understood beliefs, clearly stated boundaries.

Now, however, we find ourselves in a society full of problems. We have the highest standard of living in the world; yet there are thousands of people in the United States who actually go hungry every day, while we pay farmers *not* to raise more food. We have the technology to send human beings to the moon and beyond; yet we do not solve the problem of pollution of our air and water and poison in our food. A little over a quarter of a century ago, we fought a war against a society that believed in racism and on the basis of that belief exterminated human beings by the millions; yet now we are involved in the most severe racial crisis this country has ever had. We are a nation committed to peace; yet we have been involved in wars almost continuously for many years, and violence has become a part of our way of life. A college education is available to more people in our society than in any society in history; yet there are strong protests against our system of higher education among both students and non-students. We are traditionally an idealistic nation; yet living life with the goal of earning money to buy material things seems to be much more common than living life for an ideal.

You will be investigating various aspects of our topsy-turvy society in later sections in this book. But in this section, as you think about society as a whole, try to evaluate your *own* role within the society of which you are a part. What do you want from it? What are you willing to give to it? What are the things you like about our society? What are the things you dislike? How might you go about helping to change the "bad" things?

Society is, in large measure, an extension of ourselves, of what we want it to be. Read — think — talk — write. Can *you* help to create a better society?

To an Angry Young Man

Leo Rosten

I have been getting lusty cheers and jeers for a rueful little paragraph I recently wrote about student riots. The most eloquent (and savage) letter ended: "Drop dead!!!" Another diatribe was signed "Columbia Senior." I wish I knew where to send this reply to both:

Dear ?:

It will upset you to learn that I agree with many things you said. For instance: "Don't question our sincerity!" I don't. You are about as sincere as anyone can be. You are sincerely unhappy, sincerely frustrated and sincerely confused. You are also sincerely wrong about the few facts you cite, and sincerely illogical in the violent conclusions you reach. Besides, what does "sincerity" have to do with issues? Any insane asylum is full of sincere patients. Hitler was undoubtedly sincere. So are the followers of Voliva, who think the world is sincerely flat.

I sadly agree that your college courses have been "outrageously irrelevant to the times"— because your letter reveals that you could not pass a freshman exam in at least three fields in which you pass such sweeping judgments: economics, history, political theory.

You say, "Destroy a system that has not abolished unemployment, exploitation and war!" By the same reasoning, you should blow up all hospitals (and perhaps execute all doctors, biologists and researchers): they have not abolished disease.

Before you destroy a system, propose another that *will* solve (not hide, shift or disguise) unemployment, "exploitation," war. Anyone can promise Utopia — without specifying a program. Tom Hayden, idol of the New Left, has said: "First we'll make the revolution — then we'll find out what for." Would you employ a plumber who rips out all the pipes in your house before he learned how to repair a leak?

You say, "The mass media are not telling us the truth." Then how and from whom did *you* learn the "evils" you currently deplore? After all, your information comes from one or another organ of — the mass media.

"This society is only interested in higher prices and profits!" You apparently do not understand this society, or *a* society, or the function of prices (and profits) in *any* economy. Has it never occurred to you that the marketplace is a polling booth? That buying is voting? That no economic system is possible without *some* form of pricing, without some measure of efficacy or worth? Has it never occurred to you that profits are a form of *proof* (that something gives satisfaction to those who pay for it)? Perhaps you should examine the public *uses* that we make of private profits — through taxation.

The countries that follow your platitude, "production for use," *without exception* produce far less for their people to enjoy, of much shoddier quality, at much higher prices (measured by the hours of work needed to buy something). Don't you know that "Socialist" countries are smuggling "capitalist" incentives into their systems? Has it not dawned on you that wherever and whenever there is no free market, there is no free thought, no free art, no free politics, no free life?

You rage against "a heartless country in which the poor get poorer." Alas, poor Yoricks: The *decline* in poverty in the U.S. is among the more astonishing and hopeful facts of human history. (In 1900, about 90% of our population was poor; in $1920 - 50\%$; in $1930 - 34\%$; in $1968 - 15\%$). You will cry that 15% is outrageous. Agreed. The question is: How best abolish it? (A negative income tax makes more sense than anything your colleagues propose.)

"The middle class exploits the unemployed." Please examine that cliché. Would the middle class be worse off or better off if all the unemployed magically disappeared? Obviously, *much* better off: Think of the enormous saving in taxes, the enormous improvement in public services, the enormous benefits from refocused energies now used to ameliorate poverty's abominable toll.

You say your generation "wants to be understood." Well, so does mine. How much have you tried to understand others? You pillory us for injustices not of our making, frictions not of our choice, dilemmas that history (or our forebears or the sheer intractability of events) presented to us. You say we "failed" because you face so many awful problems. Will you then accept blame for all the problems that exist (and they will) when you are 20 years older? And how do you know that all problems are soluble? Or soluble swiftly? Or soluble peacefully? Or soluble, given the never-infinite resources, brains and experience any generation is endowed with?

I say that *you* are failing *us* — in failing to learn and respect discomforting facts; in failing to learn how to *think* (it is easier to complain); in using violence to shut down colleges; in shamefully denying the freedom of others to study and to teach; in barbarously slandering and abusing and shouting down those who disagree with you; in looting, stealing and defiling; in failing to see how much more complicated social problems are than you blindly assume; in acting out of an ignorance for which idealism is no excuse, and a hysteria for which youth is no defense. "Understanding"? You don't even understand that when you call me a "mother − − − − −" you are projecting your unresolved incestuous wishes onto me. The technical name for such projection, in advanced form, is paranoia.

Again and again, you say, "the American people want" or "demand" or "insist." How do you know? *Every poll I have seen puts your position in a minority.* You just say, "the American people demand"— then add whatever *you* prefer. This is intellectually sloppy at best, and corrupt at worst.

You want to "wreck this slow, inefficient democratic system." It took the human race centuries of thought and pain and suffering and hard experiment to devise it. Democracy is not a "state" but a process; it is a way of solving human problems, a way of hobbling power, a way of protecting every minority from the awful fatal tyranny of either the few or the many.

Whatever its imperfections, democracy is the only system man has discovered that makes possible *change without violence.* Do you really prefer bloodshed to debate? Quick dictates to slow law? This democracy made possible a great revolution in the past 35 years (a profound transfer of power, a distribution of wealth, an improvement of living and health) without "liquidating" millions, without suppressing free speech, without the obscenities of dogma enforced by terror.

This "slow, inefficient" system protects people like me against people like you; and (though you don't realize it) protects innocents like you against those "reactionary...fascist forces" you fear: They, like you, prefer "action to talk." As for "security"— at what price? The most "secure" of human institutions is a prison; would you choose to live in one?

You want "a society in which the young speak their minds against the Establishment." Where have the young more freely, recklessly and intransigently attacked "the Establishment"? (*Every* political order has one.) Wherever "our heroes — Marx, Mao, Che" have prevailed, students, writers, teachers, scientists have been punished with hard labor or death — for what? For their opinions. Where but in "fake democracies" are mass demonstrations possible, or your bitter (and legitimate) dissent televised?

You rail against "leaders crazed with power," who "deceive the people." Your leaders are self-dramatizers who demand that power, which would craze them, and they deceive you in not telling you how they plan to use force, whose excesses I hate more than you do. *I*, unlike you, want no one put "up against the wall." No "cheap politician" more cynically deceived you than fanatical militants did — and will. Your support feeds their neurotic (because extremist) needs. Washington's " 'Non-Violent' Coordinating Committee" has engaged in gunfire for three days as I write this.

You say Marcuse "shows that capitalist freedom actually enslaves." (He doesn't "show"— he only *says*.) He certainly does not sound enslaved. And does mouthing fragments of 19th-century ideology (Marx, Bakunin) really liberate? And is not Marcuse 40 years "older than 30," your cutoff on credibility? Incidentally, would you trust your life to a surgeon under 30 — who never finished medical school?

Your irrationality makes me wonder how you were ever admitted *into* Columbia. You confuse rhetoric with reasoning. Assertions are not facts. Passion is no substitute for knowledge. Slogans are not solutions. Your idealism takes no brains. And when you dismiss our differences with contempt, you become contemptible.

Very *sincerely* yours,
LEO ROSTEN

P. S. Please don't take any more courses in sociology, which seduces the immature into thinking they understand a problem if they discuss it in polysyllables. Jargon is not insight. Vocabulary is the opiate of radicals.

For Thinking, Talking, Writing

1. Mr. Rosten, in this article, discusses some important social issues. React with your own knowledge and opinions to the major issues he discusses. Analyze the arguments of the "angry young man" and Mr. Rosten's replies. Decide in each case which point of view you think makes better sense:
   (a) The lack of relevance of college courses to the times
   (b) Unemployment
   (c) War
   (d) Lack of truth in the mass media
   (e) High prices and high profits

(f) Poverty

(g) Exploitation of the poor by the middle class

2. Throughout the article, Mr. Rosten uses *analogies* to help make his points clear. An *analogy* is a kind of comparison that points out a similarity between things that are otherwise unlike each other. The first analogy he uses is in the second paragraph of the article, where he is trying to point out that sincerity has nothing to do with logical thinking about issues. He uses examples of insane asylums, Hitler, and Voliva to make this point, although insane asylums, Hitler, and Voliva are all very unlike college students in other ways.

Find the other analogies Mr. Rosten uses in the article. In each case, analyze the analogy: does it make sense? Does it make his point clearer? Does it help his argument?

The Earth Is
Still Our Home

Stewart L. Udall

This article first appeared in the April 6,1969, issue of THIS WEEK *Magazine. Since that time, men have walked on the moon and returned safely to Earth. However, the questions of national priorities that faced us in 1969 are still with us today.*

In a moment of frustration not long ago, the mayor of one of our largest cities expressed the concern of environmental planners, conservationists and most of his fellow mayors when he complained in public:

"If we aren't careful, we will be remembered as the generation that put a man on the moon while standing knee-deep in garbage."

In July, with a little luck and the matchless technical skill of our scientists and engineers, we will place men on the moon and return them safely. Appropriate expressions of national pride and self-congratulation will follow. There will be another spate of editorials and news stories about American ingenuity and the spirit of adventure that successfully took us into outer space.

But in 1969 we will also come face to face with many critical questions of national priorities that test our sense of national purpose as never before.

Can a country which has perfected the assembling of infinitely sophisticated space rockets and nuclear missiles also eradicate slums and master the art of building balanced, yet vibrant cities?

Is a nation which is willing to spend $5,000,000,000 for 120 "flying boxcars" to increase its military mobility, also willing to rethink and rebuild its transportation systems to make the everyday travel of millions a pleasure instead of an ordeal?

Is a society capable of creating a habitat for explorers on the moon, prepared to spend whatever is necessary to cleanse the polluted waters of the Hudson, the Connecticut, the Missouri and all the other rivers that course through our hometowns? (One of the really significant emotional experiences that the Apollo 8 astronauts had was the deep realization of how beautiful the Earth is and how incredibly rich as a place for human habitation.)

And, more important, does a people contemplating the building of an infinitely costly (and perhaps unwise) anti-ballistic missile system, have the will to carry out those projects and social programs that will build new bridges between the races and the minorities in our land?

Economists tell us of the near certainty that the sum of goods and services available — the gross national prodct — will be rising by as much as $40,000,000,000 a year. We have an abundance of wealth to apply and a historic opportunity to decide that a major proportion of it be directed to reshaping and restoring this continent — this country.

In the long run, a nation reveals itself by the quality of life it offers to its citizens. I believe that we have reached a point in our history when excessive and thoughtlessly conceived new machines and goods and gadgets that are unrelated to our actual domestic needs will be both demeaning and, in the end, self-defeating. We must be more concerned with the condition of our cities and the educational opportunities that we should offer our children than with half-empty new triumphs of engineering. Not only our personal lives — but our capacity for leadership in the world community — will rest on the reassessment we make of our national priorities.

I am not opposed to the further exploration of outer space. But let it be a modest program based on scientific inquiry, not cold war competition. The time has come to give paramount priority to the pressing problems of the inner space that is our home. What will it profit us if we put a whole colony of men on the moon and fail to create a broadening brotherhood and more livable cities in these limited States, on this Earth which is our home, which is the natural habitat of man?

I am convinced that we not only need new priorities, but a new adventure in nation building as well. We need a new teamwork of governments and industry and labor that can produce the beautiful, balanced cities that are the hallmark of a mature civilization. We need the kind of education (it will cost much more, but it will be much more productive) that will cause a new flowering of the individual. We need the kind of total environmental conservation that will permit nature to surround and add life-giving options to our daily lives.

If, in a decade, we could master space, so in a decade can we also conquer squalor. If computers can direct vehicles to the moon and back, computers must be used to focus man's promise and potential on Earth. If engineers can create a closed capsule to preserve life beyond our atmosphere, engineering must teach us how to preserve and improve the air we breathe, the water we use, the environment we inhabit.

The issue of our era is not whether we have the wealth, but whether we have the wisdom and the will. We possess the knowledge to produce cities that are handsome not just by design, but by the human scale and by the measure of vibrant instead of vicious inter-group relations. For example, we have the ability to produce a safe and clean automobile and quiet, clean and comfortable urban mass transportation systems. We can and must also produce a social order that commands the loyalty and enlists the inspiration of all youth.

These are *not* impossible dreams, not unattainable goals. To bring them to fruition, however, will require a renewal of our institutions and a commitment to the individual and social excellence that has too long eluded us.

My plea is for a practical earth-mindedness, for a fresh determination that, with the highest human attributes and ambitions in mind, redirects and controls science and engineering for the benefit of man on Earth.

I believe that our citizens are beginning to recognize that the worth of a society is determined by the richness and variety of life that it offers to each individual. American life must be far more than a money game or a space spectacular. It must rest on achievement, not ease; on human betterment, not materialistic achievement. I am convinced that we will begin to renew our purposes and reshape our institutions to make this nation, once again (in Lincoln's noble phrase) "the last, best hope on Earth."

For Thinking, Talking, Writing

1. In this article, Mr. Udall urges us to pay more attention to the serious problems we are having on the earth and less attention to the exploration of outer space for the sake of "cold war competition." Would you agree with him that we should cut down on the money and time spent for space exploration and put more money and time into solving these "earth" problems? Why or why not?
2. Have you any good ideas for possible solutions to the specific problems that Mr. Udall mentions?
   (a) Slums
   (b) Decaying cities
   (c) Lack of adequate transportation systems
   (d) Pollution of our water sources
   (e) Social and racial tensions

Signs of Status

Artist: Bob Clark
Writer: Al Jaffee

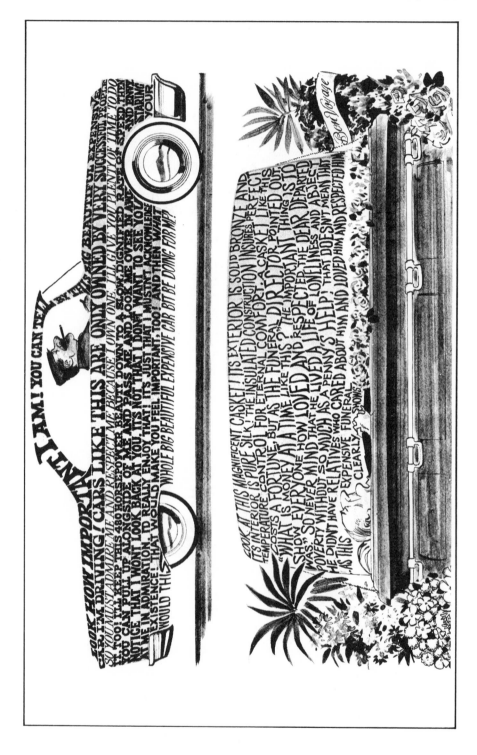

For Thinking, Talking, Writing

1. Do you agree that most of the "things" we acquire are to impress other people? Are there other reasons, too, for acquiring "things"? Why do you and your family acquire things? Think over the new things you have gotten during the last year and try to analyze the real reason *why* you got them.

2. "Signs of Status" first appeared in MAD magazine. The author thought of all these "things" as symbols of some kind for various people. There are certainly other reasons besides status, to become a doctor or to own a nice house. Which of the "status symbols" that appear in this series would you like to have? Why?

   (a) A mink coat
   (b) An expensive car
   (c) A lavish funeral (when you are dead anyway!)
   (d) To be a doctor, or something like one in terms of social status (or to have a husband who is one)
   (e) An expensive and beautifully-cared-for house

How Some Families Survive

Linda Rockey

Juanita Slaton lives in an all-black West Side housing project with her seven children and her daughter Shirley Ann's four. She will probably never know Lula Couch, who resides with her husband and six children in poor white Uptown, or Maria Lopez, who is awaiting the birth of her second child in a Spanish-speaking Wicker Park tenement.

Yet they share one common trait — their families are hungry. Their stories provide ample evidence that hunger...knows no color line.

Nor is it restricted to public aid recipients. The Slatons are hungry because they are on welfare. The Couches are hungry because Mrs. Couch is ill and cannot work. The Lopezes are hungry because Mr. Lopez is underemployed.

The Slaton home at 2145 W. Lake is a tiny 3-bedroom apartment with cement walls and cheap tile floors. It's not large enough for the 13 people who occupy it but Mrs. Slaton keeps it neat and attractive with plastic coverings on the furniture, candle holders on the walls, artificial flowers in the corners and colorful throw pillows on the sofa.

"Almost everything we have I bought when I was working," said Mrs. Slaton, 41, a tall, heavy woman who must have been pretty once, before she gained weight and lost her front teeth. She worked as a sewing machine operator for seven years, making good money until April of 1967 when her diabetes got so bad she had to quit. She applied for public aid right away, but by the time her first welfare check came in August, the family had been evicted from their apartment.

"I never knew what it's like to be poor until I got too sick for work," she said. Now she knows poverty and its ever-present companion, hunger.

The Slatons are hungry. It doesn't take long to detect the symptoms.

The youngest in the family, Shirley Ann's 13-month-old twins, ought to be lively and noisy, but they sit listlessly for hours, not uttering a sound. The older children are almost as lethargic, bringing to mind the medical evidence that children deprived of adequate food appear dull and lifeless.

Everyone has a cold or cough and many have had serious infectious disease. Shirley Ann's first set of twins died of pneumonia in infancy. Here is a family ready for the much-needed study to confirm doctor's suspicions that the high infant mortality rate and incidence of infectious disease in poverty areas is related to malnutrition.

Mrs. Slaton and her daughter Shirley are overweight, a sign that their diets, though adequate in calories, may be deficient in important nutrients. They are eating the food that comes cheapest, starches and carbohydrates, which are also the most fattening.

It would be easy to say that the Slatons are hungry because they are ignorant of proper dietary habits. On the early spring day of this interview, it was past noon before anyone in the family had anything to eat.

However, Mrs. Slaton knows that her family should eat breakfast. She should follow her doctor's instructions to have three small, nonfattening meals each day. She cannot afford it. She gives priority to milk for the children and a big dinner meal for the entire family. Beyond that, there isn't enough money.

She receives $293 a month from the Cook County Department of Public Aid. Her daughter Shirley is paid $96 a month in child support through a court order. Welfare is supposed to supplement that, but since Dec. 24, when she was burned out of her apartment and came to live with her mother, she has received only $30.

Mrs. Slaton's food allowance is $122 a month. With food stamps, she can buy $160 worth of food. But to take advantage of the stamp program, she must spend 80 per cent of her food allowance at once.

She doesn't like to, because it means that she will not have a cushion if emergencies arise during the month. But most of the time she does, traveling 25 blocks west to a Jewel supermarket, which costs 45 cents bus fare there, and $3 to $4 for cab fare back.

"There's a store across the street and another around the corner, but they're too expensive," she said. (A food pricing survey by the Church Federation of Greater Chicago has confirmed that food costs are higher in low-income areas.) However, she must patronize these stores for items that she needs daily, like milk, which sells for $1.09 a gallon in her neighborhood and 98 cents farther west.

She has a freezer from her more affluent days, but it doesn't work. "Movers broke the gas pipe, and I can't afford to have it fixed," she said. She has a freezer compartment in her refrigerator, but it is not large enough to store a month's supply of meat. For dinner the previous night, she had served rice and beans cooked with a piece of hambone. That night she planned to fix chicken wings.

Out of her food budget also must come 37 cents a day for each of five children in school. Only one gets a free lunch because "she has a nice counselor who asked for it." Under the National School Lunch Act all five children should qualify for free lunches, but Mrs. Slaton said she had never heard of a free program at the schools the other four attend.

Her family has fresh fruit only once a week and never goes out to a restaurant. She laughed when asked about the latter. "I can hardly go to a show once every six months," she said.

After food, Mrs. Slaton has $171 a month which is supposed to cover rent ($86.50) and all the other essentials of life. Sometimes it doesn't, and she has to dip into the food money, a regular habit among welfare recipients.

She still owes $200 on the furniture she bought when she was working. She needs new mattresses, but public aid won't give her extra money for them because she received $165 last year for six beds, an ironing board and a dresser.

Mrs. Slaton hates being on welfare and wants to go back to work. "I love to sew and I'm tired of staying in the house all day," she said. "But I can't work as long as my diabetes is this bad. The doctor says it would be better if I didn't worry so much."

Dewey Couch, 33, worries, too. Maybe that's why he has bleeding ulcers and lost the job in a Greyhound garage that gave him a weekly take-home pay of $118 or more. Now he draws $65 a week in sick pay, $30 of which must go to rent a 5-room apartment at 4527 N. Racine. What's left is not enough to keep his wife and six children properly fed and clothed.

And that's why his wife Lula often goes to the Chicago Southern Center for free food and clothing. Sometimes she gets it. Other times, the supply has already been exhausted by other poor white families who came to Chicago because they thought they could make a living.

"We don't eat half as well as we did in Kentucky," said Mrs. Couch. "We grew our own food, raised our own chickens and someone always had a cow."

Why, then did they leave?

"Same reason as everybody else," she replied. "There's no more work down there."

"I worked in the coal mines, but it was too dangerous," her husband added. "We thought we could do better here."

He did, until he had to quit work Jan. 31. His sick pay didn't start until March 17. In the meantime, he went to public aid and received $64 in emergency assistance. He has since been told that welfare can't help him if he draws more than $200 a month in sick pay.

The Couches are a close family where affection flows freely and pride inhibits candor about their plight — until Mrs. Couch gets mad enough.

What makes her angry? Prejudice against Southern people, crime in Uptown, junked cars and drunks, and the United States beautification program. "If you want to beautify America, fatten up a child. Trees won't fill his stomach or put a smile on his mother's face."

In the kitchen, where she was fixing hot dogs and corn-on-the-cob for dinner, she apologized for the emptiness of the refrigerator. "To be honest," she said, "we don't even have enough for food. I can't afford milk except for the baby."

The Couches eat "mostly ground beef, hot dogs, rice and greens." The children have been getting free lunch at school since their father stopped working; but their teeth, like their parents', have the telltale dark stains of dietary deficiences. They rarely eat fresh fruits and vegetables. The Southern Center cannot give away that kind of food.

A scrawny toy wire-haired terrier named Too-Too brightens the lives of the Couch children, but his master cannot afford dog food. "He eats what we eat."

The Couches have been in Chicago since 1956, moving many times because "people are prejudiced against Southern people. I really like it in Uptown because Southern people can live together," said Mrs. Couch. "But we could use more help to fix things up."

Dewey Couch knows that he could rent a place cheaper on a monthly basis, but he has never been able to save enough money for all the necessary deposits. What he and his family would really like to do is go back to Hazard, Ky. "The South is home to me," said his wife.

Maria Lopez's husband is working, but he doesn't have enough either. He is a skilled machine operator, but since a hernia operation, he has not felt well enough to handle more than a $60-a-week messenger job in the Loop.

During his illness, the family was on public aid, but after the surgery he was disqualified, "even though his Spanish doctor said he shouldn't go back to work yet," said his wife Maria, mother of one and about to have another.

"I've gained too much weight during my pregnancy, so the clinic (Board of Health) put me on a low salt diet. I'm supposed to have meat, fresh vegetables and fruit once a day, but I can't."

She cooks "mostly Spanish food, usually rice and beans," and tries to have meat once a week. She has fresh vegetables "once in a while but not often. Food is very expensive in this neighborhood."

The Lopezes don't have enough money for food now, but Maria said that it was even worse when they received $155 a month on welfare.

"I usually ran out of food a week before the check was due and had to borrow money from the Latin American Defense Organization for the baby's milk. Most of the people in this neighborhood are hungry because most of them are on welfare."

For Thinking, Talking, Writing

1. This article gives examples of three families who, living in the wealthiest society which has ever existed in the world, often go *hungry*. What do you think is the basic cause of hunger in the midst of our affluent society: laziness? lack of education? something wrong in the way the government is run? too much "red tape" in the agencies that help the poor? Is there some cause other than these possibilities?
2. Study the stories of each family in this article. What might be done so that these people could get enough nourishing food? Would you suggest that they make changes in their own lives? Would you suggest changes in the laws or rules of the agencies from which they get help? What else?
3. What can you, as an individual member of society, do to help change this strange social situation in which a very wealthy society has within it many people who go hungry most of the time? Or do you want it changed?

Chicago's Runaway Hippies

Mary Merryfield

"When you're pushed just so far and can't take it any more, you'll run. You'll just take off. I have four sisters and brothers and had to be mother and father both. My mother worked, and my stepfather drank; so I was really trapped."

The 17-year-old girl telling me this is now in a foster home in Chicago's so-called hippie community north of Old Town. Remembering how it used to be, her hand shook as she lifted her coffee cup, and she dragged harder on her cigaret.

"The whole year I was 15, I had just one date because I had to go home to feed the kids, get them ready for bed, stay with them. That's why I started cutting school—to have some fun during the day. Then I'd dread going home to clean, cook, and tend the kids again. My mother didn't see that anything was wrong, even when I told her."

Pam (that isn't her real name) was having coffee with me and a shaggy teen-age boy runaway who was wearing an old army jacket. We were in a favorite hangout, The Cellar, a weekend coffee shop in North Park Avenue, which is managed by a group of clergymen calling themselves the Vanguard ministry. . . .

These clergymen come from various faiths and are typical of the roaming pastors who counsel and minister to the needs of young people on the near north side and in Old Town and the surrounding area which embraces the city's hippie community of several thousand, most of them between the ages of 18 and 23. They also work with runaways.

"Runaways usually head for the hippie community, which is the heart of Chicago's 18th police district," says Sgt. Charles Glass of the 18th's youth division. . . .

"Most kids leave home because parents don't know their children," he continues. "They've stopped listening. And they don't seem to communicate that boundaries are flexible and how the kids can live within them. About 75 per cent of the runaways come from middle and upper-middle class homes—with lots of their folks making around $20,000 to $30,000 a year."

Reprinted, courtesy of the *Chicago Tribune*.

The average runaway has problems, but won't find the answers among other kids with the same problems, Sgt. Glass says. "These kids are hopefully searching for some type of direction they don't get at home. The lucky ones are steered to one of the area churches handling runaways...where pastors reunite them with their families or help them work things out in the community.

"Otherwise they're apt to get caught in the drug and sex pattern of an older group of unstable persons who tell them it's a thrill to be dirty, to sleep around with different people in filthy places, smoke pot, or worse. These older misfits can't adjust to society and seem to need the kids following them."

Jim, the 16-year-old boy with Pam, says "I got into such a situation. Someone gave me a ganja cigaret saying, 'Smoking pot is your initiation, man!' But ganja had stronger stuff in it, like hashish, and I was really zonked out of my gourd. I couldn't go home, since my mother ran out on me and I don't know where my father is. There was another guy who had run away from a wealthy home on the north shore, and we made it back there, but his folks wouldn't let me stay. Then I ran into Jonathan Tuttle, a roving minister, who got me in touch with Rev. Bigelow of the Grace Lutheran church. He got me a place to live.

"This community can be very dangerous for kids. There are gangs that hunt you down and the mean kind of hippie who is living here just for the drug scene—and then the folks who work hard for a living tend to resent any of us with long hair who look different, although there's a difference in why people come here."

A long-haired guitar player, a working man who lives in a three-room flat with a married couple and several other singles, says:

"Lots of us move in here just for the sense of community and being able to live our own life style and dress as we please. There's a brotherhood here. All races and backgrounds. A sort of sharing attitude of possessions if anybody has any. You know, love and human compassion toward everybody. Not like the establishment where you must stay in your own little box and reach out because the other person wants to stay in his own little box, too. You find happiness is someone reaching out to you and you reaching back."

"Some of my congregation and I are experimenting with the idea of a group family for some of the young people coming here," reports the Rev. Phillip D. Bigelow of Grace Lutheran church. "It's an extended family that takes off the pressures of the regular family structure. Sort of a combination of old fashioned, small town rooming house, an adult adviser, and plain, real people. We feel that a church in a community like this must meet the problems—drugs, public health, runaways, whatever. In some neighborhoods, people wouldn't want their children exposed to groups of runaways, I suppose."

Yet the young people living in the community don't topple easily, I find—not unless they, too, have serious problems. In a discussion with Pastor Miller and a group of boys from his church, St. Paul's in Fullerton, a 17-year-old boy expressed his feeling about the 2,000 hippies and yippies who took sanctuary at the church during the Democratic convention.

"I heard hippies telling younger runaway kids to go back home, it wasn't their thing. Being close to these people here in our community and during the convention especially, helped me understand them better and the whole scene.

"Several asked me to drop out of school and go to New York with them. I was tempted to duck the 9-to-5 school and part-time job, to toss it all up and go on the road. But listening to them, I could see how you'd be disillusioned. I want to make something of myself; so I stuck with my obligations. A lot of them talk about 'finding themselves' when you ask why they're hippies. I think that's just what I'm doing now. Joining them wouldn't help me."

What is the hippie community? The Rev. Stephen Whitehead of Vanguard ministry discussed it with me in between counseling sessions in the back room of the Vanguard book store in State street at 2 a.m. on a Sunday morning. He sees it as a sort of fifth choice. In addition to staying home, going to school, going into the army, or getting a job, you can now join the free community.

"It's a subculture within the young adult society," he says. "It even has its own underground press and movies. It's interracial. People who join it feel they can communicate best with those people who allow them to do their thing. If it's the sex scene, they want that freedom; if it's the drug scene, they want that freedom. The same with the political scene. Some are even willing to fight for it to a certain extent. Most do not work but spend time finding someone who will support them. They find the communal life style most beneficial for doing their thing and still eating and having a place to sleep."

Who supports those who want to lie around reading, painting, playing music, "rapping" (talking), or to wander through parks and on beaches, doing their thing? "There are always several willing to do this, and oftentimes they're girls who get jobs as waitresses or in clerical and sales fields to pay for the groceries and a communal pad."

Do they feel abused? "No, the girls believe in work, they like to be needed, the hippies tell me. And of course, failing someone to support them, they will get jobs from time to time, pushing a broom or whatever, although they're usually highly intelligent people and more often than not have gone to college."

But the hippie life is not always so harmless. There are drugs.

"The drug use of course is an escape and is negative, bad," the Rev. Mr. Whitehead says. "Most do not use drugs to turn themselves onto the realities of the world and build from there. They just use them for escape. This is especially dangerous today since the criminal elements and more violent types are rumored to be moving into the hippie community here. The speed freaks have hit here, too—those who shoot speed (a derivative of the amphetamine drugs)—and more hard drugs are appearing. This has happened on the west and east coasts already."

The Rev. Jonathan Tuttle, a roving minister who works with 21 churches in the 18th district, has office hours in Lincoln park on Sundays, helps people who need him wherever he finds them, and thinks the community volunteer workers—especially the clergy, teaming up with the city's youth workers—can help the hippie community remain viable.

The Rev. Mr. Tuttle towers 6 feet 6 inches tall and looks like a tender, loving Rasputin with his enveloping beard and long hair.

"If someone smokes marijuana, I tell him the best medical and best legal opinion on drugs and hope he'll see a better way," he says. "Or I help them get off a bad trip if that's needed. I counsel many runaways and refer them to church or an agency which will negotiate with parents and the police if necessary. A middle-class youngster who leaves three meals a day and a warm bed usually is looking for more than a week-end adventure."

"Between 17 and 23, this community can be a thrill and an experience for some kid trying to find a mold he can fit into," Sgt. Glass says. "Many do this and then reenter society. In the three years I've been here, the community has diminished, although we still get a continuous influx of hang-arounds, kids looking for the big adventure, who don't know where they're going and are getting into trouble or real danger.

"Lots of groups in the hippie area who complain about the seedy-looking characters in their neighborhood really have racial hangups, resent seeing an increase in the black kids around. The kids with problems do gravitate to each other without any reference to ethnic background or race. We might say that these kids show us some of our own hangups as well.

"Of course, I wouldn't want my 10-year-old ever to get into this community, but one thing we should think about is that we can't just discard these kids. We can help them."

For Thinking, Talking, Writing

1. Many of the young people described in this article come from comfortable, middle-class homes. Others are from home situations with many obvious problems. What do you think young people from such very different backgrounds have in common that causes them to come together in a hippie community?

2. Why do you think so *many* young people want to leave the kind of home they grew up in and lead such a different kind of life? Is "society" as a whole to blame? If so, how? Is the particular family to blame? Are the young people just "quitters," too lazy to face up to their responsibilties?

3. If you seriously disagree with your parents about the way of life you think is best, what can you do to solve the problem besides run away from it? Compare the advantages and disadvantages of staying at home, even in an uncomfortable situation, to the advantages and disadvantages of leaving home to be on your own.

The Young:
The Party of Hope

Alfred Kazin

The other day on Fifth Avenue in New York I saw a truck crammed with students from a Catholic university who are volunteers on a "reclamation" project in Harlem. One of the students held up a placard which read, "God is not dead. We are." When a teacher of my age gets to remembering too fondly his ideals, struggles, and hopes as a college student in the 1930's, it is important for him to see a placard like that on Fifth Avenue, to recognize—in the midst of so much money, ostentation, and waste—that the extraordinarily widespread feelings of moral outrage filling our students today are incomparably purer and are likely to be more lasting than those that arose from the politics of deprivation in the thirties.

In the thirties, the economic and social order had visibly collapsed, and between hunger at home and Fascism-Nazism in Europe, a student had good reason to feel that there was no way to elementary human sanity and satisfaction but through a militant and wholesale reconstruction of society from top to bottom. As I look back upon it now, it occurs to me that comparatively few students indeed were involved in whatever was particularly "militant"—and this militancy was often more the mark of a fanatical ideology than of any idealistic, generous, *feeling* participation in the suffering of the time....

By contrast, students today seem to me the visible conscience of society. I have never known a time when students were so regularly a jump ahead of their elders in reacting to the horrors of napalm, the idiocy of making political war on a whole people, the banalities of middle-class life, the intolerability of so much aggression, hatred, and human inequality in our national life. What is so exciting to me about the present generation of students is the fact that concern about "society" has sprouted up, seemingly unmotivated in the richest and most powerful nation in the world, from moral awareness, moral sensitivity, moral intelligence. Not power over everybody else in the name of a cruelly unrealizable ideal, not power for the sake of universal abstractions, but a creative unrest is what distinguishes the thinking of so many young people today. What they have, very simply, is a refreshing freedom from the materialism that in one way or another drives so many middle-aged Americans crazy.

It may be that as one gets older one becomes more property conscious, more cautious, and so, by degrees, more and more disenchanted with oneself. Certainly the "guilt" that is one of the more insistent maladies of our time often springs from the middle-aged man's dislike of what he has become, what he is forced to do, by contrast with the joyous self-affirmation so natural to feel in youth. Of course there is much more to say about "guilt" than this, but anyone who has seen what adult "responsibility" can do to one's youthful idealism must admit that everything the young say about the old is only too true. Though we all have understandable excuses to make on the subject and the worst seem to have no "guilt" at all, it is a fact that only youth is poor enough and "irresponsible" enough to look life straight in the face and to see the anxiety and bad conscience that weigh down so many "successes" in our society.

In any event, society is always the hub of the matter nowadays, and so long as you are not wholly preoccupied by your career and are still relatively unconsumed by the pressures, you can see how insane and unjust much of society is, you can still compare the human potential with the sufferings of a very large part of the human race. Above all, if you are young enough to be drafted, you can admit what the leaders of government do not, that "war is the health of the state," that most people are more and more committed to any economy that rests on war and on war as a necessary and permanent part of culture.

In the 1930's, the social order was certainly breaking up and a "new" society was supposed to replace it, but even radicals did not really feel committed to *awareness* of every human victim in the world—in fact, radicals especially were strikingly indifferent to the victims of the G.P.U., the old Soviet secret police. But today students even in Russia, Poland and Czechoslovakia, France and other countries seem to be refreshingly free of totalitarian ideologies and are as skeptical about the wholly "new" man manufactured by Communism as our students are about the corrupt old politicians we always have right at home. There is a universalism about the thinking of students everywhere that is one of the few checkmates to the ever-recurrent dreariness of national pomp and power, national interests and national mythification. I have seen this at Stony Brook and at Berkeley, at Harvard, in Berlin, and even in Moscow.

A whole generation has unexpectedly (perhaps to its surprise more than to ours) become the leaven in the lump, the party of hope, the spirit of change, the conscience of our time. For the first time in many years one can see what it means to persist in that healthy criticism of society that makes alternatives seem possible, that makes human faith possible again.

When this faith goes, as it has for so many middle-class, middle-aged Americans, life loses its savour. When it goes, one becomes sick with the bad faith of people who are defending nothing but their own interests even when they talk of saving Viet Nam from "Communism." But when the spirit of change is present, it lights up everything one is unconsciously striving for.

What I notice most about students today, and don't always approve, is their essential meekness. I am aware that after a certain age, one insists upon "quiet," control, submission, and that the exasperated line that depleted energies take is always to accuse young people of being noisy, irreverent, and generally aggressive. But looked at in terms of their very real expectations and attitudes, our students are indeed meek. I mean by this that they do not believe in egotism, dominance, aggression, exploitation, and war.

For the first time perhaps since Christianity arose, one sees what a concerted philosophy of peace, here and everywhere in the world, shared in and acted on by young people everywhere could mean to a world sickened by its unending violence. So far as I understand anything about my students, I understand that they are saying this: Without peace and without brotherhood nothing from here on out is possible. The meekness also follows from a marked lack of interest in business and moneymaking, from a lack of the old aggressive "individualism," from a sense of solidarity with all people of a certain age and with all people on the firing line of social crisis.

After the age of caution has come upon you, it takes a certain effort to admit that there are people around who want more for the human race than they want for themselves, that nothing likely to be gained by them as individual citizens matters so much to them as checking the moral deterioration of our society. That is why I am on the side of students today. With such young people the external commotion is to be firmly disregarded in favour of admiration—and gratitude.

For Thinking, Talking, Writing

1. Mr. Kazin feels that most young people today are far more concerned about the evils of society and far more willing to work hard to change

those evils than young people in our country have ever been before. Do you agree or disagree with him? Why?

2. Do you think young people today are less interested in business and moneymaking, as Mr. Kazin believes, than their parents are? Explain your answer.

3. Do you think that the real reason for war is that our economy depends on it—that war is a necessary and permanent part of our culture? Why or why not?

Good Days
To Be Living In!

Sydney J. Harris

Things just seem to be worse than they used to be. In reality, they're much better, in almost every area of our national life. It's just the rate of change that dizzies and frightens us.

When I began writing this column, more than 25 years ago, the United States was mentally asleep, morally stunted and emotionally constipated. We were passive, dully accepting citizenry, corny and credulous almost beyond belief.

In the intervening quarter-century, we have grown up enormously —and, of course, we have experienced the growing pains that accompany the trip through adolescence. But we shouldn't confuse the process with the state.

Today, as a nation, we are far more sophisticated, knowledgeable, concerned, oriented toward action, aware of power structures and processes, less vulnerable to being pushed around by self-serving interests. If that isn't growth and betterment, I don't know what is.

We are questioning all the old verities, which is the beginning of wisdom (but not, as so many young people seem to think, the end of it); and we are learning that a small and dedicated group can make a big difference in communities, churches, and colleges.

These are good days to be living in, not bad ones, and I have little sympathy with people my age who yearn nostalgically for the time of our youth. We were trivial and uninformed, smug and unconcerned, while the great elemental forces of change were building up enormous charges of revolutionary electricity in the social atmosphere.

One need not approve everything that is going on today—for all change breeds its own excesses and perversions—to appreciate that the motive-power behind all this churning activity is the desire to lead a fuller life, to be more the master of one's own fate, to reject authority that is not based on the realities of humanhood, to make true "individualism" an essential part of the whole social fabric, and

SYDNEY J. HARRIS courtesy of *Chicago Daily News* and Publishers–Hall Syndicate.

not just a slogan of the market place.

For we are going through a revolution as far-reaching and important as the first American Revolution—not in the 18th Century sense of changing our rulers, but in the 20th Century sense of changing the rules. We don't like the ball game, which has come to belong more to the managers and umpires and associations than to the players (and it is no accident, by the way, that baseball players have become organized and dissident in a manner no one could have predicted a quarter-century ago).

What hurts today is the radical surgery we are calling for; but if it cuts out the old malignancies, without killing the patient, hurrah!

For Thinking, Talking, Writing

In this section you have read both negative and positive things about our society. Mr. Harris' statement, in this column, is certainly a positive one. Now that you have concluded the section, analyze your own feelings, beliefs, and opinions about our society as it exists today. Would you agree with Mr. Harris that, essentially, these are "good days to be living in"? Or do you feel that we are in the midst of a decaying and disintegrating society? Defend your answer.

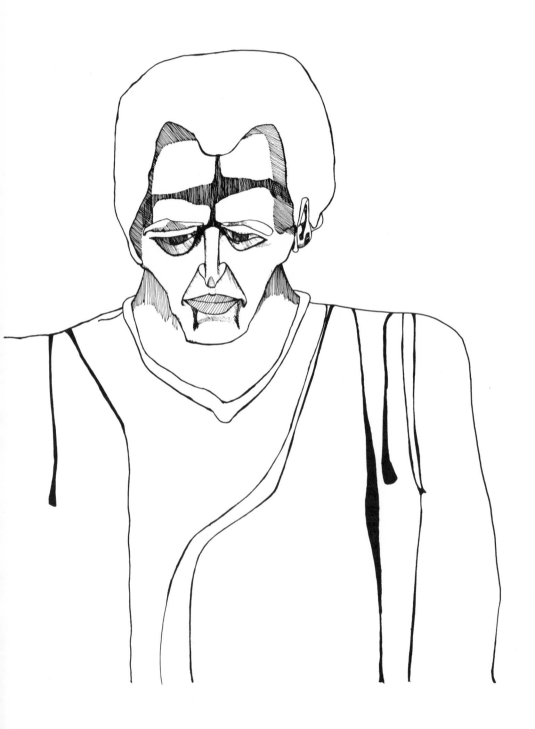

4

MYSELF:
who am I—and what?

Introduction

The search for self is probably the most important and most intense search you will ever undertake. Every human being goes through the questions about self: Who am I? What am I? Why am I whatever I am? How would I like to change? Where am I going?

The search for self has another dimension, too: the fact that we do not live alone. Sometimes we see ourselves not as *we* really think we are, but as we are reflected through other people's eyes. All of us behave very differently when we are alone than when we are with others. Which is real? Are both selves real? What's "real"?

In the *Talmud,* the authoritative body of Jewish law and tradition, there is a quotation which expresses well each man's constant search for self:

> If I am not for myself, who will be for me, but if I am only for myself, what am I, and if not now, when?

In this section you will explore various aspects of the search for self: how your personality may relate to your position in your family; how every man must face the problem of evil; the usefulness of psychiatry; the worthiness of praise; the commitment of the younger generation to social betterment. William Faulkner, one of the three American writers ever to win the Nobel Prize for Literature, said in his speech of acceptance for that award:

> I decline to accept the end of man. It is easy enough to say that man is immortal simply because he will endure; that when the last ding-dong of doom has clanged and faded from the last worthless rock hanging tideless in the last red and dying evening, that even then there will still be one more sound: that one of his puny inexhaustible voice, still talking. I refuse to accept this. I believe that man will not merely endure; he will prevail. He is immortal, not because he alone among creatures has an inexhaustible voice but because he has a soul, a spirit capable of compassion and sacrifice and endurance.

Read—think—talk—write. Can you, while studying this section, come closer to knowing your *self?*

SIBS:
A Personality Game
So Accurate
It's Frightening

Charles W. Slack

*The Game is like a map of personality and interpersonal relationships
... territories yet uncharted. A shock of recognition will often occur when
we see ourselves and others on the map for the first time.*
*The Game was defined by Dr. Walter Toman, associate professor of psy-
chology at Brandeis University.... From the works of Sigmund Freud
and others who stress the importance of early years in shaping personality, Dr. Toman has distilled a great amount of data into deceptively
simple principles.*

Guarantee: No one can help Playing the Game. Some may resist ac-
knowledging the rules, which, once learned, are unforgettable. Interestingly enough, your own reaction to the Game will depend upon which
player you are.... If this is confusing, Play the Game.

Warning: If you Play the Game with a friend, be careful. It can
strengthen or weaken, or even break relationships. Playing the Game
may give you a sense of power over others and/or a distressingly fatalistic
attitude about yourself.

RULES OF THE GAME

Do not count any sister or brother six or more years older or younger
than you.
Siblings lost through death, permanent hospitalization or complete mental retardation before you were six years old should be discounted. However, if you find a discrepancy, it may be due to this early influence.
Middle child reads both positions of the oldest and the youngest and
blends these traits together. Middles are moderate. For example, a girl
who has an older brother and a younger brother combines "Youngest
Sister of Brother(s)" with "Oldest Sister of Brother(s)" *but can ignore
the worst faults and problems.* Extremes have been shaded into temperate
traits.

Youngest or oldest of both sister(s) and brother(s) will also be a blend. The oldest brother of a brother and a sister should mingle the "Oldest Brother of Brother(s)" and "Oldest Brother of Sister(s)" together. He may find he has inherited the best of both.

Parental influence may be the cause if you find you are not quite as described in the charts. For example, if your father is an orphan and you are a boy, you may tend to take on his "unwanted" feelings. If your mother was unwed and you are a girl, you may reflect her emotions of being unloved. If your father was absent for many years when you were young, or your mother was overdominant because she was the oldest sister of sister(s), you may find this has been a definite influence in your life. To determine the reason for any further differences between your personality and the chart descriptions, you may wish to read a fuller explanation by Dr. Toman in his book, *Family Constellation.*

IF YOU ARE: AN OLDEST BROTHER OF SISTER(S)

What You Want in a Mate:
You can accept many modes of attractiveness in girls. External appearance, such as complexion, hair, face and body-build, or the way she dresses, will be secondary to what she is like as a person. You will have no sex conflict, because you have been used to girls in your family. You are used to being the leader, will want a junior as your mate. She will not have to transform into a bit of a boy or some kind of mother. Your wife will always come first—even over children.

Your Best Match:
YOUNGEST SISTER OF BROTHER(S) could be perfect for you. She has been used to boys and to being a junior. No conflict over sex or rank. She needs your leadership and you need her dependency.

Next Best Match:
MIDDLE SISTER if she has had at least one older brother. You will have no sex conflicts, and she will have only a small rank conflict. After all, she is used to looking up to her older brother and can transfer this adoration to you.

Other Possible Matches:
OLDEST SISTER OF BROTHER(S), but conflicts over seniority rights, a problem of who is boss will plague you. Each will want to transform the other into a younger sibling. Children will help.
YOUNGEST SISTER OF SISTER(S), but she will have a sex conflict—accepting you as a man.

MIDDLE GIRL OF SISTER(S) will have sex conflict within herself and small rank conflict.

ONLY CHILD if her mother is youngest sister of brother(s) and father is oldest brother of sister(s).

Worst Match:

OLDEST SISTER OF SISTER(S) only—although the fact that you have been used to girls will reduce conflicts over acceptance of other sex. You will both want to be the senior and will have a problem giving in to each other, or even compromising. Both will want to dominate. There may be ceaseless arguments, conflicts, fights.

Children?

You would rather have some children than none, but you and your wife might be happy as things are. You will take great care of your children.

Personality

He prefers a leading position to a subordinate one, not so much because he feels a calling for it but because he wants to set his own pace. Love of the tender sex is the most important of his concerns. If necessary, he will undergo hardship, but at the end of the road there must be a woman, or two, or ten. No trophy is good enough by itself. Obtaining it must help him win the lady of his choice. A realist, he does not aspire to the impossible.

Friends

Almost all types of male friends would be compatible, even though not eagerly sought. Only other oldest brothers of sisters would not last long as friends. He is not usually "one of the boys." He may go for games, sports and the like, but he has to be home on time; his wife and children expect him to.

Politics

He tends to prefer a moderately conservative government, and noninterference with business, family life, and a person's ways of thinking. Everybody should be permitted to make up his mind by himself. Everything is all right if a satisfactory love and family life are assured.

Religion

He believes in life and love. He is somewhat indifferent to, or skeptical of, God. He does not insist on any ism. He may be an atheist, but wouldn't make a point of it. He may be a member of a conventional faith because he believes that some religion is probably good for the children.

With the Opposite Sex

Kind and considerate with women, he can court for a long time without getting discouraged, go out of his way to demonstrate interest. But he can also assess his chances with women better than other men. She must be interested in him, too. Once that is established, he lets her take her time. That's her right. That's what he'd want his sisters to do. If the girl of his choice decides otherwise, he bears no grudge. He will want to show off his wife—she is the best.

Work

He is not exactly absorbed by his job but may be a good worker as long as there are female colleagues or co-workers. Only if he is happily betrothed or married will he tolerate the exclusive company of men. He would rather not get into any field of work where women are scarce. He will accept men as superiors at work if they are better than he is and if they are not favorites with women.

Financial

He is a fair-to-good preserver of property, but will not expand it greatly himself. He may create new enterprises as an accidental by-product of his efforts to please the woman who attracts him. As long as he and his family survive, things cannot be so bad. After all, what matters more than love?

Philosophy

He tends to be an Epicurean or Stoic. Either he believes in the pursuit of pleasure and happiness, or, he is a heroic, calm nonbeliever, a friend of intellectual discipline over all emotions and accidents of fate. He does not like mysticism and existentialism. Psychotherapy does not attract him.

AN OLDEST BROTHER OF BROTHER(S)

What You Want in a Mate:

You will want a girl who has learned to be somewhat like a boy herself, yet admires and adores boys. She should be your inferior in being youngest and in being "only a girl." She should have learned at home to do everything possible for boys. She must be kind and cater out of timidity. She should be a virgin. You admire elflike beauty and want everyone to see and envy your luck with her. You will secretly be looking for a mother — the only female you had in your family.

Your Best Match:
YOUNGEST SISTER OF BROTHER(S) may be your best match. Though you may have some sex conflict, she will have none. There will be no conflict over rank because she will accept you implicitly as the boss.

Next Best Match:
MIDDLE GIRL if she has had at least one older brother. She will have no sex conflict and is used to acting the part of the junior and by looking up to a senior, like yourself, for guidance.

Other Possible Matches:
OLDEST SISTER OF BROTHER(S), but there will be a conflict over seniority. She may remind you of mother and thus be compatible. You can divide your empires: You reign in business, she at home.
YOUNGEST SISTER OF SISTER(S), although you will both be in for trouble in attempting to accept the other sex, however you will have no seniority conflicts.
ONLY CHILD if father is oldest brother of sister(s) and mother is youngest sister of brother(s).

Worst Match:
OLDEST SISTER OF SISTER(S) only. You will have full rank and sex conflict. Your quarrels may be unending. You are both used to being in control of others and neither will want to let go. Arrival of children, especially of boys, will make life easier for both.

Children?
You will take pains to care for them with future plans. You will maintain order and discipline and reign somewhat self-righteously like an autocrat.

Personality
He is the leader, master of other men. He can inspire others and take the greatest hardships upon himself. Yet he will be only second most daring in matters of life and death, because he may feel, unconsciously, that his survival is more important than that of any other single person. If someone is in deadly danger, however, he will aid him even if it may cost his life. He has a solid memory for relevant facts and events, likes tight concepts, and hates big empty words.

Friends
He is on good terms with other males with the exception of another oldest brother of brother(s). His best male friend is often a youngest brother of

brother(s). He can cooperate with him, guide him, and this youngest brother will let him take the lead. Generally speaking, friendships tend to be a strong supplement of marriage.

Politics
He believes in strong leadership — even dictatorships if necessary. He may be a revolutionary in his younger years, but will come to terms with complexities of reality sooner than others and end up a conservative. He prefers working behind the scenes as the expert diplomat, economist or master racketeer.

Religion
He believes God set the world right in the beginning, and it has been functioning rationally ever since without Him. Or he insists that God's strongest manifestation is mankind's moral code. Or he is an atheist. Or a materialist who makes matter his God. He can rarely be an ordinary pious person.

With the Opposite Sex
He is tough with women. He will not fall for them, but will be delighted and thrilled if *they* fall for him. He will tend to treat girls like younger brothers — expect them to live up to his assignments, admire only him, and be content with very little in return. He will prefer them to be slim and boyish rather than heavy and voluptuous. He may try to have many girls, and since he cannot keep up with them all at once, he may put them to work for him. Obedient, respectful, and efficient, they are hardly real girls.

Work
He is a good worker when he chooses, and a good leader in any situation where work and leadership can be combined. He can accept the authority of a superior male like his boss, but he will tend to do it one of two ways. Either he will mold himself in the image of the authority figure or he will operate with a vengeance. He will look for loopholes in his idol's authority, belittling him and discarding him bit by bit. He wants to assume the role of authority himself.

Financial
He builds up property — spiritual, financial or domestic. He hates to live off capital or to be in debt. He may incur debts, but they will be only a fraction of his collateral. Perhaps he may despise finances and everyday reality altogether, but stay far ahead of his moral, intellectual, or spiritual commitments.

Philosophy
He believes in hard cash, common sense, clear purposes and relationships.
If he should turn romantic, he will not merely be the practitioner, but the
enforcer of the creed. If he accepts advice or psychotherapy, he dislikes
his dependence on another person.

A YOUNGEST BROTHER OF SISTER(S)

What You Want in a Mate:
You will want a dominant and protective wife, who has been used to boys
her junior. Since you have had girls in your family, you will have no sex
conflict. She may be attractive and even beautiful, but your choice appears
to come about by accident. What matters more to you is that she promises unconsciously and instinctively to be good with "little" boys. She must
be kind, soft and maternal, will have to overlook a lot and count on little
support from you except in real emergencies.

Your Best Match:
OLDEST SISTER OF BROTHER(S) can make you a truly perfect
match. She has been used to boys her junior. You will be the more dependent one, no matter how independent and efficient you look in the
areas of greatest talents.

Next Best Match:
OLDEST SISTER OF SISTER(S) will be willing to act the senior, to be
the dominant and responsible one. She may not be fully reconciled to the
fact she is married to a man. She may be belligerent, may not be willing
to suffer.

Other Possible Matches:
YOUNGEST SISTER OF BROTHER(S) will make a possible match,
but it will probably be difficult. She has been used to other sex, but she
cannot act the part of the senior you are looking for.
ONLY CHILD will be a possible match if her mother is oldest sister of
brother(s) and father is the youngest brother of sister(s).

Worst Match:
YOUNGEST SISTER OF SISTER(S), who will neither provide guidance
nor even know too well how to handle the other sex. You will need a third

party to supply you with guidance, although that could also break up the marriage. One child may be too much for you. Both of you are looking for a senior to guide you.

Children?
Hard for you to take. You might feel threatened in your own status. There should be only one darling little genius: yourself. You will do little planning for their future. You may be on a par with the children, rather than their superior.

Personality
He is a girls' boy. They dote on him. He evokes their maternal instincts. It does not matter what he undertakes or where he is heading, they will be around to assist and take care of him. He often lacks psychological understanding of people as he did not have to acquire insight during his early life. He is quick to compliment but remains un-involved.

Friends
He is not too popular with the boys. They resent the way he takes help and support for granted. Only with men who are by far his juniors can he ordinarily avoid trouble and quarrels. He may establish friendships or platonic relationships with older women.

Politics
He has either almost no opinions or strictly technical, limited viewpoints. He believes any of the historic or present-day systems may work, if only certain basic principles of economy are observed. He lacks the global outlook.

Religion
He is either indifferent or conventional. He tends to believe what has been taught him, even to lead a life which the minister of his church would recommend as a compromise between the pursuits of the world and those of God.

With the Opposite Sex
He can be nice to women, adore and flatter them, surprise them by his tact and care, but he does not always do so. Often he takes them for granted as he always has. Thus his efforts to win their favors are playful or even mildly sarcastic. The woman he wins has to be very kind, soft and maternal, and count on little support from him except in real emergencies.

Work

He is not a very regular and systematic worker. He may want to satisfy childish goals by making a living from playing bridge, the xylophone, or horses. Where his talents are great, he is capable of real accomplishment, preferably as an individual or as the star of a team. He may stumble along carelessly, sometimes succeeding, other times failing.

Financial

He does not ordinarily build up or preserve property well and may even squander it. With proper management by a responsible female, his talents and abilities may be directed toward highly productive and profitable goals.

Philosophy

Philosophy does not usually have a grip on him. He does not believe in anything that tries to pervade and change the individual. Things are best as they are. If in need, he is a ready candidate for psychotherapy provided he can get a motherly therapist.

A YOUNGEST BROTHER OF BROTHER(S)

What You Want in a Mate:

You will want a mate who can assume the role of a senior and be able to handle younger, somewhat dependent and guidance-seeking boys. She need not be very feminine in appearance, although you will want her to be beautiful — a cool or plain kind of beauty. Only if she is very maternal and lets you pursue all of your many and often short-lived interests, only if she is the secret boss, will you be capable of happiness with her. She can guide your professional conduct subtly.

Your Best Match:

OLDEST SISTER OF BROTHER(S). If she has coped with brother(s) at home, she can usually cope with you. She has no sex conflict; there is no seniority conflict for either of you.

Next Best Match:

MIDDLE SISTER with at least one younger brother. She will have no sex conflict, although you do. There will be slight rank conflict, since she has had a junior in her early family life. She will be able to manage.

Other Possible Matches:
OLDEST SISTER OF SISTER(S) might do, although you will both have sex conflicts. She can act as leader and give you guidance and support. YOUNGEST SISTER OF BROTHER(S) will be a possibility. She will be ready to accept you as a man, and some close friend can substitute as a guide for both.
ONLY CHILD will be acceptable, providing her father has been youngest brother of sister(s) and mother has been oldest sister of brother(s). She may like her "gifted little boy."

Worst Match:
YOUNGEST SISTER OF SISTER(S). Neither of you can afford the other the guidance, support and responsibility you long for. You may find guidance outside of marriage, or if you find work that suits you and your talents, the situation may be better. Neither of you will want children.

Children?
A bit of a nuisance to you. Child is rival for all the favors coming from your wife. You may lose yourself more than ever in work and profession. You may come home rarely or go on long business trips. Wife will have to raise children.

Personality
He is a capricious and willful man — a person who can surprise and amaze his elders but also antagonize them. He will give in to no one, yet needs others to react against. If he were really free, he would not know what to do. He seeks people with whom he can pick arguments or conduct elaborate conversations. Not only can he accept authority, but loves it.

Friends
He gets along best with older brothers of brother(s) and may occasionally enjoy the friendship of another youngest brother because of the empathy between them. So important are male friends, he may be willing to sacrifice a girl in order to keep a boy.

Politics
He is against monarchy, dictatorships and even strong leadership within a democracy. Laissez-faire is his motto. In spirit he will be a revolutionary. Yet, if he achieves power himself, he will no longer desire change.

Religion
He believes in God's incessant interference with the world that He has created, in mystic unions, flashes of revelations, miracles, and the brotherhood of all men, especially if he is their dearest brother. Emotions constitute the world.

With the Opposite Sex
He is soft with women — a gentleman, even when he plays the tough one or the cynic. He is shy, awkward, almost innocent and women are often willing to give him much more than he asks. He tends to win their favors but does not quite know what to do with them. He does not seem to understand women; all he wants is to be understood himself. Women must play mother to him.

Work
He is an irregular worker, sometimes quite excellent in his achievements and other times unproductive. He is good at work when he can compete or when somebody superior in status is watching. He is at his best in free artistic or scientific endeavors where his livelihood is taken care of by an impersonal institution or kind sponsor.

Financial
He does not create or preserve property. He takes and spends easily with no concern from where the next donation will come. He will live beyond his means and reach far above what he can reasonably hope to get. Debts and riches mean nothing.

Philosophy
He is the mystic, the romtantic, the experimentalist and existentialist. Philosophy is a mood rather than a system. He flocks to prophets, advisors, and psychotherapy. If called upon to give advice, he believes that things will take care of themselves.

ONLY CHILD — MALE —

What You Want in a Mate:
You will want someone who will pamper you, give in to you, suffer your whims, let you have your own way, though you do not want to lead. You will be looking for a father or a mother in your future spouse. You cannot really stand a peer.

Your Best Match:
YOUNGEST SISTER OF BROTHER(S) is a junior who will not try to boss you; she has no sex conflict.

Next Best Match:
MIDDLE SISTER with an older brother or possibly with a younger brother; she will have no sex conflict.

Other Possible Matches:
OLDEST SISTER OF BROTHER(S), a logical but not the best choice. There will be no sex conflict but you may not want a domineering spouse nor may you want to lead. You want your own way.

Worst Match:
YOUNGEST SISTER OF SISTER(S), particularly if your father is younger brother of brother(s) and mother is young sister of sister(s). ONLY CHILD if parents are ill-matched.

Children?
The only male child will want to remain childless, so that he can be the "child" throughout his life.

ONLY CHILD – FEMALE –

What You Want in a Mate:
You will want a mate who will love your whims as part of the display of your beauty or charm, somebody who does not mind suffering all kinds of little tortures at your hands. You, too, want a father or mother and may prefer a much older partner.

Your Best Match:
OLDEST BROTHER OF SISTER(s) will be kind, tolerant, mature, particularly if older than you.

Next Best Match:
YOUNGEST BROTHER OF SISTER(S) will have no sex conflict, but he is a junior and cannot lead you.

Other Possible Matches:
MIDDLE BROTHER with older or younger sister. There will be no sex conflict with him. There will always be a seniority conflict with an only child.
OLDEST BROTHER OF BROTHER(S) faintly possible.

Worst Match:
ONLY CHILD, particularly if parents are ill-matched. They will probably remain childless; the few who don't prove they should. Only chance is if both have powerful interests in common.

Children?
You can do without children. If there are any children, husband will have to take care of them, or provide servants.

ONLY CHILD — MALE AND FEMALE —

Family Constellation (Male and Female)
Both male and female are apt to take after their same-sex parent. For example, if a male only child has a father who was the oldest brother of brothers, then the child may resemble him (see oldest brother of brothers). And if the girl's mother was the youngest sister of sisters, the daughter may take on these characteristics herself. Yet in a situation of stress, fatigue, boredom, physical or social restriction, the only child may become an egocentric and moody singleton. If the parent has been an only child, the parent's parent's sibling position has to be investigated.

Personality
Male: The chief characteristic of the only child is that he is the only one of his kind, and remains a child often way into adulthood. He is used to being his parents' pride and joy. He is used to arousing sympathy and concern; getting all possible support on a moment's notice.
Female: She is somewhat more capricious, extravagant and selfish than other girls. It is difficult for her to understand what really goes on in other people's minds, except for those few who seem to understand hers. She comes to believe she is the most precious of all princesses, and hardly anyone would be good enough for her. After she has condescended to marry, she is prone to run back to her parents and have them comfort her.

Friends

Male: He is prepared for all types of friends, yet not ready for a peer relationship. His friends had better count on no great sacrifices, although, for the heck of it, he may sometimes make them.

Female: Her friends will be chosen from those who are kind, tolerant, mature, and preferably much older than she. She can only stand parents.

With the Opposite Sex

Male: With women, he is prepared for all types of partners yet not a real peer relationship. Rather he looks for mother-figures. They may have to let him be the infant prodigy forever.

Female: She too is prepared for all types of spouses and yet for none, because she cannot really stand a peer. Marriage will work out only if she finds a kind and preferably (much) older partner. She is at her best with someone who loves her whims and does not mind suffering all kinds of little tortures at her hands.

Work

Male: He is used to winning acclaim at home, hence he will tend to believe that at work too he should be the center of his peers' and his superiors' attention. He may believe his entire work situation has been arranged so that he may display his talents.

Female: At work, if ever she gets around to it, she is often a nuisance. She may have excellent capabilities but only where she finds a congenial milieu, preferably with older, kind and extremely tolerant superiors, may she live up to expectations.

Financial

Male: Material possessions are of little importance in and of themselves. Implicitly, he knows that his greatest assets, other than his own talents, are his parents or those who are willing to assume their roles. But he will take whatever they bestow on him for granted and have it end right there. That is, he would not of his own accord tend to think of improving his estate and finally passing it on to others.

Female: She wants everything on which she sets her mind, but her mind appears whimsical. She may ask for the most fantastic presents and favors, along with very trivial ones, and can get equally upset if they do not arrive. She makes her demands known, needs parents, parentlike friends or even "lovers" to satisfy them.

AN OLDEST SISTER OF BROTHER(S)

What You Want in a Mate:
You will want a man who will accept your leadership. You must lead, so your mate must love to be led in all but his favorite endeavors. Even there, you will want to help. You want to furnish your mate with all the things he needs in order to remain a little boy; a genius of sorts would be perfect. You are used to peers of the opposite sex, so you will have no sex conflict and will have little trouble accepting a man as a man.

Your Best Match:
YOUNGEST BROTHER OF SISTER(S) will be the ideal person to accept what you have to offer. He will want you to be the senior; he is used to being the junior. Neither of you will have any sex conflict.

Next Best Match:
YOUNGEST BROTHER OF BROTHER(S) may have conflicts about accepting you as a woman. He may waiver between rebelling against your sex and submitting to you. You can buffer his outbursts and usually comfort him.

Other Possible Matches:
MIDDLE BROTHER with an older sister.
ONLY CHILD if his mother is an oldest sister of a long row of brothers.
OLDEST BROTHER OF SISTER(S) may not be too good a match, but at least you will be used to a peer of the other sex. Children will help the marriage, because you will both want juniors to guide in the family.

Worst Match:
OLDEST BROTHER OF BROTHER(S). He will have a conflict over your sex as well as seniority. He wants a motherly person and he wants to be the one in authority, yet you want to take over the guidance of the family. Children will help because you both will want juniors to dominate.

Children?
You will want them regardless of the match you make. You want to take care of husband and any number of children you decide to have. You make up your mind about children. They will come to you rather than father.

Personality
She is independent and strong in an inconspicuous way. Often one only notices in retrospect how well-taken, foresighted and competent her actions have been. She is practical, concrete, of a healthy egotism, though sometimes self-effacing for her men. She wants to retain the men she has, find new ones, and win old ones back. Men flock to her. She will not compete with them but will assist them.

Friends
Female friends are not too important. They will not be loved for their own sakes. If they have a man at their side, they may be appreciated. If she chooses a girl friend for what she is rather than for the man she brings along, she may prefer the youngest sister of sister(s) who will look up to her as an idol.

Politics
She advocates moderation above all. She believes that, through mediation and discussion — if possible under her auspices — everybody on earth could come to an understanding. If wives were all like her, they would guide their husbands to do the things that would bring peace and comfort.

Religion
In religion, she tends to be above it all. Religion is a matter of inspiration and genius, but neither would amount to much without caring females. They have always helped the prophets along. Even God Himself can be really understood only by loving women.

With the Opposite Sex
She wields no great power of fascination. She reminds men of home and mother, and sometimes they do not notice they are in love with her. She may have to do the proposing. If she has had many brothers, it will be harder for her to settle for one man. She may marry, but keep a whole flock around . . . old friends, friends of her husband, or her brothers. She may be the woman to whom men come for advice. She may nurse budding writers or be the patron of scientists.

Work
Officially in a leading position, she is tactful and unoffensive, shows a strict, yet kind efficiency, and is able to relegate work gracefully and expediently. She relegates work when she considers it unimportant. She creates an atmosphere that is conducive to good work. She will mediate between quarreling parties. Her boss will listen to her because she does not challenge his technical or administrative competence.

Financial

Material possessions are insignificant compared to the possession of men. She may prefer her man to be a money-maker, or rich to begin with, but she can be content with much or little. If their assets lie in the same field, she will renounce her career for him.

Philosophy

She believes that all philosophy starts in the kitchen. Where would the philosophers be were it not for women who looked after them and enabled them to sit back and think? She must be in a bad way in order to seek psychological help. Usually, she can take care of herself as well as of others.

AN OLDEST SISTER OF SISTER(S)

What You Want in a Mate:

You are looking for someone submissive, someone to mould. You must dominate and must find a mate who will tolerate this. You will not budge in arguments, may turn obstinate even in a most physical sense. You will handle household problems, merchants and parties in your own stubborn way and choke his mere attempts to get in a remark. He may be superior in technical competence and talents, but you will top him by common sense, female logic or occasionally by plain meanness.

Your Best Match:

YOUNGEST BROTHER OF SISTER(S) will seek you out for your seniority, your dominance and leadership. He will not mind as long as you take care of him and the family and let him pursue his interests.

Next Best Match:

YOUNGEST BROTHER OF BROTHER(S) will accept your guidance, no matter how numerous and violent your struggles and arguments may be. Neither will be too ready to accept the other sex. He will like you as a comrade.

Other Possible Matches:

MIDDLE BROTHER if he has had an older sister.
ONLY CHILD if his mother is oldest sister of brother(s) and father is youngest brother of sister(s).
OLDEST BROTHER OF SISTER(S) may do, but he prefers a junior female, while you want a junior who is not too much of a male.

Worst Match:

OLDEST BROTHER OF BROTHER(S). You will both have rank and sex conflicts and a hard time coming to any kind of terms with each other. Children will be a welcome relief, although both of you will tend to wage war against each other by recruiting children of own sex and by agitating against those of opposite sex.

Children?

Children will be a relief even in the best of matches. You can let go of your husband and tend to them. You are a proud, protective mother, who will retain some belligerence toward males.

Personality

She can stand on her own feet, take care of others, and even overpower them to an extent. She pretends to be surer of herself than she really is, but usually succeeds in conveying that impression. She can cut people short who know much more than she does on the subject in question. If she cannot dominate, she may be unhappy, angry or aggressively mute. Taken in all, she is a kind of queen, both conscientious and self-righteous, accepting orders only from her king.

Friends

Her best female friends will be younger sisters of sisters, who will have very little trouble subordinating themselves. Oldest sisters of sisters will make good friends as long as their fields of interest do not overlap too closely. She can understand their problems. Generally, she believes no friendship with a female can match one with a male.

Politics

She tends to be a conservative, even outright antirevolutionary. She believes in legitimate authority. Above all, she believes in her father. She will be feared rather than loved by the people over whom she reigns, but this is what she wants. All government must be lawful and the law must be obeyed.

Religion

She believes in the absolute reign of God but also in her own infallibility, as long as she lives by God's commandments. God takes an active part in everything that happens, but He also helps nobody who does not help himself. Justice and morality are His important areas of concern.

With the Opposite Sex

For men she is a hard girl to make. She tends to rebuff advances and often she appears so independent that she discourages them anyway. She may be beautiful, but men simply do not think of her as wanting to be conquered or seduced. A somewhat passive or feminine man may relax her sufficiently to bring her more tender and even motherly sides to the fore. She is not all that cool and belligerent as she appears at first. If she makes an inept marriage, she will stick to it with fatal persistence.

Work

She is likely to be competent and get things done, particularly when she is the leader. Her superior must be male and older or more distinguished for her to accept his authority. Females will have to bow to her in order to win mere tolerance. Secretly she despises them and will not rest until she has surpassed them. She behaves somewhat like a male, which makes it difficult for girls under her control to identify with her and hard for men to love her.

Financial

She likes to spend freely. She will not incur debts on her own behalf, but may do so for the sake of those entrusted to her. At work, she likes to draw big salaries as a token of appreciation She will hold on to some form of control over the people of her career, business or family.

Philosophy

If she has an interest in philosophy, she is most likely to be interested in principles and their consequences for her. She wants a gospel, and whoever is strong enough to have produced one can be her potential hero. Romantics, existentialists or mystics have little chance with her unless they have a simple system.

YOUNGEST SISTER OF BROTHER(S)

What You Want in a Mate:

You will want a man who is a senior, who will dominate you, who will give you guidance. You are neither strong nor domineering but tender and patient. You are most likely of all girls to make an optimal match. In character, you are a true woman. You will have no sex conflict because you have been used to brother(s) at home. You will almost instinctively find the man who will be good for you. In all matters except your firm character, you are like wax and honey.

Your Best Match:
OLDEST BROTHER OF SISTER(S) is looking for you and knows enough about girls to sense you are perfect for him. He will dominate and you will like this. You will have no sex or seniority conflicts.

Next Best Match:
OLDEST BROTHER OF BROTHER(S) will be attracted by your sweet womanliness, by your submissiveness, which he adores. He will want you to be a timid doe. He will not want you to have a will of your own.

Other Possible Matches:
MIDDLE BROTHER who has had at least one younger sister.
YOUNGEST BROTHER OF SISTER(S) might be possible; however he will be off on a tangent, professionally or otherwise. There will be a serious seniority conflict.
ONLY CHILD if father is oldest brother of sister(s). But he may not let you continue your role as the only girl of boys. He may not satisfy you.

Worst Match:
YOUNGEST BROTHER OF BROTHER(S) is not used to a female peer and will have trouble accepting your sex. Both of you will want a partner to guide you; you cannot find that guidance with each other. You will enter this match only if external circumstances limit your freedom, or if you have had early losses that have shaken your confidence.

Children?
You will have them because — and when — your husband wants you to, or when you feel like presenting your husband with a child. You do not want children for yourself. You will not force your children but will seduce them to be obedient in freedom.

Personality
She is usually everything a man wants a girl to be: feminine, friendly, kind, sensitive and tactful; submissive without being subservient, devoted, a good companion of men, a rather good sport. She attracts men better than other girls. She is a little nondescript in other respects. She may start a career, but any worthwhile man can sway her into marriage and motherhood. She is guided by her feelings and instincts.

Friends
Female friends matter very little. Girls seek her out, frequently for the boys she has at her command. But they may also be trying, unconsciously,

to win her away from boys and substitute themselves. She might get along with the youngest sister of sister(s) who will try to learn about boys from her.

Politics
Politically, she is anything that her brother(s), her father, her boyfriend or her husband is. Beyond that, she believes that women should support their men in their convictions, assist them in their obligations, and that their own virtues should be feminine above all.

Religion
She is conventional, believing in submission to God's will, in humbly appealing to Him in prayer, and in the necessity to please Him. God wants her to look beautiful, she might well believe. She is no great moralist and almost never a fanatic.

With the Opposite Sex
Men tend to adore her. She is likely to attract suitors wherever she goes and she will never abuse an easy conquest. She is charming with everyone. She has learned to take her time with her brothers and continues to feel that the supply of men is ample. She is convinced it is never too late, so that occasionally this girl becomes an old maid. But she will retain her charm and rarely be without some kind of suitor or lover. Old or married men fall for her, dote on her.

Work
She is the ideal employee, the best person to work under somebody's guidance. She is an excellent secretary, particularly to men. She keeps track of everything she is supposed to and does not have to be watched. Women do not always like her; she is not friendly enough to them. She understands men instinctively but not objectively.

Financial
Material possessions mean almost nothing to her, because they seem to come so easily. She is the little one and the only girl among the children in the family. Her brother(s), if they have any influence on her choice of suitors, may try to get her the richest. What she retains financially will depend on her husband.

Philosophy
She has no outspoken philosophy but she may well have that inner, feminine wisdom that can outdo all philosophy. Where she is, she will bring gaiety, fun and love. Because of her ease with men, she is not too likely to look for psychological guidance.

YOUNGEST SISTER OF SISTER(S)

What You Want in a Mate:
You will want a man who will lead you and dominate you, but you may
have some difficulty coming close to each other as man and woman. You
will want to remain the child, the darling. You may surprise a man because you will have an urge to compete with him on all sorts of issues.
If he recognizes you do not have to win, you may both arrive at a good
understanding. You will want your man to see through your willfulness,
your capriciousness, through your maneuvers and difficulties.

Your Best Match:
OLDEST BROTHER OF SISTER(S) will know what a junior girl wants
and you will be willing to submit to a senior. But you are not used to a
man; he is a man, and that makes a difference.

Next Best Match:
OLDEST BROTHER OF BROTHER(S)—you will have little difficulty
accepting his leadership, and he is able to provide it. You may plan and
agree on financial aspects of marriage, but he may not awaken the woman
in you. Children will help.

Other Possible Matches:
MIDDLE BROTHER if he has a younger sister.
ONLY CHILD if his father is an oldest brother of sister(s) and mother
is youngest sister of brother(s), or a close equivalent.
YOUNGEST BROTHER OF SISTER(S); however there may be a serious rank conflict. He will be used to sisters, and so will have no sex conflict. But both of you want guidance. Neither wants to dominate or lead.

Worst Match:
YOUNGEST BROTHER OF BROTHER(S). Both of you will lack
experience with a peer of opposite sex, and be in rank conflict. Both will
try to be the little one and look for leadership in the other, and neither is
able to furnish it. Children will not help, will not be welcome. Both will
try to make a senior out of child. One child will be too much.

Children?
You may have trouble with children. You will need a nurse, maid or
governess or your own mother to help you. You want to remain the
child. Once you have children, and find you are not happy, you may
discard your family for another husband.

Personality

She likes an adventurous and colorful life. She wants entertainment and change, often on the spur of the moment. She is ready to throw her beliefs, achievements, and friends overboard and go for new sets altogether. She can seduce men better than most girls, partly because of her greater inclination to submit.

Friends

Her best female friends will be older sisters of sisters. She likes to be guided. The greater the number of sisters, the greater her predilection for girl friends, and the less her inclination to marriage. She is often sought out by strong women, feminine men.

Politics

She may be anything, switching from one to the other extreme, or declare to have no opinion at all, depending on her whim and opponents.

Religion

Her attitudes range from utter indifference to fervent concern, from theism to deisim and atheism. She may have erratic debates within herself about God, her feelings changing with her moods.

With the Opposite Sex

She is attractive to men and fairly inventive in getting to them. She can sparkle in conversation, impress by her dress and makeup, although both may be a little loud. Gradually, however, men notice they are not getting very far with her. Unconsciously she would love to be coerced to give up all her nonsense, but on the surface her arrogance discourages force.

Work

She can be excellent or erratic in her accomplishments. In almost no case would she be a good leader. Only with a male boss who knows how to take her as a worker and as a woman, who is fatherly enough to overlook her little faults and old enough not to qualify as a potential lover, would she be in a position to utilize all she is able to do.

Financial

Property may mean a lot to her, but she cannot be expected to preserve it. If she marries into wealth, she may waste it all, if he lets her. Very seldom will she contribute to any kind of estate. She is too fond of gambling to be able to save for long.

Philosophy
She tends to go out on a limb, believing in the basic goodness of man.
Therefore everything should be permitted to man and . . . more often . . .
to herself. She may be a sucker for psychotherapy which could go on
forever.

For Thinking, Talking, Writing

1. After finding and reading about yourself in these charts, do you think
   they are fairly accurate?
2. Have you gained any new insights about yourself from these charts?
   Do you know any more about "Who am I — and what?"
3. Look up your brothers and/or sisters, your parents, your close friends,
   and read about them. Does the information seem accurate, from what
   you already know about these people? Do you have any more insight
   into what they are really like?

A Conversation
with Abraham Maslow

Mary Harrington Hall

Abraham Maslow is a famous and respected psychologist. He is President of the American Psychological Association and chairman of the Department of Psychology at Brandeis University, and he has written a number of books. The following are some of Dr. Maslow's observations concerning the problem of evil.

...Why are people cruel and why are they nice? Evil people are rare, but you find evil behavior in the majority of people.... Most people are nice people. Evil behavior is caused by ignorance, by thoughtlessness, by fear or even by the desire for popularity with your gang.... The thing is to try to understand, to realize how it is possible for people who are capable of being angels and heroes and saints to be bastards and killers and quitters.... Watch out for anybody who is mean or cruel. Watch out for sadism, watch out for people who delight in destruction, especially in people who agree with you.

Youngsters are tempted. If they have their own complex about their fathers, that runs over to all authority; if they're trying to destroy daddy, they all want to join the "spit on daddy club." The one who is most rebellious becomes a leader and we have the crazy situation where the nastiest kid is apt to be leader....

I gave up everything I was fascinated with in a selfish way around 1941. I felt I must try to save the world and to prevent these horrible wars and this awful hatred and prejudice.... I felt we didn't understand—not Hitler, nor the Germans, nor Stalin, nor the Communists. We didn't understand any of them. I felt that if we could understand, then we could make progress. I had a vision of a peace table, with people sitting around it, talking about human nature and hatred and war and peace and brotherhood...I realized that the rest of my life must be devoted to discovering a psychology for the peace table...I wanted to prove that human beings are capable of something grander than war and prejudice and hatred....

For Thinking, Talking, Writing

1. Do you recognize in yourself the double capability of being a "hero" and a "bastard"?
2. Why does Dr. Maslow mention that we should watch out for meanness, cruelty, sadism, and delight in destruction, *especially in people who agree with us?* What is the particular danger in that situation?
3. Have you ever been involved in a situation in which the nastiest kid is the leader? What happens to the group in such a situation?
4. What are the implications for finding out more about who and what you are in learning something about evil?
5. Do you agree with Dr. Maslow that if we can learn to understand evil, we can cope with it more adequately? Or do you think that evil is so much a part of human nature that no matter how thoroughly we understand it, we will never be able to do much about it?
6. *Are* human beings "capable of something grander than war and prejudice and hatred"?

When to See a Shrink

Lois Libien

Two Columbia College seniors sit in a grimy Greenwich Village café, a place for philosophizing, for dark-bar talk. Chad, the blond one, whose looks say "nothing can go wrong in life," is talking.... He runs his fingers through his hair, waits for the barman to take the order, then leans across the table. "I hate to say this," he blurts out. "It sounds so hippy... I would really like to find out who I am." He blushes. *Imagine me, Chad, saying such a thing. Life is all set for me,* he thinks, *nice and tidy... college, law school, the Army, my father's firm. I have nothing to complain about....*

"But it's not me," Chad says, aloud, feeling somehow abandoned and guilty as the words come out, guilty maybe at letting his parents down... at letting himself down, maybe. *Is it me or my father I am becoming?* he asks himself. It is almost June, almost graduation, the decision-making time. Chad is not ready for decisions.

Jeff, sitting across the table, is. He is dropping out of school, now, a month before he is due to graduate. If that means the Army, Vietnam, it is, anyway, time to think. The only decisions he will have to make will be those necessary to save his skin. His only goal, to live. There will be no long-term thinking to do... for two years, at least.

Chad is not sure he will take the same route as Jeff. But he cannot study. He has been drifting along these last two months, coasting on his good-student reputation and the almost effortless hard work of the past three and a half years in school. Now, he is locked in a state of nothingness. He can't move forward. He can't drop out. He can't move. Stalemate.

Back on Columbia's uptown Manhattan campus the next day, Chad makes the only move he can.... He walks into the student psychiatric clinic. No, he hasn't cracked up. In fact, what he's going through is considered a very normal, even healthy part of becoming an adult.

For lack of a better term, psychiatrists call it an "identity crisis."

Psychoanalyst Erik Erikson terms it "a normative crisis...a normal phase of increased conflict characterized by a seeming fluctuation in ego strength and yet also by a high growth potential."

Big words. Everyone goes through it, this phase when you leave the family and become your own person, take *your* place in the world. Some people do it quickly, easily. By the time they finish high school, they know exactly who they are and what they are going to do in life.

For others, the transition from childhood to adulthood is a shaking-up time. There are so many decisions to be made — What to do... What to be...Where to go...How to live....

There are so many questions to be answered — Can I make it? In a job? In sex? In the world? *Will* I make it? What am I going to do? What do I believe in? And what about my family? How can I convince them that I'm not a child? But who am I? That's it! Who am I?

Decide!

The pressure is on...really on!

And while it's on, with all the decisions yet to be made and all the questions yet to be answered, who are you? Who are you at this very moment? You're no longer your old, child self. You're not yet your adult self. What are you? The limbo man, that's who.

And limbo-ness is vulnerability. When the pressure is on, the limbo man bends a little. But maybe this is a good thing, a way to see inside, just a little bit.

So big, blond, confident-looking Chad, jammed into a stalemate, the crisis of decision clanging against his insides, walks into the Columbia College psychiatric clinic for some emotional first-aid.

He's not alone.

Seeing the campus psychiatrist has become standard operating procedure for thousands of college students (10 to 15 percent of the population at some schools), and that says nothing of the thousands more who see psychotherapists in private practice.

Nobody knows exactly how many that is, "but the number has definitely accelerated in the past five years," says one psychiatrist. "We're full up."

Why?

For one thing, it has become more acceptable to see a psychiatrist now than it used to be. "It's as if we've been primed since our Dr. Spock days to be aware of our feelings and to know that if we're suffering, we have a right to some relief," says a University of California senior who spreads the gospel of psychotherapy with an almost religious fervor.

And maybe that's because, as one student health-psychologist speculates, psychotherapy has taken the place of religion in this uncertain age of ours.

But there may be other reasons why so many young people are asking for help.

Erik Erikson has written about the efficacy of the "moratorium," a prolongation of the interval between youth and adulthood...taking time off from the decision-making for a while in order to experiment with life, to find out all about yourself, what you like, what you dislike, what you want, and then finally deciding who you are.

Taking a moratorium sounds like a fine idea, doesn't it? But is it possible in 1968? For a girl, perhaps it is. She can drop out of college, take a not-too-demanding job for a year, do some serious soul-searching, and then drop back in again. She can put off choosing a major and flounder around a bit without much trouble. But what happens to a draftable male when he does the same thing?

Right. He's in the Army. And not very many young men are as eager to join the Army as Chad's friend Jeff is.

What is one of the pressures the college man feels most? Right again! The push to make good grades so he can stay *out* of the Army, at least for another year or two. ("I love my country," says a University of Maryland junior, "but Vietnam is not my war. The thing is, I really wouldn't mind being in the Army; it sounds like a pretty great place. Someone else does all your thinking for you!")

So, with pressures zooming in on all sides and no easy way to siphon off the steam, a guy has a pretty tough time of it.

Is it any easier for a girl?

Does a girl have an easier time of it, without any fears about going into the Army, making it big in a career, leaving her parents and finding her place in the world? Can she just sit home and wait for some nice young man to marry her and do all the worrying for them both? Just like grandmother did?

The answer is No.

"This is a tough time for everybody — for both sexes," says Dr. Edward J. Hornich, a Manhattan psychiatrist. "At eighteen, at twenty, at twenty-five, *everybody* is still solving the problems of growing up."

And how many "problems" are there?

There are four, says Dr. Hornich:

(1) Deciding what sex you belong to. (Don't laugh. In the transition to adulthood, homosexual fears are almost as common as heterosexual fears. "Can I make it sexually?" is a big question...but so is "Am I a man?" or "Am I a woman?")

(2) Deciding on your vocation and how to get there. (Involved here are fears of making a commitment, fears of failure, and fears of success, as well. Really. Some people are afraid of success.)

(3) Separating yourself from your family. (Leaving Mamma and Papa may mean more than just moving out of the house or to another city. Chad asked, "Is it me or my father I am becoming?" He capsuled the feelings he had about taking his place as an adult ... but what kind of an adult would he be? That's what caused him anguish, what jammed him up inside.)

(4) Deciding your value system. What do you believe in? (Once you've decided that, you're pretty well on your way to finding out who you are.)

These are the *real* problems that bring people to the psychiatrist's office. Of course, Chad walked into Columbia's clinic because he couldn't study. But not being able to study was only a symptom of a deeper problem.

Other people go into therapy with other symptoms.

Unlike Chad, Liz can study. No problem there. She made Phi Beta Kappa her junior year and is still going strong. A tall, brunette sorority-princess type, Liz's looks camouflage her troubles — perhaps too well. If you use Dr. Hornich's pointers, Liz falls into Category 1. Her question is: Can I make it sexually? It's not that she has no dates. She has as many as she can fit into her rigorous study schedule. But nothing goes anywhere — ever. Just little flits into a relationship and then, *zoom*, out again. While other girls are settling into engagements and marriage, Liz sees herself repeating her pattern, always feeling the let-down partner in her broken, rather tawdry, short romances. Why? Liz couldn't answer that question herself. She needed help.

Her problem was different from Bill's though similar in a way. Bill walked into his school's psychiatric clinic one day in a deep depression brought on by overwhelming fears that he was a homosexual. A sophomore in an Eastern college, he lived in a two-bedroom suite with a pair of classmates, each of whom used the rooms to make love with his girl of the moment. Both boys expressed contempt and surprise that Bill did not do the same, and one day they arranged a date for him with the most promiscuous girl on campus. Failing in his first attempt at a sexual experience, Bill became convinced he was hopelessly perverted. His roommates were concerned enough to urge him to see a psychiatrist.

Carla's case was not so tumultuous, but unnerving nevertheless. Fresh out of college, she went back to her hometown, Chicago, and easily got a good job as an apprentice copywriter in an advertising agency. But she was living at home, with her parents. And after four years away at school, she grew to resent the child treatment she was receiving from them now. So she rented an apartment with two girls she'd met at the ad agency — and then came trouble. For the first time in their lives, Carla's parents didn't put any obstacles in her way. They didn't urge her to keep living with them. In fact, they all but packed her suitcase for her. It was Carla, herself, who balked. "I had my foot across the threshold, literally, ready to move out, when all of a sudden, I was paralyzed. I couldn't move," she says. "I wanted so badly to be independent, and now I could pay my own way...I was miserable." Carla walked back into her parents' apartment, her would-be room-mates found another girl to take her place, and life suddenly turned dark gray. "Little girl Carla couldn't leave her mommy and daddy," she says.

Joel, case No. 4, never even made an attempt to leave home. How could he? He was dying of ulcerative colitis. "Too bad," everyone would say. "Such a nice boy." But that was it — exactly. Joel was so nice, everybody walked all over him. But he never complained. That was his problem. Joel couldn't express his anger. He just bled inside. Before his colitis got so bad that he had to drop out of school, Joel commuted to Los Angeles City College. He was part of a car pool, and sometimes the boys would just forget, really forget, to stop by and pick up Joel. Did he complain? Of course not. Everybody took advantage of Joel. People would scream at him when they were angry at someone else. Girls stood him up. Even his physician would leave him sitting in the waiting room longer than anybody else. Finally, when it was a case of try anything or die, Joel's doctor suggested psychiatric treatment.

And what happened?

Well, Joel isn't such a nice guy any more. In fact, he's something of an angry young man, though his psychiatrist says that this, too, will pass. Yes, Joel is still in psychotherapy. He may be in it for another year. But he doesn't have ulcerative colitis any more.

And Carla? After two years of therapy, she's living in her own apartment (no roommates) and has just been promoted into a top copy-writing job in her advertising agency. A few months ago, she became engaged to someone "very special." They'll be married in June.

Liz? She was married a year ago. Right now, she's teaching school while her husband gets his Ph.D. and when he does, she's thinking of going on for hers.

Bill's problem was solved successfully, too. After six sessions in the student health clinic, he realized that he needn't have been shamed into a situation for which he was unprepared. Does he still have doubts about making it sexually? A little... but he's doing OK.

And Chad? He's in law school. He decided that that was what he wanted after all, although he may not join his father's firm or be the same type of lawyer his father is.

OK, so psychotherapy helped make their lives better. Is it for me? How do I know?

In psychiatric circles, there is this rule of thumb: If you *think* you need help, you probably *do* need it.

Dr. Dana Farnsworth, Harvard psychiatrist, puts it this way: "Anyone who has been working quite efficiently for years, and in the course of a few weeks or months becomes ineffectual for reasons which are obscure to him should seek help."

By the same token, you may be able to work quite efficiently and still need psychotherapy.

"Most of the people who come to the mental health clinic are functioning rather well in *most* areas of their lives," says Dr. Richard Moy, director of student health at the University of Chicago. "But they suffer.... In some way, they can't do what they want to do. They want help."

As one psychiatrist explained, "You may be making it.... You may be a good student, have no sex problems; you're just sailing along and still you're not happy. You're not at ease with yourself. There's no meaning in your life. Well, you're suffering as much as the guy at the bottom of the heap."

What — exactly — is psychotherapy? How does it work?

Psychotherapy literally means "treatment of the psyche." It's a *talking* treatment. The patient sits in a chair, facing the psychotherapist, and the two of them talk together for about fifty minutes.

But seeing a psychotherapist is not "just having someone to talk to"; you can always find someone who will listen to your problems.

The psychotherapist's job is to help the patient — not by telling him what to do, but by helping him see things more clearly so he can decide for himself how to solve his problems most effectively.

For most people under twenty-five, psychotherapy is usually "short-term" treatment. In most college psychiatric clinics, the psychotherapist sees a patient an average of five or six times; sometimes only once.

"Long-term" therapy, which is sometimes offered in college clinics, "gets into the real nitty-gritty. It's the working out of a conflict which has roots that go far back into the person's life." Long-term therapy may last a year or longer, with the patient seeing the therapist once or twice a week.

Are psychiatrists the only psychotherapists?

No. Psychoanalysts, psychologists and social workers may also be psychotherapists. But their training differs to some extent.

The psychiatrist has a medical degree and has specialized in the study and treatment of emotional disorders. The psychoanalyst is a psychiatrist who has taken several years' more training at a special psychoanalytic institute. Most psychoanalysts give both psychotherapy and psychoanalysis, which probes more deeply into the psyche (the patient must lie on a couch so he can think more freely) and for that reason is more costly and time-consuming (requiring four or five visits a week over a period of two, three or four years). Psychoanalysis is rarely the recommended treatment for those under twenty-five.

In addition, there are a few psychologists and social workers who are trained in analytic theory and call themselves "lay analysts."

How do you get into psychotherapy?

If you're in college, you're lucky. You just walk into the student mental-health clinic and ask for an appointment with a psychotherapist. Walk in? Yes. Very few students who receive treatment in school-supported clinics are referred there by a dean or a student health physician. "We prefer it that way," says Dr. Harvey Powelson, director of the psychiatric clinic at the University of California at Berkeley. Come in on your own and we know it's *your* problem.

Even if you are in college, getting psychotherapy may be a problem. A surprising number of colleges and universities employ only a part-time psychiatrist or psychologist who is on campus only one or two days a week. Some schools have no mental health facilities....

How do you go about finding a good psychotherapist?

To get the name of a qualified psychotherapist, ask your family doctor or minister, consult your local mental health society or family service agency, psychiatric and psychoanalytic institutes or a good psychoanalyst who will give you a consultation and then recommend the names of several experts. Talk with all of them and then decide which you prefer. The therapist should feel that he can help you. Occasionally every psychotherapist comes upon someone he is unable to help — for his own personal reasons.

There are more than fifty different systems of psychotherapy, ranging alphabetically from Active Analytic Psychotherapy to something called Will Therapy. Though the most popular form of psychotherapy in the United States today is Psychoanalytic Psychotherapy, many professionals are eclectics, using a blend of several systems.

"The question is — does he make sense to you?" says Dr. Balter. "Do you understand yourself better for having seen him?

"If you're not comfortable with him, no matter how good he is according to his recommendations, you're starting out with one more problem than you need."

And what about cost?

In college mental-health clinics, psychiatric treatment is included in the student health plan or is available at a very slight charge. If you're not in school, or choose a therapist in private practice, it can be very expensive — costing anywhere from $15 to $35 an hour.

But there are many good, low-cost clinics run by hospitals and psychiatric or psychoanalytic institutes, where payment is on a sliding scale — ranging from $1 to $30 an hour, depending on what the patient can afford to pay.

Group therapy is also a less expensive treatment because you share the cost with others. A session may run as low as $5 or as high as $25.

Any counseling or psychiatric service that is attached to a responsible institution should keep the confidentiality of the person seeking help very strictly. Just recently, a code regarding this has been approved by all the major professional organizations involved. It provides that psychiatric records shall always be kept confidential, even after death and in cases of crimes against society, unless there is a court-ordered legal subpoena.

And some therapists feel that confidentiality is a two-way responsibility. "Neither the psychiatrist nor the patient should discuss the details outside," says Dr. Farnsworth.

Lastly, what good does psychotherapy do? How do you know it works?

"There are no objective standards for judging the success of treatment," says Dr. Balter. "Each patient must subjectively evaluate it for himself. It's all in the patient. Does he feel better, is his life better because of therapy? Usually people enter psychotherapy when they've tried everything else, and nothing works. If they're leading a satisfying life when therapy is over, then maybe it has helped."

Following are centers where low-cost psychiatric treatment is available on a sliding scale:
New York:

Columbia Presbyterian Medical Center Psychoanalytic Clinic
Psychoanalytic Treatment Center

Department of Psychiatry, Downstate Medical Center, State University of New York, Brooklyn

Chicago:

Chicago Psychoanalysis Clinic

Southern California:

Los Angeles Psychoanalytic Institute, Beverly Hills

Southern California Psychoanalytic Institute, Beverly Hills

San Francisco:

San Francisco Psychoanalytic Institute

Boston:

Boston Psychoanalytic Society and Institute

Cleveland:

Psychoanalytic Institute of the School of Medicine, Western Reserve University

St. Louis:

Psychoanalytic Foundation

In other areas, the local mental health society can direct you to low-cost treatment centers.

For Thinking, Talking, Writing

1. How do *you* feel about the "acceptability" of seeing a psychiatrist or psychologist? Does the idea embarrass you, or do you feel that it is as acceptable as other kinds of medical treatment?
2. Does reading this article give you any new attitudes or feelings about getting psychiatric help if you're confused about yourself? If so, what are they?
3. Do you believe that psychotherapy has somewhat "taken the place of religion in this uncertain age of ours"?
4. Attempt to determine for yourself where you are in the decision-making process of growing up, in relation to the four problems outlined by Dr. Edward Hornich:
   (a) Your sexual identity
   (b) Your vocation
   (c) Separation from your family
   (d) Your value system

Profits of Praise

Janet Graham

It was the end of my exhausting first day as trainee-waitress in a busy New York drugstore. My cap had gone awry, my apron was stained, my feet ached. The loaded trays I carried felt heavier and heavier. Weary and discouraged, I didn't seem able to do anything right. As I made out a complicated check for a family with several children who had changed their ice-cream order a dozen times, I was ready to quit.

Then the father smiled at me as he handed me my tip. "Well done," he said. "You've looked after us real well."

Suddenly my tiredness vanished. I smiled back, and later, when the manager asked me how I'd liked my first day, I said, "Fine!" Those few words of praise had changed everything.

Praise is like sunlight to the human spirit; we cannot flower and grow without it. And yet, while most of us are only too ready to apply to others the cold wind of criticism, we are somehow reluctant to give our fellows the warm sunshine of praise.

Why — when one word can bring such pleasure? A friend of mine who travels widely always tries to learn a little of the language of any place she visits. She's not much of a linguist, but she does know how to say one word —"beautiful"— in several languages. Wherever she finds herself, she can turn to the foreigner beside her and say *beau*, *schön*, *bello*, *hermoso* — a word of universal praise. She can use it to a mother holding her baby, or to a lonely salesman fishing out pictures of his family. The ability has earned her friends all over the world.

An old farmer who has been happily married for nearly 50 years told me once, "I reckon the best marriages are really mutual-admiration societies. No good keeping quiet about it, though. Elsie likes a little compliment from time to time — and so do I." I thought of Oliver Wendell Holmes' description of friendship as "the pleasing game of interchanging praise." How many wives praise their husbands when they *have* driven carefully? How many husbands praise their wives when they *have* remembered to sew on the shirt buttons?

It's strange how chary we are about praising. Perhaps it's because few of us know how to accept compliments gracefully. Instead, we are embarrassed and shrug off the words we are really so glad to hear. Because of this defensive reaction, direct compliments are surprisingly difficult to give. That is why some of the most valued pats on the back are those which come to us indirectly, in a letter or passed on by a friend. When one thinks of the speed with which *spiteful* remarks are conveyed on this sort of grapevine, it seems a pity that there isn't more effort to relay pleasing and flattering comments.

It's especially rewarding — in both directions — to give praise in areas in which effort generally goes unnoticed or unmentioned. An artist gets complimented for a glorious picture, a cook for a perfect soufflé. But do you ever tell your laundry manager how pleased you are when the shirts are done just right? Do you ever praise your paper boy for getting the paper to you on time 350 days a year — or do you wait for the day he is late and then unleash your wrath on him?

I was talking with a group of housewives one day about the difficulty of getting a really good steak. "I don't know what to do except keep on complaining to my butcher," said one. "*I* just throw it back at him, or bawl him out when it's tough," said another. "What do *you* do?" I asked my friend Marcia, who always seems to serve marvelous steaks. "Well," said Marcia, "I guess I just praise him when it seems especially good."

Praise is particularly appreciated by those doing routine jobs: gas-station attendants, waitresses — even housewives. Do you ever go into a house and say, "*What* a tidy room"? Hardly anybody does. That's why housework is considered such a dreary grind. Comment is often made about activities which are relatively easy and satisfying, like arranging flowers; but not about jobs which are hard and dirty, like scrubbing floors. Shakespeare said, "Our praises are our wages." Since so often praise is the *only* wage a housewife receives, surely she of all people should get her measure.

Mothers know instinctively that, where children are concerned, an ounce of praise is worth a pound of scolding. Still, we're not always as perceptive as we might be about applying the rule. One day I was criticizing my children for squabbling. "Can you *never* play peacefully?" I raged. Susanna looked at me quizzically. "Of course we can," she said. "But you don't notice us when we do." I decided not to take good behavior for granted in the future.

Teachers agree about the value of praise. Paul B. Diedrich, in the *Journal of the National Education Association,* writes that instead of drowning students' themes in critical red ink, the teacher will get far more constructive results by looking for one or two things which have been done better than last time, and commenting favorably on them. "I believe that a student knows when he has handed in something above his usual standard," writes Diedrich, "and that he waits hungrily for a brief comment in the margin to show him that the teacher is aware of it, too."

Behavioral scientists have done countless experiments to prove that any human being tends to repeat an act which has been immediately followed by a pleasant result. In one such experiment, a number of schoolchildren in Harrisburg, Pennsylvania, were divided into three groups and given arithmetic tests daily for five days. One group was consistently praised for its previous performance; another group was criticized; the third was ignored.

Not surprisingly, those who were praised improved dramatically. Those who were criticized improved also, but not so much. And the scores of the children who were ignored hardly improved at all. Interestingly, the brightest children were helped just as much by criticism as by praise, but the less able children reacted badly to criticism, needed praise the most. Yet the latter are the very youngsters who, in most schools, fail to get the pat on the back.

To give praise costs the giver nothing but a moment's thought and a moment's effort — perhaps a quick phone call to pass on a compliment, or five minutes spent writing an appreciative letter. Such a small investment — and yet consider the results in terms of appreciation. "I can live for two months on a good compliment," said Mark Twain.

So, let's be alert to the small excellences around us — and comment on them. We will not only bring joy into other people's lives, but also, very often, added happiness into our own.

For Thinking, Talking, Writing

1. Do you agree that we are often eager to criticize but reluctant to praise other people? Has this article made you any more aware of your own behavior in regard to praise versus criticism? Evaluate yourself in this respect: do you often tell others how *good* they are in some way, or are you more likely to tell them about things they do wrong?

2. Have you noticed the different results of praise and criticism in your own family? When your parents praise you for something, do you

feel better towards them than when they criticize? Are you more likely to react favorably towards them when they praise you? What about *your* behavior towards *them*? Are they more tolerant and understanding of you when you praise *them* for what *they* do right? Might this praise-versus-criticism behavior have something to do with helping to overcome the generation gap you studied in Section 2?

3. What does this article have to do with your learning to understand yourself better?

Defiant Kids
Will Make the Best Adults

Dr. Povl W. Toussieng with Arthur Henley

It has become increasingly apparent that more and more children do *not* want to be like their parents; they dress differently, think differently and aspire to different goals. Youth seems to be going its own way, not the way its elders want it to go. But is this necessarily so bad?

My answer, as a child psychiatrist, is a resounding "No!"

Working with teen-agers has always been one of the things I enjoyed most and thought I did best. We always seemed to "dig" each other. About a year ago, I became aware that I wasn't getting through to them any longer, and I began to worry about it. Finally, after a lengthy and intense personal crisis, I began to understand why these young people and I had ceased to communicate. It wasn't the kids who had become estranged from me; it was I who had not kept pace with them. This changed my thinking a great deal, as well as my views on what is happening in our increasingly youthful society.

As things fell into place for me, I made a surprising discovery. The "ideal children" who are the envy of the neighborhood because they are "such good kids and no trouble to anyone" aren't really growing up, or even trying to solve the crucial problems of adolescence. Yet many children whose behavior worries their elders most *are* actively struggling with the tasks of growing up and are likely to do better as adults than their "ideal" contemporaries.

The last task of childhood, the one that makes it possible to reach maturity, is the adolescent's achievement of a firm sense of knowing just who he is in relation to others and to events around him. For the child to become a stable adult, these relationships must have stability — a difficult task in our uncertain world.

From the time of these youngsters' birth, mankind has shuddered under the menace of possible nuclear conflict. Electronic communications have shrunk the world into one village where everyone everywhere shares the impact of any emotional experience anywhere. Almost all aspects of our lives change so abruptly, so frequently and so unpredictably that many adults have a terrible time adapting to such changes.

Fear is the result of such profound and constant change in one's accustomed way of life. Adults, by and large, have become so insecure, anxious and bewildered that fears of all kinds tend to dominate their lives: fear of death, fear of Communism, fear of growing old, fear of bad breath and body odor, fear of atheism, fear of breast-feeding and mother's milk (only in America!), fear of homosexuality, fear of non-conformity, fear of losing, fear of being alone (without a television set), fear of silence, fear of other social classes and other ethnic groups, fear of boys with long hair and girls with short skirts, and so on.

The increase in attacks on our social order has increased adult fearfulness. Those who rightly seek to protect the young from such legitimate dangers as narcotics addiction and sexual promiscuity sometimes extend their protection to include dangers, such as those imposed by social change, that they themselves fear. So their protectiveness is sometimes a disguised appeal to the younger generation to save *them* from perils *they* feel threatened by.

However, today's youth is not generally persuaded by such emotional appeals, nor are young people deluded by the double standards practiced by too many adults. While still very young, children learn from references in the news media and from conversations in their own homes about important grown-ups who are caught lying, cheating and stealing and often get away with breaking the rules.

Such hypocrisy leaves youngsters with fewer admirable adult models to pattern themselves after, and they must work out their own answers to the key questions of adolescence: *Who am I? Who should I be?* These used to be difficult questions to answer even with adult support; they are overwhelming when the young have to do it alone, while being undermined for trying to be themselves, and pressed to identify with outmoded styles of living — especially in the middle and upper classes. The only kids choosing to follow in their parents' footsteps are America's "ideal children." This large group of youngsters has neither the courage nor the stamina to fight back against adult attempts to keep them chained to a world that no longer exists. Despite their high intelligence generally, these young people question nothing. They are products of schools that still resist relevance to contemporary life.

Battered Moral Standards

Our affluent society emphasizes the joys of leisure, and the once-sturdy virtues of hard work and long hours are not esteemed as highly as they used to be. Unfortunately, many who cling to these virtues feel so guilty about their leisure time that they fail to learn how to enjoy and use it constructively.

Yesterday's moral standards have taken a battering, too. It is no longer a simple question of to steal or not to steal. More sophisticated ethical questions are now being raised. For example, how should we resolve the problem of pesticides that preserve the crops but endanger the food? Or the problem of industrial wastes that are by-products of increased production vital for today's living standards — but pollute air, jeopardizing the health of all?

"Ideal children" rarely weigh such issues or entertain doubts. They follow orders of authority figures with the blind obedience that their parents condemned at the time of the Nuremberg Trials, which condemned Nazi officials for having followed orders instead of listening to their consciences. Yet these same adults applaud obedience by their children, cheering these brain-washed youngsters on in hope that somehow they will bring back the "good old days."

"The Living Dead"

Since such hopes are futile, these "ideal" young people have sacrificed their dignity and individuality for a fictitious cause. They are walking backward into the future, so far removed from what is happening that they are nothing more than their grandparents disguised in teenage bodies. I have begun to call them "the living dead."

They will grow up going through all the right motions but will rarely touch the real world. For a time they will manage well enough — completing their education, marrying and procreating, doing what is "proper" and delighting their parents with their tractability — but sooner or later they will begin to experience the same kinds of fears, uncertainties and anxieties that beset their parents. They will seek escape in the protected suburban environment, only to discover that this protection is a sham. Many will be forced to seek escape through other means, perhaps alcohol, drugs, or illicit sex. Like most contemporary adults, they will become people for whom love is nothing more than a flight from loneliness; sex nothing but a more acceptable form of masturbation; social relationships nothing but occasions to get drunk together; for whom religious faith in measured only by tithing and weekly church attendance; for whom "truth" comes neatly pre-packaged in hygienic "see-through" cellophane — and who are senile before they have been young.

They will, in short, become a dangling generation, detached from their contemporaries and from their time, perpetuating their discomfort in their own children who will come crippled into a world they cannot comprehend.

The younger generation has *never* known a world that did not bristle with overwhelming stimulation, and was not always in ferment. So it seems to me tragic that so many adults choose to look down on young people (except the "ideal kids") with dismay, equating "decadence" of youth and such manifestations as legitimate student protests with juvenile delinquency, teen-age vandalism, illegitimacy, venereal disease, and youthful abuse of drugs and alcohol.

Such behavior represents serious, even dangerous, national problems and many youngsters will be scarred permanently by such experiences. But adults tend to label *all* vigorously independent behavior as "delinquent," and seem convinced that these "misbehaving" kids either have deep-seated character disorders or are emotionally disturbed. Some of these young people *are* warped psychologically, but we find that an increasingly large percentage do not show sufficient signs of emotional disturbance or character defects to explain their behavior. So the question is whether their defiant behavior really reflects a wish to be bad or to rebel, or whether they are fighting in the only way they know how to avoid "living death."

In my experience, many of these "bad" youngsters, unruly though some may be, are searching stubbornly for a workable and meaningful identity that will lead them to maturity in the style of the second half of the 20th century. They do not see their behavior as being bad, nor do they want to be bad.

Adults make an even bigger mistake when they automatically view the behavior of all young people who drink, sample drugs, indulge in sex, drop out of school or run away as passive, escapist behavior. I, too, deplore such excesses. But 100 million "grown-up" Americans regularly turn to alcohol and tranquilizers to banish anxiety and discomfort — impressive evidence that it is the adult generation that seeks oblivion by "copping out." Nearly all researchers agree that these "bad" young people are not looking for escape, but are actively seeking — sometimes in foolish, even dangerous, ways — how to tolerate and integrate the intense overstimulation that is built into the society they have inherited from us. They want to *find* out, not *drop* out; to learn to live with and conquer the pain, not bury it as so many of their elders do.

Actually, adults need not be afraid of this search by the young. They are simply taking the old value systems and trying to give them new form, new expression and new, intensely personal meanings that require deep commitment — not to escape or indulge in empty rebellion, but to seek a more meaningful life for themselves and all of society.

In this category are those youngsters who disdain business careers because they do not think making money is that important; who participate in the Peace Corps, Vista and other people-to-people enterprises; who leave their church when they feel it does not respond to the social responsibilities of our time — departing not because of a loss of faith but to practice through unselfish service to others what they consider the essence of the Judaeo-Christian ethic.

It behooves us to listen to these kids, to their music, to their protests, and not turn our backs on them even if they choose not to emulate us. Although most older people feel like fish out of water in this youthful society, the parent generation still has a wider perspective on many things. And young people *are* eager to listen to their elders, so long as they are not given sermons. Supportive concern and understanding by adults would go a long way to keeping our sometimes "wayward" youth from getting sidetracked dangerously en route to self-discovery and self-realization.

It's these youngsters — not the "ideal" ones — who are most likely to find ways to build a bridge from a disordered present to a more substantial future for themselves, their children and us as well. The times are indeed changing, and we have to change with them.

For Thinking, Talking, Writing

1. Discuss *your* feelings about these statements from the article:
   (a) "From the time of these youngsters' birth, mankind has shuddered under the menace of possible nuclear conflict."
   (b) "Electronic communications have shrunk the world into one village where everyone everywhere shares the impact of any emotional experience anywhere."
   (c) "Fear is the result of ... profound and constant change in one's accustomed way of life."
2. Evaluate your own point of view about some of the complicated moral and ethical questions the author mentions, that you face as a young adult in this society:
   (a) The value of hard work versus the value of leisure.
   (b) The problem of pesticides that preserve the crop but endanger the food.

    (c) The problem of industrial wastes that pollute the air and the water but are by-products of the increased production vital for today's living standards.
3. Do you believe, from your experience, that most contemporary adults are people for whom
    (a) "love is nothing more than a flight from loneliness"
    (b) "sex nothing but a more acceptable form of masturbation"
    (c) "social relationships nothing but occasions to get drunk together"?
4. Relate Dr. Toussieng's opinions to your own life and experience. What has he said that is relevant to your answers to the question, "Who am I — and what?"

A Short History of Man in Search of Himself

Natural Man
In the light of the silvery moon god.

Crusading Man
Salvation through good works.

Daemonic Man
The devil is thought to consort with the good ladies of Salem.

Revolutionary Man
Marie-Antoinette makes her unfortunate remark.

20th Century Psychological Man
The whole world seen through the mind's "I."

Economic Man
Two capitalists in every pot.

Reprinted by permission from *Careers Today,* a publication of Communications|Research|Machines, Inc.

For Thinking, Talking, Writing

This short picture-essay is intended to make the point that the things people are most concerned about *change* from one period of history to another. During the times of "Crusading Man" and "Daemonic Man," for instance, no one would ever have *asked* the question, "Who am I — and what?" Everyone *knew* that man was created and put on earth by God for the single purpose of serving God for His greater glory. There would have been no need for a section on "Myself" in a college textbook in those times. In the first place, only a few people went to college, and they usually went to train for the ministry; that's the purpose for which universities were set up. Naturally, the problem of identity simply didn't exist for these men.

But as the picture-essay points out, the people of the twentieth century are concerned with *self*-knowledge as much as they are with exterior knowledge; and with our world as complicated as it has become, identity *does* sometimes become a problem.

1. If you could, would you choose to live in any of the other historical periods mentioned in the picture-essay, rather than in the twentieth century? Why or why not? If you *would* choose one of the others, which one, and why?
2. List the areas of *your* "self" that you feel need further exploration. How can you go about exploring them — what specific steps can you take toward learning more about "Myself: who am I — and what?"

selective service system

ORDER TO REPORT FOR ARMED FORCES PHYSICAL EXAMINATION

TO: Keith Dwayne
3703 Wilke Road
Rolling Meadows, Illinois

LOCAL BOARD NO. 101
SELECTIVE SERVICE SYSTEM
2474 DEMPSTER ST.
DES PLAINES, ILL. 60018

19 June ____

selective service no.			
11	101	48	1460

You are hereby directed to present yourself for Armed Forces Physical Examination by reporting at:

CHICAGO & NORTH WESTERN RAILWAY
———— STATION ————
CENTER TRACK TRAIN
DES PLAINES, ILLINOIS

on __ 24 July ____ at __ 6:15 A.M. sharp

(Mrs.) R.G. Brook
member or clerk of local board

IMPORTANT NOTICE

To All Registrants:

When you report pursuant to this order you will be forwarded to an Armed Forces Examining Station where it will be determined whether you are qualified for military service under current standards. Upon completion of your examination, you will be returned to the place of reporting designated above. It is possible that you may be retained at the Examining Station for more than 1 day for the purpose of further testing or for medical consultation. You will be furnished transportation, and meals and lodging when necessary, from the place of reporting designated.

5

WAR AND
THE DRAFT:

what's right?

**what
should
I do?**

Introduction

Since the beginning of human history, men have fought one another — sometimes individually, sometimes as group against group. And since the beginning of human civilization, some men have objected to war. Shortly after the birth of Christ, Seneca, a Roman philosopher, said:

> We are mad, not only individually, but nationally. We check manslaughter and isolated murders; but what of war and the much vaunted crime of slaughtering whole peoples?

Other men have upheld the validity of going to war, especially for a purpose they considered noble and just. In 1777 Thomas Paine, talking about the American Revolution, said:

> We fight not to enslave but to set a country free, and to make room upon the earth for honest men to live in.

And in 1965 President Lyndon Johnson justified our involvement in Vietnam because of the *cause* for which we were fighting:

> Most of the non-Communist nations of Asia cannot, by themselves and alone, resist the growing might and grasping ambition of Asian Communism. Our power, therefore, is a vital shield. If we are driven from the field in Vietnam, then no nation can ever again have the same confidence in American promise, or in American protection. In each land the forces of independence would be considerably weakened. And an Asia so threatened by Communist domination would imperil the security of the United States itself.

The practice of drafting men to serve in an army has been almost as controversial an issue as war itself. Early in this century, before there was such a thing as a draft in the United States, large numbers of young men from European nations emigrated to this country in order to avoid compulsory military service in their homelands. Now large numbers of young men from the United States are leaving this country to live in Canada, in order to avoid compulsory military service here.

Because more people are opposed to the war in Vietnam than to any previous war in our history, and because, for the first time, there is a great deal of violent protest against the draft, many young people are confused about what is right and the stand they should take in relation to war and the draft. Read — think — talk — write. Hopefully, the articles in this section will help you clarify your own beliefs about war and the draft in general, and the Vietnam war in particular.

Now That He's Home Again

Alice Lake

Since the start of the war in Vietnam, close to a million and a half young Americans have fought in the steamy heat and then returned home, to be husbands, sons, sweethearts again.

War has changed these young men, as all wars do. Like the veterans of Korea and World War II, they are thinner, more cynical, painfully eager to forget. Yet the scars left by Vietnam may go deeper, for the participants have been different, and so has the war to which they went.

For one thing, these have been the youngest boys the United States has ever sent to fight overseas, just over twenty when they entered the service — two years younger than those who fought in Korea. Three-quarters of the officers and over a third of the enlisted men have been married, probably more than in any war.

Yet these are not settled young men, prepared to return to a civilian life already charted. Many of them were high-school or college dropouts, drafted at a time of adolescent confusion and rootlessness. Others finished high school and merely drifted from one odd job to another until the Army tapped them.

These men entered battle and withdrew from it with bewildering speed. Flown to Vietnam about five months after induction, they remained only a year, under the Pentagon's policy of rotating its fighting men. Twenty hours after leaving the 126-degree heat of Saigon, they dropped down to an air-conditioned airport at Oakland, California, an abrupt change that shocks both body and spirit. Moreover, during their year in Vietnam, they took a vacation from the war, flying to Bangkok, Hong Kong, Honolulu for rest and recreation — in service parlance, an R & R. Sometimes their wives joined them for a second honeymoon, or they telephoned home at a rate of four dollars a minute. Although these humane aspects of modern war have helped reduce to new lows the number of men withdrawn from the battlefield because of emotional breakdown, in some cases they have only postponed the psychological impact until a soldier's return home.

Seldom was a war ever so downright uncomfortable. The heat in Vietnam is searing. Feet have often been wet, clothes unchanged for weeks. Disease has been a threat: malaria, cholera, plague — illnesses that may incubate until after a soldier is home.

Because it probably has been the most brutal war Americans have ever fought, its memories are not easily erased. At the moment one young man lobbed a hand grenade into a village hut, he heard an infant cry. His grenade killed the baby, her mother, and two other children. Another soldier shot a nine-year-old, mistaking him for a sniper. The dead child's "weapon" turned out to be a three-inch penknife. Three years later, this soldier's hands still shake uncontrollably when he talks about the incident. Black humor has typified this war. According to one service joke, Vietnam is the only place where a soldier's match could light a cigarette and a house at the same time.

Suspicion of an ally heightened battle tension. A smiling Vietnamese by day might become a sniper at night, and even a child could hide a hand grenade in her skimpy cotton dress. "In Korea," says a flier who served in both wars, "we and our ally were two people standing side by side. In Vietnam, you trusted no one."

Because of the rotation policy, men have drifted back to the States in small groups, instead of returning en masse to ticker-tape victory parades. But victory has not been in the air at home: far from it. There have been no free drinks for the hero, but more likely disinterest and from some even gibes about "war criminals." In this war, one brother has fought in Vietnam while another burned his draft card.

For a year, soldiers have talked of home and counted each day. Once back, they are eager to snatch all the comforts of civilization. One man drank half a gallon of cold milk on his first day home and then doubled up with stomach cramps. Another greedily spooned down five scoops of ice cream and promptly threw up. Soldiers want two and three hot showers a day and sometimes stand under the steamy water for an hour at a stretch. Modern plumbing has a new fascination. While one wife waited expectantly in her nightgown, her Marine husband remained in the bathroom, flushing the toilet again and again.

Overanticipated by soldier and family alike, the first day home is usually a bitter letdown, like a New Year's Eve party gone sour. For one thing, the returning serviceman, fighting for cross-country plane reservations, seldom arrives when he's expected. One boy turned up in Connecticut at 3:00 A.M., eighteen hours after he was due. His mother had managed a day off from her job to welcome him. By then it was already over. Another arrived home three days early to an uncleaned house, a wife in blue jeans, and his favorite leg of lamb still in the refrigerator.

The experience of 19-year-old Bettiann Di Biccari, of Rye, a New York suburb, and her husband, Michael, 21, is typical. They had married while Bettiann was a high-school senior and Michael was at Marine boot camp. He went to Vietnam less than two months after the wedding. When Bettiann met him at the airport a year later, Mike had dropped twenty-five pounds. He chain-smoked, three packs a day, and kept jiggling his cigarette lighter in nervous fingers. If a door slammed, he jumped. Bettiann brushed against him during her sleep the first night, and he sat bolt upright, grabbing her arm hard.

Her mother had started cooking the homecoming dinner at seven in the morning. She loaded the table with Michael's favorite dishes: shrimp cocktail, lasagna, roast beef, banana cream pie. He ate the shrimp, pushed the lasagna around his plate, and ignored the rest of the meal.

Mike dodged all questions about his battle experience. During the evening, he discovered his sister looking curiously over his combat record. He grabbed the paper from her and said, "This is my business. I've done my job. Now let's forget it." Later he took all the letters he and his wife had exchanged and burned them in the fireplace....

Mike Di Biccari's jumpiness disappeared within a month; but for some young veterans, nervousness, insomnia, spurts of irrational anger last for a year or more. When a truck backfired on a city street, one ex-soldier made everyone in his apartment flatten out on the floor until the firing stopped. At Fort Dix, New Jersey, a cannon booms retreat at the end of each day. "It's easy to spot the boys who've been in Vietnam," says Captain Daniel Greenson, an Army psychiatrist. "They automatically dive for the nearest cover."

Some soldiers stationed at Fort Dix, men with spotless Army records, start getting into trouble for the first time when they return from Vietnam. They are insolent to their officers; they start fistfights with other soldiers and then go home to battle with their wives. "Many are afraid to go to sleep," Captain Greenson says. "They'd rather stay awake until three in the morning than relive the war in bad dreams."

One young veteran to whom I spoke was confused and even frightened by the temper he still could not control six months after his return from Vietnam. Anthony Alipo, of Eastchester, New York, is 23. In Vietnam he was wounded in the leg while fighting with the Green Berets, and he brought home several citations for bravery. "I was never nervous before, never," Tony says. "If a fight broke out, I'd leave. Now I'm the first one in it." Friends describe him as having "a very short fuse," and his girl friend, 19-year-old Carlina Renda, says, "He yells."

Most young veterans clam up if asked about killing another man. "You get used to it. It's strictly me or them," they are likely to answer briefly. But Tony Alipo bursts out, "I keep dreaming about killing people over there. Believe it or not, when you kill a person, that night you go to the club and they buy you drinks. Now that you're home, you're supposed to forget. But I don't think I'll ever forget."

Other young men find it impossible to brush away their own closeness with death. "It has a very sobering effect," says one 22-year-old. "You can never again believe that youth is immortal." William M. Molloy, 24, of Fairfield, Connecticut, was a company clerk in a safe area south of Saigon until a week before he returned home. Then, for two nights in a row, the replacement center to which he was sent came under mortar attack. Sleeping outdoors, Molloy flattened himself on the ground, pulling his mattress over his body. He prayed, "Dear God, let me get out alive." A mortar shell landed twenty yards away. "For the first time, I realized that someone out there wanted me dead," Molloy says. "The idea kept bothering me – that someone you haven't done anything to wants to kill you. The whole idea of war seemed so stupid."

Soldiers who have returned home keep thinking of their dead comrades, their emotions a mixture of relief –"I'm glad it wasn't me"– and guilt over their own survival. It took one young man a year and a half to share with his wife his worst memory, the body of a man next to him in a foxhole, muscles still twitching after his head had been blown off. Another, a former captain in the Green Berets, still blames himself for the death of a soldier in his outfit. "I was the fifth man in line to walk safely over a booby trap," he says. "The sixth stepped on it and was blown to bits. I still feel immense relief, but also great sorrow. I'm haunted by the thought – if only I'd chosen a different trail, he might have lived."

Such experiences provide some explanation of why a man returns from Vietnam a nervous, irritable stranger to his wife and family. Compounding the problem, many wives change, too, during the year's separation. They become independent; they manage the family finances, discipline the children, make the decisions. A peanut-butter sandwich in the kitchen takes the place of real cooking. In small ways, the return of a husband turns out to be a chore as well as a pleasure.

While her husband Greg, an Air Force captain, was in Vietnam, Sue Hosterman took an apartment with her two children near her family in San Antonio, Texas. When Greg returned, she had to pack and move to Homestead Air Force Base in Florida. "My mother spoiled me when I was home," Sue says. "It took months to get adjusted to the new work load. It made me irritable, and Greg had forgotten the demands and the annoyances of little children. It wasn't heaven by any means."

Captain Hosterman, who had done his own laundry in Vietnam, had little sympathy for his wife's complaints about the chore of washing. "Greg kept talking about how easy it was. He couldn't understand that three cycles of diapers are more work than one man's underpants." The change in discipline was another irritant. "Greg was sure I needed his strong arm with the boys, but I thought he was too tough. There were tears from the children." One blowup came when Captain Hosterman insisted on taking Jack, their three-year-old for a ride on his motorcycle. The little boy had loved the machine a year earlier, but now he was terrified. "Greg just couldn't understand this. He got disgusted and ordered me to march the child into the house."

Another wife, Jeanne Corey, 32, of Memphis, Tennessee, began to cry as she described the problems of readjustment with her husband, Robert, an Air Force sergeant. "He's a completely different person. He used to be happy-go-lucky and laugh a lot. We played canasta and entertained friends. Now he more or less stays to himself. As for me, I'm sick of staying home all the time." Sergeant Corey agreed that the couple had troubles. "Being away for a year is a gap you just can't seem to fill," he said. "Part of your life as a family has gone down the drain. It's almost like meeting for the first time."

A settled marriage is not too likely to founder under the blows that follow a wartime separation. But the boy-and-girl unions, often contracted only weeks before a soldier left for Vietnam, are more fragile. No statistics are available on divorces among men who served in Vietnam or Korea, but from 1945 to 1947, the three years after World War II, divorce rates hit an all-time peak.

After returning from Vietnam, Robert Lee Adams, of Elyria, Ohio, finished out his service with the Marines at Camp Pendleton, California, and his wife, Diane, joined him there. She is 24, he is 25, and they were the oldest couple among the Marine families living at Oceanside, near the base. Many of the wives were still in their teens. "They found it difficult to understand the change in their husbands," Diane Adams says. "The girls who were older were very patient, but the younger ones couldn't see why the men weren't the same. One boy started drinking a lot; he'd seen bad action over there. Others wanted to play cards and swap war experiences, instead of spending evenings with their wives."

Among seven young men I interviewed who had been engaged or

going steady before they went to Vietnam, five broke off with their girls shortly after their return. Robert Adams was one of these. After landing in California, he flew directly to see Diane in White Plains, New York, remained two days, broke the engagement, and left. "I just didn't care about anybody," he says. "I didn't give a damn. Nothing seemed important any more, certainly not marriage." Happily, the mood didn't last. He went to Ohio, shopped for a car, and telephoned Diane to find out what color she preferred. They were married two months later.

When a young man is not married, his parents are often the ones to feel the full force of his irritability. Shortly after his return from Vietnam, Tony Alipo started palling around with another veteran, John F. Peters, Jr., 20, who lost an eye while on patrol in the Central Highlands. The two had in common the war and the fact that neither was able to get along with his mother. Peters, who was convalescing, complained of his mother's oversolicitude. "If I wanted something, I could get up and get it myself, but she wouldn't let me," Peters says. "It got to the point where I actually thought I was going crazy." Tony's mother kept worrying because, after five months at home, he still hadn't gone out and got a job. "Every time we have an argument," Tony says, "I can't sleep. I wake up at night and remember all of Vietnam."

Young men once respectful to their parents do not hesitate to criticize them openly. One couple, whose marriage had always been stormy, were interrupted in their nightly bickering by an outburst from their veteran son. "I just can't stand this," he said. "If you two don't stop, I'll just move out of the house." Other returned servicemen complain that their parents still treat them as juveniles. "They tried to tell me what time to get home from a date," says Bill Molloy. "They couldn't seem to accept the fact that their little Billy wasn't a child any more."

Yet many mothers, at least when a son is not around, speak with pride of his new maturity. "He went away a boy and came back a man" is the way several put it. (One added, however: "In little ways where mothers hope their sons might change, they don't. The Army didn't teach him to stand up straight. He was always lousy helping around the house, and he still is.") Most young veterans also believe that their war experience has made them more mature. It is hard, however, to distinguish the growing up that occurs in any young man in a year far away from home from the changes due to this particular year of dirt and heat and danger.

Dr. Arthur Blank, Jr., a Yale University psychiatrist who served in Vietnam in 1967, suggests that two years in the Peace Corps might make young Americans even more mature. He adds this, however: "There is a significant number of young men who need to kill or to participate effectively in violence in order to establish their masculine identity. For these, war does provide maturity."

When young veterans try to explain the ways in which they feel more grown-up, they talk of increased self-confidence, an ability to get along with others, the discovery of a life goal, great compassion. "For someone of my middle-class suburban background, just being in the Army was an important experience," James Mackenzie, of Westport, Connecticut, says. "I lived with Americans really for the first time. I'll never talk again about Middle Western hicks."

Jim was drafted, at the age of 19, when he flunked out of Beloit College, in Wisconsin. He is back as a Beloit student now, enthusiastic about his courses and working hard. "Don't be like me," he warned his younger brother recently. "Do your homework." His father, Cameron, a public-relations executive, feels that Jim might never have returned to school without the interlude in the service. "The war gave Jim two years in which to grow up," he says. "It made him look at life with a little more realism. He had lived in sort of personal dreamland before."

Jim's experience is being duplicated by thousands of high-school and college dropouts, who are back in school and making a go of it. Preliminary figures from the Veterans Administration, which grants funds for education under the GI Bill of Rights, indicate that the number may eventually be higher than the 47 percent of World War II veterans who returned to school. (This figure includes soldiers who fought in the war and those who remained in the United States or were sent to other overseas bases.) It is impossible to estimate, however, how many other young men might have sought more schooling if the armed services had not taken two or three years out of their lives. One veteran told me that he had reluctantly given up his dream of law school because, at 24, he felt he ought to start making a living.

Some young men who drifted from one inconsequential job to another before being drafted emerged from the Army with a clearer sense of job goals. William Maronet, of North Miami, Florida, drafted at 19 shortly after his marriage, now plans to become an electrician. "For the first time in my life, I'm pretty well sure of what I want," he says. "If it weren't for the service, I might have just coasted along." His 20-year-old wife, Cheryl, believes both have changed for the better. "We used to have a ball," she says. "If we stayed home at night, it seemed like we were trapped. Now we're more homebodies. Just having fun doesn't seem to mean so much any more."

Like most young men who have served in Vietnam, Bill Maronet was shaken by the living conditions he saw there. "I felt sorry for the people in the villages," he said. "I wouldn't want an animal to live the way some of them do. The ones in town I didn't like. They exploit Americans. They make a mint off us, and they love it."

Whether travel and the observation of another culture have had a maturing influence on young men who went to Vietnam seems to depend largely on how wide they opened their eyes. Soldiers were often stationed in huge Army bases, almost like small American cities, and because of fear of the Vietcong, were forbidden even to visit the local village. They talked only to the Vietnamese who worked on the base and the bar girls they picked up in Saigon. "The only ones I met were whores and houseboys," one young man says.

Some, deeply disturbed by seeing 14-year-old prostitutes and hungry children rooting in garbage, shocked by the devastation to a green and beautiful land, have developed new awareness of hunger and poverty. Some of these have changed their life plans and now want to dedicate themselves to helping the people of Vietnam.

Captain Livio Pardi was graduated from West Point as an infantryman and planned to make a career in that branch of the Army. Now he is about to enter medical school. "I want to go back to Vietnam as a healer instead of a killer," he says. "Force can accomplish a limited amount, but I'm convinced that people can only be won by acts of good will."

Born in Italy, raised in Florida, Captain Pardi adds that he has returned from Vietnam with another important change in attitude. "I always felt segregation was a bad thing, but I never did anything about it," he says. "I've seen Negroes go through hell in Vietnam and then come home to be told they can't go into a bowling alley. That gets me. I wouldn't stand for it if I were a Negro. I don't get physical about things except in extreme cases. Now I'd love to get my hands on some triple-K fellow and beat him down to the ground."

Will other Vietnam soldiers, white and black, return with more tolerance for each other? Will men who have slept beside black Americans now be willing to live next door to them? Certainly the experience has made some white servicemen less racist, but far from all. Officially, the armed services are the least segregated institutions in the United States; soldiers of both colors agree that color is forgotten in combat. One white soldier says, "Everyone pulls together in the jungle. You don't stop to think if a guy is black when he might save your life." But back at base camp, deep-seated prejudice too often reappeared. And once home, some soldiers, in the same breath that they describe the bravery of individual black companions, mouth the old clichés: "I wouldn't want one living next door to me" and "How would you like him to marry your sister?"

Lonney Amos, 23, of Mount Vernon, New York, attained the rank of sergeant in Vietnam, a fairly impressive accomplishment for a draftee. He is optimistic that the prejudice of some white servicemen has been shaken by knowing him and others like him. "They're more aware that we're humans," he says. "They've seen we can perform just as well as they can and that we want just the same things out of life." Nevertheless, in Vietnam, Amos suffered humiliation from a fellow soldier who told him frankly, "I can't stand colored people." "I hit him," Amos says. "It didn't change either of us, but he left me alone after that."

Amos is far from the only black soldier who learned to hit back in Vietnam. After living there as an equal with white men, Robert Adams does not expect now to settle for a lesser share of America's abundance. He recalls that in high school he was passed over for a Jaycee football trophy because of his color. "I just overlooked it then. I was dumb." Dumb no longer, Adams is deeply resentful that a white veteran of his acquaintance was recently able to obtain a loan for a house, while the bank turned Adams down.

Like soldiers in any war, the men in Vietnam pick up bad habits: they drink heavily; they gamble; they visit prostitutes. But this war has contributed a new experience—marijuana. The weed from which marijuana cigarettes are made grows wild throughout Vietnam. "It's as common as grass," one soldier says.

The Pentagon estimates that less than one percent of servicemen in Vietnam have been brought up on charges of using or possessing marijuana, but ordinary soldiers report that the consumption is much greater than this figure indicates.

Many boys who drank to excess in the battle zone settle down as social drinkers when they are home. It is likely that marijuana smoking will also lose its lure for many veterans when the tensions of war diminish. But one thoughtful veteran says, "Whether we keep using pot in civilian life or not, thousands of us have now lost our irrational fear of it. The fact that it's a felony to smoke pot in the United States strikes us as ridiculous. At home, we won't keep quiet about it."

In some, a new cynicism, but more often merely disinterest, has shaken old attitudes toward religion. Mike Di Biccari, a former altar boy, prayed while in Vietnam for the Virgin Mary's protection. He returned, vowing to attend church every Sunday, but after eight months home, he hasn't been to church once. Others, whose observance was largely conventional, find now that convention concerns them less. "Stan went to church because he thought it was the nice thing to do," says Linda Scholl, of Ames, Iowa, about her husband. "Now he just doesn't bother. It disturbs his parents, but to me his attitude is much more honest."

Friends say that Ace Rubin has not changed as a result of Vietnam, although this husky young man now rolls himself to college classes in a wheelchair, prosthetic legs dangling. Ace is cheerful, active, and displays no bitterness. But he reports one significant change: "The war has made me an agnostic. I'm supposed to be Jewish. I always just accepted this and the fact that there was a God." Ace started questioning his religion during training, when he talked with soldiers of other faiths. His questioning continued during the year he spent in military hospitals after the amputation of his legs. "I wanted nothing to do with religion," he says now. "Too many boys got killed in Vietnam for no reason. I can't believe that if there were a God, He would allow these things to happen."

The vast majority of Vietnam veterans do not ever want to fight again. Over 30,000 men have already been classified by the Veterans Administration as partly or totally disabled. Their scars are easy to see. But none has come back without invisible scars—cynicism, fear, and a deep sadness.

For Thinking, Talking, Writing

1. Some of you may be Vietnam veterans, or have a good friend who is one, or you may have heard someone talk about his experiences in Vietnam. Compare whatever *you* know about the attitudes of the men who have fought in Vietnam and come back with the situations described in this article. Do you think the article is accurate in its descriptions and conclusions or not? How and why?

2. Discuss the statement in the article by one Vietnam veteran, William Molloy, "The idea kept bothering me—that someone you haven't done anything to wants to kill you. The whole idea of war seemed so stupid." How does this statement compare with *your* beliefs about war? How does it seem to compare with the beliefs of most people in the United States?

3. Dr. Arthur Blank, a psychiatrist, states in this article, "There is a significant number of young men who need to kill or to participate effectively in violence in order to establish their masculine identity. For these, war does provide maturity." Evaluate your own feelings

in relation to this statement. Is there something in you that feels more "manly" when you participate in violence of some kind — or, if you are a woman, do you find that you respect and admire more the man who engages in some kind of violence, in sports, or rebellion, or war, for instance?

4. This article discusses both positive and negative aspects of participating in war, as far as the veterans are concerned. Some of the positive aspects mentioned are the possibility of greater maturity, the discovery of a life goal, greater self-confidence, and increased tolerance. Some of the negative aspects discussed are a sense of guilt, increased suspiciousness, nervousness, the feeling of lack of support from the public, and difficulties in re-establishing relationships with loved ones. Evaluate the negative factors against the positive ones; taking the experience as a whole, would you say that serving in the armed forces during a war is generally a "good" or a "bad" experience for most young men?

Letters from a Dead GI

Robert Ransom, Jr.

Robert Ransom, Jr., was born October 2, 1944, in Bronxville, New York, the first of six sons. Mike, as he was called, grew up handsome and likable. He played on the Bronxville High soccer team, sang a leading role in "Kiss Me Kate," was literary editor of the yearbook, and president of the Reformed Church Youth Fellowship Group. He went to Colby College in Waterville, Maine, and then joined the Army as a second lieutenant.... On March 8, 1968, Mike arrived in Vietnam.... He died painfully on May 11, 1968, leaving family, friends, and a powerful, though an unintended, document on war.

9 March 1968

Dearest Family,

Greetings from Cam Ranh Bay. My big news is that I have been diverted from the 1st Cav. I am now headed for Chu Lai, H.Q. of the American Division about eighty miles south of the DMZ. I have no real emotion yet regarding the change, mainly because I know almost nothing about the American except that its patch is not as good-looking as the Cav's. I do know that it is sort of a hybrid division made up of random, unassigned brigades. My only disappointment at my change is that from my group at Jungle School which traveled here intact I am the only one sent to the American. We were all originally scheduled for the 1st Cav., but all the rest were sent to the 25th Inf. in and around Saigon. I do not know why I was singled out because I have neither special qualifications nor restrictions nor am I numerically or alphabetically worthy of individual selection. So, who knows?...

Reprinted from the *Washingtonian Magazine*, January, 1969. Copyright © 1968 by Washington Magazine, Inc. Also by permission of Robert C. Ransom.

While still quite separate and secure, due to processing, from all the fighting here one still knows that there's a war going on. From our billets we could hear machine gun and mortar fire from the perimeter two or three miles away. We could also see illuminating flares in the sky to light up the battlefield. Yes, I am scared. But I think it's more of the unknown than of bullets. I expect to learn a lot during the next year; I'm not sure what it'll be, but I'll learn a lot.

I am now in flight to Chu Lai, which is about an hour by air from Cam Ranh. I am in a C-130 transport plane sitting on my duffel bag with about thirty others. All are low enlisted men except for a Signal Corps Major, a chaplain Lt. Col., and me. I hope we don't crash somewhere out in the boonies because only two men here have weapons and, being Infantry, I'll probably have to take charge and engineer the exfiltration. Not the best crew for one's first command. Daydreaming!

So long for now.

All love to all, MIKE

16 March

Dear Mom and Dad,

A big hello from sunny Chu Lai and the Americal Division. I am now undergoing a week of final in-country training prior to being assigned to my unit.

Chu Lai is situated on the South China Sea about 200 miles south of DMZ with our camp being right on the beach. I am told that the monsoon season is in its final stages and that we'll be moving into the hot dry season. This is good because the rice paddies dry up and we won't have to hump through endless swamps. But the temp reportedly rises as high as 130 degrees at its peak....

I am...sending a letter to Robert Komer, the Hamiltons' friend in charge of the pacification efforts here, in the hopes of getting a job on his staff. I am really getting quite scared about being a platoon leader and so this is a last-ditch effort to avoid it.

I will say so long for now. I can't wait 'til I have a permanent address so I can start receiving mail. I miss you all very much and can't wait 'til I'm settled enough to hear from you.

All love, MIKE

27 March

Dear Mom and Dad,

Would you believe I am now officially assigned to a unit? It's taken so long that it's quite a relief.

After I left Qui Nhon last Friday, I went back up to Chu Lai to finish up my training, which ended Sunday. On Monday, I flew down to Duc Pho or LZ (landing zone) Bronco, the base camp of the 11th Brigade. From there I was assigned down to the 4th of the 3rd, "The Old Guard." This battalion has its headquarters here at Duc Pho, but its AO (area of operations) is back about five miles south of Chu Lai. Therefore all logistics are handled out of Chu Lai.

I am told that our AO is quite a good one. There is almost no contact with Charlie and what little there is rarely turns into much of a fight because he runs away. The principal danger here is from mines and booby traps, which account for about 75 percent of all casualties. The enemy here is mostly VC guerrillas, with a few hardcore VC. To my knowledge, there has been no contact at all with the North Vietnamese.

From the people I've talked to over here I've come up with some new ideas on the war here. For the most part, nobody is particularly wild with patriotic feeling for the war. There are of course those who just get a real charge out of killing people. One Lieutenant I talked to said what a kick it had been to roll a gook one hundred yards down the beach with his machine gun. But most people generate their enthusiasm for two reasons: One is self-preservation—if I don't shoot him, he'll eventually shoot me—and the other is revenge. It's apparently quite something to see a good friend blown apart by a VC booby trap and you want to retaliate in kind. . . .

I now have one last editorial comment about the war and then I'll sign off. I am extremely impressed by almost every report I've heard about the enemy I am about to go and fight. He is a master of guerrilla warfare and is holding his own rather nicely with what should be the strongest military power in the world. But it is mostly his perseverance that amazes me. He works so hard and has been doing so for so long. You've heard of his tunneling capability? A captured VC said that in coming from North Vietnam down to Saigon, he walked over 200 miles completely underground. Anyone who would dig a 200-mile tunnel and who would still do it after being at war for some thirty years must be right!

All love, MIKE

3 April

Dear Mom and Dad,

Well, your eldest is now a combat leader. So far I haven't even fired
a shot, nor have I been under any sort of fire. Our company is currently
involved in an operation to prevent the local rice harvest from falling
into VC hands. Our tactic is to remain in a company base during the day,
since it is too hot for any long, arduous movement. At night each platoon sends out two or three squad-size ambush patrols.

Two days ago we went on a heliborne combat assault. Our mission
was to cordon a village that was suspected of having a platoon of VC
hidden in it. It was an extremely well-executed mission. We were air-
lifted out of our defensive position and then were dropped in around the
village about fifteen miles south. Once we were in position a group of
Vietnamese Popular Forces moved in through our lines searching the
village. It was an all-day operation that netted one VC killed, six captured, and three weapons captured. It is in operations like this that we
hurt the VC most. As you know, the local VC are terribly underequipped.
So when we capture two or three weapons we put ten or fifteen enemy
out of commission, at least for a while. At the end of the day we were
again helilifted back to our company base. It was basically a simple
school problem, but for me, since it was really the first operation I had
been on, it was quite exciting.

Our primary danger here though is not Charlie himself, but the
mines and booby traps he sets. The first night I spent in the field an
ambush patrol from the first platoon had three men wounded when they
set off a booby-trap grenade. This morning, the second platoon took
fourteen casualties, including one killed, when they set off two mines
while on a road-clearing mission. So far, my platoon, the 3rd, hasn't had
any trouble, but these booby traps are so well hidden that no matter
how good you are, they get you. . . .

Things aren't all bad—I've got a really good company commander
and a good platoon sergeant. In my job these are the most important
people in the world to me. Also on the bright side, I'm getting the best
suntan I've ever had.

New pen, All love, MIKE

Dear Mom and Dad,

I just got my first letter from you plus the clippings on Johnson
and my pictures. I can't tell you how great it is to be back in touch with
you again.

In Vietnam nearly every GI has a portable radio which he carries to pick up AFVN Radio. It's really a terrible station, being designed to offend no one and please the majority. It plays the same pap all day long in its effort to appeal to the same Midwestern anti-Communist you mention in your letter. But they do present reasonably uncensored news every hour. This plus *Stars and Stripes,* which we get twice a week, keeps me pretty well posted, at least as far as headlines go.

I did hear Johnson's speech of deescalation and noncandidacy and thought it the best of his career, not just the way he said it. It created in me a great sense of hope that this foolishness over here will end fairly shortly. There is not a man over here that wants to see this war go on any longer. This is not to say that anybody shrinks from doing a job. But everyone is as confused as I as to exactly what, if anything, we're accomplishing and wants the war over ASAP.

I lost my first man last week. He was killed by accident by another man in the platoon. I had sent a squad out on night ambush. They had been set up in position for a few hours when the flank man crawled away to take a leak or something and as he was crawling back to position another man mistook him for a dink and shot him. He died on the chopper that dusted him off. Of course it really tears me up to lose a man, especially like that, but I must not show any emotion over it. I've got to press on, keep doing my job. Even among my men this is universal. They are saddened by the death of a buddy, but he is gone. The concern among the team (for that is what we are) is how it will affect the man who shot him. Will he fall to pieces over this and be unable to perform his function? This is what we're worried about first and foremost. War is Hell!

You know that joke about how hard it is to tell the good guys from the bad guys over here? Well, it's funny in Bronxville or Dorset, but it isn't over here. The enemy in our area of operations is a farmer by day and VC by night. Every male is required to register at his provincial capital. He is further required to carry an ID showing his picture, fingerprints, age, etc. But anyone with a VC background is supposedly denied an ID. Simple, you say? All we have to do is come to a village and police up everyone without an ID, right? Well, about three months ago we captured a VC printing plant that manufactured ID cards. Every man we pick up says "Me Vietnamese, Numbah 1. VC, Numbah 10," so we have to let him go. But more than once we have captured or killed people with weapons whom we recognized as one of those smiling faces we had picked up and released earlier. It's maddening because we know damn well that they're dinks, but we can't do anything to them until we catch them with a weapon or actually shooting at us.

By the way, *Number 1* means real good and *Number 10* means real bad in pidgin Vietnamese-English. Other handy phrases, just in case you're planning a vacation in this tropical paradise are: *teetee*—very little; *boo coo* (a bastardization of *beau-coup*)—very much; *boom boom* —whore; *deedee mow*—not out here. What more do you need to know?

Would you also like to know an interesting facet of Vietnamese economy? GI's at the large installations can buy cokes or beer for $2 or $3 a case. They can sell it on the black market for $10 or $15. The black market distributes it around the country for lord knows what price. The village peasants sell it back to GI's in the field who never see a PX from one month to the next at a dollar per can or $24 a case. To the GI in the field a coke or a beer is such a delicacy that he is all too willing to pay the exorbitant price. Oh, well!

More soon.

Love, MIKE

Dear Mom and Dad,

Well, I've had my baptism by fire and it's changed me, I think. Two days ago my platoon was on a mission to clear three suspected minefields. We were working with a mechanized platoon with four tracks, and our tactic was to put the tracks on line and just roar through the minefields, hoping to blow them. Since the majority of the VC mines are anti-personnel, the tracks could absorb the explosions with no damage done to them or the people inside. My platoon rode along just as security in case we were attacked. We spent the whole day clearing the three fields and came up with a big zero.

The tracks were then returning us to where we would stay over-night. When we reached our spot we jumped off the tracks and one of my men jumped right on a mine. Both his feet were blown off, both legs were torn to shreds; his entire groin area was completely blown away. It was the most horrible sight I've ever seen. Fortunately he never knew what hit him. I tried to revive him with mouth-to-mouth resuscitation but it was hopeless to begin with.

In addition, the explosion wounded seven other people (four seri-ously) who were dusted off by Medevac, and three others lightly, who were not dusted off. Of the four seriously wounded, one received a piece of shrapnel in the heart and may not survive; the other three were almost completely riddled with shrapnel and while they will be completely all right, it will be a slow and painful recovery.

I was one of the slightly wounded. I got three pieces in my left arm, one in my right knee, and about 20 in both legs. I am completely all right, in fact I thought I had only gotten one in the arm and one in the knee. It was not until last night when I took off my clothes to take a shower that I noticed the other spots where I had been hit.

I came back to Chu Lai yesterday because my knee is now quite stiff and swollen and will probably be here a couple of days, what with X-rays and what not. Believe it or not, I am extremely anxious to get back to the platoon. Having been through this, I am now a bonafide member of the platoon. They have always followed my orders but I was an outsider. Now I'm a member of the team and it feels good.

I want to assure you that I am perfectly all right. You will probably get some sort of notification that I was lightly wounded and I just don't want you to worry about it at all. I will receive a Purple Heart for it. People over here talk about the million dollar wound. It is one which is serious enough to warrant evacuation to the States but which will heal entirely. Therefore you might call mine a half-million dollar wound. My RTO who was on my track, sitting right next to me, caught a piece of shrapnel in his tail, and since he had caught a piece in his arm about two months ago, he'll get out of the field with wounds about as serious as a couple of mosquito bites.

I said earlier that the incident changed me. I am now filled with both respect and hate for the VC and the Vietnamese. Respect because the enemy knows that he can't stand up to us in a fire fight, due to our superior training, equipment, and our vast arsenal of weapons. Yet he is able. Via his mines and booby traps, he can whittle our ranks down piecemeal until we cannot muster an effective fighting force.

In the month that I have been with the company, we have lost four killed and about 30 wounded. We have not seen a single verified dink the whole time, nor have we even shot a single round at anything. I've developed hate for the Vietnamese because they come around selling cokes and beer to us and then run back and tell the VC how many we are, where our positions are, and where the leaders position themselves. In the place where we got hit we discovered four other mines, all of them placed in the spots where I, my platoon sergeant, and two squad leaders had been sitting. I talked to the mech platoon leader who is with us and he said that as he left the area to return to his fire base, the people in the village he went through were laughing at him because they knew we had been hit. I felt like turning my machine guns on the village to kill every man, woman and child in it.

Sorry this has been an unpleasant letter, but I'm in a rather unpleasant mood.

All love, MIKE

2 May

Dear Mom and Dad,

I am now sitting in a little hooch in a village in which we're operating. Company A is still situated on LZ Sue, securing the artillery battery which supports our battalion. The way things are working is that two platoons secure the hill, while the third goes off into the villages on patrol. Each platoon stays down for three days and then moves back up to get relieved by another. On Sue it's relatively safe, with large strong bunkers, several layers of barbed wire around the outside.

We still have to man the perimeter at night, which means not much sleep and we're always subject to mortar attacks, but Charlie would need a fully equipped battalion-sized force to take it, so I don't think he'll try. Basically, being on Sue means a rest and security, so it's good to be there. Right now, though, we are on our three days down in the field and I have to tell you that ever since we hit that minefield I am nervous all the time. My platoon is way under strength right now and I feel that we are too small a force to be operating as independently as we do. My authorized strength is forty-three. I had thirty-six when I first joined the platoon and am now operating with twenty. That minefield cost me several people, plus I am hit with a rash of people on profile and people on R&R at this time.

Last night I split my element into two ambushes. I took one and my platoon sergeant took the other. Sergeant Western's patrol was in position about an hour and a half when some dink sneaked up and threw a grenade into their perimeter. Sgt. Western saw it come in and managed to grab it and threw it back out where it exploded harmlessly. It was, needless to say, an awfully close call. I put him in for a Silver Star today for his courageous action.

Sergeant Western is a really good guy and I wish we didn't have to maintain a professional relationship because I'd love for him and me to be friends. He is twenty years old and comes from Larchmont and we are very similar in both background and temperament. He has been very lucky in achieving rank as fast as he has, but he also has the competency to merit his rank. He and I have jokingly suggested that you and his mother should get together and talk about your sons in faraway Vietnam.

Despite losing people and being scared all the time, I find being an infantry platoon leader an exhilarating, exciting, and, yes, rewarding job. I have ambitions to go higher, even in my short two years in the Army, but I don't really want to because platoon level is the last at which I still can have close working contact with my men. I think I've developed a pretty good relationship with my people, one in which they depend on me for leadership, but they know that I must be able to depend on them too. It's very healthy and as I say, rewarding. I am doing all the politicking I can to get a staff job, but if I do get one, I will hate to leave my men (not enough to turn it down, though!)....

I have a couple of requests which I wonder if you would mind filling. (1) Have you been able to change the address on the *Newsweek* subscription you said you ordered? I live in quite a vacuum for news over here and *Newsweek* seems about the best and easiest way to pull myself out. (2) Could you check the status of my bank account and send me a report. (3) Could you send me half a dozen black mechanical grease pencils. I use these to mark my maps which are covered with acetate. (4) Could you keep me supplied with felt tip pencils (blue) like this one. About two a month should do me fine. As you can probably tell, it's a cold day in hell (or Vietnam, for that matter) when I get a chance to get to a PX.

This is all for now (both requests and deathless prose). More soon.

Love to all, MIKE

P.S. You might tell any friends you have in Washington to get off their fat asses, quit quibbling, and start talking about ways to end this foolishness over here. Aside from being opposed to the damn war, it really gives me a case that LBJ, who claims to want peace and who says he'll go anywhere, anytime, to talk peace, has taken over a month without being able to find an acceptable site. Anywhere, according to his promise, ought to be "acceptable."

Dear Susan,

I realize that I'm a little late, but I want to wish you a Happy Easter.

As you probably know by the time you get this, I picked up a Purple Heart the other day when I got hit with about twenty pieces of shrapnel from a mine explosion. The mine killed one man and wounded ten, including four quite seriously. I was lucky, I suppose, to get off quite lightly.

You know what—this mine incident has changed me. I'm still as opposed to the war on moral and political grounds as ever. But since I am here, and when I see the gory mess that mine made of my people, I want revenge. I want to kill every little slant-eyed bastard I see. I just wish to hell the VC would come out and fight. We never see them, just their damn mines and booby traps. Do you know that in the month I've been with this company we've had over thirty people killed or wounded and we haven't seen a dink or fired a single shot. . . .

Needless to say, the life I lead is fairly miserable. But there are a lot of compensations in the "thank heavens for small pleasures" department. For instance, you can't believe how great it is to get coke with our resupply each night. The coke is hot and it's been so shaken up by being thrown on and off of the choppers that you invariably lose half of it when you open it, but it tastes just fabulous. Another thing is ice cream, which we get about once a week for chow; again it is usually melted and warm, but it's ice cream and it's yummy. Probably the greatest morale builder of all is mail. A word from home which can sail you millions of miles away from Vietnam. Of course, though, Vietnam is actually quite a beautiful place. If we weren't at war, this would probably be quite a nice assignment. I imagine that when this idiocy is finished the truce will allow for several U.S. bases here. Most of our bases now are right on the South China Sea which is, like most oceans, beautiful. I think therefore that you'll see lots of people requesting tours in Vietnam.

I had a funny experience last night. I'm sure you're familiar with Orientals and the importance of face. My platoon was holed up for the day in a village with three or four people in a hooch. . . . In the late afternoon we got resupplied with hot chow, and I was sitting down on the front porch with my hamburger, beans, potatoes, and ice cream, which doesn't sound that great, but after eating C rations for the previous two meals this was to have been quite a treat. No sooner had I sat down than Papasan comes out of the house and motions for me to come inside, which I did. The family was just sitting down to their own dinner and it seems they had set a place for me. Before I knew it, Mamasan had grabbed my plate with my own food and took it away while Papasan urged me over to take my place on the dirt floor around a tray of food. I didn't really want to give up my food or eat theirs, but I felt obliged; so I crossed my legs and sat down and was served a bowl of rice, a grungy pair of chopsticks, and was urged to help myself to the variety of dishes on the tray. I don't know what any of it was, but one looked like fish, another spinach, tomatoes, and noodles. I sampled them all and still don't know, but each bite tasted the same, super-salty, and each bite made me feel like vomiting. I ate as little as I thought polite, managing to avoid throwing up. As soon as I finished, I got up, bowed to the family, thanking them profusely for the delicious meal. I left them and as soon as I got around the corner of the house, I blew lunch all over the place.

MIKE

11 May

Dear Mr. and Mrs. Ransom,

It is with great difficulty that I write this letter expressing my deepest sympathy over the loss of your son Robert—known as Mike to us. I have never written a letter like this before, but then, in my six years of nursing I have never met as courageous an individual as your son.

I was able to care for Mike daily and I want you to know that his sense of humor and will to live made my work much easier. Things he could no longer do for himself—like brushing his teeth—things that surely brought him discomfort—like turning him—brought only thank-yous, humorous remarks, a gleaming smile, or a twinkle from his eyes.

Mike fought hard, terribly hard, to overcome his body's wounded condition. But, strong as he was, his body could only endure so much. Mike was never afraid and although I'm sure he realized what was happening, he never, never lost his smile or his courage.

I guess I really wanted you to know that Mike did not die alone, with no one caring. I care, we all cared—we all share your sorrow.

Be ever so proud of Mike!

Most sincerely,

CONNIE SCHLASSER, CPT. ANC
2nd Surgical Hospital MA

For Thinking, Talking, Writing

1. Mike said in an early letter, "There are of course those who just get a real charge out of killing people. One lieutenant I talked to said what a kick it had been to roll a gook 100 yards down the beach with his machine gun." Does this seem to you to support the statement that the psychiatrist made in the last article, that "There is a signifi-

cant number of young men who need to kill or to participate effectively in violence in order to establish their masculine identity"?
Discuss.

2. Mike's attitudes during the short time he was in Vietnam before his
   death changed somewhat. He remained "opposed to the war on moral
   and political grounds," but began to "want revenge" for the killing
   and maiming of the men in his platoon. What do you think this means
   in terms of how people react emotionally in a crisis situation?

3. Mike was a young man who, although he was opposed to the war on
   moral grounds, chose to go into the service rather than refuse to do
   so. Do you respect him more for this decision, or do you feel he
   should have refused to serve? According to Mike, most of the soldiers
   in Vietnam did not believe in the war in which they were fighting
   when he was there. Why, then, did they go? What does their decision
   mean morally, in terms of patriotism and personal morality?

The Decision

Priscilla Long

December 29, 1966. For Peter and me, this is the day that marks the before and after. The day that changed everything, though not through any fault of its own. For others, it must have marked a turning point, as well. People must have died that day: in a car, in some field in Vietnam, in their beds. Others got married or were born. For us, it was the last day we were to be together as free human beings for a long, long time. As we waited for Peter's plane at the San Francisco airport, we were only dimly aware of what a huge step we were taking.

My fiancé is a political prisoner. He is now serving a three-year sentence in a federal penitentiary for his refusal to serve in the United States Army.

He returned his draft card some years ago, because of his growing conviction that it was wrong to kill, especially in the service of our cold-war foreign policy, which he believed was misguided. He also believed that the draft was out of place in any free society—that if a free nation wanted to go to war, it should have voluntary consent of those who were to risk their lives in that war.

We were not a particularly unusual couple before he went in. We were graduated from a small Midwestern college, after which I took a job teaching disturbed children and Peter began his graduate work. I was happy, rather disorganized, and more or less dependent on others, especially Peter, to take care of me. Peter worked hard, studying, teaching his course, and working on his research project. We had many friends, and it was hard to imagine living without them. Although we knew he would have to go to prison sometime, we didn't known when; so life went on rather routinely.

When his case was finally decided, everything changed. Peter was suddenly taken away, and I was alone. To be near him, I had to move to a strange part of the country, where I knew no one. I had to get a job fairly quickly, as I had only a small amount of money, and I had to find a place to live. I managed all of this because I had to, as people do manage things. The kaleidoscope of life shifted; I discovered that I had fears I had never admitted to before: of flying, of being run over by a car, of strangers, of flying saucers. But these fears did not interfere with the things I had to do. Perhaps they enabled me to carry on. If I had, instead, been afraid of the real problems that lay ahead, I might not have been able to cope with them.

I had lived for so long with the possibility of Peter's having to go to prison that when I moved to Ann Arbor to be closer to him, I was startled by people's reactions to our situation. My new roommates discussed what they would tell their parents about *their* new roommate. My employer's face fell when I answered her question about what my fiancé was doing. My student assistants were amazed to discover that men could be put in jail for refusing the draft. I met other people who thought that the situation was rather romantic and that knowing me added to their prestige.

Everyone was curious and impressed in one way or another. Yet my experience has been a very private one, in that I've never met anyone in the same position. It became difficult for me to describe how I felt about it, because it was so much outside the context of the lives of the people around me. Now I hope to communicate to others what these years have been like.

As I was riding on the bus, on my way to visit Peter for the first time, I was both pleased and anxious. What would the prison be like? Would we have to talk through bars or a screen? Would Peter have changed? Would he seem strange or unreal as a federal prisoner?

I entered the prison grounds through unmarked gates. The red brick buildings, standing against the gray sky and frozen Michigan fields, looked more like a factory than a prison. The lobby, with its tile floor and bland green walls, might have belonged to any institution. I signed in and heard Peter's name barked into the speaker system. Gates were opened, doors unlocked, and I found myself in the visiting room, which was filled with chairs facing each other and with men in khaki visiting with their families. I sat down to wait for Peter.

It was strange to see him without his mustache. He was dressed in ill-fitting prison khaki, and his black hair had been cut by an unprofessional inmate barber. He had not had enough cigarettes to pay for a good haircut. I learned that cigarettes were used as money inside prison walls.

We sat rather formally, facing each other studiously ignoring the fifty-odd other people in the room. They were bank robbers, car thieves, check forgers, and narcotics pushers, with their families. They looked like ordinary people, their mothers like ordinary mothers, and their wives like ordinary wives. I asked myself what I had expected them to look like. I realized that I had just never thought about what kind of person a bank robber might be.

Our conversation was hesitant and strained at first, but we gradually got used to each other in this unnatural context. We talked about the prison, the food, the routine, about my new job and where I was going to live. Then the visit was over.

Days and weeks passed. I learned to enjoy my work and to take pride in it, partially as a result of Peter's continuous support and encouragement. The support he gave me is still amazing and wonderful to me.

He was then adjusting to prison life—to the impossibility of moving more than two hundred yards in any direction; to almost unbroken male companionship; to utter lack of privacy, ever; to the problem of rebuking the advances of inmate homosexuals without getting beaten up in the process; to the scant supply of good reading material; and to other daily indignities.

It might have been easy for him to succumb to discouragement and frustration, yet he never did. In fact, he adjusted to all of this more cheerfully than I did.

When I first moved to Ann Arbor, my evenings were sometimes lonely. I read, browsed through book shops, and went to the movies every time they changed. Things were not bad, but they were not always good. I sometimes became intensely dissatisfied with myself and my stagnant life. On these occasions, I would write Peter a scathingly unpleasant letter. While he could understand my feelings, he was helpless to do anything, and I gradually realized that he had enough to worry about without my adding to his problems. I learned to cope with my frustrations without dumping them on him or on anyone else. I met more people, and gradually life began to seem almost normal, and my fears began to dwindle.

Every week, we had a beautiful three and a half hours together. When spring came, we could visit in a walled-in patio, complete with a lawn and café tables. At these times, we forgot that he was in prison. We laughed, planned, gossiped, and discussed everything under the sun.

We had a good summer. Peter learned to play chess, improved his tennis game (there was a court inside the prison compound), and became browned by the sun. He won the tennis championship and was the recipient of three hundred candy bars. He had, by that time, several good friends, including an ex-drug addict and the prison chaplain. I had also found some good friends in Ann Arbor and was busy with various projects. The sun seemed to soften everything, and life, although it could have been better, was good.

It was one week before Labor Day when Peter learned that he was to be transferred to another prison. He found out by accident. The usual practice is to tell inmates one hour before they leave that they are going to be transferred. The reason stated in the memo concerning his transfer was "Outside contacts too influential." The reason stated to Peter was "You are too old for this prison." The fact that there were many inmates older than he was apparently irrelevant. The occasional dishonesty of prison staff members is a fact of life.

The next week, Peter was put on a bus, chained to other men, and driven away. He would not arrive at his final destination for an indefinite time, and for that amount of time he couldn't write. He "made the prison circuit," which meant that he was taken from prison to prison, each one closer to the one to which he was being sent, until he arrived at the specified one. In some cases, this takes as long as a year. Fortunately, Peter arrived at Danbury, Connecticut, in a month. It was an agonizing month of waiting and worrying. I finally got a letter from him saying he was there and safe.

I stayed in Ann Arbor for another three months before I moved again to be near him. During this time, his parole board was to meet and decide whether or not he was to be paroled. Conscientious objectors had been paroled rather routinely in the past, since, except for the discomfort caused by their inquiring minds, they make "good" prisoners. Peter's record was flawless, but as we watched the government's position on the war hardening, we were prepared for the worst.

A few days before Christmas, he found out that his parole was denied. But we had a good Christmas in spite of it, an orgy of visiting, since visiting hours were expanded to eight hours a day for the vacation.

Then I went to Boston, again found a new job, an apartment, a new home. . . .

The second year wears on. Prison for most men, and for Peter, and for me, is like water slowly dripping on a rock, slowly wearing it down. There are some things that we've got used to; for example, the fact that all our letters are read and censored doesn't bother us any more, in the sense that we just don't think about it. The visiting hours at Danbury are only three hours a month, and this is hard.

With an occasional sadistic exception, most of the guards are fairly decent men, working for their living. There are subtle ways, however, of treating inmates as animals rather than men. Many of the inmates become almost walking vegetables after an extended period of this kind of existence. That Peter has not lost his dignity as a man is a tribute to his courage and his manhood.

Twelve long months or more loom ahead before Peter will be a free man again. What will we think of all this when it is over? Although I can't know that now, we have learned much already. The meaning of freedom has become clearer to us both, but especially to Peter. He has won the freedom to think what he likes, a luxury few men of draft age have. As one of the many people who are opposed to our government's involvement in Vietnam, he does not have to make the distasteful choice between tailoring his objections to the Army's specifications and acting against his convictions about our government's policy.

Also, he has come to see that freedom is a relative thing—a prisoner who has dignity and love is more free in some ways than the man on the outside who feels burdened by his job and family and has drifted into a way of life, rather than has chosen one. Peter has given himself the choice to do with his life what he thinks best, by making one of the hardest choices he'll ever have to make.

Both of us have experienced the incredible power of our love for each other to grow and deepen in spite of long separations. I have learned to know what I want and to live for what I want; to make choices, to depend on my own resources. I have defined better for myself what is valuable in life and in society, perhaps because I've had a long time to think and not much to take for granted.

I believe that when it is over, we will remember this time as a long day, a day of pain and of waiting. Perhaps we will wonder how we did it, or perhaps we will not want to think about it at all. But our final reward will come much later, when our children learn that their father would not go to war, that he would not raise a gun to kill another human being.

For Thinking, Talking, Writing

1. Priscilla Long, the woman who wrote this article, believes deeply that her fiancé's decision to go to jail was morally right. The last sentence in the article, "But our final reward will come much later, when our children learn that their father would not go to war, that he would not raise a gun to kill another human being," indicates that she is proud of what Peter is doing. You may agree or disagree with Peter's beliefs. If you agree, would you also choose to make the de-

cision to go to jail rather than "raise a gun to kill another human being"? If you disagree, do you respect Peter for acting according to his beliefs, or do you think he is wrong in refusing to conform to the requirements of his own country? The basic question here is, does personal morality rank higher than patriotism, or should patriotism come before personal morality?

2. Suppose that much later, when the two people in this article marry and have children, the children believe that their father's action was wrong. Then there would be a conflict of beliefs about what is "moral," what is "right." Do you think that these people, who believe strongly that each person should follow his personal morality above everything else, will allow their children such a difference of opinion without being angry about it? Do you think parents *should* allow their children serious differences of belief? Do your parents allow *you* such differences without being angry? Do you plan to allow your own children to believe different things from what you believe without getting upset?

Draft Board No. 13,
Springfield, Ohio

Anthony Wolff

After the first flush of coming of age, an 18-year-old boy may begin to sweat. In his wallet, keeping company with his driver's license as part of the thin dossier that proves he's a man, is a card from Uncle Sam that says the Government has a lien on his life. In most states, he may not buy a drink, vote, marry without parental consent or sign a legal contract, but he knows that his Government can arrogate to its own purpose two years of his irreplaceable youth and subject it to unfamiliar indignities, perhaps to death.

For a lucky boy, in a lucky time and place, the draft is a remote threat. If the military is not hard up for men, his number may not come up for five or six years: an eternity to an 18-year-old, plenty of time to start a family, parlay a draft-proof education into a draft-free job or somehow avoid the draft's reach if he wants to.

Springfield, Ohio, U.S.A., this year is not a lucky time or place. The Vietnam war is forcing the draft to dig deep, and in Springfield, as elsewhere, it is reaching for 19-year-olds and tightening up on deferments.

Most boys go to war when the Government calls. Some, who don't want to go, and who know that most men will never have to go, seek deferment. The willing and the unwilling, those who go and those who will never go, all are subject to their local draft board. In Springfield, that's Local Board No. 13.

A boy who is able and willing has only to wait his turn. Each month, from the Department of Defense, via national and state Selective Service Headquarters, a call comes to Local Board No. 13 for a certain number of men. The board has individual file folders for each of its 25,000-odd registrants, indexed by draft classification and birthdate; it simply deals from the top of the 1-A deck, oldest eligible men first, and mails out the required number of notices to report for induction. It is all as neat and impersonal as clerks and files and regulations can make it. Jeannette Johnson, the grandmotherly clerk of the Springfield board, says with satisfaction, "We are like an obstetrician—we deliver them."

A boy who doesn't want to go may claim the board's personal attention at its brief weekly meeting, after the cut-and-dried classification work has been ratified. While a registrant waits to request a deferment, he may take whatever comfort he can from the printed credo thumbtacked on the bulletin board above the official list of delinquents: "AMERICANISM ... is an eagerness to defend ... [the country] against all enemies...."

The board's patriotic orthodoxy is tempered by the law, but the law also reserves to the board the sole right to classify free men for conscription. Its decision is subject only to appeal within the draft system and protected by law from judicial review. Unqualified either by examination or election, the three men sitting around a gray-steel table at Local Board No. 13, Springfield, Ohio, are among the most powerful men in America.

Tom McKeever, 19, is one who waits to see the board. He is a conscientious objector the hard way: not by subscription to an official creed; rather, by conviction that human life is sacred. He waits, armed with fragments of Camus, Socrates and Sartre, the bibliography of his unorthodox faith.

Fred Cole, the Government Appeal Agent appointed to advise the Springfield board and its registrants, has already warned Tom that "they're not going to have the remotest idea what you're talking about." From years of experience with the board, Cole knows that "They have a bias about CO's: they don't like them."

Tom has already heard his mother-in-law call him a Communist and a coward. He does not have to hear the members of the board discussing CO's:

Ed Lewis, the 74-year-old chairman, with 25 years on draft boards, says: "We get a few oddballs ... like one fellow said he couldn't kill a fly, that if a little fly was flying around this room, he'd go get a cup ... and he'd capture that fly and take it outside and let it loose. We get our smiles! He's 1-A, or probably in Vietnam."

John Patterson, the board secretary, tells of a boy who "sent in he was a CO. Then he flew in here and brought another man with him which we couldn't hear. You see, you can't bring anybody else with you before the board. The law is specific: your father, mother or your wife." (The law is specific: "... the local board may ... permit any person to appear before it with or on behalf of a registrant....")

Ed Lewis again: "The Government sets up so many religions, you know, that they consider as conscientious objectors, like the Brethrens, I think the Seventh Day Adventists, the Quakers...." (The Government "sets up" no religions that give anyone CO status, probably because the Constitution wouldn't stand for it.) Both Mr. Lewis and Mr. Patterson have definite ideas about pacifists, whom they do not consider to be CO's. Mr. Patterson thinks "A pacifist just doesn't want to do *anything* —he's like the hippies." Mr. Lewis concludes, "There's nothing in the regulations to take care of a pacifist. We classify him 1-A."

The board's interview with Tom McKeever is brief and polite. They ask him the questions on the CO form, which he has already answered in writing. Mr. Patterson, who has two years of college, cannot believe that McKeever, who has none, could have written such a "brilliant paper" without a "ghostwriter." Softly, in a monotone, punctuated by the peck of typewriters from the outer office, McKeever repeats his answers substantially as he had written them. Mr. Patterson remains unconvinced of his authorship. All three—Lewis, Patterson and Harold Crabtree—are swayed by McKeever's lack of certified church affiliation. Unanimously, they classify him 1-A.

Local Board No. 13 opens early on Tuesday morning, but the cold fluorescent lights in the basement office do not show in the predawn darkness above. The only sign that something is going on is the empty bus at the curb and the small group of women waiting on the front steps in the chill, wet morning.

Below, 34 chosen men wait. Each man waits alone, quietly, as though unaccustomed to the company of strangers at 6:30 in the morning. Their murmured conversations are unsmiling and brief. No one moves around very much, and the room does not seem crowded, even though men are sitting on all the tables and many stand.

Ed Lewis and Harold Crabtree are absent. Lewis says: "I never attend those sessions. I used to, way back years ago, but I felt as though it would be better . . . there might be some people who get overly wrought up, you know . . . and make some nasty remarks . . . so I don't come down any more."

Mr. Patterson and the clerks seem anxious to get the business over with quickly and smoothly. Still, it is something of a ritual occasion, and such occasions require speeches.

A nervous, soft-spoken man from the Gideon society assures the draftees that America's cause is God's cause, and that Christ is their friend in battle. He offers a free vest-pocket Testament to anyone who wants one. The little volume is indexed: "WHERE TO FIND HELP, When: *Afraid*—Psalms 4:8, 27 . . . *Discouraged*—Matthew 5:4, 11, 12 . . . *Needing God's Protection*—Romans 8:31-39. . . ."

John Patterson's speech is short and man-to-man, memorized for use on these monthly occasions. "Those of us on the local board who have had experience in the service know that there are two ways to do anything: the right way and the Army way. Do it the Army way, and you'll be all right."

The speeches are over, the men are ready to go, and so far, there has been no untoward incident. A tall, gaunt boy asks to speak with Mrs. Johnson in the narrow hallway. He is a volunteer for the draft, but now, he says his wife of two days is ill, and he can't leave.

Mrs. Johnson and Patterson refuse to accept his story. The quota has been filled, the papers have been filed, the bus is ready to go. The boy sweats, pales, and falls to the floor.

Mrs. Johnson tries to raise him, but she can only get him halfway up before he slides down the wall to the floor again. Mr. Patterson, who is a practicing undertaker, and so presumably qualified to handle the situation, picks up the boy's arm and releases it. It drops limply, his hand slapping the tile. They conclude that he is faking.

As the rest of the draftees file upstairs to the waiting bus, Mrs. Johnson rushes back into the office. "He's faking, he's just *faking,*" she cries several times. "He's going to get his way. He's not going to get on that bus!"

The police arrive after the bus has gone, to revive the boy and take him home. Later, they return to his home to take his wife to the hospital.

It is raining in the cold gray dawn as the bus moves toward Fort Hayes, in Columbus. Inside, the windows are fogged, creating a world apart. Idly, a boy traces a design with his finger in the condensed moisture. Some smoke, a few sleep; one boy opens his Testament, but the print is too small for him to read in the early light. There is some hushed casual conversation, about softball games and girls, the trivia of just yesterday. Nobody talks about the adventure they are about to share. Nobody knows anything about it, and nobody wants to guess.

One boy mentions a newly pregnant wife at home; another, over-hearing, claims one child at home with another on the way. Perhaps they are lying. If so, it is a futile gesture. If they are telling the truth, why didn't they tell the local board? They might have won automatic deferments. Somehow, at this late date, on the bus for Fort Hayes, the truth of the matter seems superfluous.

Two claims provoke a third. One seat away, a man says he went to Local Board 13 under the impression that by volunteering, he could get the educational benefits the Army holds out to encourage enlistments. He says that no one at the board told him the crucial difference between volunteering for enlistment and volunteering for the draft: that all a volunteer for the draft gets is precedence on the 1-A list. The board signed him up as a volunteer for the draft, and now it is too late to correct the oversight: Local Board No. 13 has filled its quota.

The bus pulls through the gates of the fort and delivers the draftees into the hands of the Army. Almost all of them will go to sleep this night in boot camp in South Carolina. As the men file out of the chartered bus, no one seems to notice the words on its side: "DISCOVER AMERICA . . . AND LEAVE THE DRIVING TO US."

For Thinking, Talking, Writing

1. This article states only things people said and things that happened at Draft Board No. 13, Springfield, Ohio. However, the author is really attempting to state his opinion about the way that local draft boards administer the draft system as it has been set up in the past. *What* is the author trying to say?
2. What is your opinion of the sign on the bulletin board of Draft Board No. 13: "AMERICANISM . . . is an eagerness to defend . . . [the country] against all enemies. . . ." Do you agree? Why or why not? What does AMERICANISM mean to you?
3. What do you think of the lottery system for the draft instead of the kind of control by local boards described in this article? Is the lottery more fair, less fair, or about as fair as the old system? Do you think there are other, better ways to handle the Army's need for men? If so, what would you suggest?

The Draft —
What Are Your Alternatives?

Anthony Scaduto

. . . It is likely that for some years to come we will be forced to maintain a large army. And although more voices are now arguing that the draft is unfair and ought to be changed, transforming it into a more equitable animal will take time. Meanwhile, young men of draft age must deal with the system as it now stands.

The Selective Service Act permits exemptions. Every man has the right to seek legal exemption. But the draft law is intricate; many do not know the alternatives open to them. And no one can reasonably plan his future without knowing all his rights under the law.

"There are seventeen broad categories of legal deferment," says Stephen Sandler, a bearded, nervous, slightly unhappy-looking man of twenty-five. Sandler is a professional draft counselor; he and other members of the National Lawyers Guild in New York advise potential draftees on their legal rights. "Many kids aren't aware that they have a legal deferment coming to them. A lot of them don't realize they have a 3-A hardship, for example, and wouldn't ever apply for it if we didn't discover it. We help the prospective draftee come up with the information he needs to help him get the best possible classification."

The broad categories look like this:

Class I

Class I-A: Available for military service.

Class I-A-O: Conscientious Objector. Available for noncombatant military service only.

Class I-C: Member of the Armed Forces of the United States, the Environmental Science Services Administration, or the Public Health Service.

Class I-D: Member of reserve component or student taking military training.

Class I-O: Conscientious Objector. Available for civilian work contributing to the maintenance of the national health, safety or interest.

Class I-S: Student deferred by statute.

Class I-W: Conscientious Objector performing civilian work contributing to the maintenance of the national health, safety or interest.

Class I-Y: Registrant not eligible for a lower class who would be qualified for military service in time of war or national emergency.

Class II

Class II-A: Registrant deferred because of civilian occupation (except agriculture and activity in study).

Class II-C: Registrant deferred because of agricultural occupation.

Class II-S: Registrant deferred because of activity in study.

Class III

Class III-A: Registrant with a child or children; and registrant deferred by reason of extreme hardship to dependents.

Class IV

Class IV-A: Registrant who has completed service; sole surviving son.

Class IV-B: Officials deferred by law.

Class IV-C: Aliens.

Class IV-D: Minister of religion or divinity student.

Class IV-F: Registrant not qualified for any military service.

Class V

Class V-A: Registrant over the age of liability for military service.

Each candidate for the draft who has not yet registered must keep two things in mind about his potential deferment:

Most important is that it is up to *you* to let the draft board know that you have a basis for deferment. The draft board has no obligation to discover reasons to defer you; the burden is on *you* to notify it *in writing at once* if there is a change in status that may legally mean your deferment.

Second, the lower in the scale from 1-A to 5-A a man is classified, the less chance he will eventually be called into uniform. The 4-F, for example, is *exempt* while the 1-Y is only *deferred* and is subject to re-examination and possible reclassification. Yet many of those in 1-Y have physical defects and emotional problems similar to those in 4-F.

About 25 percent of all men are considered 4-F, or not fit for the armed forces, because their bodies or their emotions are not up to pre-scribed minimum standards. Among them are men who are hypersensi-tive to bee stings, who are above 80 inches or below 60 inches in height, who have extensive tattoos (or obscene ones), who have a severe in-grown toenail that can't be remedied, who don't have the midportion of the index, middle or ring finger, or who have hemorrhoids or perfo-rated eardrums.

The diseases and defects that cause draft rejection are these:

Muscular-skeletal: Arms, legs, spine, sacroiliac, flat feet, amputa-tions, fingers and toes, stiffening of joints, club foot.

Heart and vascular disease: High blood pressure, rheumatic heart disease, rapid heartbeat, hemophilia, varicose veins.

Psychiatric Disorder: Character and behavior disorders, mental de-ficiency, psychoneurosis, psychosis.

Over and Underweight

Gastro-intestinal disease: Hernia, ulcers, malformation of the di-gestive system.

Allergic disease: Asthma, hay fever. (History and documentation important.)

Eyes and Vision: Strabismus, visual defects, corneal degeneration.

Genital-urinary: Kidney diseases and defects, undescended testicle, nephritis, nephrosis, hydrocele.

Neurological disorder: Nerve injury defects, epilepsy, peripheral nerve disease, cerebral paralysis.

Dermatological disease: Psoriasis, acne, eczema, athlete's foot, ring-worm.

Neoplasm: Cancer, benign tumors.

Endocrine and metabolism: Diabetes, avitaminosis.

Respiratory system: Bronchial asthma, etc.

Says an Army induction doctor: "I can't advise too strongly that if you are suffering from an ailment which could mean a rejection for you, the best thing to do is come in with medical documentation — a doctor's letter, X-rays, medical reports — anything you can get your hands on to back up your claim for deferment. We don't want you if you are physically unfit, but if it is something not very obvious, you have to call it to our attention."

The 1-Y category is the great catch-basin of deferment. Into this classification are thrown all those considered society's misfits. Among them are men with serious police records, men with emotional problems (including homosexuals), sometimes the militant antidraft demonstrators (especially if they've been to jail), even members of radical or "subversive" organizations if they are not just hangers-on but serious extreme-Left activists. Many of them belong in 4-F but they are classified 1-Y because officials suspect deliberate evasion and want to check them every few months. (4-F's are hardly ever called in for reexamination.)

Class II in the Selective Service Act includes men with student deferments and those who are deferred because of occupation. In this category falls one newly popular way for a healthy man to stay out of the Army without going to jail or taking off for Canada. It not only pays a better wage than the Army but is also a service to the community. They call it *teaching*. With the teacher shortage what it is, most draft boards will defer a male teacher who is otherwise eligible to carry an M-14 or a brace of grenades, as long as school officials certify he is desperately needed. (Practically any still-warm body that hasn't been lobotomized is considered desperately needed.)

"I'm going to be a lawyer," says twenty-three-year-old Gary Herold (a pseudonym; he asked that his real name not be used), "but I'm going to teach until I'm twenty-six, when the Army won't want me anymore. Then I'll start my real career."

Gary concedes he is teaching because he doesn't want to be drafted. He deliberately sought deferment as graduation approached. In March, 1967, a couple of months before he was scheduled to get his degree at Brooklyn Law School (when his 2-S graduate-student deferment would become 1-A), a draft-evasion counselor pointed the way: The managers of the New York public school system had set up Intensive Teacher Training, a ten-week summer course designed to take college grads who had no training in education, and transform them into teachers.

"Three months after I got my law degree I was teaching history in a grade school," Gary says. "As soon as my principal shook my hand and welcomed me to the staff, he wrote a letter to my draft board explaining how important I was to the country's health, honor, Mother, God and all that. The draft board gave me a 2-A critical occupation deferment."

Graduate schools in every section of the nation, particularly those offering courses leading to nonmedical degrees, are quietly advising their students to teach by day, take law, accounting, philosophy or whatever by night. By the time they've reached twenty-six, they'll be able to embark on their preferred careers. It is legal and, in the eyes of many educators, not immoral to take advantage of the law.

There is nothing permanent about teaching deferments, however. Col. Arthur Alpert, Deputy Director of the Selective Service in New York City, points out: "There is no blanket deferment for any class except students. All others are at the option of the local boards, depending on local conditions. In New York there is a definite teacher shortage, so we have been granting immunity to teachers for some time. But teachers have been drafted in the past and will be drafted again if the need for them slackens off."

There aren't too many such deferments remaining. As a result of a tightening by Selective Service Director Lewis B. Hershey, the options are undergoing a trimming process.

General Hershey's orders [in] February [1968] ruled out further deferment of either first- or second-year graduate students...except in the fields of medicine, dentistry, veterinary medicine, osteopathy and divinity — which hit law and science students, who had been granted such deferments in the past, especially hard. It also indefinitely suspended the list of critical occupations and essential activities under which about 250,000 men — mostly engineers and scientists — had been deferred. (However it left untouched category II-C, the deferment of men working on farms. They are still not to be drafted under *any* circumstances — even if there is a surplus of the particular agricultural crop they happen to be farming.)

In the past, college has always been the choice deferment. Now a student's 2-S deferment is as warm a haven as Linus' security blanket — and just as illusory — for it is a temporary deferment. Once a man has completed his four or five years of college, he is prime draft-bait.

"A man who is graduating college this June is in a lot of trouble," draft counselor Sandler says. "Besides possibly getting deferred for teaching, almost all that is left is the Peace Corps or Vista, which are trying to get 2-A deferments for their people. But 2-A is discretionary with each of the 4,000 local boards, and there is no guessing what a local board will do.

"If divinity school or the ministry is a man's bag," Sandler adds, "then he can qualify for a 4-D. That's another possibility left. There are very few others."

There is one condition that will insure total and legal immunity from the draft, but is considered by some to be worse than beaming down to a Vietnam rice paddy: getting married and having a child! But it is a very legal and socially acceptable form of deferment. The child, in fact, is more important than the marriage. A man must be given a 3-A deferment if he is supporting a child, even if he is not married to the mother and the child is someone else's. All that is required is "a relationship similar to that of parent and child," as the Selective Service Act puts it. As long as there is a legitimate family relationship, even without benefit of marriage license, a man must be deferred.

If a man is married and his wife gives birth to their first child, or if he marries a woman who has a child (or lives with and supports her and the child), he must promptly send a letter to his draft board asking for 3-A deferment. The moment a prospective draftee's wife or girl friend becomes pregnant he should notify the draft board, enclosing a doctor's certificate and asking for a change in deferment.

However, 3-A is barred to some college students. A man who requests, and is granted, a 2-S deferment after July 1, 1967, is no longer eligible for 3-A based on support of a wife and child — even if he happens to be legitimately married and the father of a dozen children. That's because in the past, students would pyramid their 2-S deferments through graduate school and then to marriage, fatherhood, and safety from the draft, while kids whose fathers couldn't afford to send them along the same road were getting drafted. It was patently unfair, and the law was overhauled.

There is still a legal out, though. The law applies to those students who have *requested* the 2-S. But a large number apparently have been given the deferment without asking for it because their schools sent out a form every year attesting to their good standing, and the draft board automatically continued the old classification. "Whatever you do," says one counselor, "don't request the 2-S unless the board realizes its mistake and forces you to do so."

The new limitation on 3-A deferments for students does not apply to those who come under the George Hamilton Escape Hatch. George won his 3-A because he convinced Local Board #8, in New York City, that if he was forced to serve, his widowed mother would no longer be able to live in the style to which she had become attached — a style that included a thirty-nine-room Beverly Hills mansion, a Rolls-Royce and many other civilities. The section of the draft law that Hamilton made so famous means that even a student who has been granted a 2-S deferment *must* be classified 3-A as long as he can prove he supports someone else besides a wife and child: His mother, brothers or sisters, grandparents, anyone under eighteen and any handicapped person of any age.

More than 25,000 men have been granted Conscientious Objector status. The CO's fall into two categories. The 1-A-O is drafted but performs only noncombat duties, usually in the medics. This is not an escape for the man who wants to stay out of Vietnam, because that's where most of the medics eventually end up. The second class is 1-O. It is difficult to get; even members of legitimate pacifist religious sects are sometimes turned down by draft boards. The 1-O is not drafted, but must put in two years of "alternative service" in the national interest. Vindictive draft boards frequently force 1-O's to accept the most menial hospital jobs, but sometimes they are permitted to work for the Peace Corps or do social work in local community organizations.

Draft counselors urge kids who think they may eventually claim a CO deferment to file for it *the first time* they register. "The draft boards get up tight if a kid files for a CO after he's been 2-S all the time," Sandler says. "He's on much more solid ground if he signs the CO section on Form 100 — the first thing he is required to fill out when he registers — than if he puts off signing a couple of years. He'll then be given a CO Form 150.

Even if he is claiming a 2-S as a student, he should file a Form 150 right off if he is going to eventually claim a CO. The board must grant him the 2-S and then consider the CO claim after the student deferment runs out."

Conscientious objection is one of the more complex areas of the Draft Act. It involves a landmark Supreme Court decision making it easier to qualify as a CO, a rewrite of the laws by Congress in an attempt to nullify that decision, and the certainty of further litigation. All draft experts advise draft-eligible men who intend to seek a CO to contact those organizations most active in this area. They are the Central Committee for Conscientious Objectors (CCCO) at 2006 Walnut St., Philadelphia, LOcust 3-1480, and the National Service Board for Religious Objectors, Washington Building, 15th and New York Ave., N.W., Washington, D.C., EXecutive 3-4868. The American Friends Service Committee (the Quakers) are located in every major city and will provide guidance even to non-Quakers.

Organizations like these, like the National Lawyer's Guild for which Steve Sandler works, and dozens more, have mushroomed in every city, advising young men on how to find the legal deferment that may exist for them. Almost every college has one, either within the administration or off-campus.

The remaining deferment categories include, in Class I, the high school students not yet 20 (1-S), enlistees in the National Guard, and students enrolled in Military Reserve Training Corps (1-D). These are temporary deferments and those who hold them are still eligible for military service. In class 4-B are Federal and local officials (only a handful qualify because most are overage), and 4-C covers aliens who have not been admitted for permanent residence in the United States.

Class 4-A is one of the more obscure. It provides that a youth who is the only surviving male in a family in which "the father or one or more sons or daughters were killed in action or died in the line of duty while serving in the Armed Forces of the United States, or subsequently died as a result of injuries received or disease incurred during such service..." is exempt. This is a permanent exemption from all military service.

A considerable number of men are trying to beat the draft illegally. Last year some 1,300 men were indicted on draft evasion charges, twice the number the year before and the highest since WWII. Convictions have also climbed steeply, and with the creation of a "special unit" in the Justice Department to prosecute more forcefully, the number is expected to rise even more sharply....

The other complete cop-out is to run off — most noticeably to Canada. (Lately Sweden has come into its share of publicity.) There may be as many as 10,000 draft-age Americans living in Canada, plus an unknown number of wives and girl friends who have gone along. These evaders are safe because Canada will not extradite anyone charged with a crime in the United States that is not a crime in Canada. Since there is no draft in Canada, there can be no draft evasion.

Many of the Americans in Canada are radicals who insist they hate the United States, that they worship Che and Mao and the 'Cong and want to light a fuse under the United States. For others though, there are hangups: They can never return to the United States without being arrested and facing up to ten years in prison, and they are homesick. The Federal crackdown that is just getting under way will be directed not only at those who have gone underground or fled to Canada, but also at the draft evaders who illegally twist the draft laws....

"Ridiculous," says one draft counselor. "For every man who gets away with it another is caught and ends up on a fast express to the penetentiary, or an even faster train to boot camp.

"I tell kids that come for advice, 'Rather than cop out, rather than run around headless at the last minute because 1-A is rushing at you, why not plan a little in advance and try to adapt your life to the realities of the draft law? And why not make yourself felt by getting behind those people who are trying to come up with a sensible draft law?' "

Many influential citizens are demanding changes in the Selective

Service Act to eliminate its inequities and to make it unnecessary for draft-eligible men to break the law or bend their lives attempting to fit themselves into the law's shelter. The proposals — by both Kennedys, by Mark Hatfield, and many others — include drafting 19-year-olds first, so that a man can get his military service out of the way before starting college and not have to worry about his career being disrupted later; a lottery in which everyone would be eligible; a combination lottery and 19-year-old draft; and the establishment of an all-volunteer army by tripling enlistees' pay — to about $5,000 a year — thus eliminating the need for a draft.

"One big trouble with the draft law," says a draft counselor, "is that it has been written by those who've been 5-A for a lot of years. It's about time some of the 1-A and 2-S guys had a say in writing a new law. If enough of them got out and made themselves heard, we might get a good law some day."

For Thinking, Talking, Writing

If you are a man, of draft age, and without any special deferment except your student 2-S deferment, you must make a basic philosophical decision: are you willing to serve in the armed forces if you are called to do so, or not? If you are, you have little need for this article; you will simply go into the service when you are called. If you are *not* willing to serve, however, this article may give you some information about planning a legal deferment which is appropriate for you. Analyze your own situation in regard to the draft at this time. Discuss the basic philosophical question involved in all the controversy about the draft and the war today: should a man serve in the armed forces of his country when he is called to do so, whether or not he believes in the war that is being carried on? Is such service a moral duty, or not? Should a man act on the philosophy, "My country, right or wrong," or on his own personal philosophy?

6

VIOLENCE–
EVERYWHERE:

what does it mean?
what can I do?

Introduction

Suddenly, all of us are conscious of violence everywhere around us. Some of it is violence on an individual basis: murders, "muggings," unprovoked attacks by strangers. Some of it is by groups: riots, street-gang crimes, destruction of property by student activists. Parts of some cities are no longer safe to go into, even in the daytime. People are frightened, and many ask, "What does it mean? What can I do?"

Daniel P. Moynihan, of the M.I.T.-Harvard Joint Center for Urban Studies, stated recently:

> Violence has rarely been altogether absent from American life, and it has ever been part of our fantasies.... But I think the violence of this age is different: It is greater, more real, more personal, suffused throughout the society, associated with not one but a dozen issues and causes. It is invoked by the most rational, public and respected of our institutions, as well as by the most obscure and piteous lunatic.

Some people believe that violence is simply a part of our American heritage — that we are a violent people, and that nothing can be done about it. Others believe that Americans are not violent by nature, and that the violence we are now experiencing is a symptom of a sickness in our society. In this section you will read about various kinds of violence: assassinations, riots, the "lust for blood" in sports, and capital punishment as a form of societal violence, like war. You will read the opinions of different kinds of people concerning violence and its expression, and consider some suggestions for overcoming it.

Read — think — talk — write. At the end of your study of this section, see if *you* have formed some opinions about the causes of violence in our society and possible solutions for it.

"Millions in His Firing Squad"

Mike Royko

This column was written in April, 1968, immediately after the assassination of Dr. Martin Luther King. Dr. King's assassin was found; we now have a different president; but the problems of violence in our society remain as great as the day this column was written.

FBI agents are looking for the man who pulled the trigger and surely they will find him.

But it doesn't matter if they do or they don't. They can't catch everybody, and Martin Luther King was executed by a firing squad that numbered in the millions.

They took part, from all over the country, pouring words of hate into the ear of the assassin.

The man with the gun did what he was told. Millions of bigots, subtle and obvious, put it in his hand and assured him he was doing the right thing.

It would be easy to point at the Southern redneck and say he did it. But what of the Northern disk-jockey-turned-commentator with his slippery words of hate every morning?

What about the Northern mayor who steps all over every poverty program advancement, thinking only of political expediency, until riots fester, whites react with more hate and the gap between races grows bigger?

Toss in the congressman with the stupid arguments against bussing. And the pathetic women who turn out with eggs in their hands to throw at children.

Let us not forget the law-and-order type politicians who are in favor of arresting all the Negro prostitutes in the vice districts. When you ask them to vote for laws that would eliminate some of the causes of prostitution, they babble like the boobs they are.

Throw in a Steve Telow or two: the Eastern and Southern European immigrant or his kid who seems to be convinced that in 40 or 50 years, they built this country. There was nothing here until he arrived, you see, so that gives him the right to pitch rocks when Martin Luther King walks down the street in his neighborhood.

They all took their place in King's firing squad.

And behind them were the subtle ones, those who never say anything bad but just nod when the bigot throws out his strong opinions.

He is actually the worst, the nodder is, because sometimes he believes differently but he says nothing. He doesn't want to cause trouble. For Pete's sake, don't cause trouble!

So when his brother-in-law or his card-playing buddy from across the alley spews out the racial filth, he nods.

Give some more credit to the most subtle of the subtle. That distinction belongs to the FBI, now looking for King's killer.

That agency took part in a mud-slinging campaign against him that to this day demands an investigation.

The bullet that hit King came from all directions. Every two-bit politician or incompetent editorial writer found in him, not themselves, the cause of our racial problems.

It was almost ludicrous. The man came on the American scene preaching nonviolence from the first day he sat at the wrong end of a bus. He preached it in the North and was hit with rocks. He talked it the day he was murdered.

Hypocrites all over this country would kneel every Sunday morning and mouth messages to Jesus Christ. Then they would come out and tell each other, after reading the papers, that somebody should string up King, who was living Christianity like few Americans ever have.

Maybe it was the simplicity of his goal that confused people. Or the way he dramatized it.

He wanted only that black Americans have their constitutional rights, that they get an equal shot at this country's benefits, the same thing we give to the last guy who jumped off the boat.

So we killed him. Just as we killed Abraham Lincoln and John F. Kennedy. No other country kills so many of its best people.

Last Sunday night the President said he was quitting after this term. He said this country is so filled with hate it might help if he got out. Four days later we killed a Nobel Peace Prize winner.

We have pointed a gun at our own head and we are squeezing the trigger. And nobody we elect is going to help us. It is our head and our finger.

For Thinking, Talking, Writing

1. Do you agree or disagree that the person Mr. Royko calls "the nodder," the person who "doesn't want to cause trouble," is just as guilty

of contributing to violence as those who actually participate in it? Explain.

2. Mr. Royko says, "No other country kills so many of its best people." From what you know of history, do you think this is an accurate statement?

3. React to Mr. Royko's statement that "We have pointed a gun at our own head and we are squeezing the trigger." He is talking about the assassination of Dr. Martin Luther King as an example of the great amount of hatred and violence in our country now; do you agree with him that we are destroying our society with this violence?

The Riot

Magazine Staff Writer

The Place

The other day I rode a Madison Street bus out to Homan Avenue, a journey that passes through some of the ugliest slums in America. Here dope addiction and prostitution are as commonplace as crabgrass. ...Here unemployment becomes a career. Here the sidewalks crumble, the storm sewers back up, and the buses make their final, weary runs before succumbing to the embrace of the junk yard baler. And here one week-end last April the residents in a manic outburst set fire to the buildings, looted the stores, and frolicked in the streets by the light of the flames.

When the bus reached Garfield Park, I dismounted and retraced my route, walking 24 blocks through what has come to be called the ghetto, a term that formerly described the Jewish neighborhoods before the Jews prospered and moved. ... Now it means the black slums where Negroes live. The Negroes haven't prospered. They're still stuck in the ghetto, and it is a dreadful place. The reason that the cocktail-party liberal sounds so vapid is that he has never traveled here and seen for himself the filth and despondency that he tries to summarize in pat phrases about "the socially disadvantaged" and "the culturally deprived." He never stepped inside one of those ramshackle doorways where the broken stairs ascend into blackness and the smell of urine fills the air. He never ventured into an establishment like Pigmeat's Bar where all conversation stops as the white man enters and every black head turns to stare in smouldering hostility....

One Maxwell Street homicide detective, himself a Negro, says: "Ninety-eight per cent of these people like policemen. They're trying to lead good lives, but it's pretty hard out here. They have to bring their children in off the street because it isn't safe."

That 98 per cent lives in terrified bondage. If the black man inhabits a jungle, it is he who most often falls victim to the beasts. Almost 70 per cent of Chicago's murders are committed by blacks against blacks.

Reprinted, courtesy of the *Chicago Tribune*.

Among young black men the homicide rate is 12 times greater than among whites and ranks as the second or third leading cause of death.

Nor is murder the only misfortune that kills the black race at an earlier age than the white. Because the black man is usually poor, he lives in a badly heated and unsanitary building where he becomes ill. Because he is badly educated, he holds a hard and frequently dangerous job that injures him. Because he cannot afford it and mistrusts it even when it is offered to him free, he does not receive good medical care. Genetics conspires against him by making him almost uniquely vulnerable to the blood disease called sickle-cell anemia. His woman faces greater hazards in childbirth because of her higher rate of illegitimate pregnancy. In fact, except for suicide, the black death rate exceeds the white in every major category. And so the white man who shrinks from his black brother in fear of criminal assault could conceivably face worse perils. He might himself be black and live in a place like West Madison Street.

I hurried through the riot area, past the scorched tracts where once stores had stood, taking care not to trip on the shattered sidewalks. Things like sidewalks and streets don't seem to get fixed out here. . . .

I paused to stare into a poolroom, loud with the noise of jukebox rock and dark against the glare of the afternoon sun outside. A fat black woman moved toward me, her immense bulk gliding with surprising speed. "Sir, who you looking for?" she called to me. I turned and scurried down the sidewalk, but she came to the door, and her voice pursued me down the street. "Sir, who you looking for?". . .

I had come out here to talk to these people, to ask them why they had set fire to the buildings and looted the stores and frolicked in the streets by the light of the flames. . . . But I was a foreigner here. I did not speak their language, and I would not have understood them. I am not sure that any white man fully understands them. The whites know that something out there is terribly wrong, but they cannot guess the particulars of the illness nor begin to find a remedy. . . .

The Crime

Almost no one believes any more that the blacks rioted to protest the murder of Martin Luther King.

"That was an alibi," says Harold Prohaska, chief of the Chicago Fire Department's 2nd Battalion.

"King was only the immediate catalyst that activated a lifetime of frustration and inhibition," says Kermit B. Coleman, a lawyer for the

American Civil Liberties Union, which battles in the cause of civil rights.

But from the moment of King's assassination at 6 P.M. on Thursday, April 4, Chicagoans sensed the inevitability of violence. It hung on the horizon like an advancing storm, and you could tell from looking at its roiling clouds and flickering lightning that it would scourge the city. And it was this that was most terrifying about it, that it could be foreseen but could not be avoided.

Some tried to prepare for it. Police Superintendent James B. Conlisk, Jr., met with his top aides shortly after 7 P.M. and canceled all days off for the city's 11,500 policemen. Brig. Gen. Richard T. Dunn, a Bloomington lawyer who commands the Illinois National Guard, was already in the city, trying to bring order out of the chaos of a reorganization in which the old 33rd Division was dismembered and two new brigades formed. . . . And out on West Madison Street black friends and customers warned a few merchants to flee because their stores were marked for destruction.

The destruction did not begin until the next day — Friday, April 5 — and surprisingly it was the children who started it. They had gone to school in feverish excitement, and as the morning wore on, agitators appeared and urged them to leave their classes. (In some schools as much as 25 per cent of the student body had never showed up in the first place.) Soon teachers began to lose their grip and discipline evaporated. At Farragut High school, 2345 S. Christiana, Principal Joseph Carroll was booed off the stage during a memorial service for King, and the black students took over. False alarms emptied many schools. Whites went home to avoid beatings. By lunch time 85 per cent of the students had left some schools. More than 80 ghetto schools closed that afternoon, sending their pupils out into the streets to find what excitement they could.

In the threatened areas — generally any black neighborhood but particularly the West Madison street jungle — businesses began to close down. Thousands of employes, dismissed early from their jobs, poured into the streets to mingle with the children. Through this massed humanity the police tried to send reinforcements and "incident control teams." Later, firemen and guardsmen would also try to force a passage, worsening the congestion. These dense crowds presented a highly inflammable tinder on which would fall the sparks of disorder. If only the people had gone home, the riots might have been averted.

"I was praying for a little rain and cold weather to dampen down the enthusiasm," says General Dunn, but the day remained warm and fair. . . .

The first report of violence came in at 10 A.M. when students from Lindblom High school began breaking windows on 63rd street near Wolcott avenue. "Around noon," Police Superintendent Conlisk later testified, "we got reports that gangs of 10 to 20 youths were assaulting pedestrians in the Loop, breaking windows, and causing disorder, forcing motorists to turn on their lights as a tribute to Doctor King."

At 3:39 P.M. on Friday the first building went up in flames, a furniture store at 2235 Madison street. The fire spread—faster than the wind, faster than bad news, faster than a man running. . . . From a helicopter overhead Fire Commissioner Quinn watched it happen, watched as gangs of as many as 500 blacks, mostly teen-agers, roamed the west side looting and starting fires. No accident, no spontaneous demonstration could have spread the flames so far and so rapidly. Only men who had prepared thoroughly and well in advance.

"Where would these men get this much gasoline and fire bombs," demands Chief Prohaska, "to start fires on four major streets? You couldn't do it in five hours." But somebody did it and made a good job of it, too.

"They supplied us with plenty of fires," says Prohaska ruefully. . . .

Just getting the firemen to the fires presented major problems. Ordinarily the fire stations are manned by three shifts, only one of which is on duty at a time. When the burning started, every man not already working was called to report at the fire academy on De Koven street. From there they were thrown into combat. Some rode on a few spare pieces of apparatus. Many traveled in borrowed CTA buses. Some men contrived to stop by at their regular stations to pick up their fire clothes; others already had a spare fire coat and helmet in their cars. Officers rounded up what men they could find, and men worked under officers they had never known. . . .

But the fire was not the worst of it. The worst was the people who swarmed through the streets, attacking the firemen with stones and bricks, trying to shove the men away from the hoses, stealing axes and pike poles from the trucks. Six youths threatened to beat up the driver and steal Lieutenant Maul's hook and ladder truck. Chief Prohaska was attacked by a man with a knife. (The attacker fared badly. "When a man threatens my life," says Prohaska, a husky ex-boxer, "he's fooling with his own.")

Some rioters, not content with rocks and knives, used guns to snipe at firemen and police. You could see the muzzle flashes in the dark doors and windows. Walter Rzonca, a fire-department engineer, was shot in the leg. A sniper drew a bead on Patrolman Frederick Pirjevec in the

Fillmore police station parking lot and shot him in the left arm. At times the sniper fire grew so intense that the firemen were pinned down like infantrymen in a war, flat on the ground while bullets whistled over them, until the police moved in.

And always, as they fought the walls of fire, was the uncertainty, the unpredictability of the flames and of the mob. "We had no idea how far this was going to go," says Lieutenant Maul.

And always the people — jostling, shoving, cursing, threatening. "They'd come dancing down the street," says Chief Prohaska, "and they'd say: 'How do you like it? We're going to burn this city down and what are you going to do about it? You can't do nothing.' And these weren't kids. These were grown men, 24 or 25 years old. All you can do is, you turn your back on them, but you feel like grabbing them and shaking them up." (Prohaska speaks from anger rather than bigotry. He takes pride in the fact that his son rooms with a black classmate at Millikin university.)

For the firemen the riots came as a shock. . . . They had been aware of a rising hostility, but usually they could still travel in neighborhoods where even the police preferred not to go. Until the night of April 5. On that night they became, not saviors of lives and property but representatives of the hated city administration, and they were stoned, cursed, and shot at. It was an unsettling experience for all of them. . . .

If it was bad for the firemen, it was worse for the police. Everyone loves a fireman — or at least they used to — but policemen arouse hostility wherever they go. Whenever they arrive on the scene with billy club and summons book, someone is going to get it in the neck and leave the encounter smouldering with resentment. Ask any motorist. American policemen have not customarily been loved, and never less so than on the night of April 5 on West Madison street.

Some policemen felt that even their commanders no longer loved them. Some believed that they were deserted out there, faced with the decision to shoot or not to shoot into the rampaging mob, and with only their sergeants and lieutenants to guide them. . . . But the brass could not be everywhere. General Dunn, who was on the streets with his men, says he saw the top commanders on the scene and working hard. . . .

Whether decided by patrolmen or by Superintendent Conlisk himself, the question of firing on the mob was fraught with danger. Many of those who jammed the streets were neighborhood residents, spectators, curiosity seekers, guilty of no crime more serious than turning out to watch the excitement. Many were children, 12 years old and even younger, and though they were plainly looting every store in sight, the police hesitated to restore them to the path of virtue with a bullet in the liver. Even if a man found nothing objectionable in shooting down children, every police officer knows that in the wake of a shooting will follow inquests, inquiries, boards of examination, and endless criticism in the press. In the climate of 1968, the weight of official and public opinion is likely to go against the policeman.

And so in most instances the police withheld their fire. Many observers praised them for their restraint, asserting that police gunfire would have goaded the mob to unimagined excesses.... But others condemned the police, declaring that repressive action would have halted the arson and looting. This stand is perhaps more easily taken after the fact than before. There were only 2,500 policemen there to control about 300,000 blacks.

In the end it was the massive use of manpower that stopped the rampage — that and the fact that the rioters grew weary from their exertions and went home to sleep. Not until 3 o'clock Friday afternoon, when disorder was already sweeping the city, did Conlisk and Mayor Daley call upon the national guard for help. The request, as it must, came in the form of an official letter which specified the guardsmen's "mission" (e.g., "protection of life and property, suppression of violence ...prevention of vandalism and looting") and in which geographic areas they were to operate....

Unlike many general officers in the national guard, Dunn is no politician. He is instead a disciplinarian, a successful lawyer, a practicing Roman Catholic, and a competent soldier. He knew what had to be done and how he intended to do it.

"The arson is the toughest nut to crack," he says, "because the arsonist is not visible. He operates in shadows and back alleys." But he can be flushed out, given enough manpower. Dunn had 7,079 troops. "The looting you stop by clearing the streets. Then you send men into buildings and clear them. And you keep everyone out of the area."

That's what eventually happened, though it took some stern measures. One MP platoon loosed a few rounds to suppress sniper fire in the Mother Cabrini project at Division and Laramie, but mostly they did the job without shooting. Dunn prefers tear gas and nauseating gas, which the guard used to disperse peace demonstrators who marched on Dunn's headquarters in the Chicago avenue armory. Although it may shock public sensibilities, most military men would rather incapacitate a man with tear gas than wound him with a bullet. This time, curiously, there was little outcry against the use of chemical agents, and the guard has seldom enjoyed better public relations.

But the guard did not turn the tide alone. At the height of the rioting, besides Dunn's 7,000 men and Conlisk's 2,500 in the west side riot
area, the city deployed 2,000 firemen with 100 pieces of apparatus and
1,000 sanitation workers. And even that wasn't enough. On Saturday
afternoon Conlisk asked Mayor Daley to request the help of federal
troops, and at 11:30 P.M. the first of 5,000 United States army men
arrived. By Sunday morning, the worst had already ended, but the presence of these 5,000 hard-nosed troops, many of them veterans of Viet
Nam combat, exerted a valuable psychological force.

Saturday night's rioting, though not so bad as Friday's, still caused
enough mischief. Madison street burned for the second night, and on
Roosevelt road nearly 40 buildings blazed between Kedzie and Homan
avenues. Again the firemen and police were exposed to sniping. Again
the looters roamed through the stores like legitimate shoppers, taking
what they wanted or could carry, wheeling it off down the street in
shopping carts. Many stores were stripped absolutely bare. What the
mob didn't take they destroyed or burned on the spot.

All sorts of reasons were later advanced to explain or excuse this
looting. It was said the blacks were looting because they had always
yearned for these goods while being denied the means to buy them; they
looted because the storekeepers had tricked them into signing usurious
instalment contracts or sold them shoddy goods or lived away from their
businesses and never used any of their profits to benefit the neighborhood. Some theorized that the blacks broke into the stores to destroy
the records of their indebtedness.

But perhaps the most likely explanation for looting, offered by a
couple of Ohio State university sociologists, is that — in this sort of time
and place — it just doesn't strike the participants as immoral. Here was
the whole city going up in flames, and here were all those lovely television sets and all that lovely liquor and all the furniture and nylons
and canned peas — deserted. The merchants had just run off and left the
stuff there. Why, it would almost be a sin to leave it lying around where
it might be damaged. So they just stepped through the store windows
and picked it up and saved it.

Yet despite their sudden and easy acquisition of liquor and canned
peas and television sets, it was the black man who paid in the end. Of
the seven who died, all were black. Of the 500 injured and 2,931 arrested, virtually all were black. Two hundred and thirty families were
driven from their homes, and all were black. One hundred and seventy-
five buildings were destroyed by fire, and almost all were in the black
ghetto, serving black people. Dan's Dollar Variety Store, Lane's Wom-

en's Shop, Neisner Brothers' Five & Dime, Imperial theater, Robert Hall Clothing, Certified Food store, S & R Liquor store—no matter how generous or penurious their owners—could no longer serve their black customers if they were burned to the ground. Some merchants had been gouging the poor for years and deserved what they got, but others had been good friends to the black man. Some, indeed, were black themselves but saw their stores put to the torch nevertheless, though they had scrawled the words "Soul Brother" on their windows, which was supposed to grant them immunity. And many of the businesses carried no insurance. "Who will give it to you?" asked one burned-out automobile dealer.

And so, if the blacks did it, the blacks suffered for it. And in this lies a sort of poetic justice—if you can take any satisfaction from poetic justice.

The Post-Mortem

One of the happiest aspects of a race riot is that it supplies food for critics on both sides of the ideological fence. From it the white supremacist can argue with perfect correctness that it all goes to show the need for quicker and more effective repression. He might also add that the more you give them, the more they want and the less grateful they become. The advocate of civil rights (which today means Negro rights, American Indian rights not yet having come into vogue and Jewish rights being considered a dead issue) can argue with equal probity that the riots proved the need for fewer restraints upon the black and more assistance. . . .

To make any sense out of the riot, you need all the help you can get. Your opinion can shift with the passage of events and the revelation of additional facts. Mayor Daley, for instance, as the west side was about to explode in flames, pleaded for peace. "Let's show the United States and the world what the citizenry of Chicago is made of," he said. Later, when it turned out that the citizenry of Chicago was made in large part out of hatred and terror, he committed every man he could find to combat and called for 12,000 troops to back them up. He, himself, supported them with all his heart. . . .

The practice of shooting looters has a long and honorable history, dating back to the San Francisco earthquake of 1906 and before, and no one had ever thought to criticize it. But now for the first time the looters had a measure of sympathy—almost the sanction—of a large part of society. They were identified with the black community, toward which large numbers of whites felt a new sense of guilt and obligation. Many whites were angry; many were scared.... But for every angry, terrified white man, there was one who wanted to help the blacks. Thousands donated food — 220 tons of it — and clothing for the riot victims (though it was generally thought prudent to get black men to drive the relief trucks into the ghetto)....

Besides, it's not as easy as it sounds to shoot the right man in a riot. Under a departmental order issued by former Police Supt. O. W. Wilson, policemen mustn't fire into crowds or over the heads of crowds (except when ordered to do so by an officer above the rank of captain), nor may they fire warning shots where they might hit a bystander nor may they shoot into buildings or through doors unless their quarry is clearly visible. That just about rules out most of the possible shooting on the west side that night. And any policeman, knowing of this order, knowing that he might have to answer for it at a trial, could be forgiven for keeping the safety on his pistol.

The national guard, on the other hand, suffered from no such dilemma about the use of firearms. Despite a recent report that the Pentagon had ordered guardsmen to carry nothing but blanks on riot duty, Dunn declared firmly that his men would be armed with live ammunition and the authority to use it. "There's nothing worse than a bluff in this game," says Dunn.

The guard emerged from the riot looking pretty good, and so did the firemen and police.... The blacks wound up worse off than ever — with fewer stores and homes, with buildings still more dilapidated, with almost 3,000 blacks jailed. Two months later some of them still waited in their cells, waited for bonds, waited for hearings, waited for someone to tell them what to do....

Undoubtedly Chicago had failed to do its homework in preparation for the riot, and yet who could have guessed that this would happen here? Detroit, Newark, Cleveland, Washington, but surely not Chicago. And yet it did happen here, and people are still trying to figure out why.

For Thinking, Talking, Writing

Although this article is a description of a particular riot in one American city, it describes quite thoroughly both the background and the process of rioting that has been taking place at various times in many major cities in the United States. Now that you have read this report, try to analyze the situation as it happened and answer the following questions:

1. Should the police have used their guns more than they did to control the rioters? Why or why not?
2. Can you think of things that might have been done to *prevent* this riot — and other riots?
3. What do you think is the significance of the fact that rioting has almost become an expected part of American life? What does it *mean?*
4. Do you consider rioting the most dangerous, the most destructive kind of violence we have in the United States today, or are there other kinds that are worse?

The Real Theater of the Absurd: Wrestling

F. K. Plous, Jr.

... Wrestling — yes, wrestling — is enjoying its greatest era since the glorious days of the early '50s, when television made everyone wrestling-conscious and arenas were stuffed all over America....

Wrestling as *sport* is in a rather moribund state. What is vibrantly alive is wrestling as *show,* wrestling as *spectacle,* wrestling — in other words — as *theater.*

It may even be a form of guerrilla theater, for the people around the ring ... are chiefly of one class, watching a dramatization inside the ropes of some of their class's private fears, frustrations and hates. Sociologists are fond of calling this class "lower middle," and sometimes they pronounce those words with a sneer.

It would be better to forget the sneering, however, for the love of violence is not confined to this class.... It would be better to admit that these people are having fun — perhaps a lot more fun than their self-appointed superiors at a "real" theater. Here ... there are heroes to cheer, heroes bigger than life itself. And there are villains so evil, so hulking and ugly and mean, that only a massed scream of hatred from the crowd and a salvo of trash and litter from the balconies are sufficient to express the contempt in which they are held.

This audience is not subtle; delicate shadings of meaning are lost here. Emotions are simple, straightforward: One of the wrestlers is the goodguy; he is to be cheered on, worshipped, encouraged. The other wrestler is the badguy; he is to be hated, and notified of that hate, with all the ammunition in the spectator's oral armamentarium. And the contest is to be resolved in only one way: brute strength, violence, carnage.

Once aware of these basics, you're ready to watch wrestling and derive the maximum of joy from your participation as a spectator. So watch these wrestlers closely, but, more important, watch and listen to the audience.

Reprinted with permission of the author and the *Chicago Sun–Times* from *Midwest* magazine of the *Chicago Sun–Times*, January 5, 1969.

Especially the women and children. That's where the real hate is. Sometimes it seems as if Dad is along only to keep an eye on the family. Mostly it's the young girls in slacks and leather jackets and hair that looks like steel shavings on the floor of a machine shop who cluster around the entrance to the dressing room, waiting for the heroes to emerge. It's the young boys — say from 8 to 15 — who make up the largest part of the crowd that follows the wrestler to the ring. And it's the women and children who have to be quieted down by the Burns guards (all of them dressed as cops and carrying night sticks) when the badguy does something so outrageous that the fans edge forward to hold kangaroo court at ringside. When that happens it seems as if adrenalin has been released in gaseous form into the ventilating system. . . . The women and children leap to their feet, their eyes on the ring, and you hear, in distinct cadence:

WE WANT BLOOD! WE WANT BLOOD! WE WANT BLOOD!

The fans seldom see much real blood (though there was a genuine spilling of it on the night of which I speak); what is important is not the presence of absence of blood, or broken bones or torn skin. As in real theater, the illusion in wrestling is all-important: the *illusion* of violence, the *illusion* of anger, the *illusion* of intense physical pain. The wrestlers are not so much fighting as dramatizing a fight. To the spectators, the thing and the symbol of the thing are often identical.

It's all done via conventions: There is a conventional way to hit a man in the face (and a conventional way to show you've just been hit in the face); there's a conventional way to bounce a man into the corner post (and a conventional way to bounce off); there's a conventional way to stare down an opponent and threaten him (and a conventional way to show you're scared by the threat). None of this is lost on the audience.

Injuries are a good example of convention. It isn't enough that you've been hurt; you've got to *look* like you've been hurt. After a nasty fall Black Jack Lanza staggers around like Charlie Chaplin — even to the extent of crossing his eyes. Then suddenly he recovers and goes after his opponent. The stagger doesn't last long, but it shows the audience that he took a licking, and they love it. . . .

And Black Jack Lanza has his own style of whipping the fans into a synthetic rage: He always appears with his manager, Pretty Boy Bobby Heenan, who sports dyed blond hair and a red brocade dinner jacket. Heenan hops around the ropes, threatening Lanza's opponents and enjoining the ringsiders to do likewise.

Absurd, you say? Do they really pay to go and watch this stuff? Are these fans serious? Go and ask some of them as they wait outside the dressing room for their heroes. A young girl in slacks and leather jacket, leaning on the wooden barrier, doesn't even take her eyes off the doorway when you ask her who's her favorite.

"Black Jack," she says, not even breaking rhythm as she pops her gum. "But I love 'em all.". . .

It may not be the noblest variety of hero worship around, but it's hero worship all the same. Moose Cholak is fast becoming the kind of wrestler who inspires a following, especially among the kids. Except for his enormous pectorals, which make him a sort of human Parthenon, Moose looks like he might be the proprietor of some enormously successful kiddie show on television. Attired in his $350 custom-tailored silk-and-satin robe of gold and blue (the colors of his *alma mater,* Chicago Vocation), Moose steps gingerly into the ring and is immediately waylaid by a posse of autograph-hunters. "Me, Moose!" they shout. "Mine, Moose! Sign mine!" "Hey, Moose — please?" The ringside is a forest of waving programs thrust forward for the hero's signature.

When Moose is introduced it is the kids who supply most of the healthy cheering, and when his opponent, a smaller man named Johnny Kace, is introduced, they fill the Amphitheatre with boos. And when Moose scores on his opponent the kids add their own needle:

"Ya don' like dat, do ya, Johnny?"

"C'mon, Moose — the bear hug!"

"Kill 'im, Moose!"

Moose is big, and he looks big, but it isn't size alone that makes a man a headliner. It's his ability to put on a show and give good entertainment. Some of the wrestlers — especially the young ones who aren't established yet — try to make it on theatrics alone. These tactics inspire momentary shouts of approval, but they don't really attract a big gate. The big pullers have a way of handling themselves and their opponents that transcends mere tactics. Dick the Bruiser, himself a headliner of no mean proportions, says most of the really good performers can express the essence of violence just by wrestling.

"Naturally," he says, "you gotta be an amateur psychologist. The headliners don't have to put on a show, 'cause everything they do is a show. Everything they do you notice.". . .

Professionalism is what the Bruiser calls the key to this game. That means you not only have to wrestle well — you have to look as if you're wrestling well. You have to move, and to move like that you have to train. "All the top men work out every day," the Bruiser says. "You have to work out to be professional.". . .

Not a bad bunch of boys, actually. You could get to like them

strictly on the basis of their talk, their brimming health and the seriousness with which they do their unusual work. But the fans are there for
another reason. They want the violence. A 22-year-old resident of Lake-
view was candid enough to say, "We want blood — that's what we come
to see."

He's right. You can hear the audience being satisfied by the crunches
and groans. When the blood appears at last a change comes over the
crowd. They howl like dogs as the violence reaches the level of physical pain. And again, by the high pitch of the screaming, you can tell
it's the women and children who are contributing the most. A nice body
kick, and the crowd cheers. A series of punches to the face and the main-
floor spectators stand to get a better view. A butting into a corner post,
followed by a quick drubbing or an airplane spin, and they cheer for
blood. When they get it, the Burns guards go into action: The cops
come to attention, and one big black sergeant shakes his head with a
rueful smile and caresses his nightstick — which is not provided for the
mere adornment of his person. He is under no illusions about what a
mad wrestling crowd can do.

What would happen if the cops weren't there is anybody's guess.
When the match is over the crowd's enmity follows the badguy right
back to the dressing room, and the cops form a box around him to clear
the way. Hoots, jeers and hisses rain down from the northwest balcony
as the unfortunate one passes below, and a torrent of popcorn boxes,
plastic cups and epithets falls on his head. . . .

"These people are full of pep and they're animated," says the
Bruiser. "Sure, they get out of hand. Yeah, well, that's to be expected."

For Thinking, Talking, Writing

1. This article deals with the same "need for violence" that you read
   about in two of the articles in the section on the war and the draft.
   How do war and wrestling tie in as expressions of this need? What
   are the important differences between them?
2. Have you ever seen live, professional wrestling? If so, how did *you*
   react to it?
3. How does the sentence, "We want blood — that's what we came to
   see," fit in with your opinions about the human "need for violence"?
4. What do you think is the significance of the fact that, according to
   this author, it seems to be the women and children who are the most
   violent in their behavior at professional wrestling matches?

Excerpts from
"The MAD Gun Owners and Other Small Bores Primer"

Written by Larry Siegel
Illustrated by George Woodbridge

See the nice man .
He is hunting with one of his guns.
See him shoot the pretty deer.
Bang, bang, bang.
See the pretty deer's blood gush.
Gush, gush, gush.
What fun they are having!
See how happy the hunter is.
See how happy the hunter's dog is.
The pretty deer is not happy.
He is a spoil-sport.

See the nice sick man.
Sick, sick, sick.
He bought his gun through the mail.
What is he going to do now?
He is going to shoot someone he doesn't like.
Why don't the police arrest him?
Because he is not carrying a concealed weapon.
He is carrying it in the open for all to see.
Later on the police will arrest him.
After he shoots the person he doesn't like.
Aren't you glad that justice is blind?

See the gun store.
Anybody can buy a gun and ammunition here.
See the people shopping for guns.
Shop, shop, shop.
See the nice lady.
She is bargain-hunting.
She wants to do away with her husband.
Because he's no bargain.
See her buy a pistol for $8.00,
And a bullet for 9¢.
Wait, nice lady! Don't go yet! Think . . .
You forgot your green stamps!

For Thinking, Talking, Writing

1. Identify each one of the social or legal issues that these "cartoons" from MAD are commenting on.
2. State your opinion about each of these issues, and try to back up your point of view with good reasons.
3. How do gun ownership and the laws that control it relate to the topic of this section, *violence?*

A Letter from Death Row

Name: Caryl Chessman

Box No.: 66565, San Quentin, Calif.

Date: April 17, 1960

Dear Dr. _____ :

Earlier today you asked that I prepare a note setting out whether I thought I had matured, to what extent or degree, and specifically how. You said you would see me tomorrow, and asked me to have this note ready.

I'll answer your question to the best of my ability. First, doubtless the wisest thing to do is to heed Voltaire's perceptive injunction and define the term. Maturation means to me maturing and maturing signifies a growing up; that is, an ability to respond to life situations — and particularly conflict or frustration — with intelligence, without avoidable, emotion-clouding heat, anger or hate, and with a reasonable degree of prudence. The mature person must have long-range goals consistent with his skills and temperament. He must be able to relate to others and be able to sympathize with their aspirations and needs. He must be socially aware, although I do not think he must be a conformist in the opprobrious sense of that term. Rationally recognizing the imperfections in himself, in his neighbors and in his society, his dissent or protest against conditions, events or actions in which he perceives inequity should be, when made, of a constructive kind. He must recognize that there lurk primitive, violent impulses in all of us but that the advocacy or practice of violence not only demeans him as a person; it invites and begets counter-violence, solving nothing.

By such standards, have I matured during my 12-year stay on Death Row? I believe I have, markedly. Not only have I grown up by the objective and subjective test by which maturity may be measured, I have grown older. And, a not uncommon phenomenon, either physiologically or psychologically, to some extent there has been a "burning out"—of sociopathic reaction or reflex. Humanly, I still lose my temper, but increasingly (and, to be candid, as much a consequence of this aging process as self-discipline) I find myself trying to solve my problems with my pre-frontal lobes rather than smash at them — or a substitute for them — with my fists. It may be said that my basic character hasn't changed, that, figuratively, in grudging compliance with the physical and mental demands of these passing years, I simply have exchanged rapier for bludgeon out of necessity, and hence that, at bottom, my psychopathy or sociopathy merely has found a more subtle form of expression. You, Doctor, with your special psychiatric training, are far better equipped to answer this question authoritatively than I am. My answer is perhaps a rationalization: If those character traits or that personality pattern which impelled me as a youngster into violent criminal conflict with society (and myself) remain basically unaltered or cannot be excised wholly, at least I know they can be usefully directed. They can be made my servants rather than I theirs. Historical examples abound of men who, if they had been born into this period, would have been called psychopathic or sociopathic. Yet today we honor their names and admire their creativity.

As you know, I want to become a writer, and — here ego finds expression — I sincerely believe I possess the motivation, the self-discipline, the drive, the dedication and the gift of words to become a writer whose writings can enrich our literature and contribute significantly to some of the pressing social problems of our time. Yes, I am quite aware that notoriety has contributed appreciably to the success of my already published books. Yet, keep in mind, that I *did* write them, not simply talk about wanting to write. And now that it has served its purpose as both a desperately needed purgative and as a means of dramatically focusing attention on the question of the validity of the philosophy and practice of retributive justice, I am through with autobiography. This transition already has begun. In a few days my novel, *The Kid Was a Killer,* will be published. I am sure it will furnish you a useful insight into its author, just as I believe it will help the public understand the sociopath and thus encourage that public to demand that, in dealing with him, the men in your profession be relied upon rather than executioners.

I have at least enough writing projects in mind to occupy me for another 10 years. I want to do a biography of the late Jesse W. Carter, Associate Justice of the California Supreme Court, a jurist who taught me to respect the law. As well, there is a play I desire to do about François Villon, French lyric poet and gallows bird, that has contemporary relevance. Further, I am itching to do a series of three novels of today, a trilogy. And I want to try my hand at a novelette, which could be readily converted into a play, called *Autumn and Eve* and which, entertainingly, not ponderously, with a Malibu setting, would examine the relationship of man and woman in a swiftly changing world.

And what if I failed? What if I collected rejection slip after rejection slip? Well, I am certain I would not fail finally and I am quite prepared for a rough going along the way. The pertinent point, in my judgment, is that, at 38, I am old as a psychopathic hoodlum but young for a writer. Many of the world's best authors did not reach their full powers until their 50s and even their 60s.

There is irony, of course, in the fact that I am discussing the future as though I had one, as though I did not have a date with the executioner 14 days and a few odd hours hence. However, be assured, I am completely aware of that date and, statistically, of the overwhelming probabilities I shall keep it.

Accordingly, in seeking to answer your question, it appears appropriate to turn and look at the past. You know my criminal record; you know me clinically; you know me as a person; you know of my long struggle to survive.

In gauging maturity or the absence of it, a pertinent question doubtless in my case is: Deep inside, what do I *really* think of my past? Initially, I believe it is evident that I have in fact *thought* a great deal about it, tried to make some kind of sense out of it. I can't and I don't try to justify it insofar as shifting responsibility for it is concerned. It's there and always it is going to remain there (the changes have occurred in the black, overdrawn legend that has been built up in the public mind about me, where I have emerged as a slavering, snarling, sneering mocker of justice, an inhuman "monster" without a single redeeming quality).

No, I can't change my past, Doctor; I can't erase it, I can't forget it. But I can realize I was a damned fool, and admit it. My responsibility — legally adjudicated punishment and the question of guilt or innocence of my present crimes aside — does not end there, as I see it. I feel a need more fully to grasp the nature of what we can call the psychodynamics of my particular brand of folly (overtly expressed as criminality, and psychiatrically diagnosed as sociopathy). In sum, I damn well don't want to engage in any more irrational conduct, if I can avoid it. In this, obviously, I would need help — yours or someone like you who gave a damn about me and was professionally and personally willing to lend a hand. Reversing the coin, if I survived, perhaps I could be of some value to science and humanity by being a guinea pig. Tragically, my case is not atypical; there are thousands of youngsters filling reform schools, committing crimes, defiant and rebellious, who will end up in prison or shot dead or on Death Row.

Seemingly, although my awareness of this is only recent, another test of maturity in my case would be whether I would be willing to accept a commutation of sentence to life imprisonment, even without possibility of parole. Now, I would, and not because of any newly developed animal fear of death or compromise of what I define as integrity or principle. The reason (at least the conscious one) is that, realistically, I must accept the fact that, in the context of my situation, I cannot expect more at this time. Only an irrational fool would, and this is a logical first step in my effort to think and act rationally, without folly. At this juncture I might comment, editorially or philosophically, it would appear that another crucial test of maturity is that one must come to accept the fact that, by his standards, each of us will know injustice in our lives, and if, for the present, that injustice (real or imagined) is irremediable, that is not excuse or reason for us to seek what would amount to self-destruction. Restated, I do not want to wear posthumously, a self-invited martyr's robes. To the contrary, I have become convinced a mature man in my position should and must prefer to live and thus have an opportunity to prove, if he can, that those who judged him so harshly were wrong. In this way, I would be helping those who know that gas chambers and executioners should have no place in our society to demonstrate with a concrete example the validity of their thesis.

Many reporters have asked me: If I were commuted, how would I react to anonymity or relative anonymity. The notion behind the questions seems to be the suspicioned (and mistaken) belief that I have become so intoxicated by seeing my name in the headlines that, on finding myself just another prisoner, I might become so disenchanted I would attempt something sensationally irresponsible simply to feed my (conjectured) craving for notoriety. This is perfect but understandable nonsense. I have had my belly full and more of headlines and sensationalisms. Inwardly, I wince every time I read one of those breathless and indignant accounts of myself as a cunning "fiend" with an oversized ego who, the writers would have it, cares nothing for his fellows and seeks only the false glamor of being a notorious character. Such reporting reveals far more about those who grind it out than it remotely does about me. There is nothing I desire more than to get out of the headlines. The place I want to see my name in the future is not on the front pages of a newspaper but in the title page of books. Finally, whatever my past, I want to be a man who can respect himself and who has earned the hard way the respect of others. I do *not* want the synthetic fame of a psychopath.

Respectfully,
CHESSMAN
(Row)

For Thinking, Talking, Writing

This letter was written only two weeks before Caryl Chessman was executed in the gas chamber at San Quentin prison, after spending twelve years on Death Row. Mr. Chessman had spent those twelve years educating himself and doing a great deal of writing — and, obviously, a great deal of thinking. His letter raises important questions about both the definition and the purpose of capital punishment in our society:

1. Capital punishment, like war, is one form of legal violence practiced by society as a whole. Is there, in your opinion, a *real* difference between legal violence, decided upon by society and carried out by its agents, and illegal violence, practiced by those who do not agree with society? If so, what is the difference?

2. Mr. Chessman makes the statement that "the advocacy or practice of violence not only demeans... a person; it invites and begets counter-violence, solving nothing." Do you think this is true for the individual? Is it also true for society as a whole? Why or why not?

3. Mr. Chessman talks about "...those who know that gas chambers and executioners should have no place in our society...." This statement directly attacks capital punishment as an institution. What is *your* opinion about capital punishment? Should it be continued in our society? If so, why? If not, why not?

Liquidated Are the Meek...

Eric Hoffer

It is a paradox that the most fateful characteristics of our violent age is the non-violence, the incredible submissiveness, of the victims. Hitler and Stalin liquidated millions of men, women and children without meeting serious resistance.

In this country at present, millions of peaceful folk in city streets and ghettos, in suburbs and on campuses are submitting meekly to robbers and muggers, to black and white ideological thugs, and to foul-mouthed insults and threats. No one hits back, and hardly anyone speaks out loud in outrage.

Well-meaning people are warning us not to "over-react" against those who have turned our cities and schools into savage jungles. We are warned that action by the majority would be vigilantism, that it is the duty of the police to endure taunts and provocations without hitting back, and that we shall not have peace until we have cleansed our souls of racial arrogance and callous smugness.

The other day, at Berkeley, a class of 250 students was addressed by an intruding Negro student as mother . . . and warned not to come to class next day or have their throats slit. The punk was not thrown out. The professor, a famous teacher, begged the intruder to leave the class.

Would it have been over-reaction or vigilantism had the class rushed the foul-mouthed, bushy-faced punk and thrown him out? Was it sheer humaness that kept the famous professor meek in the face of insults and threats?

The students and the professors were plainly afraid. They would probably maintain that they practiced forbearance. When cowardice becomes a fashion its adherents are without number, and it masquerades as forbearance, reasonableness, conscience, and whatnot.

It is amazing how nobly philosophical we become when we have to rationalize our cowardice. We love our enemies, extol altruism, and see self-assertion as the root of evil.

The unavoidable impression is that it is the meekness of the majority that incites and fuels the violence around us. The muggers in the streets, the rioters and looters in the ghettos, the black and white hoodlums on the campuses are all on the lookout for tame enemies and tame battlegrounds.

We do not know what's ahead of us. It is hardly likely that the violent minorities will abruptly change their way. There is a vague feeling that a day of wrath is waiting around the corner, when the saturated resentment of the long-suffering majority crystallizes in retaliation. It is impossible to say where and how the reaction will start.

For Thinking, Talking, Writing

1. Mr. Hoffer states in this article that it is *cowardice* that prevents the majority of people from retaliating against the minority in our society who engage in violence. Do you agree with him, or not? Why? (Consider other possibilities before you answer: for instance, could our failure to fight back indicate that most people find violence repugnant? Could we, perhaps, have deep guilt feelings about the way minority groups have been treated in the past, so that we think it would not be "right" to fight back? What other possibilities can you think of?)

2. How do you think *you* would have reacted to the incident at Berkeley that Mr. Hoffer describes? Try to project yourself emotionally into that situation. Would your impulse have been to throw out the disrupting student? To ignore him? To get out — to run? If you had had the impulse to throw him out, do you think you would have acted on it? Why or why not?

3. Mr. Chessman stated in his "Letter from Death Row" that "the advocacy or practice of violence...invites and begets counter-violence. ..." Yet Mr. Hoffer points out that there is very *little* "counter-violence" going on in our society as yet. Do you agree with him that "a day of wrath is waiting around the corner"? Why or why not?

Make Love Not War in Your Own Life

Barbara Kevles

When America watched the violence televised from the Democratic Convention, most of the affluent made no connection between Chicago and their own lives. How absurd! Acts of violence happen not only beyond the hedges, the picket fences, the front doors of the middle class, but smack in their own homes. In perfectly proper families, parents beat children to a pulp; teen-agers wreck the family car on purpose; sons and daughters are evicted from their homes.

"Proper" families breed violence by substituting status symbols for love. Hugs, approval, encouragement are earned by children for doing things: keeping a stylish appearance at the family affair, scoring high grades — and are earned by parents for giving things: a Corvair for Christmas, a fun fur for the college campus. When *things* are substituted for expressing feelings, families bottle up what they want to say. Talk bottled long enough explodes into violence.

Violence: Last Resort at Communication

Violence is expressed in many ways. *The Oxford Dictionary* defines it: "Physical force to inflict injury or damage upon persons or property." How can a nice girl from a nice home destroy her mother's kitchen? How can a well brought-up boy knife a brother?

Nice girls and boys are better trained at keeping up appearances than at expressing their feelings. To most of us the language of pain is as foreign as Ubangi. Bankrupt of words to defend feelings, those hurt seem to have only one alternative to get their point across — violence. Violence is a message that often is not understood.

Some authorities extend the definition of violence beyond the physical to include the psychological impact: A white boy brings home a Negro girl and is disowned.

A girl caught sleeping with a married man is commanded by her parents to shoot her dog and, instead, shoots herself.

There are infinite ways of inflicting pain without touching. This covert violence avoids the issue. We don't have to confront the people we depend upon with our grievances. This is underground guerrilla warfare in the recreation room.

Rickie can't wait for next fall because then she moves out of the posh Manhattan apartment shared with mother (a divorcée) and into the dormitory at New York University. She and her mother battle daily. After one particularly brutal argument, mother explodes emotionally and sends Rickie to an aunt in Long Island for the summer. Long Island is Squaresville. Rickie is boxed in, frustrated, abandoned. One afternoon, she stood before the bathroom mirror and gulped down a quinine pill, then another, then several. But when the pain became excruciating, she called the doctor. Why had she tried suicide?

Rickie tried to get through to her mother, but mother discouraged the criticism with "Because..." or "I'm your mother, that's why..." or "As long as you live under my roof..." We are not taught how to criticize our family or, for that matter, ourselves. The rage that had bottled up for years inside Rickie finally turned on her.

Rickie receives help now from a psychiatrist twice a week. Through these sessions she is coming to understand how much she needs her mother and, what she didn't know, *how much her mother needs her.*

The first time Rickie's mother visited her in the hospital when she was recovering from her suicide attempt, she confessed failure as a parent. They both cried. She asked her mother to trust her even when she is making mistakes, on the faith she'll outgrow her hangups. Rickie says, "Our meeting was like a scene from a soap opera, but we've never been the same since."

Is talking about a problem a solution or a stopgap? Are we born with innate violence? Dr. Frederick Wertham, an authority on human violence, says, "No. Violence is learned behavior. It is not an instinct like sex or hunger. Animals do not kill for hate, spite, revenge, sadism or greed. Most important of all, they never systematically kill large numbers of the same species. So when we speak of massacres, extermination camps, mass bombings... we should not refer to the 'bestial' in man. It isn't the beast, it is man itself...."

Most animals have an inborn mechanism that prevents such beasts of prey as wolves or lions from killing members of their pack. Man has such an instinctive drive, too. Unfortunately, this instinct against killing his kind has been smothered by his deluxe weapon arsenal. Man's power to kill man has grown beyond his control.

But, we are not *inherently* violent. Wertham states that when a person prepares to threaten or carry out a violent act, a part of his lower brain is stimulated. But the violent urge, Wertham stresses, "can be inhibited by higher centers in the brain, the cerebral cortex."

How can we control violence in America when television, magazines, newspapers continually tell us violence is masculine?

And what is a man? Everywhere a boy looks, in most of the mass media, to be a man is to be cool, show no emotions, use physical violence. If a boy learns he-men solve problems with fists, why shouldn't he? Yet when John Glenn returned after the first man-flight in space, he cried when he saw his wife. One may catch the John Glenns of our society in a two-minute news clip, at best, while the groovy nighttime serials feature the hand-to-holster heroes in saturation. Those are society's models — men who, when they kill, never grimace or cry. So, boys try to be men with their fists.

Anthony Storr, one of Britain's most articulate psychiatrists and a man steeped in the studies of ethology — animal instinct under natural conditions — defines aggression as "a drive as innate, as natural and as powerful as sex." Freud branded the aggressive drive as what led man toward destruction and death. Today Storr and others disagree with Freud. They emphasize aggression is essential for survival and mastery of the environment. Storr writes in his book, *On Aggression,* "In adult life, the aggressive drive which in childhood enables the individual to break free of parental domination serves to preserve and define identity." On constructive control of aggression's destructive impulses, Storr guardedly warns, "There is no clear dividing line between those forms of aggression which we all deplore and those which we must not disown if we are to survive."

It's startling to speak of love in the same breath with aggression, but the facts prove aggression is essential to lovemaking. The "passive woman in sex" myth is very unsatisfactory if followed. The best possible outlet for the ever-increasing stockpile of aggression is love. Conrad Lorenz, father of modern ethology, thinks only animals capable of intense aggression are capable of intense personal ties and love since the aggressive instinct can be the energy for violence, or, redirected, the same energy can be transformed into acts of love.

In the course of writing this article, I participated involuntarily in a revealing act of violence. A friend, Barbara Connell, her husband and I were watching President Johnson announce his latest bid for peace in Vietnam and his decline to run again for the President. I persisted in making asides.

When it was all over, Barbara, who is a Democrat's Democrat, verbally attacked me, "You weren't listening from the top. You're the kind of person who approaches a situation with preconceived notions. You're one of millions of negative people who see nothing good about this country."

Rather than give vent to my anger at her, I stalked out of the house and spent the next half hour walking. When I returned, I refused to talk about Johnson, the war or my cousins in Vietnam. Barbara tried to force me to say what was bothering me. I wouldn't. I had to be polite. Barbara grabbed my shoulders and shook me, shouting, "Do you want to be my friend, do you? Then tell me what you feel."

Then, though fearful of losing the friendship, I came out and accused Barbara of maligning me. She apologized and I apologized, too, for being supersensitive. Once we said what we *really felt,* once we aired hostilities, the tension eased. After arguing, we both felt a deeper communication, a sense of ultra-frequency contact — a real high.

From this, an epiphany: It's not enough to cool it, to not act violently. The way to love other people is to express what we feel — anger and love — without aiming to hurt feelings. Open but reverent communication is how to make love in our lives.

How to Deal with Violence in Your Own Life

1. Stop playing the role of victim in your family. Step out of the role of child-student and take the role of guru-adult. Start a rap going with your parents over mutual pain points. If they've criticized your appearance, for example, compliment them on their concern for your well-being, then criticize them by opening with "I know you didn't mean to, but..." "You might have said..." "Did you consider my feelings when you...?" As long as you both show respect for each other, very difficult areas can be discussed rationally.

2. When someone hurts you, express what you feel immediately. Say: "I was embarrassed by"

"You put me down when"

"I was jealous of"

"I was hurt by"

"I tried to... but you wouldn't listen."

3. When you criticize someone else, be prepared to take some artillery fire in return. It is frightening, sometimes terrifying, to have it out because when you attack, you must also expose your vulnerabilities. Don't hold back. As poet Kahlil Gibran said: "Pain breaks the shell of understanding."

4. When you become so enraged you cannot speak in normal conversational terms, YELL!

5. If you are always put down at home, find an outlet elsewhere that will give you an intake of self-esteem. Educated people are desperately needed to help the ghetto poor. Inquire into projects where you could make a real contribution and boost *your* ego.

6. If you hear the same criticisms time and again, don't tune out on your critic. Confront and try to discover the real reasons. You may learn you have a fault, or that it is a sign of insecurity in the other person projected on you.

7. Read Dr. Fredrick Wertham's book, *A Sign for Cain: An Exploration of Human Violence; Joy* by William C. Schutz, and *Human Aggression* by Anthony Storr.

8. Whoever you are, when you have the urge to cry, *cry!*

9. When you sense you are the victim of some form of covert violence, don't ignore the fact. It may pain you to know someone dislikes you, but try to find out why.

10. When you want to express anger, begin with "I feel," not "You are." Direct accusations put people on the defensive at a time when you want them to be most open.

11. Stop pretending movie and television violence has no relationship to you. Evaluate fast-draw and fist-to-chin solutions: Do they really work as problem-*solving* devices?

12. If violence has already erupted between you and someone else, remember it is a form of communication. Try to tune in to the message: *Who* is trying to tell you *what?* That's a beginning.

For Thinking, Talking, Writing

Analyze each of the suggestions the author makes for "How to Deal with Violence in Your Own Life." Which ones have you tried? Which ones make you uncomfortable, and why? Which ones, if any, do you disapprove of? If you have the opportunity, try out the suggestions that seem to be applicable to your own situation and report back on how they worked.

THE BLACKS
AND
THE WHITES:

where are we going?

Introduction

Abraham Lincoln made the following statement in 1858, before the Civil War:

> When you have succeeded in dehumanizing the Negro; when you have put him down and made it impossible for him to be but as the beasts of the field; when you have extinguished his soul in this world and placed him where the ray of hope is blown out as in the darkness of the damned, are you quite sure that the demon you have roused will not turn and rend you?

Now, more than a hundred years later, the demon has turned and threatens to rend our society. The black people in the United States are deeply disillusioned and very angry, *and they are doing something about it.*

Many white people ask, "What do Negroes want?" A survey by FORTUNE magazine in 1968 indicated what any thinking person would know anyway: that Negroes, like whites, want good education for their children and themselves; good jobs; a decent neighborhood to live in. They want *real equality* of opportunity — a chance to participate in the American dream.

The difference between today and the past, however, is that black people are no longer satisfied with delayed promises and studies of the problem and commitments to gradual integration. Integration itself has become an issue which is largely irrelevant, as black America has become more and more angered by white racism and has begun to cultivate a black racism of its own. The FORTUNE survey indicated that only 12 percent of urban blacks were interested in complete integration; most wanted only integration of *opportunity* for jobs, education, and housing. And Mrs. Shirley Chisholm, the first Negro woman to sit in Congress, stated:

> The black people are no longer interested in a lot of conferences and meetings, or surveys and graphs and study commissions. We've been analyzed and graphed and surveyed for too long. We need

action now. We want to give white America the chance to show that there is such a thing as equality of opportunity, regardless of race, creed, or color.

Read — think — talk — write. Perhaps when you finish this section, you will have some ideas of your own to help answer the question, "Where are we going?"

After all there is but one race — humanity.
—George Moore, *Bending of the Bough*

A black man says:

Charlie Doesn't Even Know
His Daily Racism
Is a Sick Joke

Bob Teague

Bob Teague, who wrote this article and the recently published book,
Letters To A Black Boy, *is now a television newscaster in New York City.*

Mr. Teague was raised in a ghetto, but a talent for football and good grades in high school got him a scholarship to the University of Wisconsin. He was offered four tryouts by professional football teams at the end of his college football career as a star halfback and a member of the All-Big Ten team, but he decided to go into journalism instead, although a black man's chances as a journalist were slim.

He has been successful at journalism, as he was in football. His wide range of experiences and his perception and sensitivity make the article you are about to read extremely valuable as a statement of the problems and the pain of the black man in the predominantly white society of the United States today.

If you look at the racial problem from a black man's point of view, you can see the jokes as well as the injustices. Which is to say that you can then understand this: The underlying syndrome that must be attacked is much more subtle than a white policeman's nightstick. It's more like a topsy-turvy vaudeville routine in which all the funny lines come from the straight men.

A favorite comic theme among the "concerned and enlightened" elements of white society is "Let's Stamp Out Racial Hatred." Hoo boy! Hatred has very little to do with the central problem, Charlie. What is done to and withheld from black folk day by day in this country is based on neither hate nor horror. On the contrary. It is coldly impersonal. Like the brains of precocious computers.

Simply put, it seems to me that white folk are convinced, deep in their bones, that the way they run this melting pot — with black folk unmelted at the bottom — is nothing more than the natural order of things.

What happens quite naturally, for example, is that a black *bon vivant* who shows up in a clean shirt at a posh restaurant is approached by white customers who beg him to get them a good table, please. There is nothing malicious about it. They simply think of black men in clean shirts as waiters.

Similarly, a black man caught on foot near a public parking lot is likely to be buttonholed by a pale proud patrician who wants his limousine fetched in a hurry.

And even the most militant white egalitarians are prone to compliment one another by saying, "That's real white of you, Edgar." Obviously, the notion that anything white is inherently superior to its black counterpart is built into the white American idiom, and thus into the white American mind.

Do you think it's accidental that the bad guys in Western movies are the ones in black sombreros? . . .

I am exposed to the same basic joke almost every time I walk into an all-white apartment building to keep an appointment with a friend. I see panic in the eyes of the pale residents coming out as I go in — trying to recall whether they locked their doors. And the doorman himself seems to be trying to remember the standard procedure for What to Do Until the Cops Come.

Although it has taken me many years to reach this point of view — perhaps because I managed a getaway of sorts from the ghetto — I understand now that neither the doorman nor the rest of white America are motivated by hate. To their way of thinking, the business of keeping black folk at a comfortable distance is not a matter of racism, not a choice between right and wrong. It's like fearing the bomb, saluting the flag and sending a card on Mother's Day. It's an automatic reflex action. In other words, no emotion of any kind is necessarily involved.

Consider, for example, those magazine and newspaper advertisements for "flesh-colored" bandages. The color they mean blandly ignores the color of most flesh on this planet. Mine in particular. But the top bananas who dreamed up that bit would be sorely aggrieved if someone called them racists. Some of those chaps are probably card-carrying fellow-travelers in the N.A.A.C.P., and their wives probably sent food to the poor people's shantytown in Washington. Their "flesh-colored" bandages are merely a profitable manifestation of a common assumption among white folk: White skin is what human flesh is *supposed* to look like. Anything else — black skin certainly — is irrelevant. Sort of a whimsical goof by Mother Nature.

How else can a black man explain those ubiquitous cosmetic ads showing a pale proud beauty using the facial lotion that promises to give her "the natural look"? The joke here is that this same beauty, and those who swear by "flesh-colored" bandages spend as much time in the sun as possible to darken their natural looks. They even buy chemical tans in bottles. And did you ever hear a commercial Goldilocks say, "Goodness gracious, my tan is much too dark"? . . .

My experience has been that most white folk are so caught up in the seductive *mystique* of White Power that their brains are rarely brushed by the notion that the "natural order" in this country is in any way forced and unnatural.

Only last week one of my white friends — to be known here as Charlie — called my attention to one of those "flesh-colored" ads. Although Charlie is well past 35 and literate and had read similar ads over the years, he was seeing it clearly for the first time.

"Man, look at this," he said, wearing an embarrassed grin. "They even insult you in the ads, don't they?"

Charlie's insight is not yet complete, however. If it ever is, he'll say "we" instead of "they.". . .

All of which is to say that white folk are immersed in such a totally racist climate that — like fish born in the ocean — they have no reason to suspect for a moment that they might be all wet. Wherever they look in this society, there are white institutions, habits, signs, symbols, myths and realities that reinforce their notion that black folk rank somewhere between King Kong and Frankenstein's monster on the scale of lower forms of life. . . .

[On] television . . . of course, white folk control both the medium and the message.

If a superintelligent visitor from another planet were to deduce, strictly from television, the nature of the 22 million black pariahs who exist in the crevices of this society, he undoubtedly would get an impression that was 99-44/100 per cent pure nonsense. From the electronic evidence of omission, projected around the clock, the visitor might gather that black women are rather dull and sexless creatures. Apparently nothing known to science or Madison Avenue can help black girls to develop "the skin you love to touch." With scarcely a blond hair to call their own, they obviously are not the kind of broads who "have more fun." And without one toothbrush among them, they have no interest in the leading toothpaste that "gives your mouth sex appeal."

Black men are equally irrelevant among the fauna of the natural TV order. It is tacitly suggested, for instance, that they are socially backward — black Square Johns, so to speak. Otherwise they would be seen driving "the low-priced luxury car" to seduce more swinging chicks.

It's true that black satellites are sometimes seen in TV dramatic series, but usually as cardboard characters with virtually no lives of their own. They are perpetually in orbit around the full-blooded white supermen who perform brain surgery, fall in love, bounce children on their knees and worry about middle-aged spread.

My impression is that many white folk would like to portray black people in a more sophisticated manner. But, alas, they cannot forget all those Tarzan movies of their youth. These made it official that black folk are natural-born spear carriers, dangerous savages and beasts of the white man's burdens.

Then, too, there are all those cannibal cartoons in the slick magazines put out by and for white folks. Who wouldn't be somewhat repelled by a black gourmet whose favorite entree is fricassee of Charlie?

Such examples of how black folk are systematically misrepresented or shut out from the stuff that the American Dream is made of are virtually endless. The smiling faces on greeting cards are never black faces. Department-store mannikins don't resemble anyone you are likely to meet in the ghetto. And all plastic angels who symbolize the Christmas spirit are pink.

The net effect of these deceptions is that each tailor-made reality buttresses the other in the minds of whites. This explains in large measure why so many white folk are genuinely baffled by the grumbling and violence in the ghettos. Which is the basis for the popular white joke that ends with the punch line: "What do you people want?"

When black folk bother to spell out the answer to that riddle—with expectations that can only be described as naive — the consistent white responses add up to rather predictable pranks: another study of black frustration; another conference on brotherhood; another million-dollar crash program to tear down an old ghetto and replace it with a new ghetto.

As one of the best buffoons in the Federal Government observed after the riots last summer: "The very existence of the ghetto is un-American." But that line was much too oblique for most of white America to comprehend.

I am not suggesting that white folk don't even try. On the contrary. They conscientiously integrate a school here and there — even if it means doing something silly, like busing half the youngsters from A to Z and the other half vice versa. At the same time, however, they automatically prevent black families from buying or renting homes near the school in question. And they bar black folk from the jobs that pay the kind of money that would enable them to afford such a pristine neighborhood.

But getting back to how hard white people try, I witnessed one of their truly valiant efforts against insuperable odds this year. The occasion was the hint dropped by the President's Commission on Civil Disorders that the "ghetto is created by whites, maintained by white institutions and condoned by white society."

Most white folk were truly sorry about that. They rushed from their enclaves of affluence to the nearest ghetto to make amends. However, once in the wilds of Harlem and its scattered subdivisions, they simply could not resist telling corny jokes. Like the one Hitler told as he toured a concentration camp: "Jews stink."

What the Fuhrer was smelling, of course, was Nazism. And in America the heady aroma of racism is equally confusing to the thin straight noses of the master race. Otherwise it would not be possible for those deadpan middle-class comedians to come up with such boffos as: "Why can't the black man pull himself up by his bootstraps like the other minorities have done?" While guarding the boots with bull-dog tenacity day and night....

From my experience with white storekeepers over the years, I judge that many white merchants make a special hard-sell effort when a black customer shows up — to unload whatever raunchy merchandise they have in stock.

Example: One of my soul sisters overheard a white housewife chewing out a white butcher for putting rotten meat on display. "Can't you see it's not fit to eat?" she demanded.

"Lady, this is not for you," the butcher said matter-of-factly. "It's for them. Believe me, they don't know any better. They're like pigs."...

... [A] public confession was made recently ... by a self-declared white liberal — a Northern youth who had risked his life as a field worker in the civil-rights movement in Mississippi. Out of curiosity, he said, he took a trip on the LSD express. And the jig was up. Under the influence of the so-called mind-expanding drug, he realized for the first time that, in the Deep South of his soul, he honestly believed that black people were not now, never had been and never could be as deserving as whites. The immediate result of his insight was a nervous breakdown.

That young man was neither the first nor the last of his breed. The mass media these days are overpopulated with white liberals who portray themselves as "champions of the inarticulate masses." The sick joke here is that the masses — especially the black masses — are not at all inarticulate. They tell it like it is and like it ought to be — with precision, persistence and profanity.

But white society can't grasp the meaning of all that yammering — being too busy washing brains, their victims' and their own. They therefore have no real difficulty in maintaining their cool and the status quo in the face of massive protest and violence.

Being highly inventive jesters, white folk entertain themselves with a monologue that says, in effect, black folk are too stupid to realize that something phony is going on here. It goes like this: "It's the Communist agitators and Communist dupes who are behind all this violence.". . .

If black folk don't laugh out loud at such routines, it is because their funny bones are dulled from the same old stale material. Real comedy depends on surprises. So why should a black man chuckle over the annual Congressional Follies built around civil-rights legislation, for example? He knows in advance that the new Civil Rights Act is going to wind up like the so-called Open Housing Act of 1866 — unenforced and soon forgotten.

Enforcement, he is told, would "infringe on the rights" of the white minority. That's a good one, too. But it is as familiar as, "Why does a fireman wear red suspenders?"

As for the sight gags in white society's repertoire, these too have worn thin from overexposure. How many times can an individual black man be amused by the blind-cab-driver routine? After the 37th time. it no longer strikes him as suitable material for a laff-in.

Did I say "individual black man"? Actually, there is scarcely any such animal as far as white eyes can see. They recognize "the first Negro who" and "the only Negro to," but not as individuals — instead, as freaks or symbols. Which is to say that white folks have a habit of arbitrarily assigning a rather standard personality to a black man. His real self is like an iceberg, deeply submerged in a sea of white assumptions.

One of my soul brothers was recently promoted to an executive position with a giant corporation in New York City. He had earned it by bringing in more sales orders over the last five years than anyone else in his department. You can imagine how chagrined he was when several of his white colleagues dismissed his personal achievement with humorless jokes like this: "It pays to be black these days. Man, you've got it made."

Such an attitude is not founded primarily on jealousy, as it might appear on the surface. White folks are simply incapable of seeing a black man as anything beyond his blackness.

At least twice a year, for instance, I am approached for an interview by one national magazine or another. My experience as a newspaper reporter and television news broadcaster has provided me with a wealth of interesting material from face-to-face encounters with four Presidents, a half-dozen princesses, scores of prizefighters, hundreds of politicians, assorted pimps, paragons and pin-up queens. But not one white interviewer ever shows the slightest interest in anything except my blackness.

"What is the role of the black newsman?" they want to know.

"The role of a black man," I tell them off the record, "is or ought to be the same as it is for everybody else in his profession; in this case, to gather the facts and report them with as much integrity, clarity and objectivity as he can muster." End of interview.

I am also rather weary of getting letters from white television fans that read like this one:

"When you first began broadcasting the news on television, I watched you every night, but I realize now, years later, that I was so conscious of the fact that you were black that I didn't hear a word you said about the news. Now, I am happy to say, I still watch you every night, but only because you are a damn good newscaster...."

What I'm getting at here is that white folks are generally flabbergasted by a black man who can fly a plane, mix a martini, speak unbroken English or shoot a round of golf. Such a black man is something like the celebrated dog that could walk on its hind legs unassisted.

About the only realm of this society which seems to be perhaps one-third of the way toward the verge of catching the spirit of this thing called the free democratic society is professional sports. Even here a string of qualifying exceptions must be taken into account. To mention just a few: Boxing is obsessed by the search for a "white hope"; football is convinced that a black quarterback could not lead his team to the goal line; and baseball, like all the others, shuts out black men from the managerial and decision-making level. And besides all that, there is a great deal of friction and apartheid on the so-called integrated teams.

But baseball still deserves a better grade than white Americans generally. In the first place, black players are no longer required to be supermen like Jackie Robinson. If you watch baseball these days, you see black men fumbling routine grounders, dropping flies, striking out with the bases loaded and winding up the season with microscopic batting averages. Just like whites. And no one suggests that such derelictions are peculiar to one race or another.

Furthermore, if a white interviewer shows up in the locker room, he is full of questions about the spitball or the squeeze play that didn't quite work in the ninth. After all, why should a third baseman, even a black one, be limited to discussing racial jokes?

So how long is it going to take the rest of this country to evolve even as little as baseball? In my judgment, another 100 years at the very least, if this society manages to survive that long.

Why so much time? Well, it seems to me that while one side of those split personalities called white Americans is striving with all its might to open their minds and their society, the other side is being pulled in the opposite direction by what white Americans accept and automatically maintain as the natural order. As you can see for yourself, it is something of an unequal race.

For Thinking, Talking, Writing

1. Mr. Teague's main point in this article is that most white people are *unconscious* of many of the things in our culture that indicate racial prejudice; they don't even know such things are there. How many of the *everyday* examples of racism that Mr. Teague mentions were you aware of before reading about them in this article? After reading it, can you now think of others?

2. Mr. Teague states that he thinks it will take this country at least another 100 years to evolve to the point at which there is even as much racial equality as there is in baseball today. Do you agree? Why or why not?

3. Explore, as honestly as you can, your own *feelings* about people of a race other than your own. Remember the boy Mr. Teague mentions in the article, who took LSD and found out he really felt quite differently than he thought he did? *Can* you be honest about your own feelings in this matter?

Every Basement
Keeps a Captive

George W. Cornell

Some people believed it. Some thought it was just an allegory. In any case, they were shocked.

"It's savage," said a church delegate here for a merger conference to form the United Methodist Church.

"How could any parents treat a child that way?" said another.

The story was told Sunday from the pulpit of the First Methodist Church by Bishop Dwight E. Loder of Detroit.

His account also was carried by radio in the Dallas area and had listeners appalled at the case he described, recalling reactions to the Orson Welles hoax broadcast of a Mars invasion in the 1930's.

"I have a heavy heart this morning," the visiting bishop announced before starting the sermon.

He said he had received a message asking him to be a character witness for a family he knew which had kept a son hidden and locked up in a basement from birth because of disfiguring facial markings.

The bishop went on:

"They were ashamed of the way the child looked, so they put him in the basement behind the furnace and kept him confined there, letting him grow up without knowing other children or the world outside.

"They fed him leftovers from the table and forced him to do menial tasks around the basement, such as chopping wood for the fireplace.

"When the family would go on vacations, they would leave a supply of food for the boy to eat. He grew up without the barest minimum of education, yet he was a bright boy with real capacities."

Finally, the account continued, a younger brother became sympathetic and smuggled the imprisoned boy a television set, through which he learned of the wider world. As a result, he became obstreperous, trying to escape.

A household struggle ensued in which the younger brother was killed, the bishop related, and in which neighbors became involved, bringing the long-hidden secret to public attention.

"Now I am expected to come in and testify for the good character of this family," the bishop said, and then went into his sermon.

Inquiries from radio listeners about the case led newsmen to check into it with the bishop, who said he had indicated at the close of his sermon that the account was actually a parable — the imprisoned child referring to American Negroes.

"But let people think it's real," he said. "It is real. It can be documented. I can take you into the dark basements of any American city, where people have been confined there, restricted to the most menial tasks, with no chance to get out in the world."

He added that while many listeners may have missed the point, he paused at the end of his sermon and turned to them, saying: "By the way, when you go home, there's someone in your basement whom you know, someone your family has been keeping there."

For Thinking, Talking, Writing

1. How does the parable discussed in this article relate to what Mr. Teague talked about in the previous article?
2. Do you believe that if black people were *really* given a chance to get out of the "basement" of society, the tension between the races would stop? Or are there other factors involved? Discuss.
3. Have Mr. Teague's article and this one given you a clearer picture of what it is really like to be black in a white society? If so, how?

One Black Family's
Fight for Equal Rights

UNADILLA, Georgia

[In] May [1968], Roy Lee Hunter became the first black graduate of Unadilla High School.

At the school commencement — which he attended despite an offer by a purported school official to "mail him his diploma since he had done so well"— he was placed in the back row on the end, with a vacant chair to space him from the nearest boy. The Sunday before, at the baccalaureate sermon delivered by a Christian minister, two spaces intervened.

Thus, Unadilla protects itself against "black power." For the Hunter family is the mainstay of the battle for equality in Dooly County.

The story began in 1966. Mrs. Elizabeth Hunter that summer enrolled seven of her eight children in Unadilla's "white" schools. As she says now, "They wanted to go, and I thought they had as much right as anybody else. I was brought up on a farm here in Georgia. Lord knows I have worked hard. Lots of these same white people I have worked for here in Unadilla. And now they act like they don't know me." No one would hire Mrs. Hunter or any of the children once it was known they were going to go to the white school.

Despite this hostility, Roy Lee Hunter did attend Unadilla High School for two years and earned the right to graduate. Even at the end, he had no easy time. A white boy who failed his tests and could not graduate scuffled with Roy in a corridor. The principal sent Roy home.

Roy wants to be a doctor, and he now studies at the Berry Academy, a college preparatory school in Rome, Georgia. His expenses there are being met through a special grant from the Herbert Lehman Education Fund, the scholarship program the NAACP Legal Defense and Educational Fund (LDF) established to increase the enrollment of Negroes in Southern institutions formerly restricted to whites.

When white students at Berry Academy ask Roy why he smiles so much, he has a ready answer: "I just don't come from a sad family."

Reprinted by permission of the NAACP Legal Defense and Educational Fund, Inc.

Welfare, Southern Style

Help for the needy from our welfare system is often slow in many parts of the country. But when a family challenges long-standing separatist practices in the South — and then asks for public assistance — this delay can be compounded.

The decision of the Hunter children to enter the white school brought a crisis to the family's finances, which had depended in part on Mrs. Hunter's earnings. No white family in Unadilla would hire her.

Mrs. Hunter applied for Aid to the Families of Dependent Children (AFDC) in August 1966. She appears to have been clearly eligible: she could get no work and she had eight dependent children. AFDC money, though distributed through state and local agencies, comes largely from the Federal government.

At Mrs. Hunter's first interview she says the welfare lady asked her whether she was the mother of the children registered for the white schools. Then began a long series of delays and obstructions that would not end till seventeen months later after Mrs. Hunter had received assistance from a Legal Defense Fund lawyer.

In the meantime, school opened. Some of the Hunter boys were beaten by classmates. Their home was stoned. One night a dead bear's carcass was dumped in front of the house. An older friend and neighbor, Mr. Marvie Lee Howard, often spent the night in the Hunter home during this time of fear. He and his wife had known Mrs. Hunter as a little girl. They "practically reared me," she says.

Word reached the welfare lady that "a man" was sleeping at Mrs. Hunter's. The police chief was asked to verify the rumor. Neither Mrs. Hunter nor Mr. Howard and his wife were questioned about their relationship. The Dooly County Department of Family and Children's Services refused any help, ruling that the Hunter children had a "substitute father" who would have to support them.

In March of 1967, and again in January of 1968, Mrs. Hunter reapplied for AFDC. During the winter of 1967-68, there was no heat in the Hunter home. Her plight was brought to the attention of Legal Defense Fund Attorney Tom Jackson of Macon. He appeared for her at a "fair hearing" and made a formal request for investigation by the U.S. Department of Health, Education and Welfare (HEW).

Finally, in April 1968, a monthly allowance of $73 was granted for the eight Hunter children. This has now been increased to the maximum $154.

Before any welfare assistance was given, *the Hunter children had been in the white schools for almost two years*, and Mrs. Hunter was travelling 66 miles a day to earn $6 for a day's work.

She does domestic work for a woman in Warner Robbins, 33 miles from Unadilla, leaving at 6 A.M. and returning about 5:40 in the afternoon. After she pays for her ride she makes $5 a day, three days a week.

For the electric stove and light, Mrs. Hunter pays $17.62 a month. Because of the dim light in the house, the children often work standing at the edge of the porch.

Eddie says he has some white friends at school. . . ."They don't call me nigger." Roy says that they were warned last year that Faye didn't know enough to pass fourth grade. Now ten years old and in fifth grade, she's "lacking one B from being on the honor roll."

The motto on the wall [of the Hunter home] reads: "Only one life, it will soon be past; only what's done for Christ will last."

For Thinking, Talking, Writing

This material gives a brief description of some of the hardships the members of one black family have had in their struggle for equal rights. Find, in this brief article, all the different problems this family had *only because they were black* — problems that a white family of similar background and size would not have had.

"I Am the New Black"

Thee Smith

First of all, you should realize that you are white, and that I am black.... By and large, when I say that I am black, you picture one of two types of black men. But I refuse to be either; and if you listen as if I were one of them, you will never realize who and what I actually represent, and you will leave this place just as your fathers left it.

I am the New Black. I will neither babble about how much I love Jesus, nor entertain you with sparkling racial comedy. I will not eat with my fingers nor go out of my way to sit down at a dining hall table with you. I will not flunk out of this place, but neither will I participate in the childish fanaticism of raving with you about your math test, or your Phy Sci lab, or your grade in English. I want neither to be your enemy, nor your friend. I don't want your love, or your pity, or your guilt, or your fear. I demand only that you respect me....

I, the New Black, am not exactly sure why I am here.... Last year I *did* know, without being told. Last year I was to eventually become a responsible American citizen. I felt that an investment had been made in me — not merely by this school but by your whole society — to provide a "safe," well-balanced, and responsible leadership for the black revolution....

The fact that I once accepted your definition of my role as a black nauseates me. I see in your definition, and in my agreement, a continuation of what blacks in this country have been trying to do since the Civil War; a continuation of the efforts to teach blacks how to act "white," and at the same time teach them to deny the legitimacy of their own culture.

As the New Black, I shall not tolerate the teaching of other blacks to be industrious, puritanical and relatively unemotional — as you are; for I feel that we, as human beings, have much more to lose by becoming white than by remaining true to ourselves, true to our culture, and true to our blackness....

This article is excerpted from a speech made by the author when he was a junior at Phillips Exeter Academy.

The problem, again, is you people. Our minority black middle class is willing and ready to prostitute itself before you, and you still cannot see *your* sickness inside them. The problem *is* racial. All men are *not* born equal. White *is* right. In a riot, *all* blacks are suspected of theft, and rape, and murder....

I, the New Black, acknowledge my blackness, and the improbability of my ever becoming respected in your society by getting white. I, the New Black, not only accept but agree with your classification of all of us, regardless of class, as blacks. We have our blackness in common and we are united by your definition of what blacks in America are.... I am a black first, and an American when I can afford to be.

I am at Exeter, not to be like you, nor to prepare myself to enter your society as a Roy Wilkins or a James Meredith. This school's efforts to prepare me for that type of role in tomorrow's world are futile. That role no longer offers effective leadership for change, because it is based on the theory that a black leader should strive for assimilation of the black masses. Assimilation is no longer the solution, though. Civil rights, as a movement, is dying. My most effective role in tomorrow's society will be to lead the advancement of Black Power; and I, the New Black, dedicate my life to that role....

We are at Exeter to obtain knowledge of ourselves, and when we become leaders, we will derive our strength not from your friendship, or your brains, or your money, but from ourselves.

For Thinking, Talking, Writing

Mr. Smith states several opinions which are open to question by others. Explore them:

1. Whites are categorized as "industrious, puritanical, and relatively un-emotional." Do you think this is generally true? Does this seem to you to be the same sort of over-generalization that whites use about blacks when they categorize blacks as "lazy" or "stupid" or "without initiative"? What is the danger in generalizing about a *whole* race, or a *whole* religious group, or a *whole* profession, or any whole group of people?

2. Mr. Smith thinks that it is unlikely that blacks, no matter how they act, will ever become really respected in a "white" society. Do you agree? Why or why not?

3. What are the implications of being a "black first, and an American when I can afford to be"? How does this attitude contrast with the

attitude of Mike Ransom, who went to war in spite of his personal beliefs?

4. Mr. Smith believes that integration is no longer the solution to the problems of the blacks — that Black Power is more likely to solve some of these problems. What do *you* think? Why?

After Identity, What?

Youth Is Right

There is no question about it. Youth is right when it insists that Negro history should be a part of the general history of this nation. There are somewhere between 22 and 25 million black people in this country and they did not come over on recent boats. In fact, there has been no great influx of black people to this country since the last slave ship docked in the early 1800s. Black people have been kept from emigrating to this country in any numbers ever since it was first settled. It stands to reason, then, that the ancestors of the millions of blacks in this country have been here since before the American Revolution and it would be impossible to work in a growing young nation in such prodigious numbers and not have some effect on its history. Historians can write us out and whites can think us out but, face it, we were there.

Youth Looks Backward

Black youth in America today is looking backward. Young black men and young black women are seeking an identity in the past. Black history to them is a need, an answer to the question "Who am I?" They seem to feel that they must answer that question to their own satisfaction before they can travel forward as whole men and whole women into the future. They have a need for a mother country, a history of accomplishment and fathers who stood straight and tall before the enemy and, even in losing, were brave men to the end. That they had such a background is easy to establish. That there were Nat Turners, W. E. B. DuBoises, Malcolm Xs and Martin Luther Kings is a matter of record. That there were literally thousands of others who kept families together against preposterous odds, who educated children with family incomes that would scarcely have fed and clothed similar white families, who defied white authority to push forward the frontiers of Negro accomplishment year after year is a self-evident fact. Many black youths looking for an identity need look no further than their own parents and grandparents if they want to see strength and skill and character. But perhaps they are looking for the wrong thing. Perhaps they, without thinking about it, have been brainwashed into judging their own past by white standards of history and accomplishment. They cannot see that the black parents who have brought them to where they are today did it against far greater odds than faced the white parents of the same period. To barely survive in a hostile environment is a tremendous accomplishment; to progress in a hostile environment is a miracle. The black mothers and fathers of past generations, then, must have been miracle makers.

So What Is History?

Too often in insisting upon the teaching of Afro-American history in the public schools, young students emphasize the fact that students of Italian descent can look back to Columbus, that the British settled most of the U.S., that the French had a Napoleon Bonaparte and the Germans, a Richard Wagner. But at the same time, they should point out that the Italians had a Mussolini and an Al Capone, that the British sired pirates like Captain Kidd and the Germans cannot deny one of the most inhuman leaders of them all, Adolf Hitler. To look into the history of a people is only to discover that among all nations and all peoples, the scoundrels were as plentiful as the heroes and that most of the citizens of all nations were ordinary people doing usually what the black Americans have done for years — taking care of the family, trying to progress just a little further, moving up a step on the economic ladder, getting a little more education for the next generation.

So You Want an Identity?

It is normal and natural for black people in the U.S. today to look for an identity. It is to be expected that black youth — struggling, confused, ambitious, frustrated — should feel the need for an identity. It is a pity that they must spend so much valuable time in searching for it.

Do You Really Need One?

That the Negro youth is searching for an identity is apparent in his almost every action. Black students' groups in high schools and colleges, the insistence upon the teaching of black history, the wearing of naturals and African clothing, the pulling away from whites in separate caucuses in otherwise integrated groups — all these are evidence of the search for identity. But does the black youth really need this identity for himself? Or is it an attempt to show white America that the black man, too, has a history and an identity? If young black America is seeking an identity to prove his equality with whites, then he is truly wasting his time. That black people, given the training and opportunity, can do anything whites can do has long been proven. That white people do not, on the whole, believe this, is also true. But in this day and age, why should black youth try to prove himself against whites. Why cannot he try to prove himself against the field, against the unsolved problems of his time, against mathematics and psychology, against chemistry and space bio-physics.

A baby born in an alley and abandoned on a doorstep with no known natural parents can develop into a great musician, a Pulitzer Prize-winning chemist or an all-star baseball player.

It all boils down to the fact that, even with an accepted racial identity, a man is nothing if he has not been trained to use his natural accomplishments. A bright, educated foundling is much more valuable to the world than an imbecile son of a king.

For Thinking, Talking, Writing

This editorial, from *Ebony* magazine, suggests that the real challenge for the young black person today is not to seek an "identity to prove his equality with whites," because equality has already been proven, but to find his identity in proving himself against the unsolved problems of our time. How does this compare to Mr. Smith's point of view? Which do you prefer?

Black Mood on Campus

In the 1950s and early 1960s, Negro students marched under the banner of civil rights. The goal was integration and equality and the struggle was fought on such battlegrounds as Montgomery, Oxford, and Selma. Today, the revolt has redefined itself, its goals — and its battleground. The aim of the student vanguard is black independence and the dominant cry is for black pride. The battlegrounds have changed too. "The universities," says Dr. Price M. Cobbs, a black psychiatrist and co-author of "Black Rage," "have become the dusty Southern towns of today."

To white eyes, the analogy may seem somewhat exaggerated. Many U.S. colleges, after all, have responded to the black-student demands, forming new black courses and greatly increasing the enrollment of black students. The result? "As soon as there are 50 black students on campus," says Tufts' Alvin F. Poussaint, "they organize and rebel.". . .

This change in targets and rallying cries has had ambiguous and sometimes traumatic effects on many whites. Old liberal allegiances are wavering. Intellectuals on campus who backed the Selma march and the Montgomery bus boycott don't know where to begin when presented with a series of "nonnegotiable" demands made by students; scholars protest that faculty — not students — should hire and fire other faculty members, and that such decisions should be made on the basis of scholarship, not race; faculty members abhor the use of force and violence in a setting traditionally devoted to study and reason. Administrators point to their increased recruiting efforts in the ghettos — and to the fact that many of the black protesters are on student aid or scholarships — and ask: "What do these people want, anyway?" For liberals, it is a question uncomfortably like the ones asked by exasperated white Southerners a few years ago. . . .

Generalizations, of course, are notoriously difficult, especially when made about a group of young men and women as diverse as the 275,000 blacks now on U.S. campuses — out of a total college population of 6.5 million. But the case studies cited below are representative of the mood, rhetoric and goals of students at dozens of other schools. Black college

Condensed from *Newsweek*. Copyright © Newsweek, Inc., February, 1969.

students — like many white students on campus today — want to claim their own identity. They want a curriculum that will help them better serve their communities. They want institutions that let them control their own lives. But they also have a unique goal; they no longer want to be dark imitations of whites....

Prof. Charles V. Hamilton, chairman of the political-science department at Roosevelt University in Chicago and co-author (with Stokely Carmichael) of "Black Power," has been a participant in as well as an observer of what he calls "the development of a black-student social conscience." Hamilton's account of the movement:

"It began in 1960 with the student sit-ins. This was the first time on a massive scale that students in this country took the lead in anything — except, of course, for those white students who were active in the '30s. The sit-in students were very religious and influenced by the Gandhian-King notion of nonviolence. They were integrationist: most of them believed very intensely in racial cooperation between whites and blacks. Their tactics were always to be neat, polite, and nonviolent. When you go sit-in at Woolworth's, take your Plato and, by all means, wear a shirt and tie. This gained the support of a large segment of white America. Who can fault a cat with shined shoes? Then something happened to begin the transformation to radicalism: the students began to question not only the system, but their own tactics."

According to Hamilton, this change came in 1964, after the rebuffs to the delegates of the Mississippi Freedom Democratic Party at the Democratic convention and the "trauma of the Mississippi summer" — the temporary migration of Northern students to the South to work for civil rights. The disappointments in both these ventures, Hamilton believes, made many black students think the system itself was "illegitimate." Then, he adds, "Stokely went on the stump in 1966 and ... the entire language of the black student changed. We started using words like 'institutional racism.'

"Today they're understanding that they are black, and that as they go into these colleges — both black and white colleges — they are not going to be made into little middle-class black Sambos. I graduated from Roosevelt. I got a law degree from Loyola University, and I got a Ph.D. from the University of Chicago. And I'm going to tell you very clearly that my education over that twelve- to fifteen-year period was geared toward making me a middle-class black Sambo. Nothing devious in that, and I'm not blaming my professors. It's just that that was their orientation. They were saying to me in no uncertain terms that in order to succeed I would have to orient myself to a Western Anglo-Saxon culture.

"But the students today are saying that they are going to be black and skilled at the same time. They're saying that they are going to develop and keep this sense of group responsibility. Somehow or other, whatever skills they acquire, they are going to make sure that these skills can be applied to the development of black America. The big test, of course, is what they do with their skills after they leave college. When they go to IBM with their skills, are they going to make sure that they develop a legitimate hiring policy? If they go to The New York Times, are they going to make sure that they do relevant stories?"

Nevertheless, concludes Hamilton, "the black-student movement today wants 'in' in the same sense that those kids wanted it in 1960. They would deny this at first. But most of them don't talk in terms of developing a separate state; most of them talk of developing at their own institutions an Afro-American studies institute or black-history courses. But notice, they're still working with the institution. They're not saying, 'We want to throw over the university.' They're saying simply, 'We want to make it over.'" By contrast, says Hamilton, the demands made by white-radical groups like SDS are generally vague and broad — working against the system — while the blacks are "still working within the system. They're still very system-oriented, except they've got in mind a revised, restructured, reoriented system.". . .

Spelman College (enrollment: 945), a woman's college in Atlanta, is a quiet, cloistered quadrangle with tree-lined walks and somber, red-brick Georgian structures. . . .

For almost 90 years, Spelman, like most other Negro colleges, imitated middle-class white academic goals. At graduation at neighboring Morehouse two years ago the dean who handed out diplomas proudly announced the job each graduate would assume plus his starting salary — and the audience warmly applauded those with the highest figures.

"Used to be only light-skinned girls with long hair whose daddies were doctors and lawyers could come here," says Sandra Lee, a 20-year-old junior from Madison, Wis., whose father heads the equal-rights division of the state labor department. "Now there are all colors here, from light-skinned to ebony. Now you're a black sister and color doesn't make any difference." Vincent Harding, chairman of the history department, adds: "Just when we were almost white, we found out we didn't want to be."

This has created a dilemma for many Spelman students. They are being tugged on the one hand by the rhetoric of black pride and cultural affirmation and on the other by the reality of a white business world that is opening wider doors for some Negroes. Recruiting by businesses and graduate schools has increased nearly 50 per cent at the Atlanta center in just the past year. The temptation to follow traditional paths to success in the white world is strong. Job offers from the white establishment are plentiful; starting salaries are high.

"I'm here to get an education so I can help my brothers and sisters," says Sandra Lee. "If black guys can get that big job, they'll take it. But they'll still be looking out for their brothers. I don't think kids just want to make it any more."

Miss Lee has worked for SCLC and sat-in in a downtown Atlanta shoe store to protest its hiring practices. Before Spelman, she attended predominantly white schools all her life. She came to Spelman because "I just don't like the idea of black people being on display. I was on display all through high school. Being at an all-black school is like a rebirth. I don't have to prove anything here. I'm accepted for what I am."

In her white high school, she adds, "we spent three weeks on slavery and they showed us picking cotton and shuffling our feet. I had to come here to find out what brilliant, beautiful people we are." Yet she acknowledges there have been great changes in white attitudes in the last few years. "I knew in high school I could never be anybody's queen or win any scholarships. Now I see black queens and black kids going to Europe to study.

"It's not the color," she concludes. "It's what you have inside. Like Bobby Kennedy. He had soul. He was one of us.". . .

Jerry Varnado, 24-year-old campus coordinator of the Black Student Union at San Francisco State, usually wears a uniform: faded fatigue jackets, blue jeans, black beret. He is a soldier of sorts. "I am not a militant," says Varnado. "A militant is just somebody who gets mad. I would just say I'm one of the black people in the United States who can tolerate racism no more.

"I was born in Magnolia, Miss. I went to elementary school in Lerman, Miss. It was inadequate. They taught you how to read and write but the teachers spent most of their time keeping order in class and telling people who had darker skin that they were black and ugly. It didn't make any difference what color the teacher was, but there were very few that were dark at that time.

"When I was 10 I learned that the white folks were our enemies. This partner of mine in Jackson, Miss., got killed, got drowned working for this white man. The white man made him go fishing for him, and he drowned. Still I didn't hate the white man. You accepted it, you were a nigger and he was the white man and that was the way it was.

"After high school I got on the Greyhound bus and rode to San Francisco. My primary thought was that I was getting away from Mississippi. Once I was in California I was hitchhiking and couldn't get a ride until this white boy came along and stood by me. We both got a ride together. I knew from then on that it was still the same thing.

"I am now a graduate student and a lecturer in the black-studies department. What we are involved in here at State is not a reform movement. That is what the civil-rights movement was. This is a revolution. Reformists work within existing rules and regulations; revolutionists make their own rules and regulations.

"We will use any means necessary to uphold the principle that people of the third world have a right to determine what kind of human beings they want to be. Violence is the best means. It disrupts and terrorizes so that if people of the third world are not allowed to determine their own kind of education, then nobody else on that campus can get any kind of education.

"One course I teach is the sociology of black oppression. . . . Once during class we were talking about what napalm was and how it was being used. I told them how it could get on the skin and burn a hole all the way through. And for all who didn't believe it, I put a formula for napalm on the board so they could make some. They could pour it on a piece of meat or on the police or somebody and see exactly how it works."

Little-known Merritt College occupies an uneasy place on the northern fringe of the black ghetto in Oakland, Calif. What is happening at this two-year junior college has perhaps far more importance to the black community than the more publicized events at San Francisco State, Brandeis, Berkeley or Harvard. For Merritt is the "turn-around place" where poor blacks can sharpen academic work dulled by ghetto high schools and get the training for semi-professional jobs or for transfers to four-year colleges. Merritt is also the cradle of black student militancy. Among its alumni are Huey P. Newton (Class of '66), the defense minister of the Black Panther Party, and Bobby Seale (who didn't graduate), the party's chairman. Merritt has been turned around in another sense: it is a "white school" that has gone over to black control.

Five years ago, Merritt's student population was less than 10 per cent black. Today, about 40 per cent of Merritt's 10,000 students are black, it has a black president, an Afro-American Studies department with a black chairman, and it closes Feb. 21 to mark Malcolm X Day.

Merritt was one of the first mostly white schools to offer a Negro history course — in September 1964. Now it has fifteen black courses — ranging from Education 5 (contemporary education of Afro-Americans) to Philosophy 5 (implications of black cultural thought). More than 900 students (including about 90 whites) are enrolled in black courses. White students, however, are barred by the instructors from attending some classes; blacks claim that their presence slows down the course.

Merritt's black students also try to bar whites from some courses. "This course is for Black Students only!" they wrote on the blackboard at a recent session of a philosophy course. Later on in the class, Fred T. Smith, Merritt's militant student-body president, stood up and asked the only white among the 29 students to leave. "It does us no good to discuss any sort of black cultural philosophy with this white man in the room," Smith said. Several other blacks murmured in agreement. "Eldridge Cleaver states that any confrontation between white people and black people in this country is a power equation," said one. "So long as this white boy is in this class, we're going to be talking elliptically, all around and over the subject, but no one is really going to be saying anything." The white student remained silent, and the instructor finally invited him back to the next meeting if he felt he could "benefit by the instruction to be gathered here."

Merritt students say that their Soul Students Advisory Council is the model for black student unions across the country. It is certainly among the most militant. In 1966, some of the SSAC leaders formed the Black Panther Party and started carrying arms in "self-defense." Soul Students have taken rooms over for rallies; the Academic Senate was once locked in a room while the SSAC pressed its demands. Instructors have been threatened. Whether started by SSAC or off-campus hoodlums, vandalism, fire bombings, robberies and assaults have been fairly common on campus.

Last June, Merritt graduated five persons with Associate of Arts (two-year) degrees in Afro-American Studies, the first such degrees ever awarded in California. The State Board of Education, trying to attract blacks into teaching, recognized the degree as a temporary qualification to teach in elementary and high schools if the teacher also simultaneously works for a four-year degree.

Last fall Merritt acquired a new president, Norvel Smith, 43-year-old former director of Oakland's anti-poverty program, and the first black president of any California college. Since his appointment, fifteen new black faculty members have been named — there are now 30 blacks on the full-time faculty of 240 — and Smith is looking for more. The fifteen hired last fall were middle-class professionals; few lived in the ghetto. The Soul Students wanted them to become "brothers in the revolution," to fraternize on a first-name basis, to work on changing the attitudes of the white faculty. "The new black faculty was somewhat overwhelmed," says Norvel Smith. "They had expected only to teach.". . .

J. Otis Cochran, 24, has already achieved the goal of many white students — and their parents. He is a first-year law student at Yale. But Cochran, who graduated from Morehouse in Atlanta and traveled in Eastern Europe, arrived at Yale with a perspective different from most of his classmates. As he tells it:

"After a scattering of sit-ins and other civil-rights activities, I decided it was preposterous to think I could offer any particular talents on a hit-or-miss basis. I decided to try instead to organize my community. I organized the Vine City Project in a low-income area of Atlanta.

"In 1967, I became more convinced that I needed to go to Africa as I sought to identify myself in terms of my history. I first noted how white culture had ingrained in me a sense of insecurity on the Ghana airline. I saw that the pilot and crew were black. I was worried: I began to ask myself, 'are they qualified?' The landing, I can report, was smooth.

"When I got back to the U.S. I knew I had to have my own bag — which was to do something for my community. I had tremendous reservations about law school because I have a general disbelief in the law as it functions. But I talked with two black students from Yale Law and came to the conclusion that belief or support for the law is not the only relevant reason for coming to law school. In fact, you should learn the law in order to discover how the prosecutors of the system use it, and then you can use it to uphold or to undo the system.

"It came to me that black students shared the same problems here at Yale and that we should all get together to cushion the shock of living in an oppressive white environment. We had to get together to fight against becoming a part of a school that functioned so blatantly in opposion to what it held itself out to be. I was a founder and am now chairman of the Black Law Students Union. The black students' association acts in two ways — to help us get to know each other and ourselves better and to keep the law school honest."

What is the lesson that whites can learn from the black student revolt? First of all, colleges may well have to bend far beyond their traditional channels to become "relevant" to black students. Secondly, whites certainly will have to try to understand the intensity of the new black mood as a step toward meeting those demands that are just. For the mood may be here to stay. "The high schoolers about to enter college," says a black student leader at Wisconsin, "are some of the angriest blacks in the movement. Watch out next year."

For Thinking, Talking, Writing

1. Dr. Charles V. Hamilton of Roosevelt University states that the blacks are "still very system oriented, except they've got in mind a revised, restructured, reoriented system." From what you know of the militant black students on college campuses, does this seem an accurate statement to you?
2. Miss Sandra Lee states that "It's not the color. It's what you have inside." This would seem to support the integrationist point of view; yet Miss Lee also felt that in an integrated school she was "on display," while at an all-black school she is accepted for what she is. How do you reconcile these two statements?
3. In the last paragraph of this article, a black student leader states that "The high schoolers about to enter college are some of the angriest blacks in the movement. Watch out next year." Since this article was published in 1969, those "high schoolers" are now in college. From what you know of what is now going on in the black movement, do you think the situation has become more severe, as he thought it would, or less severe, or has remained about the same? Give evidence from your own reading of newspapers and magazines and from what you see of the news on TV, to support your opinion.

Proposal for a
Separate Black Nation

Robert Sherrill

One day late in May, Brother Imari, Minister of Information for the Republic of New Africa, pulled up to the United States Department of State Building in a taxi and told the driver to keep the motor going because he would be right back out. Inside, James McDermott and Charles Skippon, who introduced themselves to Imari as "special assistants to Secretary of State Dean Rusk," formally received Imari's note requesting the opening of negotiations between the United States and New Africa. The note's demands were simple but rather sizable: New Africa's officials wanted $200,000,000,000 in "damages" and they also want the U.S.A. to give up five Southern states — Louisiana, Mississippi, Alabama, Georgia, and South Carolina. McDermott and Skippon took the note politely and said they would start it through the proper diplomatic channels. Two minutes after the simple ceremony in the lobby began, Imari was back in his cab and on his way to Michigan, which is his home. . . .

The President of New Africa is Robert F. Williams, a former North Carolinian who fled this country one jump ahead of the sheriff (Williams says the charges were trumped up, and there are some grounds for thinking so), and he now commutes between Peking and friendly nations in Africa while awaiting his new kingdom to be set up by the faithful back home. But the real power behind the movement is Imari's brother, Milton R. Henry, a Michigan attorney who for six years served on Detroit's city council and who ran for United States Congress in 1964, losing to another Negro, John Conyers; Henry says the election was rigged. Milton Henry has taken the name Gaidi, which he says is Swahili for "guerrilla," although he doesn't mind if it is confused with "gorilla" because he admires King Kong.

First Vice-President in the illusive Republic, Henry is also chairman of the Malcomites, a society whose membership is secret but whose purpose is not. It seeks to establish the Republic of New Africa in these steps: (1) Arm the black communities of the North and West, and if whitey tries anything rough, blast hell out of him.... (2) Ship about a million well-armed blacks into Mississippi, take over all of the sheriffs' jobs through the ballot box, seize the government, and then move on to Alabama and repeat the process; the next three Southern states would be seized in no special order, but it would be done in the same way, by shipping in armed blacks who would first try to grab the governments by voting and, if that didn't work, by guerrilla warfare.

Inside the loosely knit community of 23,000,000 Negroes in this country, the recently revived proposal for the creation of a separate black nation from a portion of the United States has probably more support than whites would like to think.

The nation was officially alerted in 1967 to how restless the natives of Harlem and Samtown and Bootville really are when the Conference of Black Power met in Newark, New Jersey, and passed with tumultuous cheers a resolution calling for "a national dialogue on the desirability of partitioning the U.S. into two separate and independent nations," one black, one white. Most newspapers reacted with either shock or outrage, especially when the Black Power conferees illustrated what they had in mind by physically ejecting white newsmen in a rather rough style.

In the South, of course, where black militancy moves much more slowly, one will find few Negroes who are even aware of the proposal; but in the black neighborhoods in Northern and West Coast cities, the dream is dreamed quite regularly; and among the black intelligentsia, it is considered a legitimate topic for cocktail-party debates; as often as not the argument turns not around the desirability of separation but about the means to achieve it and the geographic area to be demanded of whitey....

Actually if one wipes from his mind the emotionalisms of blacks-and-whites together and just takes the proposal of a separate black state on the basis of logic, it isn't ridiculous at all. Since 1950 Indians have received $246,760,764.61 in reparations from the federal government on 261 claims and the government still has 343 claims to process, which means that the 600,000 heirs of the semi-transient redskins who lived on our portion of the continent as the U.S. expanded will probably wind up with half a billion dollars for losing "their" land. The Negroes not only lost their African lands but were forced to work for nothing for a couple of centuries. So far 50,000,000 acres have been turned over for the use of our 600,000 Indians; if the 23,000,000 Negroes received a comparable handout, they would get *sixty-three* states the size of Mississippi.

As for the business of untangling their citizenship, the Henry group is asking that the federal government be only as cavalier in freeing them of citizenship as it has been in imposing citizenship. Henry complains, "The Fourteenth Amendment was designed to unilaterally impose citizenship upon the black man. He was not asked whether he wished to become a citizen, or whether he wished to be sent back to Africa, or whether he wished some portion of land here on this continent where he could set up his own government."

Logistically, the Henry demands hold up just as well. An official in the State Department's African affairs division who has watched a dozen new nations come into being (he would like to keep his job a little longer so asks anonymity) checked over the pros and cons of New Africa's chances of survival, if it ever got started, and conceded: "If you left aside the internal political obstacles of cutting themselves off, certainly the South could be made into a very workable nation. Because you're starting with everything. You've got what we call the infrastructure — you've got the roads, the factories, the stores — they're *there* (unlike Niger, for example, where they're not) and if nobody levels them, they are going to stay there. If you have a class of people who can't keep them up (as you have in many African nations) the stuff is going to deteriorate. Your roads will have potholes. But we have educated Negroes in this country, so there's no reason for things to go to hell."

Whitey's more normal responses to the separatists range from Mississippi's ex-Governor Ross Barnett ("You know what any good Southerner thinks about *that* scheme") to the rigidly Constitutional brotherhood of Senate Majority Leader Mike Mansfield ("Oh, no, no, no. This is one nation, united, indivisible — and that's *it*")....

The standard, shocked response will open with a demurrer on the grounds that separation would "admit defeat" or would be a violation of the American dream, and closes on a more candid note, implying that Negroes are too dumb or too poor to run their own country and, anyway, it's all a warmed-over Communist plot. Governor Lester Maddox, who chased Negroes from his Atlanta restaurant with an ax handle and a pistol but doesn't want them to leave the country, expresses this position perfectly: "Two separate countries would multiply our troubles and solve none of them for any race. It would be destructive of the American civilization and the American form of government, so we don't want that...."

Why the idea is judged as nothing more than an alien Communist plot by some people, is that they are unfamiliar with some of the oldest and strongest of the underground Negro yearnings, says Dr. Herbert Aptheker, national director of the American Institute for Marxist Studies. "When Oklahoma was organized out of Indian territory there was a big discussion in Negro newspapers of that day pushing the idea of setting aside the state as a home for the black population. If white people don't know that, and if they don't know that there are about 25 towns and cities in Oklahoma that are all black today, then the whole idea just naturally hits them as some sort of a bolt out of the blue." (Aptheker is one who thinks it an impractical proposal.)...

The most effective defender the separatists have found among whites so far is W. H. Ferry, a vice-president of the Fund for the Republic, Inc., a well-known money-raiser for liberal causes, and a Fellow of the Center for the Study of Democratic Institutions in Santa Barbara, California. His writings on the theme that racial integration in this country is impossible have won for Ferry the supreme accolade from Professor Browne ("I think he must be part black") and the supreme outrage of most liberals, who look upon him as a traitor.

While he concedes that a separate nation "in the long run may prove to be the only way out," he is sticking with the idea of separate cities right now. He has proposed that boundaries be set up around the natural enclaves of black residents in urban centers, and that this be theirs: power to tax, power to police, power to educate, everything, in little colonies.... Of his city colonies, he says: "Neither white city nor black colony will be permitted to erect Berlin walls, but frontier zones will be clearly marked.... There will be no bar to whites taking up residence in the colonies, where they will be subject to colonial rule. Thus black colonists will be free to whistle at white women; deny normal services to whites and overcharge them when services are provided; expect their police to treat all whites as suspicious persons and mistreat them accordingly; and deny whites access to clubs and rest rooms. All such matters will be arranged under a Reciprocal Indignities Understanding that will be attached to the original Statute of Colonization."

The only thing unusual about Ferry's plans for blacktown independence is that it comes from a white liberal. Among urban Negro intellectuals the idea is old hat. At last fall's National Conference on Black Power in Philadelphia, the proposal winning overwhelming support among the four thousand delegates called for taking over the black towns of the country — right now — with creation of a black urban army to defend their colonies.

Even when pushed to its most generously illogical extremes, the Ferry colony plan is greeted by the Henry group as a very dangerous counterproposal, however, because even if the blacks held the central city colonies, the surrounding whites would still control the transporta-

tion system, water supply, and food supply. The blacks would be occu-
pying an isolated fortress....

But in other aspects, Ferry knows just what the militant blacks are
worrying about and why they are studying Southern road maps between
target practice.

"I don't think either my plan or the separate-nation idea is looking to the immediate future. My own judgment is that we're going to
have something that is recognizably a race war, a civil war.... As for
whether or not apartheid comes out of it, that would depend on how
many whites are killed. If just black people are killed, it won't count,
but if a lot of whites are killed it's going to count like crazy. The next
one I think is going to be a blinger...."

Meet The President...

Robert F. Williams, President of the Republic of New Africa, has
not lived in the United States for more than nine years. In 1959, as
leader of the N.A.A.C.P. in Monroe, North Carolina, he became convinced that Negroes in the South would be murdered before they were
allowed equal rights or voting privileges, and he organized an armed
self-defense group. Shortly afterward, a clash between freedom riders
and white citizens occurred in Monroe. An elderly white couple was
held at Williams' home until the authorities met his demands for medical treatment for the beaten freedom riders. Williams, warned of a
lynching, escaped with his wife during the night-long battle between police, National Guardsmen and armed Negroes. They left the country
when they learned they were among the group being sought by the F.B.I.
on abduction charges. For the past nine years Williams has lived in Cuba
and China. His statement, which follows, was issued from his present
headquarters in Tanzania:

"I envisage a Democratic socialist economy wherein the exploitation of man by man will be abolished. Racial oppression will also be
abolished. The concept of the Republic of New Africa is not a segregationist concept, but rather one of self-determination for an oppressed
people. It represents a rallying point for progressive and constructive
Black Nationalism. Some doubting Thomases and white-folks-loving Uncle Toms are loud and shrill in proclaiming the idea as fanatical and
Utopian. This is definitely not the case, and I feel as certain now of the
ultimate acceptance of the idea as I did when I advocated a policy of
meeting violence with violence during the height of the era of nonvio-

lence. America is at the crossroads. The black man is becoming consciously revolutionary. He has as much chance of succeeding as the American Revolutionaries in 1775. As people of conscience who are in sympathy with the oppressed peoples of the world, our self-respect and human dignity dictate that we separate from racist America. Our survival demands it and the concept of the Republic of New Africa is our point of rally."

For Thinking, Talking, Writing

1. Mr. Robert F. Williams, President of the proposed new black nation, says, "The concept of the Republic of New Africa is not a segregationist concept, but rather one of self-determination for an oppressed people." From what you have read here about the proposal, would you agree or disagree with this statement? Why?
2. Do you agree that this idea "has as much chance of succeeding as the American Revolutionaries in 1775"?
3. Do you think that most black people in the United States would go to live in this new black nation if it were established?
4. Do you think, as does W. H. Ferry, that we are going to have a race war before the racial problems in the United States are resolved?
5. Do you approve or disapprove of this proposal for a separate black nation? Why?

Plain Talk About
Hatred and Violence

John W. Gardner

John W. Gardner served as Secretary of Health, Education and Welfare from August 1965 until his resignation on March 1, 1968. He now heads the Urban Coalition, a private organization of business, labor, religious and other leaders whose purpose is to mobilize the nation to solve the problems of our cities.

Most white people are neither haters nor practitioners of violence. Nor are most Negroes. The majority of each race earnestly wishes that constructive, non-violent solutions could be found to the racial problems that rack — and may yet wreck — the nation.

But there are whites that hate, and whites who advocate violence. There are Negroes who do the same. And, unfortunately, the whites and Negroes who do *not* hate and destroy too often quietly tolerate those who do.

Those who hate and those who resort to violence — whether they are white or black — cannot resolve the problems that divide this nation. They can only intensify the senseless spasms of emotion and savage action.

There are many levels at which we must seek solutions to the problems which are tearing the nation apart. We must attack hard-core poverty with renewed vigor — through education, job-training, employment, housing and other measures. We must attack discrimination in every form. We must take steps to ensure civil order.

But, at the same time that we are working on such basic problems, we must cope with the upward spiral of mutual fear and corrosive hostility between white and Negro communities.

Hatred and violence used to be chiefly the stock-in-trade of the white racist. Then they became the stock-in-trade of the Negro extremist. Both justified their malevolence with cogent arguments.

But today there is a curious contrast between the two. Negro hatred of whites is often expressed openly. It is frankly defended and widely discussed. In contrast, white hatred of Negroes has gone underground. It is rarely discussed publicly, rarely debated candidly. Indeed, when the President's Commission on Civil Disorders spoke of it openly, many people thought the authors of the report had done an unseemly thing.

Yet the white hatred is there. And everyone who reads this article knows it. The long tradition of white brutality and mistreatment of the Negro has diminished but has not come to an end.

It still excludes Negroes from white neighborhoods, and bars them from many job opportunities. No Negro reaches adulthood without having been through many experiences with whites that bruise his self-respect and diminish his confidence. That is hard for him to understand, living as he does in a society that bases its moral claims on the worth and dignity of the individual.

Such attitudes on the part of whites must come to an end if this nation is to survive as a free society. Each one who adds his bit to the storm of hatred does his share to move us toward a final reckoning that no free American will like.

Negro extremists who advocate violence assert that non-violence did not work. It is untrue. The greatest gains for the American Negro came in response to the non-violent campaigns of Martin Luther King, Jr., and (before it turned violent) the Student Nonviolent Coordinating Committee.

It is the fashion now to belittle those gains, but they were great and undeniable. They were registered in historic civil-rights legislation and even more emphatically in social practice. Compare Negro voting patterns today with those prevailing as little as three years ago; or southern school desegregation today with practices of four years ago; or patterns of restaurant and hotel desegregation over the same period; or employment opportunities now and then.

The gains are not enough. They cannot satisfy our conscience. But they were substantial. And they came in response to non-violence.

The violent tactics of the past two years have brought nothing but deepened hostility between the two races and a slowing down of progress in the necessary drive toward social justice.

Many white liberals have now allied themselves with the Negro extremists in the sanctioning of violence. They speak approvingly of past riots as having "dramatized" the problem. They never speak of the negative consequences of the riots, but everyone who observed the session of Congress that followed the riots of 1967 knows that the negative reactions were a reality, and diminished the possibility of constructive solutions.

Nor do those who condone violence ever speak of the legacy of bitterness and division that will be left by increasingly harsh outburts of destructive interaction. What good will it do to dramatize the problem if, in the process, hatreds burn themselves so deep that the wounds permanently cripple our society? Nor do those who condone violence ever face up to the likelihood that the paroxysms of public disorder will lead ultimately to authoritarian countermeasures.

One of the difficulties in halting the interplay of fear and violence is the tendency toward indiscriminate indictment of one race or the other. One man killed Martin Luther King — and Stokely Carmichael indicts the whole white race. A small minority of Negroes loot and burn, and many whites indict the whole Negro race.

Where will it lead? Negro extremists shout slogans of hate. White racists whisper their rage. Each justifies himself by pointing to acts of members of the other race. Hatred triggers violence, violence stirs further hatred, savage acts bring savage responses, hostility begets hostility, and the storm rages on. At some point, the terrifying interplay must have an end.

We must break through the terrible symmetry of action and reaction, assault and counterassault, hatred and responsive hatred. And the only way to do that is to ask the moderates on each side to cope with the haters and doers of violence *within their own ranks*.

There is no way for the Negro moderate to curb the white extremist, or the white moderate to curb the Negro extremist. If they try, they just give further impetus to the interplay of hostility. That is why moderate whites must curb the haters within their own ranks, and moderate Negroes must curb their own extremists.

To date, the moderates — both Negro and white — have been all too silent. It was predictable. Moderates are alike, whatever their race. They don't want to become involved. They don't want to appear controversial. They don't like trouble.

But, increasingly, the extremists of both races are giving them trouble, whether they like it or not. And it will get worse before it gets better. It's time for the moderates to speak up and assert their strength.

This "revolt of the moderates" must go on day in and day out — in offices, factories, homes and clubs. Those who promote hatred must be called to account. Those who commit or condone destructive acts must feel the full weight of disapproval by their friends and neighbors. Each contributes his little bit to the destruction of this society.

In a curious way, the whites who hate and destroy and the Negroes who hate and destroy are allies moving the rest of us toward a terrible climax. Martin Luther King understood that, and fought against both all his life, by word and deed. And so must all of us who care about the future of this society.

For Thinking, Talking, Writing

This article is a plea for non-violence and continued work toward integration. Discuss *your* attitudes toward the following statements by Mr. Gardner. Do you agree or disagree with him, and why?

1. "The majority of each race earnestly wishes that constructive, non-violent solutions could be found to the racial problems...."
2. "The violent tactics of the past two years have brought nothing but deepened hostility between the two races and a slowing down of progress in the necessary drive toward social justice."
3. "Moderate whites must curb the haters within their own ranks, and moderate Negroes must curb their own extremists."

It Could Have Happened

Art Buchwald

WASHINGTON — I'm not saying it happened, but it could have.

A black man dressed in an African caftan walked into a bus station coffee shop and sat down next to a white man wearing a white sheet and hood with the letters KKK on the front.

"I beg your pardon," said the white man. "What is that outfit you're wearing?"

"I'm a black militant, honkie."

"What a coincidence," the other man said. "I'm a white militant. Where are you going?"

"I'm going to a demonstration to demand all-black housing for college students in black dormitories."

"That's wonderful," said the KKK man. "We've been saying for years that the blacks should live by themselves."

"You have?"

"Of course. You should have your own restaurants, your own hotels, your own movie theaters and your own place on trains."

"You putting me on?"

"I am not. You can look it up if you want to. We've worked it seems forever to see that the black people didn't have anything to do with the white people. For your benefit, of course."

"Hey, that's crazy. You white cats are working for the same thing we are. How do you feel about integrating?"

"We're absolutely against it. If it weren't for the Supreme Court, you people would have all the black things you wanted. They forced you to mix with the white man."

"The Supreme Court has no right to tell us to mix with honkies."

"They certainly don't. You should be segregated, if that's what you want. We think you should have your own drinking fountains, too."

"That's for sure. Don't want to drink from no fountain whitey's drunk out of."

"I'd feel the same way if I were you. Do you know our organization advocates black and white washrooms in railroad stations and bus terminals?"

"I didn't know there were any honkies thought that."

"You better believe it. We're on your side. Why, up until a few years ago we insisted on separate educa-

Reprinted by permission of the author.

tion for the races — blacks in black schools, whites in white schools."

"Man, that's what my demonstration's all about."

"And listen to this. We felt so strongly about the black man living in his own black neighborhood that when some Uncle Tom moved into a white neighborhood, we burned a cross on his lawn."

"Good for you," the black man said. "Black people wanting to move in white neighborhoods are nothing more than plantation slaves."

"I've never said this to a black man before, but I like the way you think."

"Thanks, honkie. You know, I usually won't talk to a white man. But you're different. You're working for the same things we're working for."

"Of course we are. Some day, if you're successful and we're successful, we won't even have to eat together in this restaurant. There will be a section for you and a section for us."

"Beautiful. I can't wait for that day."

"Well, we better get on the bus."

"Yeh. I wonder where I should sit."

"Why don't you sit in the back? It's much more comfortable there."

For Thinking, Talking, Writing

In this column, Mr. Buchwald is pointing out that the separatism now advocated by many black militants is a return to the same thing as the racism practiced in this country by many white people for a long time. After reading this whole section, which describes the daily indignities suffered by blacks in our society and the various feelings about integration versus separatism stated by the blacks and the whites, take a stand. Would *you* advocate working toward complete integration or toward black separatism? Defend your point of view, using evidence from the articles in this section.

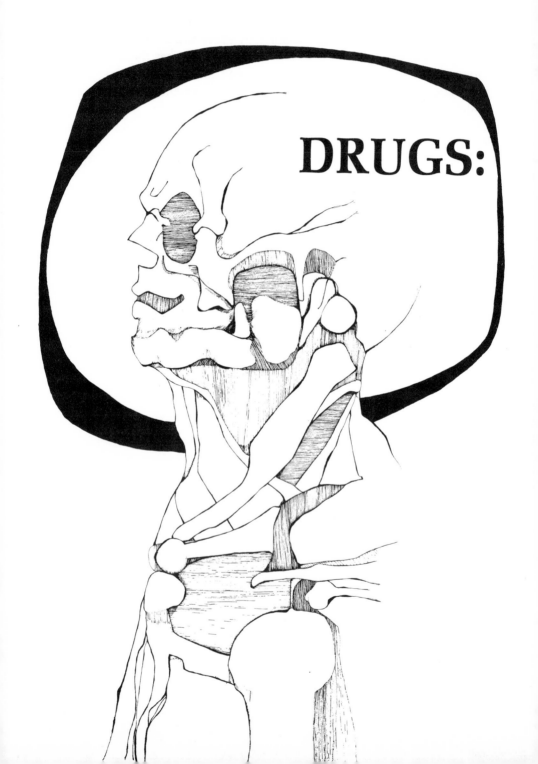

8

what's the scene?

Introduction

Mention of the word "drugs" causes an instant emotional reaction in many people. To think logically and reasonably about drug use is often difficult, because "drugs" suggests addiction, immorality, crime, the underworld, and a host of other emotionally-loaded ideas. In addition, the narcotics laws in the United States lump together drugs which *are* physically addictive with those which *are not*; so the attempt to sort out what is "right" from what is "wrong" becomes even more complicated.

But drug use in this country is certainly nothing new. Thousands of years ago, American Indians used jimpsonweed, peyote, and other "mind-changing" plants for religious and medicinal purposes. And the United States has been notorious for years for the heavy use by its citizens of more modern "mind-changing" drugs of various kinds, particularly amphetamines, barbiturates, and tranquilizers. Alcohol is a widely accepted social fact. Smoking tobacco is legal and acceptable, although its physical effects may be more harmful than those of marijuana, according to the medical evidence available so far. (Dr. Philip Handler, board chairman of the National Science Foundation, and Dr. James L. Goddard, a commissioner of the U.S. Food and Drug Administration, have both publicly testified that there is no scientific evidence that smoking marijuana is either harmful or addictive; and Dr. Goddard condemned the laws against the use of marijuana as too severe and medically unjustified.)

Three basic aspects of the problem of drug use and abuse must be considered in an attempt to sort out your opinions about this subject: Is it harmful, physically and/or psychologically? Is it moral or immoral, from your point of view? Is it legal — and if not, should it be? In this section you will explore both feelings and reasoned opinions about drug use; study a chart giving the facts about many kinds of drugs; and read about one town's attempt to solve its "drug problem." Read — think — talk — write. Perhaps you will come up with more realistic answers than you had before to the question, "What's the scene?"

Phantasmagoria

Chris Frazer

My world is ginger-smelling, free-swinging, light as dawn and dark as night, strobe lights flashing off iridescent paint, quiet and free and gentle and kind, friends to talk with and to soothe me, music that lifts me up and crashes me, bells jingling against my ankles, and unrhymed, unvoiced poetry of people like me who don't ask or take, but only give.

We live together, like a groovin' tribe of Indians. That's how I got my name, Walkin' Lonely, because it sounds like an Indian name, and because I do that sometimes, walk lonely. But people don't say your name all the time because it doesn't represent what you really are. My friends have forgotten their straight names; there's Stumble, who's short, with a chubby face and wears only black clothes and gray beads. My special friend is Lilac, because she wears a lilac behind her ear and her long robe is violet-colored. With us also are the twins we call Feather and Hop, always together. They are connected by a super-long string of carved beads.

It's nice in our place because we don't have to get up any time or answer any questions or go to sleep when someone tells us to. Food is hard, sometimes, but there's usually a broken-down truck parked at the corner of the big street, and the guys off it will feed us soup and bread and milk. Really nice, too. You don't have to pay for it, except to give them a kiss on the cheek. That's the most true payment of all, because you're giving some of yourself.

Sometimes the Man bothers us. But Stumble and Lilac and Feather and Hop and I just sit quietly or chant to ourselves. And the Man shakes his head and talks about crazy kids. You smile up at him, tell him about your heart, and he gets so worried that you'll expose his crooked straightness that he leaves you alone.

Shuffling down the street, I see Stumble and I smile. He has a soft little warm-baby face. You think, just seeing his face, that Stumble is fat. But he's skinny, and his black jeans and boots and worn jacket and dyed T-shirt make Stumble look like a lost child, a waif standing on the corners of the world. He mumbles sometimes when he talks, because he's very shy. But late at night, when I can't see his face or his honey-colored eyes, he will tell me about himself and about how he feels.

Lilac floats beside me, with her gracious robe and her beautiful black hair. She is wonderful and kind, and she plays gently on a man-dolin that she got for her shoes at the pawn shop. We met when we both came here first, and went together to find our home. When I'm with Lilac I feel very safe and warm. We are both very close to Stumble; he is like our little boy. At night sometimes, when the bad times come back to him and he lies shaking and crying on the floor, Lilac will play to Stumble and sing him to sleep.

Feather and Hop are dressed as Indians, with their lifeline-beads holding them together. I know them little, but they are very nice. Feather and Hop get us food because they know a guy who runs a kitchen. They also find us blankets and a mattress for the floor. Each Sunday, Feather and Hop go to the doctor down the street and get penicillin shots for their sickness.

We had a sixth person, a girl named Nightly, but she went away three weeks ago. None of us know where she is. At first, Lilac, Stum-ble, and I went around asking people where she was. But nobody knew so we stopped asking. Sometimes I think Nightly went home again, be-cause she was always crying and lonely. It was hard to be her friend because she would turn you out.

I don't think of my mother, because she never understood me. When I first came here, I was very bitter about her and how she treated me. Lilac talked me out of these feelings. It's hard to hate: it takes the place of true emotions. So I forced myself to forgive my mother, but I won't ever go back there. She has my younger sister, and Mother always loved her best anyway.

On the grass I sit cross-legged, my poncho covering me to my knees. Beside me, Stumble holds a joint between his fingers and makes a light. He passes it to me, kisses me on the cheek and settles back to blow a smoke ring at the falling autumn leaves. Lilac takes it from me, then she gives the joint to Feather and Hop. It is very peaceful, and I can hear temple bells inside my head.

The sky goes beautiful colors. I lie back to enjoy it. Lilac is brush-ing the strings of her mandolin, and Feather and Hop nod to the music. Stumble is smiling a soft, dimpled baby-smile. We all love him so much because he is gentle and kind. The temple bells ring with Lilac's melody. We sit there until evening, Lilac dark as the night with her mandolin. How can anyone live in a straight world when our world is so beautiful?

Together we all walk back to our home. Feather and Hop lead the way. Stumble is between Lilac and me, with his head resting on Lilac's shoulder. She is the tallest of us all, and Stumble likes to rest against her. We are all softly humming down the street and smiling at the people we meet. They smile back at us because they can see the beauty too.

Our room is very wonderful. It is a loft on the top floor of the building. Feather and Hop took different pieces of wallpaper and hung them by hooks from the ceiling. We have gotten together twelve posters that hang on the walls and from the ceiling. Edward Teller's eyes watch us from the corner. Marlon Brando and Anna Magnani stare at each other from over the door. Three Toulouse-Lautrec circus posters are on the longest wall, splashing garish color over the tired grayness of the old paint. Two op-art show ads flicker down from the skylight. Einstein blesses us from the window. Geronimo glares at us from the closet. Richard and Mimi Farina stand alongside the heater. The room is very full and fine.

Last week, Stumble and Lilac and Feather and Hop and I went to the beach. We hitched a ride with a friend who knows a guy who surfs, so the guy lent our friend his Woody. It was the last part of the warm times, which last longer at the ocean than they do inland. We spent our day walking up and down the sand, staring out at the water. Feather and Hop got tired of the salty air, so they went back to the Woody to sleep.

Lilac and Stumble and I held hands and waded deep into the surf. It was clear and we could see the tiny pebbles that lined the bottom. Lilac almost caught a little, clear-flashing fish with her hands. We were sunburned across our cheeks, and Stumble's little round nose shone like a light. Of course, Lilac didn't get tanned, because her skin doesn't color any darker than it is.

At night we couldn't believe the beauty of the beach. The jagged rocks that crust the edges of the beach were black and silver between the crashing tides. At the very lip of each breaker, there was a sparkle or green and gold, then the foaming white would drown all other colors. All the night was reflected in the water, and when Feather and Hop called to us, saying it was time to leave, we kept staring out at the glory.

Stumble dropped acid that night, to keep the beauty with him. But it was very bad, and he had terrible visions of long ocean-monsters reaching out their sea-fingers to drown him. With Lilac out wandering, and Feather and Hop at a party, I had to sit with him and help him through it. Stumble would cry out for me to kill the monsters before they pulled him into their sea-brine stomachs.

He was six hours getting it out of him. No one was around to help me; I felt so bad and so useless. When all the acid was out of his blood and mind, Stumble lay down, with his head in my lap, to sleep. He told me he loved me best of all, that he would do the same for me. But I don't drop acid because I've watched Stumble, and I am afraid.

"You're a goddess," Stumble said to me, and then he put his baby-face against my poncho and went to sleep. That made me feel good, to have someone think I was so fine.

We are now going to find the party. Posters at the corner store tell us that it is at the Crematory. That is across the park, and it takes us an hour to get there. One street away, we can hear the noise and see the light reflecting through the windows onto the sky. This is the best way to spend the night, with your friends at a party.

The Crematory is crowded, not just with us, but with teeny-boppers who giggle and try to look like us. They are little girls, just over playing with dolls. One girl tries to kiss Stumble; he holds onto my hand and hides his head. He is very shy and begins to blush. Feather and Hop find a place for us in the back and we all sit on a blanket.

With the strobe flashing off and on and whirling metallic globes in the air, the place is wonderful and groovin'. There are joints for everyone, and Lilac finds a match. We lean against the wall, smiling at our friends and smoking. Now the room is flashier and brighter and there are many more friends.

A girl from the floor below us gives me a piece of hard candy. I take it and start to suck it. I feel all floating outside myself. I lean against Stumble, and he is asking the girl:

"What is on the candy?"

She laughs. "It's acid."

Stumble is mad, and he tells me, "Spit it out!"

Now I'm afraid, because this is what I never wanted to happen. The girl thinks it's funny and she keeps on laughing. Hearing what was said, Lilac tells her where to go. The girl doesn't understand why everyone is mad at her, but she goes away.

The band is called the Undead. Their sound is bending before me, and I lean forward, feeling sick inside. Stumble asks me if I want to go outside. How can I know what to do? It's still just a little feeling and so I sit back and try to relax. Lilac, who dropped acid only once, says that I might not have gotten enough to have a bad time. But Stumble crushes the piece of hard candy with his boot. I think he knows.

They are coming to get me. With their guitars raised over their heads, the Undead are coming over the room to burn me with their strings. Screaming, I try to hide under the blanket. Now ants and cock-roaches crawl from between cracks in the floor. They climb onto my arms and legs and insidiously work their way to my face. They're biting me, chewing me ... I can't hide, I can't hide.

Stumble grabs my arms and works to hold me down. Already people are staring at me and laughing. Another acidhead off her tree, they say. And I try to scream at them that I'm in danger. Won't someone please keep the Undead from burning me with their guitar strings? Stumble, you've got to help me.

Feather and Hop have made way for Stumble and Lilac to take me outside. They cover me with the blanket and lead me out of the Crematory and into the damp evening air. Behind me, the Undead are shrieking and flashing their lights. I've gotten away. Now the earth is peaceful, temple bells ring.

"You go in, Lilac," Stumble says. "I'll watch her."

She looks frightened. Why is Lilac frightened? They aren't going to follow me out to the park. "All right. I'll be inside."

I'm looking at my bare feet, fascinated by my toes. They are beautiful and perfectly formed. My toes are the outlet of my soul. Stumble is trying to cover me with the blanket but I shrug it off. I want to absorb all the night, and cast it out through my beautiful toes, windows of my soul. The lights flashing against the sky are signs sent up by God to tell me to watch my toes. How lovely it all is!

"Lonely, how you feelin'?" he asks me, concern on his baby-face.

"Wonderful floatin' out-of-this-world, Stumble." I lean over lazily and kiss him on the mouth. Then I lean against his chest and tell him how beautiful my feet are, especially my soul-toes.

"Lonely, baby. You lie down," Stumble says.

"Want to sit and watch my toes."

"I'll watch them for you," Stumble promises.

So I lie down on the blanket and hold onto Stumble's fingers. As he promised, he is watching my wonderful feet carefully. I feel sorry for him that he can't see all their soulness. Now that the Undead are not chasing me, I am very happy. Bells ring against my ears and Stumble's soft face is getting fuzzy at the corners.

I sit up now, alone on the blanket. I am frightened and my head is hurting terribly at the sides. No one is around; all the lights in the Crematory are out. It is raining and I am very wet. My hair hangs down on my poncho, stringing and hugging my neck. When I try to stand up, things turn sideways, so I have to crawl on my hands and knees for a time.

"Stumble!" I cry out into the grayness of very early morning. There is no Stumble or Lilac or Feather and Hop. All my friends have gone away. And I forget where I am or where my home is.

Only strange, straight people are on the street. They look at me, hostile. Now I cannot smile at them, because I don't feel safe without my friends. I'm all alone, and my friends have left me. Why did they leave? Stumble! Lilac! Come back and find me and take me home again!

I sit on the cold, hard pavement at the corner. The foggy rain is seeping over me. Now I think that Stumble and Lilac and Feather and Hop aren't my friends. If they were my friends, they wouldn't leave me alone. Cars swish past me and splash my dirty bare legs with water from the street.

A woman passes by me. I reach up my hand and grab at the corner of her raincoat.

"Please, lady. What day is it?"

She looks at me distastefully. "The nineteenth. Let go of me."

The nineteenth, that seems to be familiar to me. I remember that it is my birthday, and, if this is the right month, I will be eighteen today. Happy birthday, Walkin' Lonely, I say to myself. Happy birthday, all alone.

I am free here. I am clean in a dirty, straight world of hypocrites. And these straight, evil people drive by me in cars, going home to houses with chairs and beds and heat and running water for baths. My mother has a house like that, just three hundred miles away. Well, I'm free here, but now I have no friends. I forget who I am, and where my house is.

In the wet, dragging rain I huddle under my poncho, and with my hurting head bowed to my knees, I cry.

For Thinking, Talking, Writing

This is the only selection in this book which is a short story, not an article. It was written by a student.

1. Describe as honestly and accurately as you can your *feelings* after reading this story. (Did this description of the "drug scene" as it existed for one girl attract you or repel you? Were the joints and acid worth it? Did you share Lonely's sense of desolation? What were your reactions to Lilac and Stumble?)

2. Why do you think Lonely chose the kind of life she did? (Can you pick up from the story clues about the kind of family life she ran

away from and the things about the family that made her run away?)
What other alternatives were available to her? What would you have
done?

3. Do you think Lonely and her friends were *really* living in a world as
   wonderful as she describes it at the beginning of the story — a world
   "quiet and free and gentle and kind"? Is Lonely being emotionally
   honest with herself in the way she describes her world? Or is Lonely's
   world in the story just as lonely as the world she ran from?

Why Students Turn to Drugs

A recent college graduate
who has "been there"
re-evaluates his experience —
and sounds a warning

Anonymous

Pot was hard to get three years ago, when my roommate and I connected for our first nickel bag of marijuana. We thought it would be a onetime thing, but we fell in with a "ring" of ten other Yale students and began to "turn on" regularly.

Much has happened since then. Now there is plenty of marijuana available on campus — and LSD, hashish, and pep pills as well. I'd say about 20 percent of the undergraduates at Yale this year are smoking pot — about the same, presumably, as at most comparable colleges and universities. Our own ring, on the other hand, has dwindled: two have dropped out of school, one is awaiting trial for "dealing" in marijuana, and another has taken to playing with hard narcotics.

We knew that pot was illegal. We even knew, or thought we did, the dangers involved. What, then, made us start?

Each person's experience with drugs is complicated and unique, but my own reasons seemed simple at the time. Drugs looked like an answer to many bewildering questions I faced. They would, I thought, tell me who I was and where my life was going. They provided an escape from the pressures and problems of college life. I was intrigued, too, by the stories of "dream worlds outside of time," as one friend had described it, "where colors have sounds, and music can be seen." There was the thrill of being in on what's happening. And in the bristling academic world where exploration and questioning are *required* of students, I felt little hesitation in experimenting with anything.

Once involved with pot I met a wide range of campus drug users — from the once-a-month marijuana smoker, to the turned-on dropout, to the hardened addict. They make big distinctions among themselves, but their similarities are greater than their differences: all are tampering with their minds, and all of them want to keep on using drugs.

One variety, the "social heads," smoke pot only at parties, using its buzzing lightheadedness as a social crutch. The fellow who lived across the hall was one of these. Normally a quiet, serious student, he usually seemed outside of any groups he was with. At a party, though, or before a date, he always turned on — and then became a sort of social Santa Claus. "I smoke," he explained to me once, "to be able to join in."

The true "pothead" may turn on with marijuana every evening. Consciously or not, he has renounced the "straight" world, divorcing himself from reality. "It all seems so simple when I'm high," one told me. "All I know is where I am and what I'm doing at the moment. I just don't care about the rest of the world, much less the paper I have to write for a class tomorrow."

The story with LSD —"acid"— is much different. "Tripping out" on LSD is a step few serious students are willing to take. "I guess I'm just afraid of acid," a marijuana-using friend remarked. "Even if I didn't freak out entirely, I know it still would be too hard to get back in the groove." Statistics have been mounting on the possibility of permanent psychological damage caused by LSD. Nothing brings this danger closer to home than seeing it happen to a friend.

The senior who lived upstairs from me was one of the quiet flip-outs. He tripped out on acid about once every two weeks. A carefree, zany fellow, he always seemed high in one way or another, and only afterward could we be certain whether he was clowning or serious.

I was in his room one day when he was rushing to change clothes for an appointment with the dean. A shoelace snapped. "You miserable shoe!" he bellowed. "How can you do that to me?" I told him I had a pair he could use. "Thanks," he said, and dropped his own shoes into the wastebasket. "Let's go."

Was he joking? Though he later agreed to keep the shoes he had thrown away, he never wore them again. And, in the weeks following, he began to treat every object around him as a person, caressing or abusing it in response to what he saw as acts on its part. The danger became obvious when his curiosity about "what a light bulb experiences" led him to grasp two live electrical leads. He burned both hands but couldn't understand why. Eventually he dropped out of school and is now under psychiatric care.

The acidhead rationalizes his dependence in any number of ways. I asked one who dropped out of Yale last spring if the research on LSD's link to chromosome breakage disturbed him. "Sure it's dangerous," he said. "But so is everything I enjoy. Why should I worry about my chromosomes when everything else in the world is so messed up?" Only he can answer that question, but it doesn't seem likely he ever will.

To the inexperienced, the risks of drugs may seem offset by the fantastic rewards they supposedly offer. I was enticed into the scene by these pots-of-gold:

"It's easier to make friends on a high." To a degree this was true, but only in the way that people tipsy on liquor declare undying friendship — until the hangover next morning. Smoking marijuana always made me more relaxed, inclined to talk about personal matters. It took a long time for me to realize that in these conversations none of us was actually being any more honest or open than usual. We were the same people, playing the same roles, only more giddy and simple-minded, more apt to carry on elaborate discussions about the slightest things. Are friendships like this "deeper and more meaningful"? No.

It is easy to lose friends with drugs, however. Because of the law, drug users are by necessity cliquish. I found myself forced to choose between normal society and my head friends, and soon my free time revolved totally around turning on. When I woke up to this situation I asked a number of potheads about it. Most were astonished to realize — after a moment's thought — that they, too, had lost virtually every straight friend they had.

"Drugs can tell you a lot about yourself." One effect of marijuana I often encountered was that wherever my train of thought led me, belief would follow: I would be fully convinced that any idea holding my attention was perfectly valid. But this is not insight; it is self-deception. The "truths" revealed to me on a high tended to be distorted and exaggerated. "Marijuana let me see myself in very simplistic terms," a friend told me, "like a building-block personality. But I know I'm not like that, and I doubt anyone is so uncomplicated."

"When you're high your senses are more acute." In the same way that my mind would become absorbed by a particular idea, my imagination could be rapt by certain colors, sounds and forms. But is this increased sense perception — or a *narrowing* of overall awareness? On a high I could be gassed out by the colors of a movie, and not know what the plot was. Whatever kick there is in "grooving" on simple sensuous experiences, the pot smoker eventually reaches the point where even bright colors and patterns get monotonous.

"You're more creative on a high." Another half-truth. In that I was fascinated with simple ideas and colorful images, I was more inclined to dabble with words and pictures. But is that real creativity? I asked an artist at the Rhode Island School of Design, an occasional marijuana-user, if he would paint while high. "Never," he replied. "I take my work too seriously." An honors English major at Yale said,

"I used to try to write poetry while high, but when I looked at it afterward it was gibberish. Drugs just make you think that what you're doing is art."

The truth is, drugs are in the end an enormously disappointing experience, and many students are beginning to realize it. "When I first started turning on, I thought the whole world was changing for me," a sophomore at Sarah Lawrence College told me. "But when I saw it was taking me nowhere, I quit."

"Now it's only another fad," her roommate added. "And it is playing with fire."

Unfortunately, for some the disillusionment itself becomes a cause for deeper involvement. We used to scoff at warnings that marijuana led to hard narcotics, but now it looks as if the cliché is holding true — with a twist. A Harvard Law School student put it this way: "Nobody moves up from marijuana to heroin simply for a bigger physical kick. If he does move up, it's because of frustration and disillusionment with the mind-bending stuff."

I've been through the whole business, and survived — which not everyone does. The summer before my senior year I worked in New Haven, enjoying the relaxed atmosphere of a campus on vacation. With so much free time I turned on several times a week, some weeks every evening. When school began again I was out of step, unable to concentrate, always eager to turn on again. At first this seemed laughable. Then I began to see how frightening my predicament really was. Finally I realized that pot is just not worth getting hung up about. The drug scene is not worth an overdue assignment — much less psychosis, addiction or a police record.

For Thinking, Talking, Writing

The main point of this article, by a student who has "been there," is simply that drug use is not worth its effects: physically, socially, or legally. Evaluate this point carefully in terms of the evidence presented in this article and any other information you have about the use of drugs. For instance:

1. The author tells of asking a student if the research on LSD's linkage to chromosome breakage disturbs him. Defend or oppose the student's answer: "Why should I worry about my chromosomes when everything else in the world is so messed up?"
2. What "myths" of drug experience does the author destroy? Are his arguments convincing? Why or why not?

The Complete Mind-Altering Drug and Pill Handbook

Joel Fort, M.D.

1 *Official name of drug or chemical*		2 *Slang name(s)*	
Alcohol Whisky, gin, beer, wine		Booze, Hooch, Suds	
3 *Usual single adult dose and duration of action (hours)*		4 *Method of taking*	
1½ oz. gin or whisky 12 oz. beer (2-4 hours)		Swallowing liquid	
5 *Potential for psychological dependence*	6 *Potential for tolerance (leading to increased dosage)*	7 *Potential for physical dependence*	8 *Overall potential for abuse*
High	Yes	Yes	High
9 *Legitimate medical uses (present and projected)*		10 *Reasons drug is sought by users (drug effects and social factors)*	
Rare. Sometimes used as a sedative (for tension).		To relax. To escape from tensions, problems, and inhibitions. To get "high" (euphoria). Seeking manhood or rebelling (particularly those under 21). Social custom and conformity. Massive advertising and promotion. Ready availability.	

11 Usual short-term effects (psychological, pharmacological, social)	12 Usual long-term effects (psychological, pharmacological, social)
CNS depressant. Relaxation (sedation). Sometimes euphoria. Drowsiness. Impaired judgment, reaction time, coordination, and emotional control. Frequent aggressive behavior and driving accidents.	Diversion of energy and money from more creative and productive pursuits. Habituation. Possible obesity with chronic excessive use. Irreversible damage to brain and liver, addiction with severe withdrawal illness (d.t.s).

13   Form of legal regulation and control
Available and advertised without limitation in many forms with only minimal regulation by age (21, or 18), hours of sale, location, taxation, ban on bootlegging and driving laws. Some "black market" for those under age and those evading taxes. Minimal penalties.

1 Official name of drug or chemical		2 Slang name(s)	
Caffeine Coffee, tea, Coca-Cola No-Doz, APC		Java	
3 Usual single adult dose and duration of action (hours)		4 Method of taking	
1-2 cups 1 bottle 5 mg. (2-4 hours)		Swallowing liquid	
5 Potential for psychological dependence	6 Potential for tolerance (leading to increased dosage)	7 Potential for physical dependence	8 Overall potential for abuse
Moderate	Yes	No	None
9 Legitimate medical uses (present and projected)		10 Reasons drug is sought by users (drug effects and social factors)	
Mild stimulant. Treatment of some forms of coma.		For a "pick-up" or stimulation. "Taking a Break." Social custom and low cost. Advertising. Ready availability.	
11 Usual short-term effects (psychological, pharmacological, social)		12 Usual long-term effects (psychological, pharmacological, social)	
CNS stimulant. Increased alertness. Reduction of fatigue.		Sometimes insomnia or restlessness. Habituation.	
13 Form of legal regulation and control			
Available and advertised without limit with no regulation for children or adults.			

1 Official name of drug or chemical		2 Slang name(s)	
Nicotine (and coal tar) cigarettes, cigars		Fags	
3 Usual single adult dose and duration of action (hours)		4 Method of taking	
1-2 cigarettes (1-2 hours)		Smoking (inhalation)	
5 Potential for psychological dependence	6 Potential for tolerance (leading to increased dosage)	7 Potential for physical dependence	8 Overall potential for abuse
High	Yes	No	Moderate
9 Legitimate medical uses (present and projected)		10 Reasons drug is sought by users (drug effects and social factors)	
None (used as an insecticide).		For a "pick-up" or stimulation. "Taking a Break," Social custom. Advertising. Ready availability.	
11 Usual short-term effects (psychological, pharmacological, social)		12 Usual long-term effects (psychological, pharmacological, social)	
CNS stimulant. Relaxation (or distraction) from the process of smoking.		Lung (and other) cancer, heart and blood vessel disease, cough, etc. Habituation. Diversion of energy and money. Air pollution. Fire.	
13 Form of legal regulation and control			
Available and advertised without limit with only minimal regulation by age, taxation, and labeling of packages.			

1 Official name of drug or chemical	2 Slang name(s)

Sedatives
    Alcohol—see above
    Barbiturates
        Nembutal
        Seconal
        Phenobarbital
    Doriden (Glutethimide)
    Chloral hydrate
    Miltown, Equanil
        (Meprobamate)
	
	Barbs
	Yellow jackets, dolls
	Red devils
	Phennies
	Goofers

3 Usual single adult dose and duration of action (hours)	4 Method of taking
50-100 mg. 500 mg. 500 mg. 400 mg. (4 hours)	Swallowing pills or capsules

5 Potential for psychological dependence	6 Potential for tolerance (leading to increased dosage)	7 Potential for physical dependence	8 Overall potential for abuse
High	Yes	Yes	High

9 Legitimate medical uses (present and projected)	10 Reasons drug is sought by users (drug effects and social factors)
Treatment of insomnia and tension. Induction of anesthesia.	To relax or sleep. To get "high" (euphoria). Widely prescribed by physicians, both for specific and nonspecific complaints. General climate encouraging taking pills for everything.

11 Usual short-term effects (psychological, pharmacological, social)	12 Usual long-term effects (psychological, pharmacological, social)
CNS depressants. Sleep induction. Relaxation (sedation). Sometimes euphoria. Drowsiness. Impaired judgment, reaction time, coordination, and emotional control. Relief of anxiety, tension. Muscle relaxation.	Irritability, weight loss, addiction with severe withdrawal illness (like d.t.s). Diversion of energy and money. Habituation, addiction.

13 Form of legal regulation and control

Available in large amounts by ordinary medical prescription which can be repeatedly refilled or can be obtained from more than one physician. Widely advertised and "detailed" to M.D.s and pharmacists. Other manufacture, sale, or possession prohibited under federal drug abuse and similar state (dangerous) drug laws. Moderate penalties. Widespread illicit traffic.

1 Official name of drug or chemical	2 Slang name(s)
Stimulants 　Caffeine—see above 　Nicotine—see above 　Amphetamines 　　Benzedrine 　　Methedrine 　　Dexedrine 　Preludin 　Cocaine	 Pep pills, wakeups Bennies, cartwheels Crystal, speed, Meth Dexies or Xmas trees (spansules) Coke, snow

3 Usual single adult dose and duration of action (hours)		4 Method of taking	
2.5-5.0 mg. Variable (4 hours)		Swallowing pills, capsules or injecting in vein Sniffing or injecting	

5 Potential for psychological dependence	6 Potential for tolerance (leading to increased dosage)	7 Potential for physical dependence	8 Overall potential for abuse
High	Yes	No	High

9 Legitimate medical uses (present and projected)		10 Reasons drug is sought by users (drug effects and social factors)	
Treatment of obesity, narcolepsy, fatigue, depression. Anesthesia of the eye and throat.		For stimulation and relief of fatigue. To get "high" (euphoria). General climate encouraging taking pills for everything.	

11 Usual short-term effects (psychological, pharmacological, social)		12 Usual long-term effects (psychological, pharmacological, social)	
CNS stimulants. Increased alertness, reduction of fatigue, loss of appetite, insomnia, often euphoria.		Restlessness, irritability, weight loss, toxic psychosis (mainly paranoid). Diversion of energy and money. Habituation. Extreme irritability, toxic psychosis.	

13 Form of legal regulation and control	
Amphetamines, same as Sedatives, above. Cocaine, same as Narcotics, below.	

1 Official name of drug or chemical	2 Slang name(s)

Tranquilizers
    Librium (Chlordiazepoxide)
    Phenothiazines
        Thorazine
        Compazine
        Stelazine
    Reserpine (Rauwolfia)	

3 Usual single adult dose and duration of action (hours)	4 Method of taking
5-10 mg. 10-25 mg. 10 mg. 2 mg. 1 mg.	Swallowing pills or capsules

5 Potential for psychological dependence	6 Potential for tolerance (leading to increased dosage)	7 Potential for physical dependence	8 Overall potential for abuse
Minimal	No	No	Minimal

9 Legitimate medical uses (present and projected)	10 Reasons drug is sought by users (drug effects and social factors)
Treatment of anxiety, tension, alcoholism, neurosis, psychosis, psychosomatic disorders, and vomiting.	Medical (including psychiatric) treatment of anxiety or tension states, alcoholism, psychoses, and other disorders.

11 Usual short-term effects (psychological, pharmacological, social)	12 Usual long-term effects (psychological, pharmacological, social)
Selective CNS depressants. Relaxation, relief of anxiety-tension. Suppression of hallucinations or delusions, improved functioning.	Sometimes drowsiness, dryness of mouth, blurring of vision, skin rash, tremor. Occasionally jaundice, agranulocytosis.

13 Form of legal regulation and control
Same as Sedatives, above, except not usually included under the special federal or state drug laws. Negligible illicit traffic.

1 Official name of drug or chemical	2 Slang name(s)
Cannabis (marihuana, hashish)	Pot, grass, tea, weed, stuff, reefers, joints

3 Usual single adult dose and duration of action (hours)	4 Method of taking
Variable—1 cigarette or 1 drink or cake (India) (4 hours)	Smoking (inhalation) Swallowing

5 Potential for psychological dependence	6 Potential for tolerance (leading to increased dosage)	7 Potential for physical dependence	8 Overall potential for abuse
Moderate	No	No	Moderate

9 Legitimate medical uses (present and projected)	10 Reasons drug is sought by users (drug effects and social factors)
Treatment of depression, tension, loss of appetite, sexual maladjustment, and narcotic addiction.	To get "high" (euphoria). As an escape. To relax. To socialize. To conform to various subcultures which sanction its use. For rebellion. Attraction of behavior labeled as deviant. Availability.

11 Usual short-term effects (psycho-logical, pharmacological, social)	12 Usual long-term effects (psychological, pharmacological, social)
Relaxation, euphoria, increased appetite, some alteration of time perception, possible impairment of judgment and coordination. (Probable CNS depressant.)	Usually none. Possible diversion of energy and money.

13 Form of legal regulation and control
Unavailable (although permissible) for ordinary medical prescription. Possession, sale, and cultivation prohibited by state and federal narcotic or marihuana laws. Severe penalties. Widespread illicit traffic.

1 Official name of drug or chemical	2 Slang name(s)

Narcotics (opiates, analgesics)
    Opium
    Heroin
    Morphine
    Codeine
    Percodan
    Demerol
    Methadol
    Cough syrups (Cheracol, Hycodan, Romilar, etc.)
	Op
	Horse, H, junk, smack, shit
	
	Dolly

3 Usual single adult dose and duration of action (hours)	4 Method of taking
10-12 "pipes" (Asia) Var.—bag or paper w. 5-10% Heroin 15 mg. 30 mg. 1 tablet 50-100 mg. 2-4 oz. for euphoria (4 hours)	Smoking (inhalation) Injecting in muscle or vein. Swallowing

5 Potential for psychological dependence	6 Potential for tolerance (leading to increased dosage)	7 Potential for physical dependence	8 Overall potential for abuse
High	Yes	Yes	High

9 Legitimate medical uses (present and projected)	10 Reasons drug is sought by users (drug effects and social factors)
Treatment of severe pain, diarrhea, and cough.	To get "high" (euphoria). As an escape. To avoid withdrawal symptoms. As a substitute for aggressive and sexual drives which cause anxiety. To conform to various subcultures which sanction use. For rebellion.

11 Usual short-term effects (psycho-logical, pharmacological, social)	12 Usual long-term effects (psychologi-cal, pharmacological, social)
CNS depressants. Sedation, euphoria, relief of pain, impaired intellectual functioning and coordination.	Constipation, loss of appetite and weight, temporary impotency or sterility. Habituation, addiction with unpleasant and painful withdrawal illness.

13 Form of legal regulation and control
Available (except heroin) by special (narcotics) medical prescriptions. Some available by ordinary prescription or over-the-counter. Other manufacture, sale, or possession prohibited under state and federal narcotics laws. Severe penalties. Extensive illicit traffic.

1 Official name of drug or chemical	2 Slang name(s)

LSD
  Psilocybin
  S.T.P.
  D.M.T.
  Mescaline (Peyote)
	Acid, sugar, cubes, trip
	Mushrooms
	
	Cactus

3 Usual single adult dose and duration of action (hours)	4 Method of taking
150 micrograms (10-12 hours) 25 mg. (6-8 hours) 350 mg. (12-14 hours)	Swallowing liquid, capsule, pill (or sugar cube) Chewing plant

5 Potential for psychological dependence	6 Potential for tolerance (leading to increased dosage)	7 Potential for physical dependence	8 Overall potential for abuse
Minimal	Yes (rare)	No	Moderate

9 Legitimate medical uses (present and projected)	10 Reasons drug is sought by users (drug effects and social factors)
Experimental study of mind and brain function. Enhancement of creativity and problem solving. Treatment of alcoholism, mental illness, and the dying person. (Chemical warfare)	Curiosity created by recent widespread publicity. Seeking for meaning and consciousness — expansion. Rebellion. Attraction of behavior recently labeled as deviant. Availability.

11 Usual short-term effects (psycho-logical, pharmacological, social)	12 Usual long-term effects (psychologi-cal, pharmacological, social)
Production of visual imagery, increased sensory awareness, anxiety, nausea, impaired coordination; sometimes consciousness expansion.	Usually none. Sometimes precipitates or intensifies an already existing psychosis; more commonly can produce a panic reaction when person is improperly prepared.

13   Form of legal regulation and control

Available only to a few medical researchers (or to members of the Native American Church). Other manufacture, sale, or possession prohibited by state dangerous drug or federal drug abuse laws. Moderate penalties. Extensive illicit traffic.

1 Official name of drug or chemical		2 Slang name(s)	
Antidepressants Ritalin Dibenzapines (Tofranil, Elavil) MAO inhibitors (Nardil, Parnate)			
3 Usual single adult dose and duration of action (hours)		**4 Method of taking**	
10 mg. 25 mg., 10 mg. 15 mg., 10 mg. (4-6 hours)		Swallowing pills or capsules	
5 Potential for psychological dependence	6 Potential for tolerance (leading to increased dosage)	7 Potential for physical dependence	8 Overall potential for abuse
Minimal	No	No	Minimal
9 Legitimate medical uses (present and projected)		**10 Reasons drug is sought by users (drug effects and social factors)**	
Treatment of moderate to severe depression.		Medical (including psychiatric) treatment of depression.	
11 Usual short-term effects (psychological, pharmacological, social)		**12 Usual long-term effects (psychological, pharmacological, social)**	
Relief of depression (elevation of mood), stimulation.		Basically the same as Tranquilizers, above.	
13 Form of legal regulation and control			
Same as Tranquilizers, above.			

1 Official name of drug or chemical	2 Slang name(s)
Miscellaneous Glue Gasoline Amyl nitrite Antihistaminics Nutmeg Nonprescription "sedatives"	

3 Usual single adult dose and duration of action (hours)		4 Method of taking	
Variable 1-2 ampules 25-50 mg. Variable (2 hours)		Inhalation Swallowing	

5 Potential for psychological dependence	6 Potential for tolerance (leading to increased dosage)	7 Potential for physical dependence	8 Overall potential for abuse
Minimal to Moderate	Not known	No	Moderate

9 Legitimate medical uses (present and projected)		10 Reasons drug is sought by users (drug effects and social factors)	
None except for antihistamines used for allergy and amyl nitrite for some episodes of fainting.		Curiosity. To get "high" (euphoria). Thrill seeking. Ready availability.	

11 Usual short-term effects (psychological, pharmacological, social)		12 Usual long-term effects (psychological, pharmacological, social)	
When used for mind alteration generally produces a "high" (euphoria) with impaired coordination and judgment.		Variable — some of the substances can seriously damage the liver or kidney.	

13 Form of legal regulation and control
Generally easily available. Some require prescriptions. In several states glue banned for those under 21.

For Thinking, Talking, Writing

1. On the basis of the factual information provided in this chart, evaluate the *harmfulness* of the various groups of drugs. Which ones would you categorize as really harmful? Which ones would you categorize as harmless?

2. Do you think the harmfulness of a drug is very influential in persuading people not to use it? Why or why not?

The Morality of Marijuana

Smoking pot may be against the law, but it is not necessarily a sin. That seems to be the consensus among Protestant and Roman Catholic clergy who have had any dealings with the marijuana-puffing youth of the turned-on generation.

Many churchmen are reluctant to give a definite yes or no to marijuana, on the grounds that the medical evidence as to its harmfulness is incomplete. On the other hand, Dr. Joseph F. Fletcher of Massachusetts' Episcopal Theological School, the nation's leading exponent of situation ethics, argues that "the morality of pot depends on circumstances. Social drinking is not immoral, social smoking is not immoral, social pot is not immoral — unless they are used to excess."

Cultural Rebellion

Whether or not they favor pot, many clergymen condemn strict laws against its use. Dr. James Donaldson of the Los Angeles Council of Churches believes that the severe penalties "fall not only on gangsters but on young people experimenting with cultural rebellion." Others argue that anti-marijuana laws are an unfortunate attempt to legislate morality. Like the laws of Prohibition, they feel, such laws are bound to be dropped from the books as more and more people come to accept pot as simply another of life's pleasures. Questioning the morality of marijuana, says Father Richard Mann, a Catholic priest working in East Harlem, "is like asking: 'What do you think of cheesecake?'"

Not many clergymen seem to have experimented with marijuana — or at least are willing to admit having done so. Yet it is generally agreed that students in many of the nation's seminaries have experimented with pot. Says a professor at one theological school in the San Francisco area: "Are you kidding? There probably isn't a divinity school in the country that doesn't have the problem."

A few clerics go so far as to argue that the euphoric high created by marijuana may be, for some, access to instant mysticism. Mark Welsch, a graduate of the University of Chicago Divinity School who works as a social counselor in downtown Chicago, believes that pot can be "a significant vehicle to self-realization." Others suggest that the morality of pot smoking depends on whether or not it is psychologically helpful to an individual. If marijuana is a crutch or a way of escape, says Methodist Minister Terry Cooper of Los Angeles, then it is damaging for an individual to use it. If it is a stimulus to creativity or simply a means of relaxing, there is no ethical problem.

Liberated to Care

Ministers and priests still generally disapprove of pot as a way of life. The Rev. Al Carmines, associate minister of Manhattan's Judson Memorial Church, maintains that marijuana is no incentive to Christian values. "It doesn't particularly involve one with responsibility for one's fellow man," he says. "The liberation of the Gospel has to do with being liberated to care and not being liberated for ecstasy for its own sake."

In pastoral counseling, very few ministers would think of advocating pot. The reason, however, seems to be less a matter of morality than that smoking it is against the law. Jonathan Tuttle, a United Church of Christ minister who works with teen-agers on Chicago's North Side, believes that using pot should be an individual decision. In counseling a youth, Tuttle says, "I inform him of the most pervasive medical opinions and of the legal hassle. Then I tell him to be cool about it."

For Thinking, Talking, Writing

1. After reading these various opinions as stated by Christian ministers of different denominations, and considering what you have learned about the use of drugs from the previous articles, do you consider the use of marijuana *immoral?* Why or why not?
2. Do you believe that the legal penalties for possession and use of marijuana are, in general, too severe, or too lax, or about right? Why?

A Town Fights Back
Against the
Teen-Age Drug Epidemic

Charles and Bonnie Remsberg

For the 28,000 residents of Wakefield, Massachusetts, the warning signs were isolated, and at first no one put them together.

In the summer of 1967, night patrolmen cruising the tree-lined streets of this middle-class Boston suburb encountered groups of teen-agers smoking inside cars with the windows rolled tight, despite the heat. "It seemed," recalls officer Howard Ellis, "that they wanted to keep all the smoke in with them." Later, after an auto accident involving several youths, a "nickel bag" (five-dollar packet) of marijuana was found on an ambulance stretcher that had been used to transport some of the injured.

At a football game soon after school began, two teen-age girls suddenly became ill. Another was found in convulsions on the town Common. Word spread that they had been smoking or sniffing nutmeg.

At Wakefield High School, English teacher Charles Ryan was puzzled by students who for no apparent reason burst out laughing in class or who fixed him with "an eerie, vacant stare that made it seem as if their bodies were empty shells."

"Other teachers complained: some students seemed to be undergoing radical personality changes," says Mrs. Bella Wheeler, a native of Boston and a psychiatric social worker who had been newly hired as the high school's adjustment counselor. In comparing a few students to their past yearbook pictures, she found they had suffered severe weight loss, one indication of addiction to "speed," the slang name for the amphetamine methedrine. Once Mrs. Wheeler, who had worked with drug addicts in New York City earlier in her career, detected the oregano-like odor of marijuana smoke in the girls' lavatory.

A dark-haired, vivacious woman in her forties, with a habit of stating things bluntly, Mrs. Wheeler finally confronted Schools Superintendent Thayer Wade late in October. "I hate to say it," she told him, "but I'm afraid we have a drug problem."

Thus began one of the most imaginative attacks on the rapidly worsening tragedy of teen-age drug abuse. A volunteer coalition of Wakefield citizens, including housewives, mothers, teachers, city officials and businessmen, moved to face the unpleasant facts head-on. In recent months they have hammered out an impressive array of anti-drug projects, that includes beefed-up school curricula, drug detection instruction to parents, programs for making adolescent lives exciting without drugs, and a "hot line" for addicts in distress.

Wakefield's is an approach other towns might well consider, for alarming statistics about young people who get "high" on a variety of chemical compounds are emerging from all parts of the country. Drug abuse, once thought to be confined to big-city ghettos, college campuses, and hippie enclaves, is rapidly becoming a familiar phenomenon in middle- and upper-class suburbia and small towns.

Officials of the National Council for the Prevention of Drug Abuse believe that the rate of drug users in some high schools may be as high as fifty percent of the student body. In some comfortable Chicago suburbs, drug arrests in 1968 skyrocketed more than 300 percent and, increasingly, teen-age deaths are being linked to drug use. A recent issue of *School Management* magazine, after surveying educators throughout the country, says "almost all feel the problem is deep, serious and spreading," with overtones of "a national epidemic."

Traditionally, narcotics abuse has by and large been a crime foreign to Wakefield. Though bordering "Electronics Row," Greater Boston's strip of "now" industries along Route 28, the town retains a Currier-and-Ives flavor — white spires jutting above burnished oaks, churchyards where tombstones date from the 1600s, a village Common and war monuments at the end of Main Street. Its population is a mixture of economic levels and ethnic groups, with Italian and Irish most common. About half the residents are Catholic, most of the rest Protestant. Like Boston itself, the suburb is heavily Democratic. What few narcotics arrests occurred were confined to itinerants passing forged prescriptions.

Three or four years ago, sporadic drug use among college students home on vacation became a minor annoyance, but as late as 1966 police recorded no drug arrests.

Then in 1967, in a rented loft that several college-age youths had converted into a "hippie pad," a handful of high-schoolers "turned on" to drugs. "After that," one of these students told us, "each of us turned a few others on, and the whole thing mushroomed."

Like some of his friends, this boy moved quickly from smoking "grass" (marijuana) to other drugs. He was after kicks, and much of the fascination, he recalls, lay with the "tremendous" psychedelic hallucinations of "acid" (LSD) trips. "My skin would be just a field of paisley patterns," he says. "If I looked at a friend and said, 'You're old,' he seemed to age to ninety in an instant. Furniture appeared to be fluid and dripping."

Others turned to drugs as escape. One boy, who started as a "grass" smoker, told us that he began getting "bombed" on airplane glue, sometimes to the point of unconsciousness, to hide from pressures of school and family. Within two weeks he was "living" for glue," using five tubes daily to saturate paper bags that he slipped over his head. "I could hide in the bag," he remembers, "in an endless eternity of time."

With supplies of contraband drugs available in the hippie sections of nearby Boston, or in some cases in family medicine chests, the teens of Wakefield faced an individual choice of, as Mrs. Wheeler puts it, "coping or copping out." As in most suburbs, drugs were within the financial reach of almost every student, and there seemed to be little social stigma. attached by teen-agers to their sale or use. "In a situation like this," says Mrs. Wheeler, "there aren't any dope peddlers lurking around the school yard. It's the 'nice' boy next door who's 'pushing.' "

By the fall of 1967, Wakefield's narcotics record was marred by more than a dozen arrests.

With approval of the town's Schools Committee, Mrs. Wheeler, Dr. Wade, and Police Chief Merritt Wenzel, who had fully agreed with Mrs. Wheeler's diagnosis of the problem, set to work. With the help of student volunteers, they first notified every service club, social or professional organization, and public agency in Wakefield of a special closed – and candid – meeting in November. Some 180 persons representing about 100 groups, from the Wakefield Mothers Club to the Chamber of Commerce, showed up. Police and school officials bared the disturbing facts.

Although there was no accurate measure of drug use among the high school's 1,900 students, estimates then (as now) ranged anywhere from 25 to 300 regular users, with an unknown number of irregular or one-time experimenters. Drug abuse was also felt to be prevalent among some groups of high school dropouts in Wakefield.

More important than trying to calculate numbers, Mrs. Wheeler explained, was realizing the seeming compulsion of youthful drug users to convert others. "Having even one addict in the school and not doing something about it," she said, "is like ignoring one smallpox carrier."

The first skirmish in their battle against drugs, the representatives decided, should be launched before the upcoming Christmas vacation, when many high school students would have long days of idleness and opportunities for contact with college students home for the holidays. The group appointed a committee to organize a special student assembly for mid-December to "tell the drug scene like it is."

The assembly, the first of similar ones held later in Wakefield, recognized the theory that today's young people understand and respect facts. The first speaker was Dr. Michael Baden, a pathologist and New York City's associate medical examiner.

With no hint of "thou-shalt-not" sermonizing, Dr. Baden explained in specific terms some of the known physical and social effects of drug use. As illustration, he projected colored slides of drug-addiction deaths he had investigated.

One showed an addict collapsed in a drug stupor, his face congealed against a hot radiator. Others showed close-up of needle tracks on the arms and legs of a user who lay in vomitus in a squalid apartment, frothing at the mouth and nostrils from internal strangulation. Still other slides, taken during autopsies, compared hearts and other organs of addicts to those of deceased non-addicts.

One girl fainted in her seat. Some students fled the auditorium, sick. The audience that remained was still gasping and buzzing when the pathologist turned the speaker's stand over to a man and a woman — young former addicts located by the committee through Synanon, an addicts' self-help organization in New York.

Briefly they told their stories. Both had started smoking marijuana on weekends as teen-agers and had all but destroyed their lives with heroin.

Then for more than an hour they answered anonymous written questions from the audience.

"Can you become addicted to 'pot'?" one student asked.

Marijuana does not cause a physiological addiction, the addicts replied, but a user can become psychologically dependent upon it. Regular users often become passive and introspective. They lose motivation. Strong enough doses taken by persons who unknowingly are borderline psychotics or schizophrenics may produce fearsome impressions from the subconscious that can trigger a dangerous panic. "Some personalities can smoke it," the girl addict said, "and stop there. For others, it is a bridge to hard narcotics. You have no way of knowing which category your personality falls in."

"Doesn't LSD just bring out what you really are?" asked another student.

LSD doesn't help you understand yourself, the addicts agreed. Instead, LSD distorts. It can give you a false feeling of power and invulnerability. The girl told of one friend who thought he could fly while under the influence of the drug — and plunged from a tall building in New York to his death.

The deluge of other questions included inquiries about the possible fatal effects of glue sniffing; the process of "kicking" a drug habit; the relative dangers of marijuana and alcohol; the belief that drugs heighten creativity, intelligence and alertness; and many more.

After the open assembly, the ex-addicts met with interested students — adults excluded — in small, informal "buzz sessions."

That night, a similar program was presented at a town meeting attended by about 600 parents. Among the questions asked by the adults were: "What is speed?" "What is acid?" "How can you identify a marijuana cigarette and tell if your son had smoked one?"

Differences in the level of awareness in questions from the two sessions made it crystal-clear: the high school crowd was clearly familiar with drugs, but with vague, often mythical, and potentially dangerous street-corner knowledge. The parents' questions reflected almost total ignorance, both of the local existence of drug abuse and of how to detect and cope with it. One mother recalls of the evening: "It was frightening."

Another meeting of the club and agency representatives followed quickly, and in January, 1968, the group named a permanent Drug Action Committee of nine men and women, giving them a mandate to act. The community contributed $800 to help them get started, in small donations from townspeople and local groups.

This first move was to study the enemy. "I couldn't even *spell* marijuana when we started," says a local businessman. But readings from an extensive bibliography of reference materials, attendance at university and medical society conferences, and long, probing talks with professional therapists and visiting ex-addicts, have helped DAC members understand the workings of the world of drugs.

Then came the job of passing on some of this important information to the community at large.

To every household with youngsters in the Wakefield school system, DAC members, aided by seventy volunteer mothers and students, wrote and then mailed out an arresting document titled *Is Your Child Using Drugs?* In easy-to-understand language, it explained the slang names, chemical components, dosage forms, effects and dangers of marijuana and a wide variety of hallucinogens (such as LSD), deliriants (such as airplane glue), amphetamines, and barbiturates.

Readers learned, for example, how to recognize a marijuana cigarette by looks and smell...how LSD can be concealed on a postage stamp...what speech pattern distinguishes a barbiturate user...why burned fingers and the constant wearing of sunglasses are danger signals of use of certain drugs.

Symptoms described in the document led a number of unsuspecting parents to the discovery that their children were on drugs. One mother had been baffled for months by strange changes in her seventeen-year-old son. Previously a hearty eater, he had been going three and four days without food. He would stay awake in long, talkative, hyperactive stretches, then pass out exhausted. Girls and school no longer interested him. He was so nervous and restless his hands trembled, and his suspicions of everyone around bordered on paranoia. With a shock, his mother realized he was "speeding."

Determinedly, the committee began seeing to it that students, too, learned more about drugs. As in most states, Massachusetts law requires that drug instruction be included in the school curriculum. But when school officials and teachers from grades K-12 met for a question-and-answer dialogue with ex-addicts brought to town by DAC, they realized that the school system's old-fashioned, "opium den" emphasis was far from relevant to the contemporary drug scene.

With help from DAC, high-school and junior-high-school science committees have updated their unit materials to include, for the first time, data on speed, marijuana, glue, LSD, and other current drugs. Rather than teach from "canned" educational packages, reports Dr. Wade, "Wakefield faculty members have undertaken their own research into a tremendous amount of material on drugs. From that, they are able to tailor their presentations to fit precisely their classes and the situation in this community." The presentations are continually rewritten to remain topical.

Wakefield school personnel are working on a fifth- and sixth-grade drug curriculum, too. Children as young as seven have been found using drugs in Wakefield, sometimes having been "turned on" initially by older brothers and sisters. "Enough others hear about drugs at the grade school level," says Dr. Wade, "that we want them to get the information straight."

As its projects have increased in scope and complexity, DAC, currently headed by oral surgeon Melvin Hellinger, has also grown. Today it includes twenty-five volunteers, a community cross-section of housewives; teachers; police officers; politicians; career girls; business, professional and working men; five high school students who serve as a sounding board for projected proposals; and the energetic Mrs. Wheeler.

One of their most dramatic projects is called the AID (for Addicts In Distress) Line. This telephone contact was created just over a year ago in hopes of salvaging those teen-agers already hooked and those who, from boredom, despair, or curiosity, will try drugs despite all efforts to dissuade them. The AID Line, whose special number is advertised in the local newspaper, leads any caller to the voice of Mrs. Wheeler, who can be reached for emergencies around the clock if need be.

"Kids on drugs worry most about one thing," explains Charles Ryan, a DAC member who also teaches a night course in a state hospital drug-addiction ward, " 'If something happens to me — an overdose, a bad trip, a paranoid seizure—whom do I call?' " A user "crashing" (coming off his "high") on speed may be so confused about reality, to the point of doubting his own identity, says Ryan, that he may try suicide to end the torment. Ryan knows Wakefield youths who have stayed awake in terror all night with paranoid delusions of policemen surrounding their houses to do them harm.

"Hot line" callers need not identify themselves, and the conversations are kept confidential by Mrs. Wheeler even from other members of DAC. No records are kept. In the first few months of operation the line carried fifty calls and involved Mrs. Wheeler in a kaleidoscope of human misery.

Once, a sobbing, heartbroken mother wanted to know how to approach her son, who, she had just discovered, was peddling marijuana. In another case, a teen-age runaway had to be tracked to the cemetery where she was hiding, terrified to confide her drug problem to her parents. Another time, Mrs. Wheeler picked up a boy on a post-midnight LSD "trip" and drove aimlessly around town, talking soothingly to him as he cringed from snakes he "saw" on the windshield and around the steering post. After hours of hallucinating, he finally allowed her to take him to a hospital for treatment.

Whenever possible, Mrs. Wheeler turns her "crisis contact" with an addict or his family into a program of sustained professional help. She and other DAC volunteers have thoroughly canvassed the Boston metropolitan area, pinpointing hospitals, social agencies, psychiatrists, and psychologists with experience in treating drug cases.

Sometimes she refers AID Line callers directly to these potential sources of help. In other instances, a user may not want to abandon drugs or does not realize that his habit may be anchored to deep psychological problems. Often parents fail to understand that their personalities and home environment are contributing to their child's addiction. "Then," explains Mrs. Wheeler, "I try to counsel them on my own, often working with several members of the same family, until they are ready to accept more intensive treatment."

We talked to one young man who recalled that he and his parents began seeing Mrs. Wheeler after he wobbled downstairs one day, glassy-eyed and incoherent from sniffing spray shoe polish. He had started on drugs with a marijuana cigarette given him by a hippie hitchhiker, then sunk rapidly into a nightmarish ordeal of chemical intoxication.

Once he took two dozen cold capsules with whiskey, and remembers: "I had violent hallucinations. Bugs, snakes, and rats were all around me and on me. I saw myself start to literally break apart. I could *feel* my body disintegrating. The hallucinations lasted eighteen hours, and the effects nearly killed me." Still, he stayed on drugs.

Over several months, sessions with Mrs. Wheeler led him gradually to begin to understand some of the psychological factors behind his habit, and how to cope with them. His parents realized some of the ways their behavior had affected his. He recalls, "Once my dad and I sat down and talked all night about how we each felt about life and about each other. It was the first time in seventeen years he had said much more to me than 'Pass the bread,' except to scold me."

Eventually the boy entered a hospital for deeper therapy, and other members of his family sought private psychiatric treatment. He says now he is through with drugs. He credits this to personal insights that began with the AID Line and some close relationships he was able to establish with certain of the hospital personnel. "I'm really beginning to enjoy myself as an individual," he told us. "I'm getting a tremendous 'high' out of life itself."

The list of persons who have joined Wakefield's drug battle extends far beyond DAC's permanent membership. Carefully screened mothers have volunteered to chauffeur drug users to and from appointments with therapists. Other volunteers man a speakers' bureau which DAC maintains to service any group interested in learning more about drug abuse. The local newspaper, too, has been generous in helping spread the warning on drugs. Motel owners have provided free lodging to ex-addicts and professional speakers flown to town by the committee. City officials have set aside time to interview the visitors for new insights, and Wakefield firemen and mothers have helped with DAC fund-raising.

The police, too, have been active in the town's war on drugs. Officer Ellis, a DAC member, has become the department's first drug spe-

cialist. Recently he attended a Federal school in Washington on the
latest methods of drug detection and has accompanied Federal agents
on field operations in the Boston area to sharpen Wakefield police pro-
cedures. Known drug pushers are kept under surveillance and, through
an improved intelligence network, police last summer were able to head
off plans by school dropouts to establish a hippie colony in a Wakefield
woods reservation. On several occasions, officers have destroyed patches
of marijuana found in vacant lots, and some "pot" parties have been
raided. Perhaps most important, the police have cooperated by referring
teen-age drug users they encounter to Mrs. Wheeler for counseling.
"Piling up a record of arrests is not the answer," explains Chief Wenzel.
"Prevention and help are more promising."...

The people of Wakefield are working together now. If a thousand-
mile journey begins with a single step, they are on their way.

For Thinking, Talking, Writing

This article explains very clearly the steps one town is taking to
fight its drug problem. There is no question but that the people involved
in this work are helping to solve many serious problems that exist among
both the young people and their parents in this community. However,
there are a few interesting statements in this article which *are* opinions,
or *express* opinions, yet are stated as facts. It is important that as a voting citizen of this country, you be able to identify such statements.
Evaluate the following quotations from this article in terms of their degree of *factual truth* vs. their degree of *assumption* on the part of the
authors or the people of Wakefield:

1. "In some comfortable Chicago suburbs, drug arrests in 1968 skyrocketed more than 300 percent." This is undoubtedly a *true* statement. But suppose that there are 30,000 people in such a suburb,
   and in 1967 there was *one* drug arrest. How many arrests in 1968
   would it take to "skyrocket" the statistics "more than 300 percent"?
   Only four. Would this be significant in terms of increased drug abuse?
   No. By the way, these are *not* accurate figures, and the 300 percent
   increase is undoubtedly more significant than this imaginary situation. But such a statement does point out the necessity of finding
   out what statistics really *mean*. They *can* be misleading.
2. "Then in 1967, in a rented loft that several college-age youths had
   converted into a 'hippie pad,'..." What is a "hippie pad"? This is

not clearly defined in the article, merely used in a vague, negative way. It could mean many different things.

3. "...police last summer were able to head off plans by school drop-outs to establish a hippie colony in a Wakefield woods reservation." Notice — there is no explanation of what this "hippie colony" might involve. There is an automatic assumption that such a colony would be "bad" and that it would involve drug abuse. But supposing that such a colony would have provided a refuge for teen-agers whose parents were alcoholics, or spent their evenings screaming at each other. The *proclaimed* hippie philosophy is one of love and mutual support. *If* the Wakefield hippie colony had been established with such a philosophy, might it not have been a better place for young people to be than in really bad homes? Who knows? But at least that possibility is something that needs to be evaluated; it is not fair to assume automatically that preventing the establishment of the colony was a "good" thing, without knowing more of the facts.

9

SEX, LOVE, AND MARRIAGE:

what do the
new patterns mean?

Introduction

Human sexuality and its relationship to human love have always been matters of consuming interest and concern to individuals and to society as a whole. Individually, we are concerned with our own feelings, our own morality, our own longing for closeness with other human beings. Societally, we are concerned with the structures of relationships and with the protection of children. Havelock Ellis, in his book *The New Spirit,* pointed out that

> The omnipresent process of sex, as it is woven into the whole texture of our man's or woman's body, is the pattern of all the processes of our life.

You, the college student, are probably concerned about the question of sexuality as it relates to your total life pattern. You are now at the age of making decisions about your own moral principles, how you believe sex relates to marriage, whether or not you want to get married, and why or why not.

In this section you will find varying opinions on these matters. Read — think — talk — write; perhaps after you explore the thinking of the authors, you will be better able to reach the decisions you must make in your own life about sex, love, and marriage.

"The Sexual Revolution" Is a Myth

Arno Karlen

The media constantly bombard us with stories confirming the popular legend: America is in the midst of a great sexual revolution. We're increasingly surrounded, they say, by suburban wife-swapping, single swingers, coed roommates, homosexuals, kinky undergrounds, and microboppers who take the Pill at puberty. But, in fact, scientific evidence has been piling up for years that indicates that no such thing is happening. What must be explained is our touching fidelity to the idea.

The presumed Red Square of American sexuality is the campus. The most knowledgeable researchers, however, doubt that any great sexual revolution is taking place there. Soon the biggest, most careful study of college students since Kinsey's will appear, and it will show a small, unstartling change in student sex behavior. Some 20 to 25 percent of college girls are nonvirgins, some five percent more than Kinsey estimated two decades ago — and he said it had hardly changed during the 20 years before that. Now, as in the past, most of this premarital sex is with intended husbands. Even Vance Packard, whose recent book on sex research suggests that there has been a significant change in sexual habits, admits there is "no indication that copulation has become rampant among college women in general (or males either)."

Perhaps more students live together, and perhaps more openly, but it's public attention that has increased most of all. Vast numbers of coeds sign in at 10 P.M., and the lives of many probably wouldn't be terribly different if they didn't. Those on and off campus who belong to the radical youth subculture often talk a much better game than they play.

Studies of the rest of the population also show no dramatic increases in any kind of sex activity, by people of any age, class, religion or education level. The level of masturbation, petting, intercourse, is the same, or moderately increased (that is, done a little more or begun a little younger). The overall picture is one of slow, unstriking change.

The same is true in other western countries. Sociologist Michael Schofield, after studying almost 2,000 British teen-agers, discovered that in
Swinging England, as in the United States, teen-age intercourse is not
nearly as common as we think it is.

Everyone thinks the Pill has loosed a tide of sex — just as everyone thought in the '20's that the automotive "brothel on wheels" was
bearing off our youth to new orgiastic treats. Yet no one actually knows
how many single girls take the Pill. Or whether they have sex more often.
Or enjoy it more. Or whether, in fact, the Pill is easier to get than a
diaphragm. But many of the country's top sex researchers — Dr. Paul
Gebhard, Dr. Mary Calderone, Prof. Ira L. Reiss — agree that new con-
traceptives didn't change sex behavior in the past, and probably aren't
doing so now. Fear of pregnancy never kept people out of bed. It just
made them worry afterward.

People also assume a tremendous upsurge in homosexuality. If
there is an increase (and many experts doubt it), it's a very slight one.
This is borne out by every study of American sex behavior before, including, and after Kinsey. Michael Schofield comments, "Maybe if you
put two adolescent boys in a double bed tonight, they'd be just as likely
or not to have sex as twenty years ago. The difference is that instead of
the stony silence of utter shame the next morning, there'd just be embarrassment."

Homosexuality is more talked about than 20 years ago, but so is
all sexuality. In some ways homosexuality is more open than ever before;
but 60 years ago every city of even moderate size had a red-light district,
with male brothels and male streetwalkers, which wouldn't be tolerated
today. One must remember that for almost 3,000 years westerners have
claimed there's more sex, and more homosexuality, than there was yesterday. Obviously, most of them have been wrong.

As for sadomasochistic and other baroque undergrounds, Dr. Paul
Gebhard told me, "All together, they probably number in the thousands.
They're very small groups, though they don't like to think so. When you
talk to people involved in these things, you hear the same names over
and over. It's an encapsulated little fraternity." Most knowledgeable people I've spoken to agree. More people have tried wife-swapping and
various deviant acts once or twice, but even they are a distinct minority.

Those who are familiar with sex clubs and group marriages on the
West Coast, where they are commonest, guess there are 40 to 60 of
them, with an average of 25 members each. Many meet sporadically, and
few last as long as a year. More than a century ago there were dozens
of communities in this country based on sharing property and sexual

partners. The Fourierite and Owenite communities alone numbered over 40. The Oneida group, in upstate New York, had hundreds of members and lasted for two generations. Proportionately, more of the nation may have been involved in radical sexual communities then than today, and more successfully.

Few anthropologists are surprised at how slowly sex behavior is changing, even in this century of deep social upheaval. They know that mores and sex behavior are so emotion-laden, so deeply woven into the social fabric, that quick cataclysmic change is unlikely. Kinsey concluded that one can predict when a person is 14 what his lifetime sexual patterns will be. Others believe such patterns are set far earlier, and that to change them one must radically transform the bedrock social attitudes and institutions that shape the first five to seven years of life.

If we are witnessing such a moderate evolution, why do we have such a stake in the idea of revolution? For two centuries a wave of sexual utopianism has been growing in the West. Since long before Christianity, sex had been considered a dangerous chained beast; in the eighteenth century the pre-Romantics began to see it as a beneficent force. Impulse should be released, not controlled. Early in this century, as the anti-Victorian reaction grew, debased Freudianism gave it scientific sanction. More and more people came to believe that if sexual impulses were acted out, society would end war, and individuals lose their pimples, sulks, work problems and other debilities.

Like poverty and the weather, sex had always been there, an intractable fact of life. But then poverty, the weather, and sex became "problems," to be studied and solved.

All these vectors converged on the generation born early in this century. Many Americans had recently arrived from foreign countries or moved from rural to urban areas. Their Anglicized, city-bred offspring knew a generation gap greater than any today. They invented dating. For the first time, most people chose their own spouses instead of letting their families and communities do it for them, and they did it more on the basis of love than social contract. The idea that sex is validated by marriage was extended by some people to the love that leads to marriage. By fewer, to love alone. By fewer still, to affection, caprice or simple lust.

When Kinsey compared the generation that came of age in the '20's with their parents, he found increases of 8, 15, sometimes 20 percentage points in various categories of sex activity. Of 10 young women picked at random, now five rather than four would have masturbated; three or four would have petted to orgasm, rather than one or two; by the age of 25, three or four would be nonvirgins instead of one or two. That was the dimension of the sexual revolution of the '20's, and it was the greatest the century has seen.

But people thought the change was greater, for attitudes changed more than behavior, and the rhetoric of sexual liberation had taken on a life of its own. People's ideas had run far ahead of their lives, for it took a lot of talk to work oneself up to a little more action. In 1910 most college girls would say premarital sex was a sin. In 1925 they'd say it was quite all right, if one loved the man; most would then probably add, "I just haven't met the right guy yet, myself."

Basically what had happened was that males had sex less with prostitutes, more with girls they knew. Some girls were somewhat more willing to consider sex if they expected marriage or felt love. Sex took on a more positive conscious value. Some people's inhibitions lessened, and their sexual repertoires expanded. By 1930 the upswing on the graphs almost leveled off. A slight, almost imperceptible, rise continued into the '60's.

During the past few years the line has started to climb a bit more steeply again. But there has been no change to match that of the '20's. We are talking about a few percentage points for any group of people or sexual activity. (In some areas there are actually decreases.) During this gradual erosion of old patterns the idea has persisted that sex behavior is changing rapidly. And as the change accelerates just a bit in the '60's, the clamor multiplies ten times as much.

In the '30's, when the peak of change was well past, an eminent pioneer sexologist said that if things continued the way they were going, no American girl would reach the bridal bed a virgin in 1960. Most prophets make the same mistake today, and will sound just as silly a few decades from now.

Four-letter words and mini-skirts don't mean people act very differently in bed. Anyone who thinks the most basic sexual values have changed might try bearing a child out of wedlock, or announcing publicly that he is currently enjoying adultery or homosexuality. We are less ignorant than in the past, but reading sex manuals no more enables a person to be sexually spontaneous than reading karate manuals enables a coward to leap bravely into a brawl. After a half century of sex education, social change, psychiatry and programmatic revolution, the amount of secret sexual suffering and confusion is still vast.

The distance between our rhetoric and fantasies on one hand and our daily lives on the other is greater than ever. We say sex should be guiltless and pleasurable; we are only a little better equipped for attaining this than our parents were. Where there is a greater gap between expectation and real sensual liberation, there must be more doubt and inadequacy than ever. Add to this an increasing confusion in sex roles, and one has a disturbance of the first magnitude.

One of the best defenses against this disturbance is to deny it with fake sophistication. In three years of work on a book dealing with sex problems and sex research. I've found that nothing makes people more uncomfortable than mentioning the need for accurate studies of sex behavior.

Their fantasies and self-esteem are at stake. They don't want their emotional prejudices upset by facts. Recently a very reputable sex-research foundation was turned down by two dozen leading foundations when it wanted to do a much-needed study of homosexuality. Do we think we already know all the facts? Or are we so frightened of the subject that we don't want it examined?

Many in the radical youth subculture look with lofty pity at their elders' sex lives; the elders believe the young are as sexually carefree as rodents. It proves the old psychological truism that children pick up their parents' hidden fantasies. The kids talk the sexual liberation their parents and grandparents tried so hard to attain, with such limited success.

Actually this vanguard of youth consists of several groups. Some are just talking generational party line. Others are delinquents, who 10 years ago might have joined gangs. Today they fall into society's current delinquent slot, the hippie drug scene. Others are dropouts from the middle and upper-middle class, some as well or as badly adjusted as most people, others deeply disturbed.

The trappings of that youth culture are no sign of sexual freedom or health. A New York psychiatrist says, "I see plenty of the flower children from the Lower East Side. Lots are shacked up at sixteen, but in sibling relationships. They want love, and downgrade sex. They tend to be passive and dependent. Sex without love is a problem, but love without sex is no improvement." A Philadelphia psychologist told me, "They come in here wearing beads, old dresses and soldier coats, with beautiful facades of love and freedom. They verbalize well, but they don't know how to live or love. Even the girls with lots of sexual experience usually have no sense of their bodies, no capacity for pleasure."

Like those two doctors, I object not to the idea of sexual revolution but to the illusion it has taken place. We need one badly — a real one that will allow people to live healthy, expressive, sexual lives without legal penalties and social obstacle courses. As in another emotion-laden revolution, the black man's fight for equality, the smug cant of progress lets people evade the need for deep, difficult change. You never beat the devil when you deny that he exists.

For Thinking, Talking, Writing

1. Do you agree with Mr. Karlen that "mores and sex behavior are so emotion-laden, so deeply woven into the social fabric, that quick cataclysmic change is unlikely"?
2. Do you believe, with Mr. Karlen, that the sexual revolution is more talk than action?
3. What do you think of the statement, "Sex without love is a problem, but love without sex is no improvement"?
4. Do you believe that we "need [a sexual revolution] badly — a real one that will allow people to live healthy, expressive sexual lives without legal penalties and social obstacle courses"? If so, how might young people today contribute towards such a *real* sexual revolution?

Sex for Credit

Nancy Gay Faber

I turned to the young man sitting next to me and said, "Sexual intercourse." He smiled and nodded his shaggy head. "Sexual intercourse," he repeated.

Now, before my family collectively faints from shock, and other ... readers rip out these pages, please understand that we were sitting in a great, gray lecture hall at the University of Minnesota among dozens of students who were saying the same words at the same time. The second lecture of a course called "Human Sexual Behavior" sounded like a kindergarten word drill — except for the words. Leading the class, and clearly enjoying himself, was Professor Gerhard Neubeck.

"Don't look at me when you speak," he urged us. "Turn to your neighbor. It's more embarrassing that way. Now, let me hear 'vagina.'" We all muttered the word while Neubeck stood, hands in pockets, eyes gleaming, like Victor Borge about to launch one of his mad attacks on an unsuspecting piano. "Louder, please," he demanded in a calm voice. "VAGINA," we shouted. Laughing and self-conscious, we tried "clitoris" and then "erection."

After class, Neubeck stood in the window of his office on the new West Bank campus in Minneapolis, lit a little cigar and looked down at the broad stretch of Mississippi River below. "The first big hang-up I run into with each new class is the vocabulary," he explained. "This idea that sex talk is dirty talk is deeply ingrained in us. I have to desensitize my students so that sexuality becomes less loaded for them. Saying the words out loud is a good start. If you repeat 'vagina' often enough, it loses some of its threat."

It may surprise those on the far side of the generation gap to learn that college students today — those super-wise, super-sophisticated creatures — need any sexual desensitizing, but it's true. At least the kids are smart enough to recognize their hang-ups and to make some attempt to understand them. That's more than can be said for many parents who like to pretend that sex doesn't exist.

Students at Minnesota are luckier than most — the administration has made some provision for sex education. Even more important, students find in Neubeck's class an honesty, candor, and humor that are rare on other campuses. Most universities — if sex is taught at all — either limit it to the basic biological facts, antiseptically presented by a gym teacher, or sandwich it into a marriage course, somewhere between the lectures on choosing a china pattern and balancing the family budget. Hardly any notice is taken in such courses of what Neubeck calls "the enormous emotional and psychological complexities that go along with the physiology." And yet, that is what the kids want to know about. Which is why Neubeck's course is always filled on the first registration day every quarter. Although "Family Studies 100 — Human Sexual Behavior," as it is listed in the university catalogue, is officially limited to juniors and seniors who plan professions dealing with the sex problems of others, many in the class are there to understand their own sexuality.

Sometimes Neubeck's desensitizing runs into a roadblock, like the minister's wife who thought she had accepted "those words" but couldn't remember how to spell "penis" in her notebook. I sat in on another class, near the end of the course, when the students showed just how relaxed they had become with the vocabulary. One boy wanted to know why certain words describing intercourse were considered offensive. He used the standard four-letter verb without batting an eye, and the class was equally offhand.

No word is forbidden to students in Neubeck's class (although he himself deliberately refrains from the most pungent Anglo-Saxonisms), and no question is too hot to answer. When kids ask what the Professor thinks about premarital sex, he tells them: "Americans overemphasize 'scoring' in everything they do — business, sports, and even sex. What is really important is not scoring a conquest, but rather, what happens between two people. The decision to have intercourse, made jointly by two rational people, is a lot different from the impulsive exploitation of one person by another, which is often the way it is in sex before marriage."

When a student asks if masturbation is harmful, Neubeck answers that one too: "There is no scientific evidence that masturbation leads to anything detrimental. Of course, if a person is masturbating a dozen times a day, I'd say he was concentrating on only one thing. I tend to be a little suspicious of anyone who overdoes anything."

In Neubeck's class, kids discuss everything from technical virginity to extramarital sex, from pornography to prostitution, from menstruation to menopause, from abortion to abnormal sex. The Professor quotes from the poetry of e. e. cummings, Bertrand Russell's autobiography and John Updike's *Couples* as well as Masters and Johnson's study of the physical aspects of sex. Reading assignments include Vance Packard's *The Sexual Wilderness*, a book called *Sex and Love in the Bible*, plus articles from scientific journals with titles like "Extent of Spousal Agreement of Certain Non-Sexual and Sexual Aspects of Marital Adjustment."

What is really outstanding about Neubeck's course is not so much *what* he teaches, but *how* he teaches his students to think about sex. Says the Professor: "For the first time, many of my students find in this class an adult who is willing to openly admit that he is a sexual being. I'm not defensive about sex, and I don't want them to be."

Two years ago, when Gerry Neubeck began his sex lectures, his three grown children threatened to picket the class with signs reading: "Dad is a Dirty Old Man." They were kidding, of course, but for many Americans, sex is no joke, and any man who teaches it is a little suspect. In spite of the sexual revolution we are experiencing now, the story of the birds and the bees is, at least among the hard-core middle class, still the biggest conversational taboo in the country. Neubeck is succinct: "People equate talking with doing."

It's true America has come a long way from the day in 1934 when a censor blue-penciled the word "syphilis" out of the New York health commissioner's radio script. And we're light-years from those pre-1960 movies when Hollywood put married couples into twin beds, chastely separated by a night table.

There is a sexual revolution in this country, and Neubeck points out for his students some of the signs: the growing acceptance of the pill, even among Catholics, and the first appearance of scientific journals devoted to sex. But the simple fact remains that a lot of people aren't ready for the revolution. Neubeck itemizes some of the sexual conflicts Americans are saddled with:

• Sex is considered both dirty and disgusting and sacred and beautiful.

• We regard sex as something to be treated delicately, yet by not talking about it ourselves, we encourage those who deal with it grossly.

• We acknowledge the idealism of youth, yet we are afraid to be honest with them about sex.

"I don't have all the answers for you," Neubeck explains to his students, "but you should be aware of the confusion. Somewhere along the way, sexuality got separated from the rest of life. I want to integrate it again. As soon as you try to hide something that is essentially normal, people overreact. The forbidden-fruit flavor of sex makes it all the more fascinating."

It isn't a very revolutionary idea — most intelligent Americans would agree. It's just that a lot of them don't act as though they agree. Which is probably why I sat in that Minneapolis classroom feeling uneasy as I recited what I knew in my mind were perfectly accurate and acceptable terms. It's in your conditioning. My relatives are all New Englanders. They wouldn't dream of saying "those words"— in fact, they wouldn't think of talking about sex at all. And the embarrassment of the young Midwesterners sitting around me in that early lecture, bearded and long-haired and thoroughly modern though they may be, proves my family is no exception.

One hung-up generation passes along its bits of misinformation and guilt feelings to the next. This sort of Victorianism is a long time dying. Recently, the teen-age daughter of a friend came home from school and said one of the nuns had warned the girls not to wear patent leather shoes because, in the reflection of their shiny surface, boys could see up under a young lady's skirt. I hadn't heard that chestnut in years, but here it was still making the rounds.

The question asked by one Minnesota student sums up the national conflict about sex. "Why," he wanted to know, "is it easy to tell your date a dirty joke and impossible to ask what she thinks about premarital sex?"

Proof of this conflict is found in the kind of sex information available to young people these days. College students can, for example, watch the multi-deflowerings of *Candy* at any neighborhood theater, and they can buy, quite openly on campus, underground newspapers like the *Berkeley Barb*, with frankly explicit want ads ("WANTED: one stud, well-hung, to act as houseboy...."), but only a few can walk into a classroom and learn about sex from a qualified teacher.

Academically, Neubeck has all the proper credentials for his job. For 14 years, he taught an undergraduate course in preparation for marriage at the university. He is now president of the American Association of Marriage Counselors and acting head of Minnesota's Family Study Center. He runs a post-doctoral program on marriage counseling and, in the evenings, works with his own patients.

More important for his students are the personal qualities Neubeck brings to class. He and his wife Ruth have been married for 28 years, a match described by their 22-year-old daughter Eva as a "very beautiful relationship." Both Neubeck and Ruth are German Jews who fled the Nazis in 1939. Perhaps because he barely escaped that horror, the sexual fears that preoccupy Americans seem small by comparison, and he is able to view the scene with detachment. Happy in his marriage, Neubeck brings an emotional security to the class.

He wants to show his students how better communications can take the scare out of sex. "As I see it," the Professor says, "sexuality is not a matter of whether you do or don't, but rather, the nature of it. It isn't enough just to learn how to avoid problems and resolve conflicts. You should be able to learn to enjoy what life offers."

Our breakdown in sexual communications begins early, Neubeck explains to his class: "A child sees, hears and feels sexual phenomena. To a certain extent, he is allowed to participate — watching Mommy change her clothes and Daddy take a shower — but a censorial curtain is dropped when it comes to talking about it. A child who asks what a four-letter word means quickly finds out that this is forbidden."

This conditioning turns out grown-ups who play word games. Neubeck gives three examples: the doctor who asks his patient if she has an irritation in "the sexual organ"; the divorce lawyer quizzing his client on whether her husband "had relations with" the other woman; the mother who asks her 13-year-old if he has "funny feelings" in bed at night. At this point in the lecture, Neubeck unfailingly asks his class to recite the correct words: "vagina," "sexual intercourse" and "nocturnal emission."

What he calls "silent sex" can have tragic results. Neubeck gives his students the classic case of Kathy and Keith, teen-agers who are going steady: "Holding hands came almost automatically, but when Kathy reached into Keith's pocket for change and discovered he was having an erection, she was horrified and ran off. Keith was aghast. Next time they met, both pretended nothing had happened — talking about sex wasn't 'nice.' As time went on, Keith cupped Kathy's breast, unhooked her bra and had an ejaculation — all without words. Since they could not discuss their feelings, decisions were arrived at half-heartedly until finally they drifted, still silent, into first intercourse. Later, all they could say was 'Good night, Kathy' and 'Good night, Keith.'" Neubeck finds this silent drift into intercourse appalling.

For him, sex goes far beyond a physical phenomenon. "Intercourse," Neubeck says, "cannot be described clinically." Which is, according to him, the flaw in the Masters and Johnson study, where 705 volunteers were observed in intercourse. "The researchers were only aware of what was happening physically," he says. "Nothing was known about the emotional state of the subjects."

In contrast to this clinical approach, Neubeck reads a long description written by a woman in her 30's, telling her reactions after having intercourse with a man she loves. The passage is both explicit and intense as she describes the rhythms and climax of making love. The class sits silent as he reads. No one rustles papers, no one shuffles his feet — and no one takes notes. It is painfully moving and beautiful.

Near the end of the course, I asked Neubeck to pick a few students at random for me to interview. By then, I decided, the kids would demonstrate whether the desensitizing really worked. We agreed to meet at my hotel one evening without the Professor, for a frank talk about what, if anything, they had learned in class.

While I waited for them to arrive, I thought back on my own education. I spent my adolescence fitting together pieces of sex information like a patchwork quilt because no one — at home or at school — could or would talk on the subject. There were forbidden books to read (*Forever Amber*), magazine ads alluding to "feminine hygiene" to puzzle over and always *Webster's Collegiate* to search through for very unsatisfactory definitions of words like "whore."

The closest I came to sex education in school was a textbook used in an all-girl health class that discussed such fascinating subjects as necking and petting. Of course, we were never allowed beyond the chapters on good grooming.

With this sort of conditioning, I wondered if I was ready to talk about sex with a mixed group of strangers. Would I revert to the word games? I needn't have worried. As the evening progressed, it was clear that the students were completely at ease with the topic. No one was the least embarrassed, not even me. There is, I learned, a big difference between sexy talk and sex talk.

It would be impossible to cover everything that we discussed that evening. We laughed and shouted and interrupted one another like old friends; except I had never had that kind of conversation before, even with close girl friends.

All of them were taking Neubeck's course as an elective, to learn more about their own sexuality. One divorced woman had signed up to "help me answer the questions my teen-age sons ask." Another girl was trying to unlearn what she had been taught. "I went to a Catholic grade school," she explained, "where even to think about sex was a sin." This same girl laughed as she told us how, just recently, she shocked a group of social workers by using the word "scrotum."

For the boys in the group — most of them either 19 or 20 — Neubeck's class had made them more aware of the feelings and desires of the girls they date. One young man said: "My father keeps telling me about all the girls he seduced in college. He thinks that I have to make it with every girl I date. He thinks women are *things*, to be used."

A second boy observed: "That's Neubeck's objection to *Playboy*. It treats women as objects, not people. My father pulls the same thing. Every time I take a blanket for a picnic, he has to make some remark. He's got a whole other concept of women."

"I wish my mother could take Neubeck's class," sighed the divorced student. "My sons can't even use the word 'pregnant' in front of her."

We talked nonstop for five hours, covering all kinds of sexuality, from how they learned the facts of life to homosexual TV commercials to child molesters to local dating habits. At one point, all the women were involved in a discussion of the problems of menstruating when we were young. "You couldn't swim or take a bath," one girl recalled. "My mother wouldn't let me wash my hair."

Another girl told how she watched a film on menstruation shown to girls in the fifth grade: "It was one of those Walt Disney things with the glands all blossoming into flowers. When it was over, the school nurse told the girls to remember what they had seen — but not to tell the boys. Can you imagine anyone that dumb?"

I asked the boys if they thought women over-dramatized the pain that goes with being female.

"Bill Cosby has a good answer for that," one junior said. "He has a record that says men suffer the most awful pain of all — much worse than giving birth — when they have to sit through a double feature with their arm around a girl, and the blood stops circulating and your fingers are about to drop off."

"Hey," another boy broke in. "Remember when you were young and the older kids were talking dirty and you didn't understand, but you laughed anyway? Once, in my neighborhood, they were saying 'vagina.' I thought they meant Regina — that's a Canadian city — and I didn't know what was so funny about that, but I laughed all the same."

It was an exhilarating evening. Neubeck's students were liberated by what he had taught — and almost giddy with their newfound freedom of speech.

When I left Minneapolis, it was not with the idea of forcing friends and relatives to listen to words they didn't want to hear. As Neubeck warns: "Better communications can be blocked by shock tactics. You've got to remember that others are not where you are yet, and to gauge your audience."

Minnesota is lucky to have Neubeck's course on campus. But how lucky? Out of a total enrollment of 48,000, only 120 students at a time can take the class. That means 360 liberated kids a year. America may need more than that.

For Thinking, Talking, Writing

1. What is *your* opinion of the kind of sex education described in this article?

2. Analyze *your own* feelings about one of the sexual conflicts Professor Neubeck feels that many Americans are saddled with: the fact that in our society sex is considered both dirty and disgusting and sacred and beautiful. Do you find yourself thinking about it in these different ways from time to time? If so, in what connection do you think of it as "dirty and disgusting"? In what respect does it seem "sacred and beautiful"?

3. What are your reactions to Professor Neubeck's belief that "sexuality is not a matter of whether you do or don't, but rather, the nature of it"? How does this opinion tie in with traditional moral standards? With your religious beliefs?

4. Two of the boys in the discussion group felt that their fathers thought of women as *things*, to be used, rather than as people. Do you think this is typical of male attitudes among middle-aged people? Do you think that young men, as a group, have a different attitude about women now?

Coeducation: How Far?

Pearl S. Buck

The conversation in the living room of my rambling old house was so lively this morning as I passed on my way to my desk to write this article that I yielded to temptation and sat down to listen. An argument was taking place. Subject: whether Sally, a young woman of our acquaintance now attending a university nearby, had done wisely in leaving her dormitory to live with a young man, a fellow student, in a small apartment. I remained silent while the argument waxed strong, for it had nothing to do, it seemed, with faculty or family. Sally's family, I knew, would violently disapprove, but their disapproval meant nothing in this day of relegated parents. Nor did I offer advice. I merely sat and listened for the conclusion. There was no conclusion, however, except that Susan, our young beauty, was to my surprise, firmly on the negative side.

"It's too messy for me," she declared. She was on her way to an early tennis engagement, looking as usual, very smart, with a young man in the offing. For at least five years there has always been a young man, or several, in Susan's offing. She was gone and I stole away, foreseeing no further conclusion to the argument. Here at my desk I now put down my random thoughts, not new but stirred to articulation by the talk in the living room, to which I shall put my own conclusion.

Coeducation, defined, changes with changing times and changing moral values. I can remember when coeducation was a matter merely of young men and women attending the same classes in the same institution. That argument was settled affirmatively and the next was whether they should eat at the same time at the same tables. Now, of course, it has proceeded to a much more intimate point. Classes and meals in common are taken as a matter of course. The argument today is whether men and women students shall share the same apartment, perhaps even two by two, or if in dormitories, shall they have the freedom of one another's rooms.

It is idle, I believe, to think of a return to the past. The past is dead, its recovery beyond our reach even if we wish to recover it. The apple of Eden's garden has been eaten. The only argument is how far shall the knowledge of good and evil go. The minds of young academicians today are absorbed, especially the female minds, by questions concerning virginity, abortion, pills, etc. Male academicians are not so much absorbed in or concerned about virginity. Indeed, I discover very little concern in the young male mind on any question relating to sex. Their only question is how far they can persuade the girls to go. Women of all ages are available, and the only vexation, it seems, is a matter of temporary delay due to the unhappy fact that as yet not every female is available to every male, a situation that makes for increasing masculine indignation.

I realize, of course, that I am the last person in our universe to discuss the subject of coeducation as it exists, or seems about to exist, today. Millenniums ago I attended a girls' college. In my ignorance, I was not at that time even interested in boys, although two men's colleges were in our periphery. The reason? Books! I had never in my life had enough books to read, to range through, to gobble down in order to satisfy my insatiable curiosity about everything. . . . I could not have been sufficiently tempted by any young man, however handsome, to consider, on any terms, even marriage, much less sharing with him an apartment. It was not so much morals that prevented me as the fact that I would be burdened by cooking and cleaning and otherwise caring for his needs. True, in those early days we also had the healthy preventive fear of producing an illegitimate baby and disgracing our families thereby. That inhibition is now removed, or said to be, since I am reminded by the most recent birth statistics that 300,000 children are born out of wedlock each year in the United States, most of them to high school girls, compelling me to question the universality or efficacy of the pill. Nevertheless, the pill exists and undoubtedly does prevent thousands of other births. . . .

I am nőt so old-fashioned as to believe that virginity is in itself a treasure. Still, one ought to give one's self the pleasure of enjoying the loss of it, and therefore one should save it, so to speak, until the maximum moment when all elements can contribute to that enjoyment. The first element for the enjoyment is a man whom one can completely love and the second element is a maturity in one's own self sufficiently developed for full enjoyment. Youth does not distinguish between one wine and another.

...It is natural for a girl to want to draw the attention of a man. It is when she is fearful that no man will find her desirable that she is willing to pay any price — and pay too soon — to win his pursuit.... Upon investigation...I discover that the girls pregnant too soon usually are poor students and may even be called plain stupid. An exception last year was Louise — that is not her name, of course. She was pretty, she was a good student, and everyone was more than surprised, they were shocked, when she dropped out of school to have her baby. But I knew Louise's family. Her parents were quarreling over a divorce. She was a child who had grown up without a stable home. She had led a loveless life. It was perhaps inevitable that, in her hunger for love, she yielded to an immature imitation of it....

It is all too obvious that while I believe coeducation is acceptable for those young persons mature enough not to allow themselves to be diverted from the necessity of being educated, it is a doubtful benefit for the immature who cannot reconcile themselves to what they obviously are. Instead they seek to charm through the crude implement of sex experimentation and succeed only in charming others like themselves....

This then, is my conclusion. Coeducation is admirable, advisable, impossible at this late date to prevent, but only for some, perhaps only for relatively few, will it prove a blessing. For minds and characters strong enough to benefit from contact with other minds and characters as strong, coeducation may improve education as a whole. For others it will prove only a distraction from the main purpose of education....

For Thinking, Talking, Writing

1. From your own experience and knowledge, do *you* think that, for most young men and women, living together in college distracts them from their education?
2. Discuss the alternative possibility: that living together may take the emotional pressure *off* young men and women in college and thus free them to pursue their education more intensely.

Twenty Ways
to Be More Loved

Men Want...

by Harvey Roma

Men don't know what they want in a girl. Except sex. Ask them and you get Just One Thing for an answer. Pressed to the limit, men become anatomical, physiognomical and nearly always comical. "Love" is mentioned apprehensively, if at all. "Hung up" is still the preferred term. Such anxiety. Wow!

Anything to keep from getting serious. So, Lust is still in. Love is still out. Sorry to have to say that men are still boys, but that's the report from the barroom, locker room, poolroom and schoolroom — all those rooms where sex is in the open and love is taboo — where men reveal they don't have the foggiest idea what they want, beyond the barest essentials.

But, *if* they knew, these are the things they'd say:

MEN LOVE:
1. A life of special favors.

A girl who knows how to surprise and delight is absolutely priceless. She is aware of what makes a man's eyes shine, shoulders relax. The sensitive woman somehow remembers what works, and does it again — only more so and differently. The favor can be a word, a gesture, a caress, a real gift — it doesn't matter. It must be an offering, however, with no strings attached, no negotiations, definitely nothing expected in return. Whether she gives him a glance or a glorious evening, he must know that it belongs to him alone. Then, when the return comes, it's not an obligation.

2. A world of unusual meanings.

Women are men's environment. They surround us, above and beneath. No man can resist a girl who creates a fabulous microcosm for him. And I *don't* mean interior decorating. The creating is done by attaching new meaning to common things, especially shared things — clothes, places frequented, music, even money. A man knows he's in love when the familiar is oddly fabulous: "I have often walked down this street before, but...."

3. The illusion of complete freedom.

No "mands," thank you: no demands, commands, mandates or mandibles. Freedom is deceptive, but we want the deception absolute. We will do anything for a girl if (a) she doesn't punish us when we don't, and (b) she comes across when we do. Girls who are successful in love find our special rewards.

4. Girls who dress, make up, do their hair, etc., to please us.

"Glamour," "chic," smart fashion "looks" of various kinds — all turn out to be things women do in order to show up other women. Men couldn't care less. When we tell a girl not to put on lipstick and plastic eyelashes, we mean it. Sometimes we're compelled to stare at some chick whose eyes are drawn like Minnie Mouse or whose skin resembles silent-film. We can't help watching this contraption but we wouldn't want to take it home in a plastic bag.

MEN NEED:

5. Fidelity.

It doesn't matter whether we "have a right to ask" a girl not to date others. We may be too proud to mention it. We may not, I fear, be faithful ourselves. But the man who doesn't get fidelity is soon gone. Panel discussions on "inequities of the double standard" haven't changed men's attitudes about loyalty one bit. By the way, it's not faithfulness *qua* abstract virtue that a man wants, but evidence that he reigns supreme.

6. Undivided attention at key times.

A key time is any time a man is most himself. All men need to be adored. That means looked at, listened to, touched frequently, and otherwise tendered notice that the state of grace is still going for them. A girl can hardly touch a man too much. Don't cling, just handle.

7. To feel like great lovers.

No, to *be* great lovers. This is a sensitive point. There are times when a man wants to be superior to all other men on earth. The more insecure he is, the more he needs to *know*. This is not a subtle message. A girl *must* tell a man when he has been great to her in no uncertain terms.

8. To be proud...

...of her, of himself for having her. Interestingly enough, *her* friends may not matter, but his *always* do. Clever girls worry about this and work at putting themselves across to his crowd.

9. To be allowed to pursue their thing in their own way, with help and advice, of course, but no interference.

This goes, no matter *what* it is. If his idea of the world's work is collecting old model-airplane parts or laying his life on the line for an impossible cause, no broad can say to him, nay. He means it. Love him, love his bit — and that is that.

MEN CAN'T STAND:

10. To be forced to feel what they don't, to put on an act, to have to be somebody they aren't, to be "nice" when they feel rotten, to have moods misunderstood and taken personally.

Men hate to be considered "underdeveloped." We are not in training. We are finished products. Take it or leave it. A good chick can do almost anything she wants, but she can't make us over.

Girls Want...

by Lillian Roxon

A girl knows what she wants in a man. And really experienced men have been onto the secret for years. The ones who *know* concentrate on what might be called the extras.

Men might get hung up on the numbers game and superstud fantasies. *Girls* get hung up on the one thing he said about her eyes or, better still, her lips. If he meant it, that is.

Sincerity, wretchedly overworked word that it is, is one of the things girls really want from men. Women have a truly uncanny way of knowing what's for real and what isn't. If you do fool them, it's only because they're in a mood to be fooled anyway. (A man who can do that with charm — and it's not easy — deserves to win.)

What do girls really want from men? *Really,* that is, when the cards are down and they're admitting everything.

GIRLS LOVE:

1. Infinite Tenderness...

...perhaps because it's so alien to a man's public personality and is such a private and personal thing, because it shows the man trusts her and is not afraid to show her the gentler side of himself, because even if the encounter is a brief one, it shows that he values her as one might value any beautiful and delicate object. There are men who can be tender with cars, dogs or children, but not with women. It's such a mistake because as far as a girl is concerned, there is no such thing as *too* much tenderness.

2. Surprises, an unexpected change of pace.

The thing about tenderness is that it's a surprise, especially coming from a normally tough and guarded man. A man whose usual life-style is entirely gentle and romantic will, without doubt, delight women utterly, most of the time. If he wants to delight them *all* of the time, he might well consider giving in to that nagging urge to come on tough occasionally. All girls want to be treated like goddesses *most* of the time, but no girl wants to be treated like a goddess *all* of the time. An experienced man knows exactly how to combine elements of both moods so that he never becomes entirely predictable. Unpredictability is an aphrodisiac.

3. A sense of theater.

In a romantic situation a girl invariably sees herself as acting out a role. Anything that fits in with this excites her. Girls love champagne because it feeds their sense of theater. But if they're acting out Celia Johnson in *Brief Encounter*, then a stale sardine sandwich in a railroad waiting room will do the trick, as it did in the film. Girls need to feel "onstage" because it makes them feel special. That's why, when there's no drama in their lives, they create it, often from thin air. The man who knows how to play straightman to her fantasies needs to know very little else. Eric Clapton, guitarist of the Cream, has navy blue sheets (and a red blanket) on the bed of his Chelsea flat. That's bedroom theater, never to be underestimated.

4. Harmony.

If a man wants to know how to make love to a woman, he should listen to a Beethoven symphony or a Brandenburg concerto. Nothing in the Beatles or any modern-pop rock, strangely enough, expresses better her need for decisive action one moment, violent absorption the next, and lyrically romantic adagio passages a minute later. Modern music comes on too strong, too fast, which, maybe, is what is wrong with modern man. A sonata often starts quietly and thoughtfully, building itself up, burning itself out, resting, recuperating with maybe a lively, but light, allegro sequence at the end.

5. The perfect gesture.

It could be anything – a kiss on the back of the neck, a shared cigarette, a single flower. It really doesn't matter what the gesture is. The point is that girls need them and want them. Experienced men, the cads, have a whole repertoire of them – and a magician's sense of timing when to use them. The gesture should never be expected, it should occasionally be performed in front of others because girls are very concerned with their images. And it should always be, whether it's a touch or a gift, something specifically tailored to her personality.

6. Physical Comfort.

Girls pretend they like to rough it. They lie. Girls need an enormous amount of pampering in order to be most effectively themselves. Girls don't function well when they're tired, when they need a shower, or when a chair is lumpy. They are not as involved with luxury as men imagine, but they are affected negatively by noise, dirt and the other distractions that a man finds, in romantic moments, easy to ignore. Above all, they have a strong sense of privacy. Sometimes all that is wrong is that there are too many people around — a thought that bothers men considerably less.

7. Reassurance.

Every girl in the world is full of doubts. She doubts that she's truly beautiful, and even when she believes that her face is beautiful, she doubts that her body is. And even if she believes some of it is, she doubts that all of it is. And even if all of it is — that it's all beautiful to *him* — she doubts that she is right for him. She worries about being too free, and not free enough. She wonders if she is making him happy, doing things right, acting right. And she would never dare ask. A man who can quell these doubts, and make her feel she can make no move that is a wrong move, is fulfilling one of her fiercest needs, He also has to be able to reassure her that what she is doing is right, even if it is only right for that moment. Women are more moral, even today, than any man likes to admit.

8. Tranquility.

When girls talk about what's wrong with men as lovers, they invariably complain about being rushed before they have had time to collect themselves. Girls, being wildly romantic, want to switch out of the everyday world of romance before they can accept love properly.

9. Words.

Girls really love words — and a man who can put things into words. What is said is no problem. It can be very simple. *How* it's said is something else. Men are constantly afraid of sounding corny. All they have to do is tell it like it is. Women may be intuitive, but they don't trust their intuition. You have to tell them what they already have read from you, if only to assure them they read it right. Some women are happiest with a running commentary, which for them is the best part of what's going on, because they love words so much. You can tell them much more than you think with words — command, entreat, suggest, applaud. It pays to increase your word power.

10. The exotic.

The man a girl rejects in Brooklyn, she accepts with avid eagerness in Venice. Two people meet in a desert and fall in love under the palm trees. They would have hated each other at a singles party in Chicago. Love is magic and needs magic to nourish it. That corny stuff about moonlight and strolling violinists works. It's true.

For Thinking, Talking, Writing

1. If you are a man, compare what *you* want in a woman with the things Harvey Roma says most men want. If you are a girl, evaluate yourself against Mr. Roma's criteria: how many of these items *can* you do, and *do* you do, in your relationship with a man?
2. If you are a girl, compare what *you* want in a man with the things Lillian Roxon says most girls want. If you are a man, evaluate yourself against Miss Roxon's criteria: how many of these items *can* you do, and *do* you do, in your relationship with a girl?
3. Have you learned from this article anything which you can apply to your future relationships? If so, what?

Are We the
Last Married Generation?

Harriet Van Horne

Back in the Jazz Age, when no nice girl smoked *anything* and all brides were presumed chaste unless noticeably with child, a kindly, concerned judge in Denver decided something had to be done about America's rising divorce rate. His prescription was trial marriage. Not free love, another shocking notion in the 'twenties, but a marriage that could be dissolved by mutual consent if there were no children. In consequence of his views, Judge Ben Lindsey was denounced from the pulpit and castigated in the press. He was called a Bohemian, a heathen, a defiler of the American home — and a great deal worse. Ultimately, he was dropped from the bench.

In the forty years since Judge Lindsey's advanced theories were set forth, the divorce rate has tripled, and trial marriage, in some circles, is positively old-fashioned. Living together without the benediction of marriage is the new vogue on university campuses and among young people who dwell in those giddy habitations restricted to "singles." The affair is without commitment or any assumption of permanence. A psychiatrist at the University of California in Berkeley sees such liaisons as the wave of the future. "Stable, open, nonmarital relationships are pushing the border of what society is going to face in ten years," said he.

The downfall of the Puritan ethic that began in the early 1950s was probably speeded by the pill and the loop. There were many who felt that the denial of guilt and shame about sex was all to the good. But the Puritan notion that sex can be both dangerous and sinful — particularly among the irresponsible young — had a certain merit. Every society, to hold itself together and go on functioning, must have taboos. When contraception was chancy, when a fallen woman rarely rose up again, the taboo on sex outside marriage made sense.

Today, when a respected sociologist can write that marriage now "seems more a swinging affair based on mutual involvement than execution of a solemn vow," what can we expect of courtship? Casual friends become lovers for a night or a week, drift apart, are hard put to remember each other's names a year later.

Vance Packard reports (in *The Sexual Wilderness*) that individuals who have had many sexual encounters before marriage are substantially less likely to live happily ever after when they finally enter matrimony. He also reports that girls who have had sexual experience before marriage are more prone to infidelity than those who haven't.

These are comforting statistics for worried parents and plain, dull girls who never get asked; but they are offset by certain other findings. Such as: The couple who have considerable premarital experience — *together* — report a happier adjustment after marriage. In a sense, they've had the trial, followed by the marriage. A great many doctors — and a few theologians — are now recommending such a progression.

The fallacy here seems to be in the importance attached to the role of sex in marriage. Couples who find the conjugal bed sheer heaven may find life in the rest of the house a hell. Inevitably, since sexual love must involve the whole personality, the conjugal bed takes on the storms and resentments that have swept too long through kitchen and den.

It's unfortunate that the officiating clergyman cannot amplify his ceremony to give the couple a foretaste of marriage. If he could turn to the bride and say, "Do you, Mary Lou, promise to be thrifty, punctual, and neat? Will you be crisp and smiling at breakfast? And will you promise to humor his bad moods and be very sweet to his mother?"

Saying "I do" to twenty such questions might put a bride into a thoroughly rum mood that would last through the honeymoon. But the practical aspects, the grinding reality of this most demanding of all human relationships, would be plainly set forth. The bride could not complain that nobody had warned her.

With contraception so easy and divorce so commonplace, it is obvious that we may have to live with this new marriage ethic. Dr. Margaret Mead has acknowledged the permanence of the new morality and the prevalence of sexual adventuring by suggesting that marriage take new forms. She recommends a loose, easily dissolved marriage for couples who do not wish to have children. An unstructured marriage, if you will. But for a man and wife who have begotten children and created a home, divorce would be made a great deal more difficult.

In view of the changing morality, it seems sensible to stop clucking over student cohabitation and pregnant brides and shift our concern to marriage as an institution.

In a civilized society that cares for its young, marriage is a bedrock necessity. And the notion of a loving, faithful marriage should be refurbished — with song, story, and untarnished homilies from Granny's day, if necessary.

The prevailing theory that fidelity simply doesn't work ... is one of the many idiocies we should erase from the credo of the young. It works a great deal better than infidelity. And it always will.

However commonplace trial marriage may become, it still is makeshift. And its defects are always more hurtful to women. One of the nicest elements in marriage is its public aspect. One's love for another human being is *sanctioned*. The traditionalists who see marriage as a sacrament, a civil rite, and a total commitment of mind and heart see life clearly and see it whole. Being married is "being alive in the flesh." And it is being serene and whole in spirit. Sexual appetites may fade, adversity may strike, but love — and particularly married love — bears it out to the edge of doom.

Because it's a human arrangement, always involving two groping, ordinary mortals, their progeny and kinfolk, marriage will always be an imperfect institution. Are we the last married generation? Well, if we are, prepare for anarchy, chaos, and a breakdown in all the civilized amenities.

In her fascinating book *The English Marriage*, Drusilla Beyfus quotes Lord Longford (wed many years to a writer of distinction, Elizabeth Longford) as saying: "I never think about our marriage at all. It's rather like asking myself how do I manage to breathe or how do I get off to sleep. ... Once you are in love and you have a wife who has many interests in common with you, it seems to me the relationship wouldn't need further stimulation."

This suggests that we all may be too preoccupied with the technique of marriage at the expense of the spirit. One famous psychiatrist has said flatly that great love is not necessary for a good marriage. What is? "A wide area of common interest and an individual capacity for contentment." Neither of these traits can be properly tested, one would say, in a trial spin.

For Thinking, Talking, Writing

1. The author obviously feels that real marriage, legal marriage, is highly preferable to either living together without marrying or to a loose, easily dissolved marriage. After reading the articles in this section, do you agree or disagree? Why?
2. Each of the following statements from the article is a *generalization*

— that is, a statement which expresses an idea supposed to be generally true. Generalizations are very useful things; it is good, for instance, that we learn as very small children that fire is hot and will burn us — by applying that generalization in our own lives, we avoid getting burned. However, a generalization is only useful *if* we can count on its being true. Analyze each of these generalizations; decide whether the author presents enough evidence so that we can count on her generalization; present your conclusions:

(a) "Individuals who have had many sexual encounters before marriage are substantially less likely to live happily ever after when they finally enter matrimony."

(b) "In a civilized society that cares for its young, marriage is a bedrock necessity."

(c) "Fidelity works a great deal better than infidelity. And it always will."

(d) "However commonplace trial marriage may become, it still is makeshift."

(e) "[What is necessary for a good marriage is] a wide area of common interest and an individual capacity for contentment."

10

RELIGION:
what do I believe?

Introduction

Religion is perhaps the only subject that has always been as interesting to human beings as sex. The search for significant *meaning* in life, something beyond the day-to-day problems of existence, has been a driving force in all societies. George Bernard Shaw once said:

> Religion is a great force — the only real motive force in the world
> ...but you must get at a man through his religion and not yours.

Today, especially among college students, there is a real effort to find out *what their religion is*: what its goals should be, how the traditional churches should change to better meet the needs of the people, what the significance is of religion in human life. The college generation is exploring deeply the real meaning of the term *religion,* and often coming up with answers that may be unconventional, but express a strong sense of commitment and sincerity. One teen-age girl recently wrote this of her feelings about God:

> We love God, not fear him. GOD, beauty, sensitivity, nature, GOD, people, soul, minds, tears, laughter, GOD, Pan, feeling, love, sunset, GOD, sea, daffodils, eyes, depth, silence, echoes of thoughts, happy thoughts, beautiful thoughts, GOD.*

In this section, you will find comments on the traditional churches, appeals for a new emphasis on meaning in religion, a re-telling of the story of Mary and Joseph as it might occur today, a justification of faith in both God *and* reason in our scientific world, and a description of some of the "now" roads that many are taking to explore the religious meaning of life.

Read — think — talk — write. Perhaps you can clarify your own answer to one of the important questions in your life: "What do I believe?"

*Reprinted with permission from *McCall's*. Copyright © 1968 by McCall Publishing Company.

A Cry from
the Underground Church

Malcolm Boyd

Yes, it's Christmas again, Jesus, and we're going to celebrate your birthday another time around. But are we aware you're *real,* Jesus? I mean, do we honestly accept your humanness as well as your being the Lord? I don't think so. Maybe this is why we seem to be despising humanness in our world right now.

Thank you, Jesus, for your life as a baby, a growing boy, and a man. Thank you for respecting and loving our humanness so much that you have completely shared it with us. And thank you for being real, Jesus. Please help us to understand what it means to be truly human and real, with you and the others we share life with.

"Silent night." The nights I know, Lord, are noisy and frantic now. Be there with me, in the dark of this December, in the noise and confusion, will you, Jesus? Happy birthday — I hope it's okay to say that to you, Lord. Thanks, Jesus, for being our brother, and our Lord.

Help me, Jesus. I am Malcolm, alone. Underneath a number of titles, roles, functions and images — this is who I am. In this moment, I find myself asking deep and painful questions about life. I can't help crying out in a world in which complexity and feeling lost seem to be more and more of a reality.

Many of us are speaking, and crying out, from an underground church — call it a new church, an open church, or an experimental church. It simply means that for many thousands — and maybe millions — of us, the game of church-as-usual isn't sufficient now. More and more people are joining in a cry for honesty and meaning in faith. A revolution is taking place at virtually every level of American life — in sex, politics, race, the arts, education, mass communications — while the church, largely unaware because it is out of touch, stands archaically as the chaplain of the status quo. If, God forbid, America should veer sharply toward becoming a police state, the underground church might take on a reality that now is only whispered about.

By permission of the editors from the December 24, 1968, issue of *Look Magazine.* Copyright 1968 by Cowles Communications, Inc.

Our cry comes out of real need. The meaninglessness of church-ianity is acutely painful to us. An unchanged Sunday morning — or Christmas Eve—charade with the *same* prayers, *same* form of sermon, *same* hymns, *same* separation between clergy and laymen, *same* liturgy (be it in Old English, new English, rock-and-roll jargon, or Latin) and the *same* feeling of not-touching-base is increasing a sense of despair about the church.

We feel a need of prayer and worship in our own idiom and style, reflecting our individual and social experiences and joys, dilemmas and visions. As a result, in underground-worship settings that are invariably within people's homes, indigenous liturgies and prayers are spontane-ously cropping up in every section of the U.S.

For Catholics, Protestants and Jews alike, time seems to be run-ning out. This is a time of open crisis, personally and collectively. Fami-lies recognize it: rich, poor, middle-class, white, red, black, yellow, Methodist, Jewish, agnostic, Mexican-American, Irish, Italian, in Ne-braska, California, New England, Mississippi, New York, everywhere. But it is not the expected kind of crisis.

In an age of supposed unbelief, people are yearning in a desperate way for something to believe in. Their nakedly exposed need is openly shared. The institutions of organized religion have, they feel, frustrated and betrayed this yearning again and again. These are the reasons for the summons we now hear.

What is the cry from the underground church at Christmas? If we listen carefully, it is all around us. It is contained in many different voices and tongues. It is a cry for unabashed honesty in the place of institutional public relations, courage to face the future instead of the past, an ethic rooted in human need instead of ecclesiastical legalism, a concern for people instead of statistics and things, and a passion for life rooted in Biblical faith instead of a passive living death masked by pasted-on smiles, incestuous concern for the self-perpetuation of an or-ganization, and yet another fund-raising drive to erect a new church building "to the glory of God."

What is the connection between the cry from the underground and Christmas? The basic one is that Christmas celebrates your birth, Jesus. Your whole life is the form on which Christianity is stretched out. We have locked up Christmas inside December 25th, but unless we under-stand its meaning in the holiness of everyday life, this becomes the cor-nerstone of the Big Lie. You know, people get all dressed up for church, they pray and sing, rub elbows and listen to words, and tragically may not grasp what it's really all about.

The cry at Christmas comes out of a curious common sense of loneliness that we all share. It is always more acute at times of celebration, and amid crowds and even family circles. Somehow, at such moments, we clearly catch a vision of death and our own participation in it. So, at the very moment of warm lights, traditional music, shared food and close-knit relationships, we stand more starkly alone than at any other time. We seem to be standing outside ourselves, looking on, yet still being ourselves.

In such a moment, I ruthlessly examine myself: "Who am I? Am I white or black — or human? Am I American or German, Vietnamese or Brazilian — or human? What, precisely, am I doing in this sad and beautiful world? My life is draining out of me with each heartbeat; what is its meaning? I don't want to waste it. What does my life stand for? I am Malcolm. Have I faced myself? What am I doing here, and where am I going?"

We don't want to go on crying out such questions in the midst of cold, vast, echo chambers. We need to hear one another. We need to be heard. We want, in our loneliness, to stand together. Tennessee Williams expressed this poignantly in his play *Camino Real:* "When so many are lonely as seem to be lonely, it would be inexcusably selfish to be lonely alone." Many people have been moved to search for meaning in the underground church because existing religious institutions seem bureaucratically remote and inhumanly out of touch. So-called leaders, reminiscent of the Wizard of Oz, seem to be fearfully hiding behind high walls or their own titles or roles. They are, in any event, enclosed securely within a religious ghetto. Any ghetto represents separation. It accentuates a sense of alienation from other people.

Many of us are crying out to one another. We do this in small, intimate circles of people. We seek, and are sought out by, new people in spontaneous or planned encounters. We *do* connect, and often by means of words. While nonverbal meaning may be fundamental, the word is still the vehicle. We write, and receive, letters. Mine come almost equally from students and older people. They talk to me directly, and here are some of the things they are saying:

"What a straitjacket I was in for so many years," someone wrote me recently. "There has been so much junk getting in the way for so long. Guess what, here I am after seven years again ready to acknowledge the reality of God. You and others have shown me that Jesus is the kind of person who will run with me. Who understands when I can't take being human any longer. Hang with it, Luv."

The need is acute; the pain, unsupportable by oneself.

Someone else wrote me: "When I first heard about you, I really didn't care much about civil rights, unwed mothers, or poverty. I was attending a church girls' school and was perfectly content to live a life naive of the reality of pain, suffering and frustration. Then I found that there are people who are living in a modern-day type of slavery. I found that completing high school, something I had taken for granted, was a terrific accomplishment if you have to bring up yourself and eight brothers and sisters. But most important of all, I found that the color of your skin, your religion, and where you live have nothing to do with your basic right as a human being. I learned to respect others and at the same time to truly respect myself. It took me almost 19 years to learn these things."

The need is for an honest, working faith to comprehend one's brother as well as oneself.

"I look around and see nothing I can do. (I am 15.) What can be done?" asked another letter writer who entered my life not long ago. "If I ask nuns or teachers, they say to pray. But, when people are starving, they need food, not prayers. Isn't it better to do what is right, even if everybody says it's wrong, than to go along? Malcolm, I know you are busy, thanks for listening."

What the institutional church seems so often not to understand is that prayer means sharing food with starving people and changing conditions that affect them, not comfortably saying words that request a magician-deity to do it.

"When I first read about you, I said, oh well, another damn priest trying to prove he's one of the boys; more power to him, but who cares?" someone else wrote me not long ago. "I apologize. I heard you on TV. I went out and got your books and for the first time thought maybe it is possible to be a Christian/christian. I do not want a remote, theologically-ridden Son of God, whose incomprehensibility excuses me from imitation. I do not need a church of ritual and beauty whose dogma and promises encompass humanity, yet cannot hear a human cry. I loved it and long for it, but reject it. I can relate to you because you wear your psychic wounds showing, maybe bleeding a little. I hate the good taste that cures its sores under sterile bandages and antiseptic powders of platitudes and denial."

The underground church is growing out of a deep sense of personal and corporate need. Having started from a strong, dissident-Catholic base — an indication of a rising tide of resistance to traditional centralized authority — it will rapidly embrace more and more Protestants. For people are reacting against repressive ethical and social mores in local church structures. Many protest what they believe is a betrayal of you, Jesus, in normative American church life. Lots of clergymen are underground because, if they publicly said what they believe about your relation to racism, poverty, and war, they would be swiftly unemployed.

"Except a corn of wheat fall into the ground and die, it abideth alone: but if it die, it bringeth forth much fruit." The underground feels that the institutional church, which speaks your words, Jesus, to others, must itself go through this same dying in order to be renewed by God and thus live for others.

When "my" God becomes "our" God, then something wonderful can happen. "My" world becomes "our" world. "My" life becomes "our" life. Suddenly, we are alive together. The alternative is, sadly, that we may choose to be dead together.

The chips are down. We are faced by either a distinct possibility of annihilation or a genuine promise for the betterment of human life. It is uniquely a time to sink or swim, fish or cut bait, die or face the truth about ourselves. I find truth painfully beautiful. It is the reservoir of hope.

Hope? Yes!

There is incredible hope in the clarity of alternatives. We humans are summoned to our mission of becoming human.

How?

First, by discovering what our words mean. We ought not to say "I love you" unless we mean "I love you." We ought not to say, alone or in a group, "I believe in . . ." unless we believe in it. Very specific definitions are in order. Who *is* God? Do we feel God is a man, a woman, white, black, American, a busy heavenly switchboard operator, love, Charlton Heston-in-the-sky, an angry, hating monster who runs torture chambers, a kind elderly bishop with a beard, or what? In my own experience, God is the spirit of loving instead of murder, of relationship rather than fragmentation. To me, the meaning of Jesus is God's sensitivity, involvement, nearness, and intense loving. Prayer, for me, is not asking God for either small favors or great miracles, but wanting to place my life with God in loving and relationship; and I find there is much praying in the simple act of being with people.

Second, by closely relating our words to our attitudes and actions. Communication isn't just words; it is the life-style beneath words. If we make pledges about "democracy," then we must practice it within today's cities, schools and neighborhoods. (Or else, have the plain decency to shut up, ceasing to mouth platitudes.) If we profess Christianity, then we must reject churchianity in its stead. The church is called to follow your life-style, Jesus. If one is a church member, he must not worship religion in place of God. If we say that we are "against war," then we must give ourselves — bodies, minds and souls — in working for peace. Our words by themselves are no longer taken seriously by most people, and even our actions are looked upon rather cynically. But our way of life — the expression of our whole being — is regarded with a startling seriousness.

Third, by understanding how we are a part of everybody and everything. One cannot point to the church "over there"; it is right here. I am the church, you are the church, we are the church. In the Judeo-Christian tradition, which was, is, and will be the nerve of our social conscience, this reality touches almost everybody. In today's world, Vietnam is not far away. It is just around the corner. It is where people like you and me are suffering. It is where a man whom we know — a nephew, a son, a friend, a husband — is fighting. Remember: A human face is a human face. Look into it and see. ("I see white and black, Lord. I see white teeth in a black face. I see black eyes in a white face," I wrote in *Are You Running With Me, Jesus?*) A human heart is a human heart; transplant it and see.

Fourth, by listening carefully to what people really mean. For example, if someone speaks of "revolution," he may not be speaking of anything new. He may have in mind original meanings, turning over the soil, and getting back to essentials that have undergone corruption or been forgotten in the midst of convenient idolatries. If someone says, "I'm dreaming of a white Christmas," he may really be declaring "I'm lonely." A black student saying "Black Power" may be talking about social equality, whites' recognition of the beauty of blackness, and the absence of separation in genuine opportunity. I find that I must listen to what people say underneath their words. I must listen not only in my head but in my heart. Sometimes, I have to listen painfully. Listening is, I think, a beautiful thing. It has so much to do with people.

Fifth, by jumping into life. Life is a shared experience with other people. To love means openness, spontaneity, a radical transformation of individual and social life. Let's knock down ghetto walls. And quit acting like a brother's keeper — who wants one? Does a brother want a brother? Maybe he's been burned too many times. Maybe he feels he cannot trust a brother. So we must understand now that, in terrible and great truth, we are one another. So we must live together. Shall we do this joyfully and creatively? Real life can't mean anything else.

Hope, like love, is considered by many people to be very, very corny. This year, I am 45. I have learned a few essential things during the short and long years of my life. One of them is that I cannot live without hope. If hope has substance, it is closely related to need. For me, your meaning, Jesus, is found in God's radical, total involvement in all of human need, including my own.

Will the church, claiming to be the body of Christ, develop the reality of authentic community as well as a way of life that embodies your prophetic passion and selfless love, Jesus?

This is the cry from the underground church at Christmas.

For Thinking, Talking, Writing

1. Do you agree with Father Boyd that "church-as-usual" is no longer sufficient? Has "churchianity" become meaningless to you? Why or why not?
2. Do you believe, from your own experience, that this is, generally, an age of unbelief?
3. Do you find yourself and/or your friends "yearning in a desperate way for something to believe in"? If so, does this "something" necessarily need to be *religious?* Why or why not?
4. Analyze your own beliefs and feelings about the needs Father Boyd states as the reason for the "cry from the underground church":
   (a) Unabashed honesty in the place of institutional public relations
   (b) Courage to face the future instead of the past
   (c) An ethic rooted in human need instead of eccliastical legalism
   (d) A concern for people instead of statistics and things
   (e) A passion for life rooted in Biblical faith instead of a passive living death....
5. Try to put into words your own feelings about what God is. Father Boyd defines Him as "the spirit of loving instead of murder, of relationship rather than fragmentation." What is He to you?

Yes, God Is Alive and Well and Everywhere... But Not Necessarily in Church

John Cogley

In the churches and synagogues of the United States today, the generation gap is more like a Grand Canyon. In one sense, the present crop of young people may be the most religious in our history, but by and large their pastors — or the clerics who would be their pastors if they kept up their church affiliation — don't believe so. The problem is that most of the clergy have one idea of religion, the young people another.

According to Michael Novak, a young lay theologian whose influence extends far beyond his own Roman Catholic Church: "If one wishes to be radically religious in our society — that is to say, radically committed to a vision of human brotherhood, personal integrity, openness to the future, justice and peace — one will not, commonly, seek an ecclesiastic outlet for one's energies. One will, instead, find community under secular auspices, create one's own symbols for community and integrity, and work through secular agencies for social and political reforms."

Novak adds that "the saints of the present (and perhaps of the future) are no longer ecclesiastics, churchgoers, or even, necessarily, believers in God. The saints of the present are, in the words of Albert Camus, 'secular saints.'"

This does not add up to "religion" for many of the leaders in the churches, however admirable they might find the deep social concern of the young. For them, the "religious" youth takes an active part in a worshiping community (church or synagogue), subscribes to and practices a traditional moral code, professes belief in a body of theological doctrine and finds a place for formal prayer in his busy life.

The two groups are both professedly "religious," but communication between them is minimal. Traditional ecclesiastics look upon Camus' "secular saints" as shameless secularists who, in worshiping man, have turned an idolatrous back on God. The young rebels may reject the "institutional" Church but do not believe that they have thereby cut themselves off from grace. In fact they often regard themselves as more honest, more in touch with the divine, more "religious" than those who went before them, including even the church leaders.

If they sometimes scorn the ancient moral codes propounded from the pulpit, it is because they are convinced that it often drips with hypocrisy. Traditional "religion," they feel, is life-denying. In a world torn by racial dissension, threats of war, and selfishness, they hold, the old moral code has proved its uselessness. If they take no part in the worship offered by their religious communities, it is because they feel it is by and large cut off from the lives and modes of thought of youth.

"How can I worship God by being something other than myself?" is the way one Eastern college student put it to me recently. "When I join a group of people to sing sentimental hymns in a draggy musical style, or when I sit listening to a sermon I don't agree with and that would bore me to tears even if I did, I may be pleasing my parents, but I am not pleasing myself, and I don't think I am pleasing God. How can I be true to God by doublecrossing myself that way?"

Finally, if many of the young pay no heed to the theological doctrines of their tradition, it is because for them these doctrines have lost their credibility. The very word "God" is often seen as a cover for dishonesty, injustice, and moral complacency. "The difference between me and my parents," one high school senior said, "is that while they are embarrassed to talk about sex, I am embarrassed to talk about God." The girl explained that it was the word and what it connoted that bothered her, not the idea of a Supreme Being. "Actually, I consider myself quite religious."

Many young people who feel the same way are, however, staying with their churches. They are critical of the irrelevance, hypocrisy and incredulity they claim can be found there but are nevertheless determined to push through changes: They know they cannot do so from the outside. The lucky ones have found rabbis, priests, and ministers who share their general point of view and work closely with them in a desperate effort to revitalize, modernize, and — they believe — purify the ancient traditions they stand ready to castigate but not to totally abandon.

This marks a notable difference from the religious turnoff of the past. A generation ago the young who were disillusioned with the Church simply dropped out. They counted themselves, not without a certain sense of satisfaction, among the "decent, godless ones" T. S. Eliot immortalized. For that generation, religion was identified with the Ecclesiastical Establishments. Not so today. Today young Catholics and

Protestants are more and more heard to proclaim: *"We* are the Church."

The once-young who are now the middle-aged were willing to put their faith in Science writ large, or in Politics, Psychiatry, or any number of capital-letter forces that promised salvation. Most of these gods have proved to be false and incapable of dealing with the basic problems bugging post-nuclear youth. As a result, many of the collegians of that not-so-distant past are surprised to find that their own children are listening intently to the theological voices of these times. More collegians than ever before are taking the ultimate questions of religious thought seriously.

All over the United States religious studies are popular on university and college campuses. At the same time there is a falling-off in church attendance. Religion, to many in the younger generation, is not necessarily tied to the traditional observances.

In looking for answers to the questions bothering them, young people are not only rediscovering the theological sources of their own traditions but looking beyond to the religions of the Orient. Eastern thought is particularly appealing because of its emphasis on the contemplation and introspection that are characteristic of the young.

"When you talk about meditation or contemplation, the classroom comes alive, the students listen to every word," according to Professor Novak, whose recent experience with collegians extends from California to New England.

Speakers like the Episcopalians, Father Malcolm Boyd, and [the late] Bishop James A. Pike, the Roman Catholics, Father Daniel Berrigan and the artist-nun, Sister Corita Kent, the Baptist theologian, Dr. Harvey Cox, and the prophetic rabbi, Dr. Abraham Joshua Heschel are able to attract huge audiences on college campuses from coast to coast. The young feel that such people are not selling pie in the sky but a faith related to such realities as the draft, the war, racism and the problems of poverty. Phrases like the "Fatherhood of God" and the "Brotherhood of Man" are no longer enough. The young demand that their religious mentors put their own bodies on the line if they expect their preachments to be taken seriously.

The most successful ministries to the young, then, are those based on the new religious style. Vietnam protesters, like the pacifist Jesuit Father Daniel Berrigan, Chaplain at Cornell, or Yale's Dr. William Sloane Coffin, who was indicted for counseling draft resistance with Dr. Benjamin Spock, bring religion alive for thousands of young people more by their actions than by their words, though both are highly articulate clergymen and Father Berrigan is a prize-winning poet.

Father James Groppi, the Milwaukee pastor who led civil rights marches throughout the city last winter, is one of the few white Americans able to communicate fully with militant blacks. I asked a young Negro in Milwaukee not long ago why this was so. "Father Groppi," he said, "shows that he cares. It's that simple. He doesn't preach about the dignity of black men so much as he acts on his belief. That's why so many racists here really hate him and we trust him. He could preach his head off and it wouldn't make any difference to most of them. It wouldn't make much difference to us either."

The new religious style is not confined to social action. It also has been brought into the church itself. Under the impact of youthful pressure, the traditional liturgies in most of the major churches have been deeply affected. It is not at all unusual these days to walk into a Roman Catholic or Episcopal Church and hear a familiar guitar beat that young people love, accompanying the singing of a Bob Dylan song by lines of people approaching the Communion table.

The new style, to be sure, strikes some of the oldsters in the congregation as irreverent. People used to a rigid behavior pattern in church are frequently jarred by lusty guitar masses and loose, almost casual worship. But the young feel more authentically themselves when they are permitted to "be themselves" in prayer, too. The beautiful staid liturgies of the past simply don't speak to many in the under-30 group. "It's the old question," argued a minister who has received complaints from older parishioners, "of whether man was made for the Sabbath or the Sabbath was made for man."

Along with the more formal liturgies, many are now practicing a kind of semisecular paraliturgy that takes many forms. Probably the most successful are those directed by the Los Angeles artist-nun, Sister Corita. Last winter she arranged an Evening With God at a Boston nightclub. No liquor was served, but everyone had a good time. The Baptist theologian, Harvard's Dr. Harvey Cox, served as emcee for an audience-participation show that sent everyone onto the streets, singing new-style rock hymns, thanking God not only that they were alive but that He is.

A few months later, Sister Corita was back in California leading an Awareness Weekend at a house of her order in the coastal town of Montecito. Earlier Sunday morning, at her instigation, dozens of participants went to the beach to fly homemade kites as symbols of their freedom and desire to reach beyond the banalities of daily life.

The new youthful approach to religion did not develop overnight. It owes much to the theorists among modern theologians of all faiths who laid the groundwork for what was to come.

Among them was the bearded, patriarchal Rabbi Heschel of the Jewish Theological Seminary of America. Dr. Heschel has long been insistent that religion is a unique human experience, easily confounded with its own symbols. Ten years ago, the rabbi wrote that religion, though it is ready to offer comfort, "has no courage to challenge. It is ready to offer edification," but "it has no courage to break the idols, to shatter the callousness." According to Heschel, religion had become "religion"— institutions, dogma, securities.

"It is customary to blame secular science and antireligious philosophy for the eclipse of religion in modern society," Heschel wrote. "It would be more honest to blame religion for its own defeats. Religion declined not because it was refuted, but because it became irrelevant, dull, oppressive, insipid. When faith is completely replaced by creed, worship by discipline, love by habit; when the crisis of today is ignored because of the splendor of the past; when faith becomes an heirloom rather than a living fountain; when religion speaks in the name of authority rather than the voice of compassion, its message becomes meaningless."*

Some religious leaders, at least, were listening. During the past decade his indictment has become increasingly less deserved, though there are of course still too many in the churches hung up on less-than-religious obsessions.

Dr. Harvey Cox is another theologian whose speculative writings have had tremendous practical consequences. His book *The Secular City* became a surprise best-seller three years ago and his basic thesis that *this* world is not merely a testing ground for the next but is worth saving — and enjoying — for itself was accepted by leaders of all faiths. The values once dismissed as merely secular were suddenly seen in a new light. Though the thesis was on conformity with traditional Judaism, many in the Christian churches had lost sight that theirs is an *incarnational* religion — whose ethical significance was summed up by Jesus when he asked how a man could love God whom he doesn't see if he hates his neighbor whom he did see.

With the basic idea firmly established, the search for relevance began. Not only did that search lead to a new theological vocabulary in tune with the times, it brought about radical reforms in liturgical traditions, hymnology, and what was and was not truly "religious." Social action became a new form of worship. Rabbis, ministers, priests and nuns began to appear on picket lines and in protest marches. Soon the distinction between clergy and laity began to fade. The claim made especially by the young that *"we* are the Church" antedated the popu-

*Religion in America. Meridian Books. 1958.

lar development of participational democracy by several years.

The ecumenical movement of course has had a tremendous effect on the religious life of the younger generation. The youthful leaders in the various churches have not generally given up their denominational affiliation – they just don't put much emphasis on it any more.

The older generation of Protestants and Catholics, for example, may have squabbled; the present generation read the same theological books, listen to the same lectures, share the same concerns, and frequently worship casually in each other's churches. Not long ago it was unheard of for Catholics to receive Communion in a Protestant church or Protestants to go to the altar in a Catholic church. Today, though it is not officially approved in most places, it is commonplace.

The ecumenical movement, which started off as a Christian phenomenon, has broken through the bounds of that faith-community as well. It is not unusual to find Christian and Jewish students meeting to talk about their religious concerns or to find them, together, studying the teachings of Buddhism.

Of course while all this has been going on a large number of young people have been wholly alienated from traditional religion. These are the youth who are intent on "doing their thing" without any reference to classic theology, ascetic discipline, or faith in a world-to-come. Their religion, they will tell you, is the religion of human brotherhood. Their concern is the here-and-now and the living of life to the fullest. If they do ask the ultimate questions with which religion deals, they are content with the answers arising from their own experience or with no answers at all.

The religiously oriented young are not about to convert them. The most common belief is that no one can be unfaithful to his God by being faithful to himself. The young people active in the church, with the exception of the evangelically persuaded, do not expect religion to "grow," except in individuals. Most in the Christian bodies have accepted the idea of the diaspora Church – the notion that in the future Christians will work side by side until agnostics and atheists will be small in numbers, comparatively, and that the church, as such, will have little direct influence on the secular culture.

"Religion is our thing," one young guitar-strumming worshiper told me not long ago. "We'll do it our way – and who knows, something may happen." The young lady was not depending on a vast institutional apparatus, clever clerical management, or even the power of numbers. She was extremely critical of the clerical establishment in her church, and determined that her faith would not be dissipated in the irrelevancies and formalisms that, she believed, marked the faith of her parents. "But," she explained. "I need to know *who* I am, not just *what* I am; I need community. And I can't help myself — I have to reach out for something beyond myself. Those old theological questions keep bugging me. I'd like to forget about it sometimes and drop the whole thing. But I don't know where I'd go. I wasn't sure I needed the church until I discovered the church needs me."

For Thinking, Talking, Writing

1. Analyze your own religious beliefs and attitudes in relation to the following statements from this article:
   (a) "The saints of the present . . . are no longer ecclesiastics, church-goers, or even, necessarily, believers in God. The saints of the present are . . . 'secular saints.' "
   (b) " 'Religious' youth [should] take an active part in a worshiping community, subscribe to and practice a traditional moral code, profess belief in a body of theological doctrine and find a place for formal prayer in his busy life."
   (c) "The young [religious] rebels [are] more honest, more in touch with the divine, more 'religious' than those who went before them, including even the church leaders."
   (d) "Traditional 'religion' is life-denying."
   (e) "In a world torn by racial dissension, threats of war, and selfish-ness, . . . the old moral code has proved its uselessness."
   (f) "The worship offered by religious communities is by and large cut off from the lives and modes of thought of youth."
2. Do you believe that, if you find traditional religion irrelevant to your religious needs, it is better to stay with your church and attempt to change it, or to drop out of organized religion altogether?
3. Have you had any personal experience with the new liturgies and new approaches to the meaning of religion which have developed in some churches? If so, describe how they have affected your own religious feelings and attitudes, in comparison with traditional religious services.
4. Relate this article to the article by Father Malcolm Boyd, "A Cry from the Underground Church."

Mary and Joe, Chicago-style

Mike Royko

Mary and Joe were flat broke when they got off the bus in Chicago. They didn't know anybody and she was expecting a baby.

They went to a cheap hotel. But the clerk jerked his thumb at the door when they couldn't show a day's rent in advance.

They walked the streets until they saw a police station. The desk sergeant said they couldn't sleep in a cell, but he told them how to get to the Cook County Department of Public Aid.

A man there said they couldn't get regular assistance because they hadn't been Illinois residents long enough. But he gave them the address of the emergency welfare office on the West Side.

It was a two-mile walk up Madison St. to 19 S. Damen. Someone gave them a card with a number on it and they sat down on a bench, stared at the peeling green paint, and waited for their number to be called.

Two hours later, a caseworker motioned them forward, took out blank forms and asked questions: Any relatives? Any means of getting money? Any assets?

Joe said he owned a donkey. The caseworker told him not to get smart or he'd be thrown out. Joe said he was sorry.

The caseworker finished the forms and said they were entitled to emergency CTA fare to County Hospital because of Mary's condition. And he told Joe to go to Urban Progress Center for occupational guidance.

Joe thanked him and they took a bus to the hospital. A guard told them to wait on a bench. They waited two hours, then Mary got pains and they took her away. Someone told Joe to come back tomorrow.

He went outside and asked a stranger on the street for directions to an Urban Progress Center. The stranger hit Joe on the head and took his overcoat. Joe was still lying there when a paddy wagon came along so they pinched him for being drunk on the street.

Mary had a baby boy during the night. She didn't know it, but three foreign-looking men in strange, colorful robes came to the hospital asking about her and the baby. A guard took them for hippies and

Reprinted with permission from the *Chicago Daily News*.

called the police. They found odd spices on the men so the narcotics detail took them downtown for further questioning.

The next day Mary awoke in a crowded ward. She asked for Joe. Instead, a representative of the Planned Parenthood Committee came by to give her a lecture on birth control.

Next, a social worker came for her case history. She asked Mary who the father was. Mary answered and the social worker ran for the nurse. The nurse questioned her and Mary answered. The nurse stared at her and ran for the doctor. The doctor wrote "post partum delusion" on her chart.

An ambulance took Mary to the Cook County Mental Health Clinic the next morning. A psychiatrist asked her questions and pursed his lips at the answers.

A hearing was held and a magistrate committed her to the Chicago State Hospital, Irving Park and Narragansett.

Joe got out of the House of Correction a couple of days later and went to the County Hospital for Mary. They told him she was at Chicago State and the baby had been placed in a foster home by the State Department of Children and Family Services.

When Joe got to Chicago State, a doctor told him what Mary had said about the baby's birth. Joe said Mary was telling the truth. They put Joe in a ward at the other end of the hospital.

Meanwhile, the three strangely dressed, foreign-looking men were released after the narcotics detail could find no laws prohibiting the possession of myrrh and frankincense. They returned to the hospital and were taken for civil rights demonstrators. They were held in the County Jail on $100,000 bond.

By luck, Joe and Mary met on the hospital grounds. They decided to tell the doctors what they wanted to hear. The next day they were declared sane and were released.

When they applied for custody of Mary's baby, however, they were told it was necessary for them to first establish a proper residence, earn a proper income, and create a suitable environment.

They applied at the Urban Progress Center for training under the Manpower Development Program. Joe said he was good at working with wood. He was assigned to a computer data processing class. Mary said she'd gladly do domestic work. She was assigned to a course in keypunch operating. Both got $20-a-week stipends.

Several months later they finished the training. Joe got a job in a gas station and Mary went to work as a waitress.

They saved their money and hired a lawyer. Another custody hearing was held and several days later, the baby was ordered returned to them.

Reunited finally, they got back to their two-room flat and met the landlord on the steps. He told them

Urban Renewal had ordered the building torn down. The City Relocation Bureau would get them another place.

They packed, dressed the baby and hurried to the Greyhound bus station.

Joe asked the ticket man when the next bus was leaving.

"Where to?" the ticket man asked.

"Anywhere," Joe said, "as long as it is right now."

He gave Joe three tickets and in five minutes they were on a bus heading for southern Illinois – the area known as "Little Egypt."

Just as the bus pulled out, the three strangely dressed men ran into the station. But they were too late. It was gone.

So they started hiking down U.S. 66. But at last report they were pinched on suspicion of being foreigners in illegal possession of gold.

For Thinking, Talking, Writing

1. This re-telling of the story of the birth of Jesus as it might have happened in a modern city is a *parable* – that is, a story intended to illustrate a moral or religious principle. What principle is Mr. Royko illustrating here?
2. Does the Christmas story seem more real or less real to you, told in this way? Does it enable you to think of Mary and Joseph as real people instead of religious abstractions, or does it seem offensive to you?
3. What can we learn from Mr. Royko's column about our own attitudes and religious beliefs and how we carry them out in our own lives?

Impiety Passing as Religion

Sydney J. Harris

I received a wickedly irreverent letter yesterday, from a woman who considers herself deeply religious. She wrote, in part: "A God-fearing man doesn't need to know the facts, his love of God will make him sense the truth."

What a dreadful impiety this is, masquerading as religion. For if you believe in God, and love Him, you believe that He gave man his reason to use for discovering the facts — and the faculty of reason is what makes us in God's image.

People like this woman — and there are millions like her — use "faith" as a substitute for reason, but it never can be that without disastrous consequences. Faith must begin where reason ends, not an inch before it.

Her attitude has done more to discredit religion than all the attacks of all the atheists put together. For, through the centuries, so-called God-fearing men have used their own blind sense of the truth to justify witchcraft and slavery, bigotry, and persecution, and the most vicious wars are between different "defenders" of the true faith. The rejection of reason has always been a bloody prelude to barbarism.

Refusal to push reason as far as it will go — though not further than it can legitimately take us — is a deep affront to God's creation. For if we resemble God in any way, it must be in our power to take conceptual thought. In fact, we are the only creatures who can "conceive" of the idea of God; mindless animals live in a purely contingent world.

"Faith" and "reason" are not opposed to each other, as both the falsely religious and the falsely scientific believe; they are, rather, different aspects of the same reality, and it is as foolish to talk about "faith" in knowing the facts as it is to talk about "reason" in sensing the hand of God.

Every discipline tends toward an imperialism: In the past, religion claimed more for its domain than it could responsibly handle; today, science often makes assertions that go far beyond its competence.

There are only certain questions religion can attempt to answer, and

SYDNEY J. HARRIS courtesy of *Chicago Daily News* and Publishers–Hall Syndicate.

no others; and there are only certain questions science can attempt to answer, and no others. To confuse these realms is to confound the whole thinking process, ending only in futile controversy.

A "God-fearing" man first of all respects the hard facts of the universe and doesn't try to ignore them or pervert them into conforming to his preconceived beliefs. To do this in the name of "religion" is a greater sin than the nonreligious commit in denying the realm of faith.

For Thinking, Talking, Writing

1. Explore Mr. Harris' statement, "Faith must begin where reason ends, not an inch before it." What does this mean in terms of *your* life — in terms of reconciling your knowledge of scientific fact with your religious beliefs?
2. Do you agree with Mr. Harris that "... if we resemble God in any way, it must be in our power to take conceptual thought"? Can you think of other ways in which we might resemble God?
3. Discuss Mr. Harris' statement that " 'Faith' and 'reason' are not opposed to each other ... they are, rather, different aspects of the same reality."

A Magical Mystical Tour

Gail Madonia

It is always amazing to discover how various the world is. That in the middle of football games, computers, National Sour Pickle Week, the sex revolution and soul food cookbooks, there are people who think of the time in which we live not as the Electronic Decade or the Psychedelic Revolution, but as the Age of Aquarius. That there are people in what seems to be a spectacularly secular age who are trying to fit the human jigsaw together with mystical illumination, or who explore the levels of the unconscious through psychic experiences. And, there are those who jog along for the fad value, because they are lonely, or want to lose weight. They're all here in various states of mind along the tracks of the magical mystical tour.

Perhaps we can blame this madcap impetus of interest in what used to be called for simplicity's sake the occult on the energies of the Aquarian Age. What's the Aquarian Age? According to astrologers, our time is divided into celestial cycles of 2,000 years' duration. Old Testament times comprised the Arian Age. Aries, the sign of the ram, represents in the zodiac Pure Spirit, God the Creator. It is the sign of the leader or pioneer. The time of Christ was ruled by Pisces, the fish, a water sign at the end of the zodiac cycle. Among other things, Pisces represents emotion as a universal solvent and the eventual dissolution of that emotion into chaos. In its negative aspects, Pisces is the sign of the victim.

But that is all past, according to astrologers, as we enter the Aquarian Age. Aquarius, a fixed air sign, represents the golden age of universal cooperation, brotherhood, the power that springs from knowledge, an experimental mind that hates traditional restrictions. Aquarius is also the sign of electricity and astrology. So astrologers say that the advent of the Aquarian Age, which began according to various accounts anywhere from 1933 to the present time, is responsible for increased interest not only in astrology, but in all forms of inner exploration. They cite it as a force behind the liberation of morals, the popularity of com-

Reprinted by permission of the author. This material first appeared in *Cavalier Magazine*.

munes, the attempts to make public nudity acceptable, the experimentation going on in art, science, and life styles, the waning interest in marriage as opposed to simple live-ins.

One astrologer laughed, though, saying, "That doesn't mean it's going to be all good. The signs are good. But god knows we blew the last age."

Whether you think it's due to the Aquarian Age, to some anti-computer revolt, or to the last gasp of a dissolute body politic, the fact is that interest in astrology, psychic experiences and mystic systems has risen at a phenomenal rate in the past ten years.

Twenty years ago, one hundred newspapers carried astrology columns. Today, 1,200 papers carry them....There are probably 10,000 astrologers casting horoscopes in the United States today, ranging from suburban housewives to long-time members of professional societies like the American Federation of Astrologers and the American Astrologers Guild. At any given social gathering there is bound to be at least one soul who goes around asking everyone their birth date, saying things like, "Hmmm, you just don't look like a Cancer" (thank God for small favors) or "I would have known you for a Virgo (what?) anywhere."

The subject responsible for so much convivial banter seems to have begun as early as 3000 B.C. when the Babylonians classified the twelve constellations visible to them in the night sky and gave them animal names. These became the signs of the zodiac. Over a period of time the practice of interpreting the stars spread to India and China and became more elaborate as astrologers imbued the signs with qualities and portents related to man. Astrology was popular in ancient Greece. Historians say that the personal horoscope had evolved by that time. And in Rome, too, it flourished.

The zodiac is regarded as a cycle of experience, moving organically through the seasons, the four elements, and the planets and being expressed through the twelve signs. The first sign, Aries, transmutes into an earth sign, the earth sign into an air sign and the air sign into a water sign, representing the various expressions of physical energy. Philosophically, the signs are further qualified as Fixed, Cardinal or Mutable. The symbology of the zodiac provides a fascinating source of material that falls within what psychologist Carl Jung called the "collective unconscious."...

The proponents of astrology claim that it is...organized on mathematical principles...and is logically valid as an extension of this premise: because we operate within the structure of a natural universe whose tidal and lunar movements affect everything from madness to menstruation, the message of the stars applies to human life. The logic of this would not tax any philosopher, nor does it tax astrology's critics who say that this is all hogwash, or that even if it were so, the principles under which astrology operates are so antiquated in relation to our celestial world today that star readings are no longer valid. Its critics find astrology easy to dismiss as a pseudo-science that caters to every man's secret belief that his own is the greatest story ever told.

It is likely, however, that astrology began as an attempt to decipher effects of the cosmos on mankind. And it is certainly obvious that we are affected. A recent article in *The New York Times* stated: "While no serious scientists regard the casting of horoscopes and predictions of the future as more than arcane flapdoodle, there are at least a couple who think that the electromagnetic fields of the sun and moon and the planets closest to the earth may influence life here in many still unrecognized ways."

Is this a case for astrology? Maybe — maybe not. But it is the kind of quote some nouveau-astrology buffs are fond of using. . . .

The whole thing reminded me of something I had read in John Blofeld's introduction to the Chinese *Book of Changes*, the *I-Ching*. "I have no means of convincing skeptics unless by asking them to test its powers in all sincerity, which their very disbelief will make virtually impossible. Correct interpretation of the oracles requires a particular state of mind. . . . My own experience is that the oracles, properly sought and properly interpreted, are unfailingly correct, and if the injunctions implied by them are followed strictly everything will come to pass exactly as foreseen."

Blofeld might shudder at the use of his words to end a discussion of astrology. But the *I-Ching*, like astrology, is a system of divination that is both very ancient (it is thought to have arisen around 1150 B.C.) and based upon the use of natural symbols to find a path of right living and thinking. Astrology as popularly practiced today, however, is a vestigial philosophic system compared to the *I-Ching*. Both are concerned with change, but astrology, though it illuminates individuals on their qualities, does not provide a tradition within which to live them out. It is as if astrology were an alphabet, the *I-Ching* the language constructed from it.

The *I-Ching* contains sixty-four hexagrams composed of various combinations of yin and yang lines. The premise behind them is that varying components of yin (the feminine) and yang (the masculine) illuminate the changes in the natural world and, by making us both acceptant and aware of the changes, show us the cosmic oneness that unites them. Blofeld says that within the sixty-four hexagrams one can obtain 4,096 answers to questions put to the *I-Ching*, because according to the throw of coins (or, if one is traditional, yarrow sticks), yin lines can change to yang and yang to yin, yielding entirely new hexagrams.

I-Ching is a subject worthy of serious attention. Attempting to describe its structure and ability to illuminate, I realized I had not only reached an impasse, but had not succeeded from the beginning. I decided to ask the book itself what to do; the answer it gave is both a better description of the way it works than I could ever contrive and an illustration of the stern humor that one discovers occasionally in the answers given. After several consultations with the *I-Ching*, one feels its personality as strongly as if it were a living person.

The hexagram I was given in answer to my question about how to explain the *I-Ching* was Wei Chi, titled in English *Before Completion*. The actual text of the hexagram read: "Before completion — success! Before the little fox has quite completed its crossing (of the ice), its tail gets wet. No goal (or destination) is favourable now." The commentary on the text explained that the fox getting its tail wet meant that the questioner had not yet succeeded in getting beyond the middle of the matter forming the subject for the question. This incomplete understanding makes it advisable not to push the matter to completion. So the book had told me I would be successful, but hardly through my own understanding of the subject. The *I-Ching* stands as its own best explanation.

I myself have never questioned it or felt its answer to be irrelevant. A friend once told me how he had earnestly tried to convince one of his good friends about the value of the *I-Ching*. The friend was skeptical about the book's "personality." "All right," my friend said, "even if you don't believe me, just open up the book and read it. It's beautiful." He did and enjoyed the hexagram he came across so much that he asked to toss the coins. The hexagram he arrived at then was the same as the one he had chosen at random. . . .

The abundance of people who make their living on psychic phenomena is overwhelming. A great many of them are parasites of the paranormal, people who are capitalizing on that well-known thirst in man for knowing definitely just what things are all about. There are also a great number of dedicated spiritual psychics, some whose work can only be regarded as sad self-delusion and others whose experiences in the paranormal raise questions such as prompted Freud to write in 1921: "If I had my life to live over again, I would devote it to psychical research rather than psychoanalysis." And throughout the history of mankind, there has been a continuous stream of reports of precognitive dreams, hunches, telepathy, ESP, and clairvoyance. Like the unpredictable eruptions of geysers and volcanoes, they are generally so sporadic that science has a hard time studying, much less defining them. But at an increasing number of hospitals, in universities and foundations throughout the world, research on psychic phenomena may someday give us more understanding of why a person may suddenly dream an event that occurs in the future or "know"— in a way we have not yet been able to describe — that a ship has sunk, someone has died or been born hundreds of miles away. In the Eastern world, where ideas of cause and effect and the nature of time are radically different from our Western concepts, there is an easy acceptance of what we call paranormal phenomena.

In his excellent book *Prophecy in Our Time*, Martin Ebon says, "Prophecy goes against the grain of our time-space oriented civilization." But contemporary scientific research, especially in physics, entails questions about causality and the nature of time and space that may well throw some light on the nature of parapsychological experience. If time is indeed an arbitrary label for what is actually space, then predictions of the future and telepathy become much easier to comprehend.

Research may be difficult because science has not yet defined the concepts that apply to parapsychology, but material for research is certainly not scarce. There is an abundance of material in the work of such psychics as Eileen Garrett, the founder of the Parapsychology Foundation and one of the world's greatest living psychics; Edward Cayce, who diagnosed illnesses from hundreds of miles away; Jeane Dixon, who is popularly called "the Washington seeress"; and hundreds of others less known. There are the archives of records compiled at the time of major disasters, too. The Kennedy assassination was the latest in a line of upheavals that have occasioned widely-felt psychic reverberations. Jeane Dixon, whose book *A Gift of Prophecy* was a best seller several years ago, predicted that the President would die or be assassinated in office. During the entire month of November that year she became more and more upset at the imminence of disaster she felt would soon fall on the White House. A few days before the assassination, Mrs. Dixon said to companions, "I just can't get my mind off the White House. Everywhere I go I see the White House with a dark cloud moving down on it." On November 22, at a luncheon, she was so absorbed in her thoughts someone asked what was troubling her. She said, "I'm sorry but I can't hear what you say, because the President is going to be shot."

After attending Mass on the day of the assassination, she met a friend and said, "This is the day it will happen." Later that day she toyed with lunch, saying, "I just can't. I'm too upset. Something dreadful is going to happen to the President today." (Mrs. Dixon had also counseled a friend, "Whatever you do, don't get on the same plane with Dag Hammarskjold," just before the crash that killed the UN official.) There were many individual reports of foreknowledge of the President's death the day he was shot. Astrologers, too, predicted the event. In November, 1963, an issue of *American Astrology* carried an article stating that certain constellations had in the past proven dangerous to the head of state and that for President Kennedy "November is obviously fraught with perils of several varieties." In *American Astrology* in March, 1961, an astrologer examining the President's horoscope stated, "Mercury adverse Venus presented as deadly an aspect in private life or politics as is ever known" and that "the United States will surely have to keep him well-guarded."

Knowing the twenty-year cycle of Presidents dying or being assassinated in office and having this wealth of material from astrologers and psychics on public record, it is a sad measure of our skepticism toward mysticism and paranormal knowledge that the President was *not* better guarded.

The Titanic sinking, too, had plenty of psychic corroboration, some of which can be dismissed as simple anxiety, but others of which seem to be *bona fide* predictions of the disaster. Dr. Ian Stevenson, an American psychiatrist and psychical researcher, published the known data surrounding the sinking of the Titanic in the *Journal of the American Society for Psychical Research*. Stevenson feels that the unexpectedness of the sinking of this "unsinkable" ship generated a strong psychic agency. He said that "strength of emotion is an important feature" in making extrasensory perception occur. The cases Stevenson collected included telepathic, clairvoyant and precognitive experiences. An English businessman had booked passage on the Titanic and dreamed of a sinking ship ten days before the sailing. He canceled his reservation. Only after having canceled the trip did he tell his family and friends, two of whom stated they had dreamed of floating in the air above the wreck. A British medium predicted on the day of the sailing, "a great liner will be lost." Stevenson said he would like to see more research into "motives which separate those who act upon premonitions from those who do not," feeling that "a cultural climate hostile to psychical experiences may influence percipients not to act on perceptions when a more favorable climate might encourage them to do so."

Although much psychic experience seems to be concerned with anxiety for the well-being of others, especially family members, not all is turned in that direction. There are the psychic healers. A fascinating variant on that theme is Edgar Cayce, who never healed a soul but whose accurate medical diagnoses of people he had never seen or met has made him the subject of a growing cult in the United States since his death. Cayce, who was reported to be not only unschooled, but illiterate, was a simple, devoted man, a constant churchgoer, well-loved by his Virginia Beach, Va., neighbors and friends. From 1910 to 1945 he made over 14,000 statements in trance, some medical, some prophetic or spiritual. All are carefully documented in the Cayce Memorial Association for Research and Enlightenment in Virginia Beach. His prophetic statements are at best garbled and at worst ludicrous, and it is a pity that his followers have lumped his amazing medical statements together with his abysmally unsuccessful prophecies in an attempt to hail him as a mouthpiece of the "higher entities."

Cayce often not only diagnosed the diseases and even the impending death of his questioners accurately, but also was able to see them, though they were hundreds or thousands of miles away. "The body is leaving," he said once, "going down in the elevator now," or "Is this body in bed? No, she is sitting in a large chair, talking to a man." His telepathic visions and psychic diagnoses have been subsequently corroborated by both doctors and clients....

With the growing interest in mysticism and psychic phenomena, we may someday come to the place where these subjects are better understood and accepted as a valid and healthy part of human experience.

To move from speculation into the even stranger world of reality, you see before you Scientology, a cult whose mystical or psychic magic or malefic proportions are difficult even for student scientologists to assess. Scientology grew out of Dianetics, which in book form became a best seller in the fifties. L. Ron Hubbard, its founder, has been accused of being a spiritual fascist, a muddled philosopher, and/or one of the world's greatest thinkers. It all depends on who you're talking to....

Scientology with its amalgam of ancient religions and philosophies may be the most American stew to hit the marketplace for religious fads. A *Life* magazine article said it "reaches dangerously into the mind" and quoted a three-year-old government report from Australia which called Scientology "the world's largest organization of unqualified persons engaged in dangerous techniques which masquerade as mental therapy."

Scientology involves clearing the mind of its accumulated "engrams," which are defined as picture images imprinted on the cells of the mind by experiences that are both unconscious and painful. Part of the methodology includes the use of the E-meter, which scientologists regard as a refined lie detector. Psychiatrists, including Dr. William Menninger, have cautioned on the danger of various techniques used by Scientology. But the "org" still grows with an estimated worldwide membership of two to three million. When Hubbard incorporated his theories into a church, he freed himself from many legal strictures. But the churchly aspects of Scientology are all gloss. Most people I talked to agreed that it was a super-bureaucratic, rather fanatic bunch of young people bent on solving the problems of the world by "Really Communicating."

...According to the literature "Scientology is an applied philosophy that works. It is the science of knowing how to know answers." Perhaps one of the charms of Scientology is that it leaves so many questions....The ideas Hubbard takes from philosophy and ancient religions may show him to be a man who in spite of recognizing the best recipes in the world, still makes dogmeal out of what might have been at least bouillabaise.

Hugh Lynn Cayce, Edgar Cayce's son, in his book *Venture Inward* says, "The growth of Dianetics into Scientology is of considerable interest in the light of our concern over the doorways to the unconscious. As wholesale processing got under way, a great many 'auditors' (those who process others) began to discover levels of the mind hitherto unsuspected. This included regression to what appeared to be past lives and an extension of consciousness to include clairvoyance, telepathy, and other psychic abilities." Cayce mentions, as have many others, the potential danger of techniques in the hands of untrained and inexperienced people.

So the controversy rages. Is it spiritual or is it dangerous? According to the *Life* magazine article, the endocrinologist who wrote the foreword to Dianetics broke with Hubbard, charging that he was headed toward "absolutism and authoritarianism" and that some of his patients were going insane. *Naked Lunch* author William Burroughs, who wrote some praise-filled copy for Hubbard's publicity unit, suffered a similar disillusion and disgust. Meanwhile, the cult proliferates — to the tune of tuitions that rival top psychiatric fees. This magical mystical tour does not recommend stopping at that town, where the price is high and the lectures abysmal. Better you should join the Parapsychology Foundation, or study astrology, or even become a carpenter and wait for The Second Coming.

For Thinking, Talking, Writing

1. Have you been interested in, or had friends who are interested in astrology, mysticism, or psychic experiences? If so, how would you explain such an interest? Has it come about because of a feeling that traditional religion has failed to meet the human "yearning in a desperate way for something to believe in," as Mr. Boyd suggests in "A Cry from the Underground Church"? Are there other reasons you can think of?

2. This article shows that many people in our society are developing more and more interests in all kinds of psychic phenomena, often as a substitute for traditional religion. What are the implications of this kind of interest in an otherwise super-scientific age? Are we longing to find some kind of meaning in our universe that neither science nor traditional religion has given us? If possible, make an investigation of your own community in terms of people's interest in psychic phenomena. Find out the number and specific kind of organizations for the study of such things that exist, and the number and kind of people involved in them.

11

MY CAREER:
where am I going?

Introduction

Until recently, the question of which career to choose was rarely raised in human society. It was almost impossible to move from one social class to another; it was difficult to move geographically from place to place; and there was only a limited number of occupations available in any one spot. Most young men grew up to do what their fathers had done or, at best, to choose among a small number of available ways to earn a living near the place where they were born. Young women usually married, produced children, and sometimes worked with their husbands.

Now, however, the number of careers in the United States that both men and women can enter is so staggering that choosing a career has become as much a problem as an opportunity — particularly since technology is moving so rapidly that the job you have ten years from now may not even exist today. "Blessed is he who has found his work; let him ask no other blessedness," said Thomas Carlyle in 1843; but how can you "find" work that may not yet exist? (As one example of newly developing career opportunities, the University of Colorado began in the fall of 1969 a course designed to prepare people for a new career in medicine — the "supernurse," who is something between nurse and doctor. Here is a whole new field, for both men and women!)

Thus this section, while it offers some current information on what companies want from young people and which careers seem most promising in the years immediately ahead, also attempts to help you develop personal guidelines that will apply to *any* career. Read — think — talk — write. But concentrate on the things you need to learn about *yourself* on the job, whatever the specific field may be. These things can guide you successfully to sensible answers to the question: "Where am I going?" — in terms of a career.

How to Succeed in
Business Before Graduating

Peter M. Sandman

A dozen cans of luminescent white paint, a set of stencils, and a few old brushes were all John Cobb needed last year to net more than $1500 in his spare time. As a freshman at the University of Illinois, in Urbana, John had had an idea that homeowners might like to have their street number visible on the curb in front of their house. By his junior year, he was hiring three freshmen to do the work. The boys stenciled in the number of every house on a block, then knocked on each door, pointing out the glistening numerals and accepting voluntary donations for the service. Appreciative or amused homeowners contributed enough for John to gross $7.50 an hour.

Now a senior, John continues to employ other students in his miniature business empire. He holds campus sales franchises for shirt, sweatshirt, and stationery manufacturers, operates a campus-wide sandwich agency.

John Cobb is a student entrepreneur. He is one of the thousands of "campus capitalists" who have discovered the money-making potential of a small, independent business. They represent one of the most encouraging trends on the college scene today.

Peter De Yoe and Susan Mallon felt a little bewildered and lost in their first few weeks at Middlebury College in Vermont. A year later they decided to help the next crop of freshmen by publishing and selling an informal orientation booklet. Part of the booklet went out free to all new students over the summer, and the complete booklet, *The Unofficial Guide to Middlebury College,* went on sale in the fall. Both carried extensive local advertising. The originators netted more than $300 the first year and this year's profits should be even better.

Sandy Kross, a Brigham Young University junior, noticed that many Utah high schools and civic groups were having trouble finding enter-

Reprinted with permission from the April 1968 *Reader's Digest.* Copyright 1968 by The Reader's Digest Assn., Inc.

This article is condensed from the book of the same name by Peter M. Sandman who is a graduate student at Stanford University.

tainment for their dances and conventions. He opened a booking agency. Inside of eight months his agency was sending out entertainers — most of the talent recruited right on the BYU campus — to scores of clients in six states, and was also busy providing guest lecturers, organizing barn dances, and catering posh dinners. By the time he graduated, Sandy was netting as much as $600 a week. Today he is working on setting up branch offices throughout the Pacific Northwest.

The Student Prints. At Williams College football games, fans read about the players in a 20-page program prepared by senior Mike Hall. An assistant manager helps solicit ads (which cover all costs) and helps Mike write the text. Underlings sell the programs, which yield a net profit of about $150 a game.

Not that there's anything new about earning one's way through college. Many of today's most successful people managed it, usually by putting in long hours at a succession of part-time jobs. But such jobs are harder to find now, with more students competing for them, and the typical wage of $1.25 an hour doesn't make much of a dent in today's high tuition. Therefore, the new emphasis is on student business. Many a campus enterprise nets its manager between $1000 and $3000 a year, without involving more than 15 hours' work a week. (Most authorities feel this should be the maximum for wage-earning activities, in light of today's heavy academic workloads.) At the same time, it may provide as many as ten other students with good part-time jobs.

An alphabetical list of successful collegiate enterprises today runs from Advertising, Answering Service, and Appliances to Wine Skins, Writing, Yardwork, and Yarn — with thousands of entries in between. And each item hides a lot of different businesses. Advertising, for example, has included everything from an advertising design service for corporations at M.I.T. to a broken-down hearse with painted-on ads at Northeast Louisiana State College.

Food for Thought. Roughly three-fifths of all student businesses involve the sale of goods to other students. And the easiest item to sell to a college student is food — any kind, from popcorn to potato pancakes. Ray Croxford, a senior at Ohio University, pays for his room, board and tuition peddling potato chips, sandwiches, and soda pop. It started as a one-man operation, but Ray now has four people working for him. He carries the money to the bank. Student-run snack bars get some of the trade, but the biggest profits go to the man who hawks his goods from dorm to dorm in the evening study hours.

Most students prefer to make their wad with a high-profit, once-only item. Beer mugs, magazine subscriptions, and college souvenirs are probably the most popular, but more offbeat gewgaws produce the prettiest sales charts. Dick Gregor and his roommate Chris Miller at Swarthmore College, for example, dye tee shirts. For $2 apiece they will transform a plain white tee shirt into anything from an intramural football uniform to a psychedelic extravaganza. They turn the prettiest girls on campus into walking advertisements by giving them free shirts, and the customers line up. The seniors estimate that each shirt, with dye materials, costs about 75 cents; wages for student dyers run another quarter, leaving a clear dollar profit on each sale. The business netted $150 in two weeks last spring. Chris then moved on to Cape Cod for a highly profitable summer on the beach.

Many other unusual sales items have made it big. At Carleton College it's "Records Unlimited"; at Vassar College it's wigs and knitting yarn; at Rutgers University it's a student-invented variation of chess; at Princeton University it's firewood.

Punch Bowls to Punch Cards. After sales, the next best bet is a campus service. Old standbys like typing, tutoring, and laundry are still profitable, but the big money-makers in this area are new. There are vending-machine operators, student haulers, and book exchanges. But by all standards the newest and biggest service is the one invented in 1965 by two jaded juniors at Harvard. Long on ingenuity but short on ingenues, they decided to apply computer techniques to collegiate dating. The new business, dubbed Compatibility Research, Inc., was a phenomenal success. More than 100,000 collegians have filled out questionnaires, paid $3 (later $5), and waited anxiously for their computerized lists of "ideal dates." The idea has had dozens of successful imitators, and punch cards have now replaced punch bowls as the "in" way to meet a date.

A campus travel agency is a good bet. The biggest mover of them all is a student at the University of Texas who handles discount flights for students at more than 60 Texas colleges, netting well over $10,000 a year. Others, on their own campuses, act as representatives of professional travel agencies, or handle promotion and ticket sales for airlines, railroads, bus companies. Then there are the transportation rental people. Some students work for Hertz or Avis, others rent out their own supply of motorbikes, bicycles, trailers, canoes, even horse-and-buggies. No one knows who tries hardest.

Profit With Honors. Almost any part-time job can be transformed into a challenging business. A student who works for a television repair shop may decide to open his own repair agency. A coed baby-sitter may move on to a baby-sitting referral service. A student hasher may start a campus doughnut shop, a bus driver manage his own taxi service. For most employed students the door to an independent business stands open — unless the college administration kicks it shut.

"The proper business of students is study," says one southwestern dean. A number of educators echo the fear that student entrepreneurs are likely to fall behind in classwork. But surveys show otherwise. The grades of most students stay the same when they start earning money, and some actually improve; only a few go down. "Year in, year out," says President Grady Gammage of Arizona State College at Tempe, "more top grades are captured by the worker than by the non-worker."

There is no doubt that running a business can teach a student lessons in organization and concentration that can be advantageous in classwork, and invaluable in whatever profession he later follows. Most corporation personnel managers recognize an advantage in hiring the graduate with an independent business background.

The Now Generation. Perhaps the most important benefit of collegiate business is the opportunity it gives students to stand on their own. Ambitious young people often find their urge to be independent self-supporting adults frustrated by the prolonged demands of our educational system. They see themselves as endlessly preparing for that far-off day when they will finally be able to take their place among the productive members of society. Some psychologists believe that the blocked impulse to do something meaningful in the real world *now* is a major cause of radical activism on the campus today. Student business, most would agree, is a much more constructive outlet.

Some college administrators are beginning to recognize and encourage student business. Harvard Student Agencies, Inc., is an example. An independent, self-supporting corporation, HSA acts as a central clearinghouse for all Harvard student businesses. Each contributes a set percentage of its profits into a central fund in return for technical, legal, and financial advice. The money is used to help new ventures get started and older ones to expand. Under HSA's guidance, Harvard students have inaugurated a dozen new successful businesses in the last five years, including a catering service for Back Bay hostesses, a publishing division, and an information-gathering service for businessmen. HSA now includes 20 different businesses, grossing a total of well over one million dollars a year. The manager of each receives a salary and a percentage of his profits, while student employes are paid wages that range between $2 and $10 an hour.

The student-agency concept has generated interest among college administrators, turning up on the agenda of at least four conferences on financial aid in the past few years. Financial demands on the colleges are hurrying the change. So is pressure from students, who, in the finest American tradition, show a lively interest in paying their own way.

For Thinking, Talking, Writing

1. Instead of dealing with your future career, this article suggests ways of helping to cope with the high costs of college today. However, some of the principles and ideas in the article certainly apply to successful careers later. What are these principles? *How* might you apply them to your future career?
2. Have you, personally, had much experience with part-time jobs? If so, comment on Mr. Sandman's statement that "... such jobs are harder to find now, with more students competing for them, and the typical wage of $1.25 an hour doesn't make much of a dent in today's high tuition." Has this been your experience, or have you been able to find higher-paying jobs?
3. Why do you think that the student who works often earns better grades than the student who does not work? Does this indicate anything about personality and character, or not?
4. What do you think of the statement, "Some psychologists believe that the blocked impulse to do something meaningful in the real world *now* is a major cause of radical activism on the campus today." Would you agree or disagree? Why?

A Job Is Only a Way
to Find Out Who You Are

A Conversation
with Peter F. Drucker

Mary Harrington Hall

Mary Harrington Hall: Many of the brightest students believe that ours is a sick society. Yet, here you are, Peter, a teacher who urges them to move out of school into that society.

Peter Drucker: Yes, it's like urging them out of the sick ward into the open air. They don't know, because nobody tells them, that their competitive struggles in high school and college are more desperate than any they will find outside. The pressure in the educational system is fantastic. The rest of the society may not be completely sane, but what they have experienced directly is absolutely insane. . . .

I would be happier if men and women who reach 17 could be young adults among adults. Those who wanted to go back to school could come back later. They would be better students and much happier people. Learning would be an adult activity, not a chore for children. . . .

Knowledge today exists in action, not in hard-covered books. This is one of the things that the college generation senses. The kids want relevance. So you know something, but how does it help clean up Lake Erie? You can't treat knowledge as irrelevant if it can blow up the world. The great question is the responsibility of knowledge.

This means you cannot disassociate it from its applications, from technology.

Hall: All right, how can people know where to act on what they know? How can they choose a career?

Drucker: That question, Mary, has never before had the urgency that it has today. A basic change of the last few decades is the emergence of career choice as an opportunity — and as a difficult problem. It used to be easy, because you took whatever you could get. Somebody let you have a job as a favor because he knew your uncle.

Young people can now choose — almost without limit. But no one tells them how to choose, what questions to ask, what commitments to make and which ones not to make. They are confused and bewildered by the abundance of opportunities.

And they are terribly worried, because they think that a career decision is like marriage, to be broken only by failure or by death. This just is not so. Some of today's students will work into the year 2011 A.D., if the earth is still here. How can they expect to know what the world will be like, or what they themselves will be like in 2011 A.D.?

Hall: But a student still has to decide what to do next.

Drucker: The question is much easier to answer in that form. Nobody needs to be afraid of it, or put it off. Here I am 59, and I still don't know what I'm going to do when I grow up. That sounds flippant, I know, and there is almost no way for a 22-year-old to avoid the feeling that I am being cavalier about a serious matter. My children and their respective spouses think I am kidding, but I am making a serious point. They believe that life is divided into categories, like textbooks in a library, and that to have a career you must lock yourself into one category....

Hall: O.K., but how do you begin to decide?

Drucker: First, you have to accept your uncertainties as normal. Only musicians and mathematicians and a few early-maturing people — the number is very small — know from adolescence onward what they want to do. Maybe at age 11 they are fascinated by snakes. But the rest of us have to find out. You know what you don't want to do, but what you *do* want to do, you don't know.

A job is your opportunity to find out. That's all it is. You owe no loyalty to your employer other than not betraying secrets. Be ruthless about finding out whether you belong; I am. One can always quit.

Hall: What are the things you need to know first about yourself?

Drucker: One of the most important things is to know whether you like pressure or whether you cannot take it at all. There may be people who can take pressure or leave it alone, but I have never met any of them.

Hall: What else can you know about yourself before you pick a job?

Drucker: You have to know whether you belong in a big organization. In a big organization, you don't see results; you are too far away from them. The enjoyment is being part of the big structure. If you tell people you work for General Electric, everyone knows what G.E. is.

I also think you need to know whether you want to be in daily combat as a dragon-slayer or whether you want to think things through, to analyze, prepare. Do you enjoy surmounting the daily crisis, or do you really get your satisfaction out of anticipating and preventing the crisis? These things I believe one *does* know about oneself at age 20, though it is not always comfortable to judge yourself.

Hall: What is the hardest thing to know?

Drucker: There is one great question most young people probably can't answer: Are you a perceptive or an analytical person? This is terribly important. Either you start out with an insight and then think the problem through, or you start out with a train of thought and arrive at a conclusion. One really needs to be able to do both, but most people can't. I am totally unanalytical and completely perceptive. I have never in my life understood anything that I have not seen.

Hall: What about being a listener or a reader?

Drucker: That's another thing most young people don't know. And this they can check easily. Trial lawyers both read and listen. Nobody else can. I am a listener; I can read after I listen but not before. Probably I can't even write first, but that's pathological.

Hall: But what is the most important consideration about the choice of the job, apart from the personality of the person?

Drucker: Job content. The question is not, am I interested in biology? That interest may or may not change. You can't tell. The issue is: when you work, do you want to sit down to a stack of computer readouts and plot figures for two weeks, or do you want to go around and pick people's brains? Do you enjoy being alone, or do you have to be a member of a team? Do you like pressure or can't you stand it? How do you really function? There is a fabulous amount of misinformation about jobs, because there is not one job pattern that is clear. You can't tell by the field. . . .

Hall: . . . Isn't there an inevitable war between the individual and technology?

Drucker: Only in the sense that technology brings change, and many people resist change. I don't know whether you know that the first advanced management-training course was one that the German Post Office gave in 1888. Its topic was the use of the telephone. Top management was scared of the telephone. Believe me, the coming generation looks at the computer the way we now look at the telephone. We can't get enough extensions.

Hall: I suppose that the computer looks ominous because it is used by large organizations. Isn't there an inevitable conflict between people and organization?

Drucker: That's a very different question from the one about man's war with the machine. Any time two humans live near each other, they have organization. Organization is inevitable, because it is the structure of relationships between people. . . .

The task of this generation is to make sense out of large organization, to make it responsive. They haven't really begun yet. The New Left wants to burn down Columbia University. Do they really think that its successor would look any different? How can it? And just breaking large organization into smaller units often leads to greater rigidities. The problem is to make organization your tool, like the computer, and not let it be your master.

Hall: How can you use an organization if you work for it? That's like sending Big Brother out for coffee.

Drucker: The only way to find what you want is to create a job. Even if you move into an existing position, you change it by the way you do it. Nobody worth his salt has ever simply fitted into a slot. That's for post-office clerks. Companies look formidable, and seem to know what they are doing, so it's hard to believe how susceptible some of them are to change from within. And most people don't know until they are 29 or 30 that they have to do things their own way. By then, many feel trapped because they married their job.

Hall: That's why you emphasized the things that students have to know about themselves. The problem is to find the organization and the place in it where you can start to develop your best capacities as a person.

Drucker: You want the job content to fit you. There are businesses that are wide open, like positions in the international divisions of some big banks — the Bank of America, Chase Manhattan, or First National City Bank of New York are examples. Their young men are really entrepreneurs. They invent new services and new branches, and no one says them "nay." And there are government jobs meant for the kind of imaginative fellow who draws to an inside royal flush....

Hall: Are job stereotypes changing?

Drucker: Jobs cannot be typified, cannot be classified. Ten or 20 years ago, bankers were good Anglo-Saxons who parted their hair in the middle. That is no longer necessarily so. In New York a fellow with a red beard who goes barefoot to work is vice president of a commercial bank today.

Hall: Is that *really* true, Peter Drucker?

Drucker: Yes, he can do it so long as he stays in the data-processing department. I met him at lunch recently. He's a vice president of one of the biggest banks and he is very young. I don't think it's necessary for him to pretend he's 19 any longer, but that's his business.

Hall: How old is he, really?

Drucker: About 36 I would say.

Hall: What on earth has happened to banking in the past 10 years?

Drucker: Nothing has happened to banking. Banks have discovered that if they have a computer that costs a million dollars a month, they had better have somebody who can make it produce. And if he goes barefoot and has a red beard and wears a blue undershirt, you just make sure you don't expose him to the clientele. Nobody has to see him except the computer, and the computer has no great fashion preferences. On the other hand, no university faculty would dare hire him. And for good reasons. He talks so much about love that everybody hates him....

Hall: Peter, you have not said much about the matter of field — biology or finance or education or merchandising or engineering. Do you mean that they are actually less important than job content within the field?

Drucker: Infinitely less. This, again, is very hard for students to believe. They have been brainwashed with academic categories until they forget that they — the kinds of people they are — count more than the subject they happen to have studied a bit more than other subjects. Every profession and every industry, with the partial exception of coal-mining, is short of able people, often desperately short. Over the next few years, those shortages will become far more acute. The inevitable result will be that today's students will have greater freedom than any before to pick the things they want to do, and do them in their own way. Companies and government agencies will have to be much more responsive to the expectations of the men and women they want to work for them.

Hall: I still want to ask about the fields students major in, even if they are less important than people think. If a student takes engineering, science or business administration, hasn't he made more of a career choice already than the student in liberal arts?

Drucker: Not necessarily. Or he may have regretted his choice, but decided that he can't afford to go back and start over. Many engineering students in their junior year begin to fear that they will be slotted too narrowly. Young scientists often panic over the thought that their research will be wanted mainly by weapon-makers. In business administration, there are students who have made no choice. Some have done well in math, or maybe they haven't done well enough in other subjects to want a liberal arts major — which has an unjustified reputation for being tougher.

Hall: While business administration has a justified reputation for being easy?

Drucker: No, it has a reputation for being predigested. Like engineers, the business majors tend to worry in their junior or senior year.

One has to assure them that they don't have to be accountants for the rest of their lives. . . .

Hall: As for dedicated people, what about graduates going straight into the Peace Corps?

Drucker: No! The Peace Corps is a great disappointment.

Hall: How can you say that? Why?

Drucker: I always thought the kids would get a tremendous amount out of the Peace Corps, but I have seen too many when they come back. In their personal development, they are exactly where they were when they left. It is just another postponement, a delay. My conclusion is that one belongs in the Peace Corps in his 30s, not in his 20s. In the 20s, he belongs in the city administration of Peoria, or out selling Gallo wine.

Hall: Selling wine? Gallo?

Drucker: Let me tell you about one of the nicest boys I know. He took a job as a salesman for one of the large wineries. His parents were beside themselves. I asked him why he went to work as a salesman. "To find out what I can do," he answered. "But why did you go to work for a winery?" I asked. You see, he had offers from Ford and IBM and Minneapolis-Honeywell. "At the winery," he said, "I'm the only one who can read and write."

Now, he knows exactly what he's doing. I don't think he'll stay long unless he's made president within five years. He might go back to law school. If the winery doesn't work out, nothing has happened. He is trying himself out. Too many kids with too many opportunities are just playing around.

Hall: You think that a good young person should go out and jump in somewhere, anywhere?

Drucker: Yes, and not with the typical question the kids ask the recruiters: Is this the right place to stay for the next 35 years? Hell, the answer in all likelihood is no.

There is a right question to ask the recruiter: Is this a place where I can learn something and have fun for two years, and where I will have a chance if I produce? If the answer really turns out to be yes — when you try it — then you might have good reason to stay there 35 years.

Hall: A job decision would be a lot easier if there were somebody to talk it over with. To whom should the student talk?

Drucker: That's part of the problem. The faculty is less than useless. Parents want desperately to help, but the great majority of today's students do not have a parent who went to college. These parents are frightened. I have talked with many.

The problem is not that of the few parents whose children happen to go to Harvard or Yale. They represent only a small fraction, and are not typical. But in the much larger system of higher education, the situation is serious. The University of Scranton, to take an example, is in the Pennsylvania coal fields, where it was unusual a few years ago to go on to high school. At a commencement exercise, one father there said to me, "My son wants to major in mathematics. Can one make a living in mathematics?" I had the pleasure of saying, yes, a good mathematician would never starve. The parents, many of them, simply do not know what you can do if you have an education.

There has been no reliable source of information. The need is greater than anyone realizes, except the young themselves, and they are much too tense, too hung-up to deal well with the problem. They need information, but they also need reassurance....They need not be full of agony, despair and doom.

For Thinking, Talking, Writing

1. What do you think of Mr. Drucker's statement, "I would be happier if men and women who reach 17 could be young adults among adults. Those who wanted to go back to school could come back later. They would be better students and much happier people. Learning would be an adult activity, not a chore for children." Do you think it would be better for *you* if you could postpone college for a while? Why or why not?
2. Analyze *yourself* in terms of the personal qualities that Mr. Drucker talks about as being important in helping you decide what kind of career you want:
   (a) Do you like pressure, or can't you take it?
   (b) Do you want to be a part of a big organization, where you don't see results, or are you happier when you can immediately see the results of the work you have done?
   (c) Do you like to be in "daily combat" (that is, to have constant problems to work through each day), or do you prefer to "think things through, to analyze, prepare"?
   (d) Are you, as far as you can tell, a *perceptive* or an *analytical* person?
   (e) Do you learn better by listening first and reading later, or by reading first and listening later?
3. If you have gained any new information or new insights from this article, list them and discuss how they can help you to make a decision about your career.

What Companies
Want Most
from Young People

Sterling G. Slappey

In the past 15 to 20 years possibly 15 to 20 million words have been printed on what bright-eyed, high-grade college graduates expect from companies they are willing to work for.

American companies spend millions of dollars every year...sending personnel recruiters to sound out graduates and talk with other young people who could be put on the executive track.

It's well known what the grads expect, but relatively little is written on what the companies expect of the youngsters.

The largest, best run, most progressive companies have definite ideas on what they are looking for.

Nearly every company wants communicators — young people who speak well and write clearly. Most companies now bear down hard on the search for socially conscious people. For some this is a departure from previous years.

Companies want personality projectors; they want competitors because competition from other companies increases; they want maturity (quiet enthusiasm rather than any boisterous Joe College attitude); they want people with outside interests.

And they want people who will stick with the company — loyalty. The job-hopper type is shunned.

Westinghouse Electric Corp. defines what it needs: "people interested in industry and in its desire to produce a profit while it is trying to improve society."

Qualities such as intelligence, aggressiveness, imagination, self-sufficiency are sought. In addition, Westinghouse looks for prospects who are prepared to discuss what they can contribute to the industry and to society and how they plan to use their education and training in the company's behalf.

Armstrong Cork Co. and Westinghouse were...among the first

large companies to go in for college recruiting. They started just after the turn of the century and have constantly expanded their search programs.

Armstrong needs 175 to 185 youngsters each year who stand out above the crowd. Armstrong wants to see evidence of maturity in the people to whom it is considering offering a well-paying, rewarding position.

Armstrong may not insist on the graduate being in the top half of his class if he has done extra work or had extra, attractive experiences. It is accepted that a student who is president of his senior class may have been busy and not made grades as high as he would have otherwise.

No effort is made to "sell" a man on Armstrong, the company's recruiters maintain. The student must have an interest in the company and the position. Furthermore, if he has dollar marks for eyeballs, Armstrong isn't quite so interested.

The company is now broadening its search for good students in junior colleges with the plan in mind that they will come to work for Armstrong immediately and finish their college education in night classes. This way they don't lose time and experience from work while they earn degrees. Armstrong will even assign a promising young junior college graduate to a company office in a city where special courses are available.

Every company has always wanted men of leadership, but how do you tell if a graduate has it or not? One long-recognized way is to check his outside activities. Was he an officer in campus clubs or just a member of the club? Was he on student councils?

Versatility, breadth of interest, the positive outlook, ability to express oneself, the ability to be master of one's fate and not to swim with the tide — those are hallmarks which Dow Chemical Co. is on the lookout for.

Xerox Corp. looks for many things. One tactic it dislikes is for people to try to sell themselves to the highest bidder. Xerox especially distrusts people who take a cavalier attitude toward the recruiting process.

"We do not like having to prove ourselves," the company says.

"We try to determine if the 'chemistry' is right — the intangible qualities which help a man fit in with us comfortably. And we also seek people who have interests outside the business world and can see and understand the social responsibilities of businessmen and business organizations," the company . . . [says].

Innovators are in demand at Xerox, along with communicators. Adaptability and a spirit of adventure are prized. In the future, Xerox expects computers to play an increasing role in establishing contacts between companies and likely prospects. Also in the future Xerox expects to do more vocational counseling at the freshman and sophomore levels.

Radio Corporation of America wants a man with good scholastic achievements who "has been educated beyond the classroom."

RCA's man is a participator, not a spectator. He can be a participator in football or golf, or on the debating team, just so he participates.

When looking for engineers or other technical people, RCA wants top members of classes in the top universities who get top recommendations from their professors.

E. I. du Pont de Nemours and Co. interviews hundreds of prospects and bases its decision whether to offer jobs on professional competence, personal characteristics, motivation, practical intelligence, relationship with others, maturity, communications, leadership. Du Pont, a technically oriented company, aims the bulk of recruiting at technically trained people. However, many of the same personal characteristics sought in graduates from liberal arts universities are also sought in graduates from engineering schools.

Like so many companies, Du Pont is career oriented — not a revolving door.

Hippies are not welcomed by United Air Lines, but neither are they thrown out of the interview room on their hair-covered ears. "If a young man we interview appears promising, but sports a hippie appearance," United says, "we might suggest some changes and invite him to see us at a future date."

United's big search is on for what it calls the "promotable types." These are people who must be capable, intelligent, personable and have good character, in the company's view.

United notes changes in attitudes of college applicants in the past few years. Young people are more informed about business now, and this has made screening applicants more difficult....

Department managers accompany United recruiters to campuses so they can speak more fully on specifics of 170 managerial and professional classifications.

Efforts have been made to dispense with the glamor aspects of a big airline, even in United's stewardess hiring. Job content and opportunities for individual growth are the points stressed now.

"We have found that applicants appear to be less interested in fringe benefits and more on job content," United says. "Some come to interviews armed with annual reports with various points underlined. They are interested in such things as how we finance our aircraft. They also want to know how to get to the top in the company."

This attitude tends to put them on the wanted list.

Bethlehem Steel Corp. looks for desire to advance in the people it interviews. Integrity, which may seem old-fashioned to some people, is a priceless commodity at Bethlehem.

Emphasis is not placed solely on scholarship, but rather on all-around attainment and leadership. Still, the student who ranks in the upper half of his class gets an extra-close look.

Dow Chemical . . . searches for "high energy" people. And how do you spot this? One part of the answer is: Find out what the student did with his summer vacations and spare time. If he lounged around, went swimming every day, just goofed off, he's not likely to be highly energized.

Smaller organizations without teams of recruiters use a variety of other tactics to contact and judge new, key employees. One executive, William Rosenberg, board chairman, Dunkin' Donuts of America, Inc., franchise operation, used his son, Robert, as a recruiter. After the son got out of Harvard Business School, father Bill said, "Bobby, who were the smartest people in your class?" Several were brought to the company to form a bright, young management team.

One company, which requested that its name not be used, says the initial impression of interviewers is all-important because the first minutes of a talk may decide whether the interview is pursued seriously. During these first few minutes, the applicant is appraised for his grooming, dress, poise, and general appearance and attitude.

If he looks good, then these are checked: verbal facility (another way of saying communication ability), personality, curiosity, maturity, judgment, drive, growth potential.

Curiosity is a trait that is highly valued.

Under the general heading "judgment," the company seeks to find why the applicant reached important decisions in his life. How did he select his school, his courses and, above all, why did he select his career?

This company, like practically every other one, wants people with a sense of humor.

Without it the applicant is lost in the company, as, indeed, he is in the modern world.

For Thinking, Talking, Writing

1. Re-read this article carefully and try to pick out the five characteristics which seem to you to be the most important ones that large companies look for in hiring new college graduates.

2. Rate yourself on each of these five characteristics: good, average, or poor. For any average or poor ratings you give yourself, try to think through ways you could improve your rating *now*, while you're still in college.
3. Note that this article indicates that most large companies like to hire people who want to stay with them as a career. Yet Mr. Drucker recommended that young people just starting out *not* consider their first job a lifetime career commitment. Discuss these two points of view; which do you think is more sensible? Why?

Reprinted from *U.S. News & World Report,* May 20, 1968:

Latest On Career Opportunities
for Young People

*By the time you read this, a new "Occupation Outlook Handbook"
will have been issued. However, this article will give you some general
ideas about the trends various professions are taking and alert you to
the fact that you can get for yourself, if you're interested, the latest edition of the handbook.*

A new, official study of career opportunities for American youths
in the years ahead has just been issued by the Federal Government.

This guide, entitled "Occupation Outlook Handbook," is published
by the U.S. Department of Labor every two years. It is recognized as
one of the most authoritative and comprehensive sources of information for young people setting out on their life's work.

Among the broad highlights from the 1968 edition of the handbook:

In the current decade, 1965-75, employment in the U.S. will increase by an estimated 20 per cent. By 1975, there will be 92 million
jobs in America.

Employment in government, services, and contract construction industries will increase the fastest. Job growth in service industries is put
at more than 40 per cent, in government at just under 40 per cent, and
in contract construction at almost 30 per cent.

Although jobs in manufacturing are expected to increase only half
as fast as over-all employment, factories still will employ more workers than any other one broad field of endeavor.

More and more people will be going into white-collar jobs. Employment in professional and related occupations will grow twice as fast
as the general average in the 1965-75 decade.

Education is of growing importance in preparation for jobs of all
kinds. Completion of a high-school education has become standard for
American workers. The handbook states: "Employers are hiring people
with higher levels of education because job content is more complex and
requires higher levels of skill."

The new edition of the handbook covers more than 700 occupations. It will be available in counseling offices of most U. S. high schools and colleges. Individual copies can be obtained for $4.25 each from the Superintendent of Documents, Washington, D.C. 20402.

Those preparing the guide to tomorrow's jobs assumed that relatively high levels of economic activity will continue to prevail, that there will be a national-defense effort comparable in scope to that existing before the Vietnam build-up, and that scientific and technological advances will continue.

Following is a sampling of the information given in the handbook for some of the occupations expected to offer good opportunities.

Government workers. One out of every 7 persons employed in the United States holds a job in federal, state or local government. Only a small increase in federal employment is expected between now and 1975, but rapid growth of jobs in state and local governments is predicted.

Increased use of computers and materials-handling equipment is seen as limiting employment in many clerical and blue-collar jobs offered by the Federal Government.

State and local governments, expanding services at a fast pace, will provide opportunities in a wide variety of occupations such as guidance counselors, dietitians, maintenance workers, medical-laboratory technicians, hospital attendants, foresters and electricians.

Government employment offers much job security. At state and local levels, more and more jobs are filled on the basis of a civil-service test. Health insurance, retirement programs and other fringe benefits are usually provided.

Teachers. The largest of all U.S. professions is teaching. Around 2.3 million men and women are at work in the nation's elementary and secondary schools and in colleges.

Between now and 1975, about 1.8 million teaching jobs are expected to open up in grade schools, junior high schools and senior high schools.

Competition for teaching positions in junior and senior high schools may be somewhat keener. There will be some slowing of enrollment growth in the secondary schools. At the same time, there is expected to be an increasing number of college graduates prepared for teaching at this level.

College professors. A continuing rapid increase in college enrollment is predicted. This will create many new positions on faculties. Those entering this field with Ph.D. degrees, or who are close to getting this advanced degree, will find excellent opportunities. Those with master's degrees will find positions opening up, too, especially in the junior colleges that are increasing in number and popularity across the U.S.

A survey by the American Association of University Professors found that the average pay for a full professor in the 1966-67 academic year was $14,402. For associate professors it was $10,829, and for instructors $7,122. These salaries are based on teaching nine to 10 months of the year.

Physicians and dentists. With new medical and dental schools opening up and existing ones expanding, there is to be more opportunity for training in these professions. An increase in the number of graduates, however, is not expected to result in fewer job opportunities.

Over the next decade, the number of dental-school graduates will be barely enough to maintain the present ratio of dentists to population. Average net income of self-employed dentists in 1966 was $21,000. For self-employed physicians, it was reported to be between $20,000 and $27,000.

Scientists, engineers, technicians. Employment in science and engineering will expand faster than that of professional workers as a whole. Demand for scientists is expected to increase at a faster pace than for engineers. Technicians trained in these fields also can expect excellent opportunities.

The scientific field is described as offering exciting prospects. As one example, the handbook states: "The flight of astronauts through space, the probing of the oceans' depths, or even the safety of the family car depend on research performed by physicists."

There is this comment on engineers:

"There will probably be an especially strong demand for new engineering graduates who have training in the most recently developed engineering principles and techniques and for engineers who can apply engineering principles to the medical and other sciences."

Oceanographers. This profession is typical of many described as just beginning to come into their own. Many colleges are setting up departments of oceanography and the Federal Government is expanding its work in this field, which involves study of the sea and its vast resources. It is an occupation that provides a more exciting way of life than most, often involving long voyages.

Salespeople. Close to 5 million people work in the business of selling. A need for more than 275,000 additional workers each year is predicted. Some with no more than high-school education will be able to land jobs in retail stores, but may earn as little as the federal minimum wage, now $1.60 an hour. Others, with college education followed by special training, will sell insurance or stocks and bonds and earn as much as $30,000 a year.

Selling is a diverse business in which a housewife may work part time, or a highly qualified engineer may make use of his knowledge to sell complex equipment to industry.

Hotel workers. This line of work is expanding rapidly as more and more Americans travel about their country. New hotels and motels are springing up, offering jobs that range from bellman to manager. Graduates of college training programs in hotel management can expect starting salaries ranging from $5,000 to $7,200 a year. Experienced managers earn many times those amounts.

Carpenters, bricklayers, other construction workers. Employment for skilled craftsmen in construction jobs is seen as increasing "moderately." Most authorities — including labor-management committees — recommend formal apprentice training as the best way to become proficient at carpentry, bricklaying, plastering, plumbing, sheet-metal working, cement masonry and other crafts.

Apprentices in the building trades are generally required to be between the ages of 18 and 25. A high-school education also is often required.

A sampling of average minimum wages paid to workers belonging to building-trade unions in 68 cities across the U. S. showed bricklayers drawing $5.04 an hour, carpenters $4.74, painters $4.46, plumbers $5.08 and paperhangers $4.37. Since this survey was made in mid-1966, most construction workers have been given wage increases.

Computer operators. Rapid expansion of job opportunities in this field is expected to continue even though the size of the staff needed to operate a computer installation may be reduced as more-sophisticated models are developed.

Most employers insist upon at least a high-school education for computer work. Console operators are expected to have some college training. Many console operators, through on-the-job experience, are able to move up to the position of computer programmer. A private survey in 1966 found that the average pay for beginning console operators was $101 a week and experienced ones averaged up to $180 a week.

Secretaries. Despite development of more-sophisticated office equipment, competent secretaries and stenographers are expected to have no trouble finding jobs in the foreseeable future. There may be as many as 200,000 openings each year for such workers, most of whom are women. A high-school education that includes shorthand, typing and possibly some business subjects will continue to be adequate qualification in the view of most employers. Some, however, prefer a background of academic subjects in high school, supplemented by secretarial training after graduation.

For Thinking, Talking, Writing

Which of the careers mentioned here might you be interested in, and why? If you have already chosen a career, does it appear in this article? If so, how is it rated? Does the article change your mind about anything you might have already been thinking of in terms of a career?

Encounter

The text of this book was designed by Gunther Bahrs and typeset by Central Typesetting Inc., San Diego, California, in 11-point Times Roman, with 2-point leading. The section headings are in 30-point Melior semi-bold and the article headings in 18-point Melior semi-bold. The printing was done by offset lithography by Kingsport Press, Inc., Kingsport, Tennessee and the paper is 50# Bookman Offset Wove. The book was bound by Kingsport Press, Inc., Kingsport, Tennessee in 12-point Carolina printed 1-color by offset lithography.